the definitive guide to
direct and interactive marketing

In an increasingly competitive world, we believe it's quality of thinking that will give you the edge – an idea that opens new doors, a technique that solves a problem, or an insight that simply makes sense of it all. The more you know, the smarter and faster you can go.

That's why we work with the best minds in business and finance to bring cutting-edge thinking and best learning practice to a global market.

Under a range of leading imprints, including *Financial Times Prentice Hall*, we create world-class print publications and electronic products bringing our readers knowledge, skills and understanding which can be applied whether studying or at work.

To find out more about our business publications, or tell us about the books you'd like to find, you can visit us at

www.pearsoned.co.uk

the definitive guide to
direct and interactive marketing

how to select, reach and retain
the right customers

Merlin Stone, Alison Bond and
Elizabeth Blake

with contributions from Derek Davies and Tess Moffett

FINANCIAL TIMES

An imprint of Pearson Education

Harlow, England • London • New York • Boston • San Francisco • Toronto • Sydney • Singapore • Hong Kong
Tokyo • Seoul • Taipei • New Delhi • Cape Town • Madrid • Mexico City • Amsterdam • Munich • Paris • Milan

PEARSON EDUCATION LIMITED

Head Office:
Edinburgh Gate
Harlow CM20 2JE
Tel: +44 (0)1279 623623
Fax: +44 (0)1279 431059

Website: www.pearsoned.co.uk

First published in Great Britain in 2003

© Pearson Education Limited 2003

The right of Merlin Stone, Alison Bond and Elizabeth Blake to be identified as Authors of this Work has been asserted by them in accordance with the Copyright, Designs and Patents Act 1988.

ISBN 0 273 67520 6

British Library Cataloguing in Publication Data
A CIP catalogue record for this book can be obtained from the British Library

All rights reserved; no part of this publication may be reproduced, stored in a retrieval system, or transmitted in any form or by any means, electronic, mechanical, photocopying, recording, or otherwise without either the prior written permission of the Publishers or a licence permitting restricted copying in the United Kingdom issued by the Copyright Licensing Agency Ltd, 90 Tottenham Court Road, London W1T 4LP. This book may not be lent, resold, hired out or otherwise disposed of by way of trade in any form of binding or cover other than that in which it is published, without the prior consent of the Publishers.

10 9 8 7 6 5 4 3 2 1

Typeset by Pantek Arts Ltd, Maidstone, Kent
Printed and bound in Great Britain by Bell & Bain Ltd, Glasgow

The Publishers' policy is to use paper manufactured from sustainable forests.

To Ofra, Maya and Talya from Merlin

To Trevor and Peter from Alison

To Nick from Lizzy

acknowledgements

We would like to acknowledge our friends and colleagues who have supported the work and the research that helped us write this book. The first edition of this book was co-authored by Derek Davies and we have retained some of his contributions, particularly in the area of direct marketing strategy and planning.

In particular, we would like to thank:
Merlin's many colleagues at IBM, particularly Bryan Foss
Professor Derek Holder and Neil Morris, Managing Director and Deputy Managing Director of the Institute of Direct Marketing
Trevor Millard, Alison's husband and business partner at ABA Research Ltd
Nick Chambers for his help in putting together the writing team
Neil Woodcock of Qci
Mike Clarke of Centurion Press for his print and production advice
Nick White, Head of Value Added Services at Virgin Mobile
Tess Moffett of IBM, who co-wrote Chapter 15, on electroinc and broadcast media

about the authors

Merlin Stone is the IBM Professor of Business Transformation at the University of Surrey, Business Research Leader with IBM and a director of QCi Ltd and The Database Group Ltd. He is the author of many articles and twenty books on marketing and customer service. He has consulted to companies in many sectors on CRM and customer service. He is a Founder Member of the Institute of Direct Marketing, a Fellow of the Chartered Institute of Marketing and on the editorial advisory boards of many journals. He has a first class honours degree and doctorate in economics.

Alison Bond is a director of ABA Research Ltd, a firm specialising in services research in consumer, business and public sector markets. Alison has worked in marketing and planning for two major airlines and for a customer reservation system supplier. She managed one of the country's leading data processing research companies before starting her own services research business in 1994.

Elizabeth Blake is a senior marketing manager at BSkyB. She has eight years of practical marketing experience gained at Barclaycard within the UK and European markets, and at Sky digital where she manages below the line marketing. She has broad optimisation, retention and acquisition experience across the fields of financial and subscriptions marketing and has introduced SMS marketing as a new acquisition channel to Sky digital.

contents

Acknowledgements vi
About the authors vii

1 Direct and interactive marketing and the customer 1
Direct marketing to consumers 3
Types of buying decision 3
The determinants of consumer choice 4
Summary of direct marketing to consumers 8
Business-to-business direct marketing 8
The importance of business direct marketing 8
Business buying 9
What is different about business-to-business purchasing behaviour? 10
The role of direct marketing 10
Summary 11

2 What is direct and interactive marketing? 13
Introduction 15
Technical definition 16
Main types of direct marketing 18
Benefits of direct marketing 21
Planning your direct marketing activity 22
Applications of the customer database 24
Summary 25

3 Who does direct marketing and how? 27
Direct marketing users and suppliers 29
Users 29
Suppliers 31
Media 33
The direct marketing environment 37
Summary 40

4 Direct and interactive strategy 41

Introduction 43
The principles of acquisition and retention 44
Acquisition 44
Keeping customers - the principle of retention 49
Acquisition vs retention 51
What creates loyalty? 53
Steps in a retention strategy 53
Understanding the customer base 55
Summary 55

5 Planning direct marketing 57

What makes a good direct marketing plan? 59
The planning process 61
Situation analysis 61
Customer definition – who will buy it? 62
Financial performance 63
Reviewing your key resources 64
Competition 65
Setting business objectives 65
Common direct marketing objectives 66
Strategy options and evaluation 67
Action plans 69
The essential skill - what you need in a campaign manager 75
Financial analysis 75
Summary 76

6 The customer database 77

What a customer database is and why direct marketing needs it 79
How a customer database is used 79
What has helped database marketing grow so fast? 81
The strengths of database marketing 82
The database 82
Data design 83
Sources of data 84

Types of information on the database 85
Holding the data 88
Data quality and maintenance 89
Using the database 92
Doing it yourself or outsourcing 92
Summary 92

7 Who uses the customer database and how? 95
The start of the story 97
Which industries are using databases? 97
The demand for direct and interactive marketing 103
Summary 105

8 The competitive use of the database 107
Strategic vs tactical use of your database 109
Identifying opportunities 113
Quantifying the gain 114
Quantification 117
Summary 120

9 Competitive applications of direct and interactive marketing 121
What types of application are there? 123
Strategic issues 126
Data acquisition and development 127
Maintaining the database 128
Making applications work 129
Using management applications 129
Developing accountability through applications 130
Supporting decisions 131
Day-to-day working applications 132
Sophisticated statistical applications 132
Phasing in the applications 133
The fully integrated system and its applications 133
Stepping through your system 134
Summary 136

Contents

10 Market segmentation and research 137

Introduction 139
What is segmentation? 139
Standard classification methods 140
Geo-demographic segmentation 140
Psychographic analysis 141
Lifestyle questionnaires 141
Combining sources 142
Response-based segmentation 142
How to define segments 144
Purchasing variables 144
Modelling 146
Statistical methods for finding segments 147
Using market research in direct marketing 147
Main research techniques direct marketers use 150
Summary 153

11 Making the right offer 155

The definition of an offer 157
Components of the offer 158
Are new products required? 161
Pricing the direct marketing offer 161
Promotional offers 161
Distribution channels in direct marketing 163
Summary 166

12 Direct mail 167

Targeting 169
Components of a mailing 170
Who uses direct mail? 172
Quality and the law 173
The brief for a direct mail campaign 176
Formats 177
Making your mailing more effective 177
The creative 178

Managing a direct mail campaign 182
Summary 188

13 Telemarketing 189
What is telemarketing? 191
Strengths and weaknesses 192
Why customers may like telemarketing 192
Key concepts in telemarketing 193
Functions performed 194
Telemarketing objectives 195
Contact centres 196
The technology of telemarketing 196
Productivity ratios 201
Additional targets and ratios for inbound telemarketing 203
Other important measures for inbound and outbound telemarketing 203
The importance of feedback 204
Setting targets 204
Call guides 205
Promoting the telephone number 207
The Telephone Preference Service 208
Summary 208

14 Customer relationship management (CRM) 209
Managing the relationship in stages 212
Why CRM is important 214
A model of CRM 216
Summary 218

15 Electronic and broadcast media 219
Broadcast media 221
Interactive media developments 221
Interactive TV developments 224
Mobile marketing technology 228
Key success factors 230
E-mail marketing 231
New developments 237

16 Lots more ways to contact customers 239

Targeting – always the key factor 241
Press 243
Inserts 243
Tip-ons 245
Leaflet distribution and free newspapers 246
Coupons 246
Designing press or magazine response advertising 247
Television 248
Shopping channels 250
Catalogues - offline and online 250
Exhibitions 254
Sales seminars and other company-sponsored special events 254
The sales force 255
Sales promotion 255
Posters 256
Public relations 256
E-mail and the Internet 257
Short messaging service 257
MMS 258
Third generation (3G mobile phone services) 258
Summary 258

17 The creative side 259

What does 'creative' mean in direct marketing? 261
Creativity and action 262
How can you create creativity? 263
Direct marketing vs advertising creativity 264
Developing the creative strategy 265
The creative brief 269
Summary 269

18 Production and fulfilment in direct mail 271

Production 273
The start – artwork 273
Typesetting 274

Reproduction/make-up 275
Mailing 276
Developments in direct mail technology 277
Understanding Mailsort 279
Fulfilment 280
Fulfilment tasks 281
Fulfilment steps 281
The management of handling 283
Summary 286

19 Managing the hit 289
The campaign process 291
Campaign planning 293
Campaign development 296
The offer 298
Creative 299
Promotional actions 300
Implementing targeting 301
Campaign management processes 305
Quality in campaign management 306
The management process for progressing a campaign 309
Staffing 312
Summary 314

20 Testing in direct and interactive marketing 315
What is testing and why should you test? 317
Specifying testing 317
The objective of testing 318
The aim of statistics – to generalize 319
Narrowing down what is to be tested 320
Sampling and inference 320
Distributions 324
Testing differences 324
Sampling methods 324
Test matrices 325
Split runs and other ways of varying sample treatment 326

The control group 326
Response rates vs sales rates 327
Advanced statistics 329
Summary 330

21 Profitable, cost-effective direct marketing 331
Planned and actual results 333
General budgeting 334
Campaign budgeting 335
Monitoring and control 340
Supplier quality as shown by control statistics 342
Learning from final results 342
Summary 348

22 Integrated communication 349
What is 'integrated communication'? 351
Media integration 351
The meaning of integration 352
Strengths and weaknesses of different media 353
How integration is achieved 362
The concepts of integration 364
Summary 368

23 People in direct marketing 369
Who works in direct marketing? 371
Direct marketing users in the marketing organization 373
Who's responsible for the workload? 374
Staff capabilities 374
Recruiting direct marketing staff 376
After the investment? 377
Supplier management 377
Should you contract out? 378
Supplier selection 379
Agency structure 380
Rules of good supplier management 382

Controlling supplier costs 382
Managing the strategic relationship with suppliers 384
Finalizing contracts 384
Summary 385

Glossary 387
Index 390

direct and interactive marketing and the customer

Direct marketing to consumers

Types of buying decisions

The determinants of consumer choice

Summary of direct marketing to consumers

Business-to-business direct marketing

The importance of business direct marketing

Business buying

What is different about business-to-business purchasing behaviour

The role of direct marketing

Summary

This book shows you how to make your direct and interactive marketing more effective. We won't spend too much time defining these terms in the first chapter – more on this later. In brief, we use the term 'direct marketing' to describe many ways of interacting directly with named customers and prospects, in old and new media.

Effective direct marketing depends, above all else, on our thoroughly understanding customers, and on deciding what customers are expected to do, and how, when, where and why they are expected to do it. Understanding customers is the key to developing competitive advantage. If we don't understand our customers, we can't expect our marketing to them to be very successful. We'll succeed only if we provide relevant offers to customers, and if we interact with them in ways they find easy, cost effective and perhaps even fun. Doing this means we need to know how customers think, feel and act.

Direct marketing to consumers

Customers may be business customers or consumer customers – individuals or families. Let's first look at consumer direct marketing.

Marketers play close attention to studies of consumer behaviour. The quality of such studies has grown – particularly in relation to concepts and empirical research techniques. Psychology, sociology, statistics, mathematics and information technology have all contributed to this. We are now better armed than ever before to understand consumers.

Types of buying decision

High-involvement and low-involvement decisions

Many purchases require little or no explanation. Often, it's quite clear why the consumer buys. Sometimes, especially where the consumer invests a lot of emotion in buying or using the product or service, we need to probe a bit deeper.

> **Low-involvement** products are usually basic commodities. They are bought for functional reasons and carry little or no symbolic meaning. Their unit price is low, whichever brand is selected. They are routinely purchased. There is not much economic, social or psychological risk of making the wrong brand choice.
>
> Products that we 'wear' – not just clothes, but also cigarettes, alcohol, cars, books, home furnishings and the like – are **high-involvement** products. Brands within each product class invoke and commit the consumer to such an extent that brand switching is seen as risky.

Some products are 'low involvement', e.g. impulse purchases from low-value merchandise catalogues. However, direct and interactive marketing is more strongly established, growing faster and offers greater potential for high-involvement products, such as financial services, charity fundraising, publishing, automobiles and retailing.

When devising a direct marketing strategy, consumers' buying decisions can be analyzed using the following framework:

- **existence of the need** (whether or not the consumer realizes it);
- **identification or realization of need** – the need comes to the 'front of mind';
- **problem recognition** – the need exists for a reason, typically a problem that needs to be solved;
- **search for information** – about products and services that will solve the problem;
- **evaluation** – when all the relevant accessible information required to make the choice that will resolve the problem is gathered and analyzed;
- **choice** – some choices are purely impulsive, or at least may seem so. However, many choices are deliberate and rational, based upon reasonably systematic processing of information. Such processing leads to the intention to buy;
- **post-purchase review** – the consumer re-evaluates the decision in the light of any new information, e.g. on product performance. Sometimes consumers are unhappy about what they now know. They experience doubt or anxiety if the product does not meet their expectations. This may be resolved in various ways. Consumers look for information which supports their decision, or they may focus on the 'good deal' they got, to try to convince themselves they made the right decision.

The determinants of consumer choice

Needs trigger behaviour only when consumers **perceive** the need. At this point it makes sense to examine the process of perception. Marketers focus particularly on mental processing of external information, notably advertising messages. The direct marketer is also interested in this, as much direct marketing activity includes targeted advertising. Direct marketers usually see targeting just as reaching particular target consumers with a communication.

Targeting implies much more than this. It means identifying people who are psychologically receptive to the message.

> **Warning!**
> Most consumers remember very few of the 2000 or so messages they are exposed to each day in the UK (in the US it is nearer 3000 messages!). This is because **their perception is very selective.**

Selective perception is a function of two distinct but related forces: extrinsic and intrinsic forces. **Extrinsic** forces are outside the consumer. They can be controlled or influenced by the marketer. They include:

- **where** the consumer is exposed to a message. Television, for instance, is quite an intrusive medium. If there are no other distractions in a room with the television turned on, the consumer is more likely to notice the advertisements than those placed, say, on billboards at a crowded sporting event. In this context the direct marketer should appreciate the value of inserts and direct mail. Both of these are highly *intrusive* media in the sense that the consumer cannot avoid handling them, even if it is only to throw them away. Of course, if advertising is poorly targeted (wrong audience, wrong situation), consumers may just leave the room or not pay attention;
- **when** the consumer is exposed to the message. Consumers are more likely to see and make sense of messages when they are mentally fresh and unlikely to be faced with distraction from other advertisements. Those who are freshest in the morning are more likely to notice direct mail. However, not everyone gets their post in the morning, making it necessary for direct marketers to look beyond this;
- **what** the consumer is being exposed to. This is affected by factors such as the advertisement's size, its position, or its isolation from other influences. Obviously, larger advertisements tend to capture more attention than smaller ones (though not in direct proportion to increases in size). The position of a press advertisement on a page affects attention. Advertisements on the upper half of the page tend to do better than those at the bottom of the page. Those on the left of a page do better than those on the right. The degree of isolation of the communication affects perception too. Thus, a mailing containing only one offer will gain more attention for that offer than one containing several offers.

Intrinsic forces are more important in determining what is perceived and how it is perceived. These include:

- **needs**. These may be functional, e.g. the need to replace a faulty dishwasher or a worn-out car. Such needs cause the consumer to pay more attention to communications about the product in question. Needs may be emotional. Pictures of people of the same age and lifestyle may catch a consumer's eye. The consumer may identify with and relate to the subjects of the picture. Direct marketing works most effectively when messages address current needs;
- **perceptual benchmarking**. Consumers tend to recognize more quickly words or images that relate to their own values. Thus, if a particular consumer is a regular donor to charity, that consumer will recognize and process very quickly words connoting values central to charitable giving. 'Cause', 'help', 'humanity', 'suffering', 'children' and so on will be recognized and absorbed more quickly than others. Words that tend to have a non-charitable connotation, for example 'financial', may have negative impact, causing the consumer to delay processing the information or to avoid it altogether;
- **consistency**. This is important in maintaining consumers' values and beliefs, even in the face of conflicting evidence. Consumers tend to strive for balance and to maintain a consistent view of their world. So they accept messages that support their beliefs, rejecting those that threaten them.

When consumers have concerns about products they have bought, they seek out advertising messages that support their purchase decision. Direct marketers have an edge in this area because they can pinpoint more accurately those who are likely to feel let down and they can provide potentially more reassuring messages. 'Welcome' and 'thank you' letters are particularly effective in this respect. So, too, are 'bounce-backs', i.e. further offers that are made following initial response or purchase;

◆ **motivation**. Once consumers perceive a need, they are motivated and energized to satisfy the need. Motives link needs and their satisfaction. Some types of motive are more common than others. The more common ones of interest to marketers are:

- ◆ making or saving money;
- ◆ helping the family;
- ◆ saving time or effort;
- ◆ feeling clean or secure;
- ◆ pleasure;
- ◆ impressing others;
- ◆ belonging;
- ◆ self-improvement;

Many motives work to **maintain** behaviour rather than **change** it. For example, the desire to become rich may lead to a strong savings habit.

Some factors act to sustain motivation but not to increase it. These factors are called **'hygiene'** factors (the idea being that the presence of soap and clean towels will not motivate people to work **harder**, but their absence causes people to grumble and become dissatisfied).

◆ **learning**. Direct marketing is a good knowledge builder. A direct marketer can use response rates to gauge the proportion of consumers responding to a particular marketing action and to measure the connection between stimulus and the consequent behaviour. Consumers can also learn. For example, they can learn to associate the benefits of buying from a catalogue with the reduction in unproductive shopping. The more frequently a particular offer is made, the more response behaviour is reinforced;

◆ **personality**. This plays an important role in motivation and learning. Unfortunately, personality is easier to recognize than explain or even understand. Personality *traits* include sociability, gregariousness and aggression. Advertising is often designed to appeal to consumers with particular traits;

◆ **attitudes**. Consumers may feel good about the products offered for sale through direct channels of communication, but may feel bad about the buying process in these channels. This may be reinforced through experience. For example, catalogue mail order returns are notoriously high (up to 50%). Poor experience with the medium may lead consumers to form negative attitudes towards the advertised products. This may be strong enough to inhibit further mail order purchasing.

Checklist of direct marketing campaign focus	What it means to the campaign
☐ Need	Have you assessed the likelihood of your consumer's need?
☐ Perceptual vigilance and defence	Does your message fit the types of emotions that your consumer will respond to?
☐ Cognitive consistency	Will the message challenge their views and produce a negative response?
☐ Motivation	Are there enough motivating words and messages to make consumers want to buy?
☐ Personality	Is the personality of the communication positive?

▶ Social influence processes

The above concepts relate to the psychological make-up of individual consumers. However, group behaviour also influences consumer choice, for example the need to feel valued by groups we belong to, and this often leads to a desire for status.

> For years, American Express mailings began with 'Frankly, an American Express card isn't for everybody'. You couldn't have a much more blatant appeal to status.

Conversely, some consumers need to conform rather than stand out from the crowd. To conform is to be 'in', to be different is to be 'out'. This is a strong motive. Direct marketers work hard to transform it into interest and buying. Hence the slogan: *Every home should have one!*

What is the social focus of your direct marketing message?	What it means to the campaign
☐ Status	Will status appeals make your product (and consumer) stand out from the crowd?
☐ Roles	Are role requirements clear? What are recipients of your message expected to do – buy, recommend, etc.?
☐ Conformity to norms	Have you told (threatened) consumers what will happen if they don't buy?
☐ Power	Have you empowered your prospect? Remember, visible symbols of exalted position such as special badges or cards, often work.

▶ Summary of direct marketing to consumers

Effective direct marketing depends on a thorough understanding of consumer behaviour. Traditionally, direct marketers approached markets from an instinctive, experiential perspective and denied the need to understand consumer motivations, insisting that testing and modelling behaviour was enough. This approach is no longer adequate. Markets are too competitive to allow direct marketers this luxury.

▶ Business-to-business direct marketing

> **Business-to-business marketing** is marketing by one organization to others. We abbreviate it as 'business marketing'.

Much business marketing is direct marketing. Every time a business person picks up the phone and speaks to someone in another organisation, every time a letter is sent, direct communication takes place. These kinds of communication call for a direct response, often immediately. Order taking may not be the objective, but some direct response usually is.

▶ What's the difference between consumer and business marketing?

Business direct marketing differs from consumer direct marketing because of the type of benefit that must be offered to business buyers. The latter are usually concerned with how to meet the needs of their organisation's customers, who may be other businesses or consumers. Business marketing is a key area for direct marketing. Advertising is less important than in consumer markets, typically taking up 10% or less of the marketing communications budget. More important are trade shows, sales promotions, sales incentives, sales force management and public relations.

Direct marketing typically takes up about a third of business marketing communications budgets. Telemarketing may be a large element of this – up to 50% – particularly if a business has many small customers. Direct campaigns are often run as part of a co-ordinated campaign with other media, e.g. generating leads for the sales force, inviting customers to an exhibition, drawing attention to a new catalogue or to offers in the catalogue.

▶ The importance of business direct marketing

Two key reasons for the importance of direct marketing in business markets are as follows:

- Most companies' customer and prospect universe is small enough to permit and encourage precise targeting. Whereas consumer markets may consist of millions of individuals and households, most business markets have far fewer customers. Only the very largest business marketers have more than a million customers (e.g. utilities such as telecommunications and power, branch banks) and most have a few thousand.
- A field sales call is expensive. It includes basic salary, commissions, car, expenses, pension benefits, sales support costs and corporate overheads (which may be substantial if the salesperson has an office and a team of support staff to help manage customers). As little as 42% of the 240 days a year a salesperson has available to sell will actually be spent selling (the rest will be spent on prospecting, administration, sales meetings and conferences, etc.). It may take many calls to make a sale. For this reason, many business marketers have been using direct marketing techniques to maximize exploitation of sales force time.

▶ Business buying

Much organizational buying is as routine as its consumer counterpart. For instance, the office manager's decision to restock the office cupboard with paper clips is likely to be as simple as the consumer's decision to restock with coffee or tea. In both cases, known suppliers with reliable brands will be chosen automatically. Such industrial purchases are called 'straight re-buys'. They are low-involvement decisions taken by individuals with little or no search for and evaluation of alternatives. In such cases, most purchasers rely on known suppliers. Only when the normal supplier is unreliable will a new supplier be sought. The arrival of a direct marketing communication from another supplier at the right time may be crucial in securing the switched business.

However, as the complexity of the buying task increases, the degree of search and evaluation increases. 'New buy' situations occur when buyers depart from routines to learn more about alternatives. For instance, if a decision has been taken to replace all the computers in an office, considerable search and evaluation may take place. The product form is sufficiently different to prompt research into the benefits of different machines and their suppliers. Moreover, several people may be involved. Numerous departments will have their say.

▶ The structure of the buying centre

From a seller's perspective, it is important to understand the pattern of communications within the buying centre. This, in turn, requires a clearer picture of the structure of the buying centre. Therefore it is important to research before deciding on the correct direct marketing approach.

Conflict within the buying centre

There is inevitably conflict within the buying centre. This conflict may increase the more the decision process involves other departments. The seller must anticipate conflict between different departments and build in benefits that will apply to all departments involved in buying.

What is different about business-to-business purchasing behaviour?

Business-to-business purchasing has much in common with consumer family buying. The **problem-search-evaluation-decision** model for high-involvement consumer purchases will often involve members of the family in the same way as business buying involves members of the decision-making unit. Family roles may also be initiator, influencer, user, decider and buyer. The family, too, is an organization. In business organizations, the gatekeeper role may be crucial because business buying is more likely to be highly structured and formalized than customer buying. This implies that purchasing managers know more about the products they buy. There is also usually greater buyer-seller interdependence than in consumer markets.

The role of direct marketing

The traditional tasks of business direct marketing have been lead generation and qualification, order-taking and customer development. However, there are a number of problems that relate specifically to business market data.

List problems

If you are working from externally sourced lists, you face several possible problems. External list availability and quality rarely match the standard needed to run perfect campaigns. Businesses move, personnel change and they are out of date as soon as they are complete. On the other hand, the relatively low number of customers makes list compilation, list maintenance and targeting relatively easy. Quality control, particularly telephone checking, is also likely to be more effective.

Contacting the right person

Although the buying process may be complex, the essential elements are captured in the useful mnemonic 'find the MAN' – the person with the **Means, Authority and Need**. There will be those who can afford to pay, those who need the product and those who are authorized to pay.

> **A high-cost management development programme**
>
> To generate sufficient leads, you might need to contact the potential delegate (need), the delegate's manager (need), the personnel function (means/authority) and the financial function (means/authority). The level of manager to be contacted will depend on the size of the company. In large companies it could be the HR (human resources) manager and financial controller, in smaller companies the HR director and financial director and in very small companies probably the managing director (who performs both authority and means roles).

> A UK direct marketing agency was recently asked by a client to locate and communicate to all public-sector potato buyers: schools, hospitals, care centres, prisons, etc. No list of named potato buyers was available, unsurprisingly! So the pack was addressed to 'The Potato Buyer'. The results of the campaign exceeded the client's expectations – the packs were clearly passed on to the right people.

The aim of personalization is to make your communication relevant to the recipient. For instance, if your database holds details of potential customers' lines of authority and responsibility, the number of employees in their charge, the size of their budgets, their purchasing limits, etc., you can design letters, brochures and reply devices which use this information. This is likely to increase your response rate.

Selling to businesses involves identifying the roles the different members play and tailoring messages accordingly. Mass media communications have lower potential in this situation, but direct marketing – especially using mail and telephone – is very effective at reaching the right customer with the right message. Personalization is particularly important.

▶ Summary

Direct marketing depends for its effectiveness on a deep understanding of customers and how they think, act and buy. If you don't base your direct marketing communication on sound knowledge of customers, your results are unlikely to be impressive.

what is direct and interactive marketing?

Introduction

Technical definition

Main types of direct marketing

Benefits of direct marketing

Planning your direct marketing activity

Applications of the customer database

Summary

In this chapter we describe the discipline of direct and interactive marketing – direct contact with individual customers. We show that its strengths lie in using its targetability, measurability and testability to find the best method of managing customers. We show that its focus is not just on the acquisition of new customers but on keeping customers and developing their value.

▶ Introduction

Direct marketing is now an essential part of marketing. The key principle is that at least part of the communication you have with your customer is direct – to named customers. From this simple principle has grown a whole new discipline. But it has not grown quickly. The seeds of direct marketing as we use it today were sown in the nineteenth century by the US mail-order industry, which served so well the needs of remote farmers, ranchers, settlers and new townships.

Today, direct marketing is required to cut through the hundreds of messages that people receive every day, so clarity and relevance of message and personalization wherever possible are necessary to break through the noise and reach your target. Since this can be time consuming and expensive, direct marketing must be cost effective, measurable and reliable. Technology has helped achieve this, making it much easier for us to communicate directly with our customers. Changes in tastes and media fragmentation are making conventional mass-marketing techniques less effective. However, a balance of both can be used to achieve response, brand development and presence.

Direct marketing can be summed up as essentially:

- targeted – reaching the customer in an appropriate manner for them, to prompt a response;
- direct – the communications go directly between yourself and the customer, with no intermediary. Customers can generally feel, touch, see or hear your communication to them as individuals;
- marketing – it helps meet your customers' needs and your profit, sales and other objectives.

Direct marketing has three further important characteristics:

1 It is based on **direct** responses. Direct marketing communications invite customers to respond – by mail, telephone, Internet, redeemable retail vouchers, etc. The response may range from enquiry and giving information to ordering. This opportunity for monitoring feedback is critical to direct marketing.

2 Direct marketing is **measurable**. In any direct marketing campaign responses are measured, evaluated and analyzed. Responses can be through any medium – telephone, mail, Internet hits, etc. Measuring responses leads to accountability. All costs can be related to response. Return on investment can be calculated. Traditional advertising relies mainly on market research techniques based on samples to measure effectiveness, though for some campaigns sales results can

be accurately measured (e.g. if run in test areas only). Direct marketers use transaction data to measure. This is one reason why direct marketing has been called scientific advertising – direct marketers conduct their tests in controlled environments. While environments do change, direct marketing is as near to a science as marketing achieves.

3 Direct marketing usually requires you to build and maintain a **database** of customers and prospects. This gives you better understanding of your market and can give you competitive advantage.

Technical definition

Direct marketing is the planned implementation, recording, analysis and tracking of customers' direct response behaviour over time to derive future marketing strategies, for developing long-term customer loyalty and ensuring continued business growth.

Let's consider this definition in more detail. There are eight key principles of direct marketing, as follows.

1 **Planning your marketing activity.** All direct marketing should form part of a controlled marketing strategy, which has been produced as a result of market and competitor analysis and in relation to achievable objectives. Chapter 4 explains how to do this.

2 **Targeting your customer.** Customer information should be stored and capable of manipulation and retrieval from your customer database, to contact your existing customers. Analysis of this also helps you to identify characteristics of potential future customers.

3 **Measuring your marketing activity.** The results of direct marketing should be measured to tell you what works and what doesn't.

4 **Tracking.** This involves monitoring customers' responses over time, ideally for as long as your relationship with them lasts. This enables you to measure their value and understand how much of it is a result of how you marketed to them.

5 **Customer behaviour.** Tracking the spending patterns and general behaviour of your customer can help you establish which products are popular and which aren't. This can help you determine future products and strategy.

6 **Future strategies.** One aim of marketing is to maximize the value of your customers to you. So the previous steps will ensure you have the information to plan effective and efficient marketing to achieve this aim.

7 **Developing long-term loyalty.** By targeting the right customers, offering them what they want and encouraging them to take more of your products, you will protect your customer database. Your customers will be more likely to stay with you for longer.

8 **Encouraging profitable business growth.** This is achieved by increasing the number of loyal and valuable customers you have and limiting the number of customers with low value and/or high risk. This increases turnover and profit, which can be reinvested to ensure that service and product standards are maintained and that your customers stay happy.

So, direct marketing is a continuing process of acquiring new customers, continuing to satisfy existing customers, and developing all customers so as to achieve greater loyalty and increased purchasing. This process is illustrated in Fig. 2.1.

Fig. 2.1 The spiral of prosperity

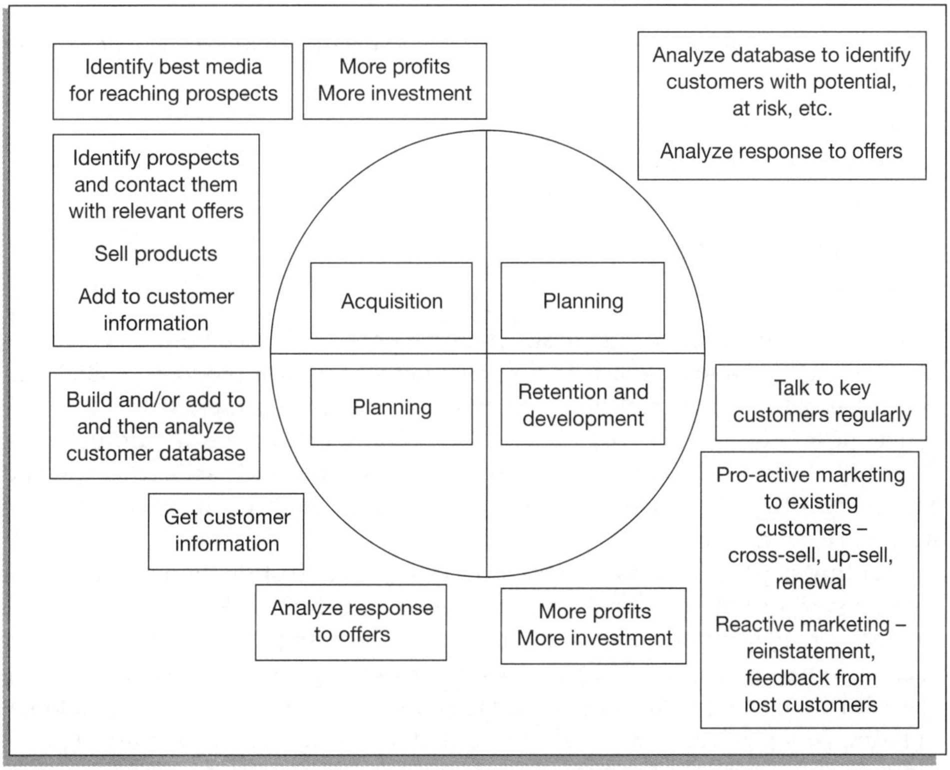

Frequent flyer programmes

Increased loyalty is needed in the highly competitive airline industry to guarantee future repurchase and provides a much-needed USP (unique selling proposition) as the customer has increased choices. BA now competes with BMI British Midland and Virgin for premium business travellers and Go, Easyjet and Ryanair for budget flyers (who now include many business flyers). For business travellers, database marketing is used to identify the most valuable customers, who are rewarded or incentivized to motivate them to continue flying and to buy more premium tickets. Rewards range from access to the airlines' silver and gold business lounges to free points and free flights.

Main types of direct marketing

These eight key principles of direct marketing can be applied to all three key business sectors:

- business to consumers;
- business to intermediaries;
- business to business.

Marketing direct to consumers

A variety of channels is used for this. The key five which may be used alone or in combination are:

- post;
- face to face – retail/branches, rarely a sales force;
- Internet/e-mail;
- fixed line telephone;
- mobile.

Notice that some of these (e.g. post, retail/branch) can be used both as a communication channel and as a distribution channel for physical products, and all can be used as both for information-based products, e.g. financial services.

The post is used widely by mail-order clothing companies including Next, Freemans, La Redoute, Boden, by credit card companies such as Barclaycard and MBNA, and by audio-visual companies including Book Club Associates, The Readers Digest and Britannia Music Club.

Retailing is performed by shops, service centres and showrooms in cities, in smaller stores such as local shops and village post offices. Some also use mail order to broaden their target audience. These can range from national chains such as Next, The Pier and Habitat to smaller independent businesses and single specialist shops such as Ye Olde Porke Pie Shoppe in Melton Mowbray (traditional sausages, pork pies, cakes) and Fortnum and Mason. Larger companies usually have more scope for controlled testing of products and communications, allowing them to optimize their marketing over hundreds, possibly thousands, of products. Banks use their branches for selling financial services products, though most insurance companies now operate entirely via distributors or direct marketing.

Retail outlets can develop direct relationships once they have captured their customers' details, so many capture names and addresses at the point of purchase and send questionnaires for feedback. Many use their mailing lists to keep the customer informed of promotions and new product ranges. Others may have their own or a shared loyalty scheme, which enables them to capture their customers' details and record their spending patterns. Supermarkets (Sainsbury Nectar Card, Tesco Clubcard), large high street retailers (Boots the Chemist, Marks and Spencer), department stores (House of Fraser Storecard, Debenhams – also a

Main types of direct marketing

partner in the Nectar Card scheme) and petrol stations use this medium widely to prompt loyalty and repeat purchase.

> Lakeland Limited, the housewares retailer, has both shops and a mail-order business. When customers buy from a Lakeland shop, staff ask them if they have found everything they need, then offer the catalogue. This is a good way of promoting the catalogue and increasing their database.

The Internet is very effective in reaching a vast target market and is quite simple and cheap to update. It has been used to good effect by travel and holiday companies or brokers (easyrentacar.com, easyjet.com, lastminute.com, cheapestflights.co.uk), audio visual (mvc.co.uk) and book clubs (amazon.com), and again clothing and homeware companies (next.co.uk, thecotswoldcompany.co.uk). Companies offering services such as flower and chocolate delivery (interflora.co.uk, thorntons.co.uk) also benefit from being able to display their products well – you can see the products clearly before buying them as a gift.

Telephone selling, or outbound telemarketing as it is usually called by marketers, is used by companies wishing to focus their marketing on customers they think are highly likely to purchase their goods. So lists of people may be bought, for instance from a lifestyle survey, to find people interested in or considering their product. This can be a cost-effective way to sell, as the price of the phone call and staff costs are the only expenses involved. Digital TV companies (BSkyB) and telecoms companies (BT) as well as credit card companies (Barclaycard, MBNA) use this channel to reach new customers, or existing customers, to sell additional products to them.

One of the latest channels in direct marketing is SMS text messaging, which involves sending text messages to the customer's mobile phone. Although in its infancy, it is proving very effective, particularly in the youth market. It is immediate, personal and cost effective. Virgin Mobile is an extensive user of this channel because it is the company's only way to reach its predominantly pre-pay customer base. Other companies such as Bacardi use SMS for tactical sales promotions, using imagery in their texts to integrate with their TV advertising.

> Virgin Mobile uses SMS to offer customers things like daily horoscopes, local cinema guide, tailored news such as celebrity and entertainment gossip, sports news, headlines and movie news. The aim is to give its customers added value and unique features so that they stay with Virgin Mobile, and to create word-of-mouth advertising through its innovative features.

▶ Marketing to and through intermediaries

Many businesses work, at least partially, through intermediaries – wholesalers, retailers, dealers, distributors. Much marketing effort is spent on moving the product along the channel. Here you face two communication challenges:

19

- marketing to the trade;
- marketing to the final consumer.

In trade marketing, mass branding was traditionally the most powerful tool used to 'pull' products through the trade. However, using direct marketing, you can mount targeted sales promotion campaigns to encourage consumers to visit retail outlets or dealerships. This is one way in which manufacturers deal with increasing retailer power and fragmenting media. To reach the consumer directly, local door drops, car window screen flyers and so on can be used to motivate the customer to visit the nearest outlet for *your* product rather than another product.

Many packaged consumer goods companies are experimenting with targeted household mailings or leaflet drops. Hair care companies and grocery FMCG (fast-moving consumer goods) product relaunches (tea bags, washing powder, etc.) often use door drops and news-share distribution to hit postcodes with their messages, often with product samples attached. Some intermediaries have developed this further and send personalized vouchers and money-off coupons, which are scannable and trackable in-store. Car manufacturers use similar techniques, often combined with local radio, to persuade individuals to visit their local dealership.

At the same time, these manufacturers collect customer information for planning. Manufacturers of consumer durables, such as washing machines and dishwashers, collate warranty and guarantee cards and store this on a database for marketing of other products and repeat products after a certain time. They also sponsor lifestyle questionnaires as issued by Claritas or Experian, and market to people expressing an interest in their product or category.

> Buyers of a vacuum cleaner may receive information on spare parts, replacement bags and servicing (cross-selling). They may also be offered an extended warranty. Later they may receive information on the latest and improved models (up-sell). Customers may also be asked for their feedback (loyalty).

Direct marketing can play an important role in marketing to the trade or to retailers. Maximizing the penetration of the market may be difficult with a limited sales force calling on retail buyers and shop owners. Direct marketing enables you to reach the entire distribution network and the most important buyers.

> BSkyB produces point-of-sale advertising for retailers to use. It provides brand guidelines and tactical offers and promotions for retailers to undertake their own direct marketing. This is supported by direct response press advertisements in the local press and local door drops to prompt store traffic, and radio advertising to raise awareness of promotions.

There are many ways in which customer data can be collected and added to the database, even when you deal with customers through retailers. They include:

- money-off coupons and other offers in the media;
- warranty guarantee cards;

- customer satisfaction questionnaires;
- loyalty cards and schemes;
- deals with credit card or store card marketers to access their customers;
- lifestyle surveys;
- e-mail addresses captured on your company web site.

▶ Business marketing

This is used to generate leads for a sales force or dealer to contact and increasingly for direct delivery – it is now possible to order a mainframe computer over the web. Direct mail, the web, e-mail, the trade press and exhibitions are probably the most widely used channels to prospect for new business, and telemarketing and direct mail are used to service existing customers. Catalogues may be used to support marketing where the product range is wide and where customers may range from the largest enterprise to very small businesses, such as with housing maintenance and decoration products (where the builder or installer is the usual target customer) and office supplies. Catalogues can be expensive to produce and post, so web sites are increasingly taking over this role. Product samples may be used to stimulate interest, with the customer directed to the web site for full product range and information. Another example of sampling is the *Mail on Sunday*'s strategy of sending copies of the paper directly to the home of its most important media buyers.

The field sales force is also a direct marketing medium. While in some cases central direct marketing is used for lead generation, it is not uncommon for field sales forces to be given direct marketing 'kits', allowing them to construct their own direct marketing campaigns.

▶ Benefits of direct marketing

▶ Direct marketing makes other communication strategies work harder, and vice versa

When brand awareness is being raised by media advertising, direct marketing response rates rise, especially when the overall marketing campaign is so well integrated that customers recognize the communication as being part of the same deal, from the same company. Direct marketing works best when deployed as part of an overall communication strategy. The use of several types of marketing communication and using the message more times in more ways means they are more likely to respond to the offer.

▶ It converts interest to sales

Direct marketing converts interest into sales by being, as its name suggests, direct. The message and call to action must be clear to generate a response. The call to action, though often perceived by brand advertisers as unsightly, does not usually reduce the creative impact of the advertisement. Brand image is important to long-term preferences, but response can be vital to short- and long-term sales and loyalty building.

▶ It can deliver prospects

If the advertisement can get the customer to respond, the sender can begin the process of capturing customer information.

▶ It reinforces brand image

Direct marketing can be used to convey general branding messages, while at the same time building goodwill, reinforcing purchase decisions or saying thank you. These are all ways to reinforce branding and generate future sales and to encourage word-of-mouth advertising, the cheapest and most effective way to acquire new customers.

▶ It creates interaction with customers

Mass marketing tends to consist of a one-way flow of messages. An essential component of direct marketing is the response mechanism. This ensures that the message has been received. The more customer information flows back to you, the better targeted, more relevant and more personalized your messages to your customers can become.

▶ It is measurable and accountable

As the pressure on advertising budgets increases, so does the need to measure the effectiveness of contacts. Direct marketing produces measurable results that can prove that spend is producing results.

Direct marketing is as near a science as marketing can ever hope to be. It allows you to carry out controlled experiments and tests. Here, one type of contact acts as a control to represent the current situation or the norm. The other part acts as the test for different approaches. In this way it is possible to measure the effect of the changes and identify stronger formats, messages, offers and lists.

▶ Planning your direct marketing activity

The basic requirements for planning include:

- sales target;
- budget;
- time frame;
- objectives.

Planning your direct marketing activity

You need to be sure of the above in order to determine what kinds of campaign are going to give you the results you need, over what time period. This information is also needed to brief the many suppliers you will need.

Campaigns can vary between a single letter to your ten customers and a multi-channel plan with a budget of £150 million, aimed at millions of customers. Each should be planned in the same thorough way.

There are three key areas to consider in planning which campaigns to run with your customers:

1. acquisition – recruiting new customers;
2. database – storing and manipulating customer information;
3. retention – customer care/loyalty programmes to keep existing customers.

These are shown in Fig. 2.1.

▶ Acquisition marketing

This involves:

- deciding what kinds of customers you want – your target market;
- finding out who they are, how many of them there are and where they are – this is assessing the market opportunity;
- understanding what motivates them – using market research and feedback to identify your key selling points and USP if you have one;
- determining which media to use to talk to them – what media do they consume? What papers do they buy, when do they have time to think about your proposition?
- developing communication and executing campaigns – what tone of voice to use, which paper and formats are cost effective and appropriate, when is the best time to communicate with them, when sales have to come in by;
- converting prospects to customers – the sale and what information is needed to quote, supporting the pricing back-end, training of sales staff, fulfilment needed.

▶ Database marketing

This involves:

- obtaining relevant customer information – who are the best customers, what attributes do they have, how many prospects are available like them?
- storing the information in a usable, retrievable and secure format;
- enhancing this information over time – making sure systems feed into the database so it is kept up to date;
- analysis of the information, to identify the customer – when and what they last bought, their value, the segment they belong to, products held;

- selection of target segments of customers for campaigns – certain segments may warrant different actions for different reasons;
- recording sales and response – it's important to know what works and what does not;
- evaluating, measurement and future business planning – for rolling and tactical strategies to maximize the value of the customer database.

▶ Retention

This involves:

- giving your customers service and product quality that meets their needs;
- building loyalty over time;
- maximizing the length and value of the relationship with customers;
- communicating to them regularly at the right time (that is right for them!);
- deepening the relationship with your customers by encouraging them to buy different types of product, to upgrade and renew;
- monitoring profitability.

▶ Future value of customers over time

If a customer's transaction data is accumulated for a long enough period, you can calculate the future value of the customer. This can be used for several purposes, such as:

- making campaign decisions which *both* generate a profit and increase future customer value. Recent buyers are nearly always among the most frequent responders to additional offers;
- setting levels of investment in customer acquisition and reactivation;
- monitoring future business prospects. An increasingly valuable list indicates a solidly growing business, while a list whose value is deteriorating indicates a business with a problematic future;
- knowing who are your best customers – who has the largest future value, their acquisition source (how they were acquired – direct mail, phone with a special offer, etc.) so that you can acquire more of the same. By matching their characteristics (where they live, age, income, etc.) with those of the rest of the population, you can target others with the same attributes. This is smart acquisition.

▶ Applications of the customer database

Customer databases can be used in:

- testing an offer or medium – keeping it and finding patterns;
- modelling the expected performance of potential customers for the offer, using these results;
- analyzing the financial implications of promotion to different types of customers;
- targeting narrowly defined market segments with specialized offers;
- defining programmes for reactivating lapsed customers;
- evaluating sources of the most valuable customers, for targeting of new ones;
- determining the optimal frequency of promotions;
- quantifying the number of customers likely to buy new products or services and researching their needs;
- testing new products or services;
- measuring marketing effectiveness when multiple distribution channels exist – provided the various channels can be tracked accurately;
- identifying groups of customers who are or will become loyal if communicated with through a programme.

Summary

In this chapter we have briefly reviewed the role of direct marketing and shown some of its uses. The main benefits of direct marketing are that:

- it is applicable to all companies;
- it is an integrative force in communications planning;
- it reaches new targetable media and provides measurable results;
- it encourages the building of customer relationships;
- it offers scientific testing opportunities;
- it reinforces distribution strategies and can add new distribution possibilities.

The cornerstone of direct marketing's strategic role is the control of customer information through the database, supporting acquisition and retention programmes, the life blood of your company's profits and growth. The reasons why you are almost certain to be relying on direct marketing to achieve profits and growth lie in our rapidly changing market environment, the subject of Chapter 3.

3
who does direct marketing and how?

Direct marketing users and suppliers

Users

Suppliers

Media

The direct marketing equipment

Summary

This chapter covers the direct marketing industry, its environment and how you should take these influences into account in direct marketing planning.

Direct marketing users and suppliers

The main users of direct marketing include financial services, travel and leisure, mobile telephony, utilities, charities, business-to-business companies and increasingly the media companies.

The main suppliers of direct marketing services to these users include:

- creative agencies – plan and produce the direct marketing material;
- media planning agencies – buy the media delivery channels (TV advertising slots, press space, door-drop distribution, radio air time);
- telemarketing bureaux – for outbound dialling;
- systems and software suppliers;
- response-handling resource – contact/call centre or paper based;
- fulfilment houses – for sending out packs to customers.

They all work in an environment of increasing regulation (e.g. data protection, product liability, industry-specific regulation – utilities and financial services), which adds to the already high level of technical competence required to succeed in direct marketing.

To deliver direct marketing requires many different decisions, different suppliers, agencies and types of support. A single campaign comprises many stages. These can be categorized broadly into six areas:

- creative;
- print/production;
- leads;
- personalization/media;
- postage/delivery;
- fulfilment.

Not all are involved in each campaign. Personalization may not be needed for a campaign where the first step involves mass advertising, for example.

Users

These are the companies which use direct marketing to influence their customers. Here are some of the main types of client.

▶ Financial services

Credit card, loan and insurance providers dominate the direct marketing expenditure league. In the past Barclaycard was one of the largest users of direct marketing in the UK, particularly through media inserts and direct mail, but it is now focusing on a more targeted audience. Direct Line Insurance, a leader in this sector for many years, has become a household name through its use of clear branding and integrated direct marketing.

▶ Charities

Without direct marketing, fundraising for charitable causes would be a lost cause. A large proportion of charities' income is generated through a mix of direct mail, media inserts, door drops, off-the-page press advertising and direct-response TV.

▶ Travel and tourism

This sector includes not only direct-sell travel companies but also airlines, flight centres, independent hotels and tourist information. They use the direct route to reach customers, particularly off-the-page press in weekend newspapers, as well as marketing to third parties such as flight brokers and travel agents. Broadcast and published media are used to attract customers to company web sites or into the travel agent. Much of the travel industry is moving towards the Internet as the main marketing platform as it can be updated easily which suits the ever-changing nature of offers, prices and flight/holiday availability. Some low-cost airlines have pioneered direct booking from web sites, offering incentives for those who use this channel. Some are now making nearly all their sales through this channel.

▶ Mobile telephony

Due to the highly competitive nature of this market, much like the credit card boom of the early 1990s, mobile tekephone companies use direct marketing aggressively, particularly via media inserts, press advertising and in-store point of sale (POS) to compare their products.

▶ Media companies

In the past few years television companies have become more competitive, and as digital TV has become more embedded in the UK's homes, so the choice has become more widely available. Direct marketing, particularly using press, media inserts and door drops, is used widely by digital TV companies to display their products and associated discount telephony deals. Direct-response TV and off-the-page advertising are also used widely by independent channels to increase their subscriptions and viewing figures.

Suppliers

Agencies

Direct marketing agencies are organized quite like advertising agencies, with account directors and executives, art directors, copywriters, media specialists and so on. They can be big, small, specialist or full service. Some of the biggest are multinationals and many more are subsidiaries of international agencies.

The difference between direct marketing and advertising agencies lies mainly in the additional range of services supplied by some of the larger direct marketing agencies, such as:

- campaign planning and management;
- database building and management;
- response handling, fulfilment;
- data processing and analysis.

They can also take on a greater strategic planning role before the above takes place, even to the extent of managing the entire process. This might include:

- market and competitive analysis;
- marketing strategy.

Direct marketing agencies are required to perform to quite exacting technical standards and to create responses to advertising which are immediate and measurable. They are therefore usually closely involved in planning and implementing the measurement approach.

Mailing houses

Mailing houses enjoy several different names, e.g. letter shop, fulfilment house. They put printed material into envelopes and deliver them to the postal service, perhaps sorted by postcode to obtain postal discounts. In its most sophisticated form, for very high-volume or complicated mailings, this requires skill, experience and much expensive equipment.

Computer bureaux

Although some of the biggest clients and some of the biggest agencies have in-house data-processing facilities, many clients of all sizes and sectors use bureaux. These bureaux perform a range of tasks for clients, from list merging and purging to the design, construction and management of large databases supporting many applications.

▶ List suppliers

List brokers act as an intermediary in the supply of lists of names and addresses from list owners (usually either clients that have built lists through transactions with their customers or companies that have compiled lists specifically for the purpose of renting them out). If you want to mail, you need a list of names and addresses. If you haven't got a list, you may turn to outside lists and sources of list suppliers, probably a list broker.

A list is a perishable commodity. It dates quickly as people move homes and jobs. Whatever efforts are made to maintain the quality of a list, some names will inevitably not be accurate or usable. This is why a 'net-names' agreement is usually employed. Here the broker will rent the list (usually for one-time use only) subject to payment for a specified percentage of names used (usually 85%). To protect the broker against the dishonesty of the client, 'seeds' will be planted in the list. These may be employees of the list-broking firm who will receive (unknown to the mailer) any subsequent mailings sent out by the company from the 'once-only' list. List brokers can also add value by ensuring you comply with data protection laws, which govern the use of personal data and how it is stored.

▶ Paper and equipment suppliers and printers

These are the backbone of the direct mail industry. They vary from the largest paper companies to small print shops running off handbills and cheap inserts for local traders. Without paper, print and inserting machines, no mail-shot could be possible. But it is a particularly fragmented industry, with local suppliers often important. Larger companies with extensive marketing budgets often employ print brokers to manage their substantial print runs. They can add real value in managing complex and large print runs, as well as putting out to tender jobs to printers across the country and abroad to get the best prices. This is useful when huge volumes need to be printed quickly and more than one printer can be used.

Types of supplier	What they can do
Mailing houses	Send out the mailing
	Sort mailing by postcode to obtain a postal discount
	Project manage the campaign
	Provide a freepost address for returns
	Fulfil the offer
Computer bureaux	Hold client data
	Clean client data
	Make the data mail friendly and produce data on tapes for mailing house
List brokers and managers	Sell lists
	Advise on best possible use of them – data selections to take
	Act as an intermediary for other lists of other clients
	Collect names and addresses to compile new lists

Paper, equipment suppliers and printers	Supply raw materials – paper and envelopes Organize stuffing of envelopes (auto or manual enclosing) Organize deliveries and collections to clients, other suppliers and the Royal Mail or another distribution company Proofread and check the personalization is running out correctly from the list and that the location on the letter is in the right place
Direct marketing agencies	Project manage all the above Advise client on suppliers of the above Produce the creative and supply the artwork Proofreading/checking at different stages

▶ Media

The major media used in direct marketing are:

Broadcast and published media	Distributed media
Press Magazines Television Radio Cinema	Take-one leaflets Media inserts Inserts (into letters, statements, etc.) Free newspapers Door drops/news-share distributions Product despatch
Direct response media	**Electronic media**
Direct mail Telephone DRTV (direct response television) Fax See also distributed media section	Internet sites and portals E-mail Interactive digital TV (also broadcast) SMS message to mobile

Figure 3.1 shows the many different ways of contacting customers. Let's take a brief look at each of these channels.

▶ Broadcast and published media

Press

This is an important and accessible medium. It includes national and local newspapers, so you're able to reach certain regions of the country. It also includes weekend supplements and TV guides. Press includes use of off-the-page advertising, which can range from full-colour page adverts to small mono (black and white) fractionals used either individually or as a series. Circulation volumes range from the millions in large national weekend newspapers to the thousands or tens of thousands of small local papers or single regions of a national paper. Press allows

Fig. 3.1 The media spectrum

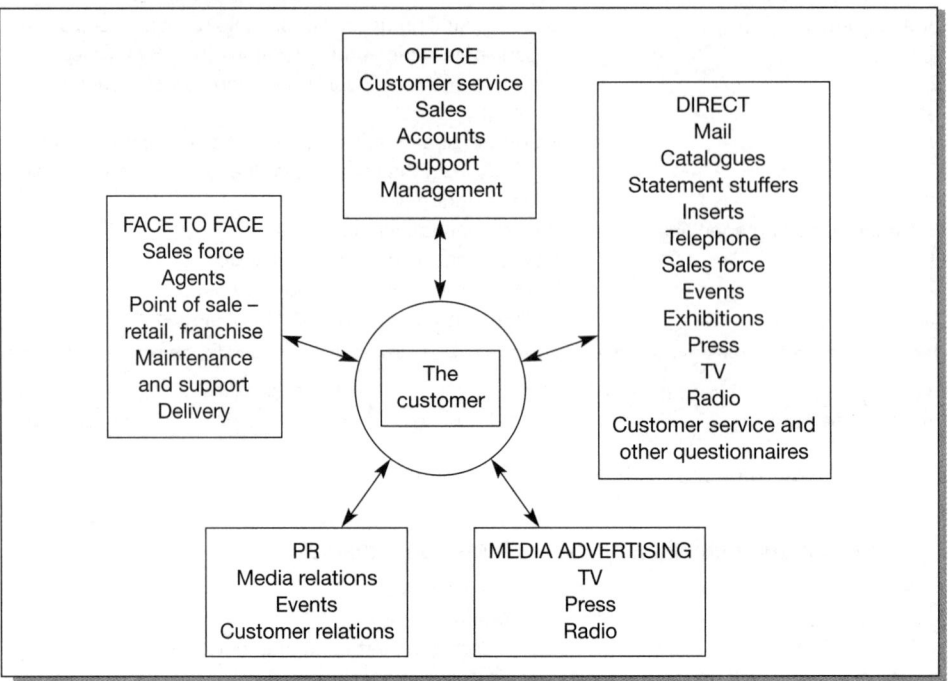

```
                    OFFICE
                Customer service
                     Sales                    DIRECT
                    Accounts                   Mail
                    Support                  Catalogues
                   Management            Statement stuffers
                                              Inserts
   FACE TO FACE                               Telephone
    Sales force                               Sales force
      Agents                                    Events
   Point of sale –                            Exhibitions
   retail, franchise                            Press
    Maintenance          The                     TV
    and support        customer                 Radio
      Delivery                          Customer service and
                                         other questionnaires


         PR                      MEDIA ADVERTISING
    Media relations                      TV
       Events                           Press
  Customer relations                    Radio
```

Note: some media appear twice because they perform more than one role

massive reach if required. Timescales are short so advertisements can be turned round quickly for tactical activity. Response from daily newspapers also tends to be instant. If the advertisement appears at the weekend, response tends to come in on the Monday and Tuesday.

Magazines

These are used in a similar way to press in newspapers, but timing is slower as they are often produced abroad and are circulated weekly or monthly. Due to their extended shelf life, they produce response over a longer period and so have more readers per issue. They are also consumed in different ways to newspapers and are generally read in greater depth for longer, so the advertisement may have greater impact. They usually have a more targeted readership, allowing direct marketers to use them as an effective way of addressing particular market segments.

Television

This is an effective method of generating awareness and works best when supported by direct marketing to convert interest to sales. The viewer will dip in and out of TV, so above all else advertising must be high impact, engaging and/or thought provoking. It needs to produce a strong reaction.

Radio

Radio is often used as background in the car, at home or at work and so the listener, in the same way as with TV, dips in and out of it while it's on. Therefore advertising must stand out to be heard and this is often achieved by the use of sound effects, music, clear or quirky voices and humour. Customers see radio as a softer, less invasive medium, so it's very effective when used in tandem with direct marketing to raise the awareness of a product or special offer. It is also useful in communicating local and time-sensitive offers which are relevant and useful to the audience. The many stations ranging from Jazz and Classic FM to popular national radio stations like Radio 1 and music stations such as XFM and Kiss FM mean that it's possible to reach different audiences and so make your message more targeted and relevant. It is also cheaper than TV, so many companies use it to support their campaigns. It is frequently used as an interactive medium, with direct response telephone numbers and web addresses included.

Cinema

This works well as it has a captive audience. However, it requires high-quality advertising features with good production values and/or relevant local messages to work effectively. It's often used as a part of a brand-building campaign and is effective in targeting different types of viewer, according to film certificate and audience profile.

▶ Distributed media

Take-one leaflets

These are often used in high footfall areas and waiting areas, where there are large numbers of people who may want to read your leaflet. Examples include shopping centres, banks, railway and bus stations, airports and even doctors' surgeries. Leaflets may offer information and an application form. Credit card companies, loan and insurance companies and travel/leisure companies use them widely. These campaigns are often supported by promotional teams handing out the leaflets, sometimes along with samples.

Media inserts

These are used in their millions by a wide variety of companies to sell subscriptions, mail-order clothing catalogues, credit cards, digital TV, magazines, wine clubs. They are also used widely by scratch card competition companies, mobile phone providers (to sell SMS text messaging and ring tones), insurance companies (to sell home, car, health, pet insurance) and loan companies. They are inserted into newspapers and magazines and can be loose or bound in and threaded through the spine of a magazine. Mass production of these can lead to very low production costs, so they tend to be planned in large quantities.

Other inserts

Similar to media inserts, loose flyers can be inserted into other customer communications (e.g. catalogues, letters, product despatch material, invoices and statements). This is an efficient way to target your existing customer base and is used by financial services and insurance companies all the time. Inserts can also be distributed through third parties' customer communications to reach another company's customer base. If the target market is similar to yours, response can be very good.

Local newspapers (free or paid for)

Local newspapers provide a good medium through which to target a particular area. They are generally trusted and perceived as non-biased and therefore are good at reaching people who would normally dismiss national papers and their contents. They can be used to carry media inserts, press and editorials, but are limited in circulation volume so are best used as part of a wider plan to gain reach.

Door drops/news-share distributions

These are organized distributions made on foot, managed by independent companies or postal companies. They involve dropping flyers, etc. through the door, usually at targeted postcodes. The number of elements being dropped and for which type of companies may not be known, though there are agreements on maximum number of items and exclusion of direct competitors from the same drop. Postcode targeting allows certain types of households to be mailed, though response is lower than direct mail as they are not personalized. Door drops are also used to good effect by supermarkets, garden centres and garages to target their local area with offers and discounts, new products, etc. The fast food sector relies largely on this method and is often highly competitive.

> In the late 1990s there was fierce war between the supermarkets, with the largest launching loyalty cards and vying with each other to win the customer. Safeway decided to withdraw its loyalty card, instead spending more below the line and cutting prices. It delivered vouchers to residents near its stores, to be redeemed against goods. This direct approach worked and allowed Safeway to survive the severe competition and build itself a new 'neighbourhood' niche.

▶ Direct response media

Direct mail

This is very targeted, reaching a single person at home or at work with your message. Due to its components (creative, print and production, postage, lead) it is quite an expensive medium. Generally, the more targeted the campaign, the higher the cost per contact, especially if the data is from a rented list, but generally the more responsive the mailing. So, if you get the format and message right, you can generate excellent results. Thus testing is key.

Telephone

This is the most personal means of communicating with a person. It is good for two-way communication, feedback and information gathering. It's also very useful to tailor the product to individual customers, to increase relevancy. However, it can be seen as intrusive, particularly if calling someone at home in the evenings. Therefore care should be taken to position the call so that it is not confrontational. The telephone is often used in gathering service feedback, for surveys, and to up-sell and cross-sell existing products to existing customers. It's also used to acquire new customers, though this can be tough.

DRTV (direct response television)

This is similar to TV advertising but uses a strong call to action (CTA), with the viewer being reminded repeatedly throughout the advert to respond – normally to call a telephone line to buy, book, donate money or get information. It is used to good effect by charitable causes (e.g. Red Nose Day, BBC's Children in Need, RSPCA advertising). DRTV is also used widely by insurance companies – the combination of emotional images or scenarios and rational action is a powerful one.

Fax

This is not used so much nowadays as e-mail has taken over much of its role. However, it is still used for cheap marketing to businesses and by office suppliers and paper merchants due to the industry's link with the medium.

> ### Electronic media
> This is an important new media which uses e-mail and short messaging to mobile phones. It is a quick and hard-hitting method of direct marketing.

▶ The direct marketing environment

This is ever changing and so will influence the success of your direct marketing campaign. The main influences are:

- political;
- economic;
- social;
- technological

or PEST.

This simple checklist can help you analyze your market and identify likely effects of changes on your direct marketing.

Political factors

A change in the government can affect consumer behaviour, usually influenced by the media interest and the reaction to changes to taxes and laws. Deregulation and privatization of businesses, often in the years after a change in government, can result in a more competitive environment where the consumer has more choice.

The deregulation of the financial services industry accelerated the development of direct marketing channels and catalyzed the development of new ways to reach the consumer, e.g. DRTV, outbound telesales, the Internet. These developments increased the focus on customer value management and segmentation, on how to find better means of penetrating new markets and launching new products.

Privatization of the telecommunications industry has created competition for the previously state-owned monopoly in many countries and has been exacerbated by the arrival of mobile telephony and companies reselling telephone time, offering competitive rates, products and increased flexibility. Direct marketing has helped all these companies attack and defend, using off-the-page press ads, door drops, direct mail and DRTV, e.g. from NTL, Virgin Home Phone and the many power utilities which offer telephony, such as Eastern Electricity.

Media liberalization has led to further choice. Multi-channel television is now very competitive. The UK saw the launch in 1998 and demise in 2002 of ITV Digital (previously OnDigital), which tried to compete with Sky digital for market share, with cable companies NTL and Telewest offering cable TV and phone packages. The multi-channel TV market is yet to change further as set-top adaptor boxes continue to offer an alternative, usually with a narrower range of channels, but free.

▶ Economic factors

Whether the country is heading for a boom or recession affects people's comfort or fear to spend money. This in turn will affect consumer confidence and the propensity to purchase your product. However, longer-term factors are also important. As population is growing slowly in most developed economies, marketers must look for areas of increase in real income and spending. The major variables involved include:

- levels of unemployment/employment;
- labour productivity;
- inflation;
- consumer/business spending;
- the savings ratio;
- investment;
- the balance of payments;
- lifestyle changes.

It is often argued that direct marketing benefits in an economic downturn as advertisers switch expenditure on advertising to direct marketing to exploit its cost effectiveness. In such circumstances, the finance director is often the strongest advocate of direct marketing, as its measurable benefits are strong compared with above-the-line advertising.

Another area to consider is the pace of technology and the different behaviour of new generations of buyers. Today children are less likely to imitate their parents' buying behaviour, preferring to find their own way to major brands. So it becomes more challenging and important to reach them. Ethical issues of marketing to young people are also involved.

▶ Social factors

Society places pressure on people to conform and as such people like not only to feel good about themselves but for others to feel good about them too. By understanding your target market better, you can start to build up a clearer picture about their values, their lives and what's important to them. You can then align your products and services with this picture and become a more natural fit into their lives.

Market information, gained by competitive research, customer feedback, lifestyle survey data and other sources, can provide the data you need to market more effectively to your customer or prospect. Examples of where this is applied include suppliers of luxury brands, which use aspirational appeal to sell expensive cosmetic products to people who buy designer clothes or to those who shop in certain prestigious stores. BSkyB positions digital TV as a market leader, offering premium choice and quality viewing in order to overcome the perception which once existed that it is for lower classes. The Body Shop provides pure and untested products to an increasingly environmentally conscious market.

▶ Technological factors

Technology enhances existing markets and creates entirely new markets and new channels of communication. Since the 1990s the mobile phone has developed into a prime communications medium. Technology created a new market that now supports additional channels such as SMS. The Internet is also a new technology that has helped shape our marketing world. We have information on any product at the touch of a button. We can send pictures, stream live video and sound, send instant messages and purchase goods from anywhere around the globe. In the direct marketing world, we have more capability than ever before to extract customer data and deliver highly segmented and tailored marketing to reintroduce more personal customer communications and drive customer value.

▶ Micro-competitive intensity

The intensity of the competition is defined not only by the number of competitors but also by their dominance. BSkyB is the dominant multi-channel TV supplier. MBNA, the credit card supplier, has around 100 different credit cards available, many with similar customer bases. Monitoring your close competition is important because they can use direct marketing to attack specific parts of your customer base.

▶ Barriers to entry

It is useful to analyze barriers to market entry as part of your direct marketing planning because direct marketing techniques are often used to break down barriers. This should include barriers to purchase, gained from feedback from people who have not yet bought your product, competitive activity and pricing. It may also include seasonal factors. Once you know your barriers you can overcome them by changing your plan.

▶ Summary

All marketers are waking up to the opportunities offered by direct marketing and are learning its tools and techniques fast. However, direct marketers need to learn from their 'above-the-line' colleagues and develop competitive approaches which go beyond measuring the response rate on the last campaign. They must open their minds to new movements, to new issues, to new ways of defining old problems, and must shift from short-term to long-term thinking. Direct marketing has for too long been a tactical response to problems based on individual campaigns and their management rather than on the achievement of long-term corporate goals or missions. Companies that have a clearly defined mission, based on an assessment of strengths, weaknesses, opportunities and threats, and the capacity to convert the mission into effective strategies and tactics, are better placed to survive and prosper.

In this chapter we've described briefly the structure of the direct marketing industry – clients, agencies and other suppliers. Each of these is a business in its own right. If you want to use direct marketing, you need to use the campaign planning and implementation methodologies of classic direct marketing. But you also need to look outward, beyond the confines of the direct marketing industry to the wider economic and social environment in which your campaigns will have to succeed. Political and legal changes may affect your market profoundly (e.g. financial services, utilities). You may be affected by economic and social change (e.g. charities) or by technological change, particularly as computing and telecommunications developments allow so much more to be achieved, more quickly, at lower cost and with fewer staff, and provide consumers with so much more choice about how to get information about your products, obtain them – and contact you afterwards to complain about them!

In the next chapter we focus on how you should develop your direct marketing strategy.

4 direct and interactive strategy

Introduction

The principles of acquisition and retention

Acquisition

Keeping customers – the principle of retention

Acquisition vs retention

What creates loyalty?

Steps in a retention strategy

Understanding the customer base

Summary

Introduction

Because of its origins as a tactical weapon, especially as direct mail, direct marketing is often seen as an operational tactic, best expressed in phrases such as: *'Let's do a mailshot'*, *'Let's e-mail our customers'*, *'Let's put something different on our web site'*, or *'Let's try to sell to customers who call in for service.'* To such suggestions, you should counter with: *'Why, to whom, when, with what objectives, what will follow on, how will my relationship with my customers change, etc., etc.?'*

Direct and interactive marketing is now an accepted part of strategic marketing planning. Direct marketing has opened up great opportunities in collection, analysis and tracking of customer information. This information, maintained on your database, is clearly a corporate planning asset. Companies have been bought and sold on the knowledge they contain. On balance sheets this is shown as 'goodwill' values, but in direct marketing terms it is an asset of tangible value – the names, addresses and all transactional and promotional information on all customers. The lifetime value of a customer is yet to appear on balance sheets but it will be an inevitable consequence of a better understanding of direct marketing.

> Next bought Grattan, a mail-order company, largely for the value of its 6 million customer names.

Direct marketing permeates all levels of strategic and marketing planning. Enhanced customer knowledge means that you can enter new markets with greater degrees of certainty. You can identify customers under competitive threat and take steps to reinforce their loyalty. You understand more about particular markets. You can use the database to identify specific market and product range opportunities. You can derive and test product specifications and promotional options. You can revolutionize the channels through which you manage your customers through direct and interactive marketing techniques.

Different ways to use your database include to:

- identify markets which have similar customers to those on your database;
- identify customers who recently have bought less and research them to see whether they are buying competitive products;
- identify customers who are loyal and develop loyalty programmes to reinforce their loyalty and encourage them to buy more (greater volumes, wider product ranges, etc.) and recommend you;
- identify customers who have bought particular products, and develop new products to suit these segments;
- develop and test campaigns to get particular types of customers to buy more;
- test promotional ideas on a sample from your database.

The principles of acquisition and retention

Your **customer attrition rate** is the percentage of your customers at the beginning of a period who cease doing business with you during that period. A single figure is not always the best way of measuring it, as its significance depends upon factors such as the average length of the buying cycle or frequency of purchase, and the range and value of products bought. For example, you might want to regard a customer as lost if they stop buying your highest-value products from you and buy only your very low-value products infrequently. So **share of wallet** is also an important measure.

Your **customer retention rate** is the converse of your attrition rate, i.e. the proportion of your customers that you had at the beginning of the period who are still doing business with you at the end of the period. For the same reasons, a single figure gives you only a rough guide to the situation.

Customer retention is similar to **loyalty**, but loyalty is strictly speaking a state of mind. A loyal customer may buy elsewhere because you don't happen to have the right product at the time. **Customer acquisition** is the process or achievement of gaining new customers. **Customer retention** is the process or achievement of keeping them.

Most objectives and strategies in direct marketing are based on the ideas of customer acquisition and retention. However good your marketing, you will always suffer some customer attrition. To stand still, you need to acquire more customers – the purpose of acquisition programmes.

Acquisition

There are usually six stages in an acquisition programme.

1 Set objectives.
2 Profile the type of customers you wish to acquire (usually similar to your existing best customers) by analysing your database.
3 Target those customers, often using acquired or rented lists.
4 Media selection – if the right lists aren't available at the right cost, use media which are targeted at the type of customer you want to acquire. This has become much easier because of the way media have developed to focus on more closely targeted markets.
5 Communication – develop the communication that will attract those customers, through an offer designed to appeal to them, sent to them at the time it is most likely to appeal, and expressed in a way – copy, images, etc. – most likely to appeal to them.
6 Sell to customers.
7 Handle them properly after the sale to retain them, sell more to them and sell a wider range to them.

▶ Objectives

Perhaps surprisingly, the starting point for any acquisition programme is not analysis of the reasons why people come to you – or don't – it is a simple financial calculation. **Lifetime value** is the value (profit) you can expect from a given customer over the expected life of that customer with you. It increases the better your retention rate, the more you can sell up and sell across, and the more strongly you can get the customer to recommend you to others. Strictly speaking, it should be calculated using discounted cash flow techniques, but most direct marketers use much simpler approaches, such as the value of the first N years of purchase. How far ahead you should look depends upon how long you can expect a customer to be interested in your category of product and the length of the buying cycle.

> **Allowable marketing cost per acquisition** is how much you can afford to spend to acquire a customer. It should be determined by the expected lifetime value of a customer, as opposed to short-term profit.

> A parent is likely to be in the market for particularly high volumes of detergents for the period in which there are children at home. This can be for as long as 20–25 years. Acquiring a customer at the beginning of this period can yield a very high lifetime value if loyalty is managed successfully. However, keeping the customer loyal in such a highly competitive market is expensive and many quite loyal customers will switch to try out competitive offers – the purchasing cycle is frequent enough for this to happen – and switch back later. This can cut the value of loyal customers.

If you haven't got the data to calculate lifetime value, you can use various short-term measures, such as:

◆ cost of achieving the initial sale(s) to the newly acquired customer – this leads to a focus on finding low-cost methods of acquisition (e.g. if the offer is price led, making it on a low-cost item). You need to be careful about using this, as customers who are easy or cheap to acquire may be customers who are always ready to leave their existing supplier. They are known as 'switchers';

◆ return on investment from the initial sale(s).

However, the closer to lifetime value the measure is, the better it is as a criterion for targeting or selecting customers to be acquired. One reason why a good customer database is so valuable is that it allows you to track the longer-term buying patterns of your customers and so calculate their lifetime value.

Acquisition and retention strategies differ according to your previous relationship with the customer. The key categories here are these:

◆ repeat customers;
◆ former customers;
◆ previous enquirers;
◆ new customers.

▶ Profiling

If your database contains data on individuals and their response and purchase histories, it is the right starting point for you to examine which media sources and communication strategies work best. Where little or no history exists, developing a profile of existing customers will help you target new customers. Many companies use customer satisfaction questionnaires for this purpose. Many have analyzed the relationship between being very satisfied and the likelihood that a customer will respond to a communication or buy.

▶ Targeting

Targeting should be based on profiling the customer base. This is clearly the best way, but not always possible. Your aim here is to look for customers with similar characteristics to your best customers.

> **Member get member** schemes (known as MGM) are often used by membership and credit card organizations as a way of recruiting similar customers. Members tend to recruit similar people to themselves. If your database does not hold enough good prospects and if relevant lists are hard to obtain, MGM should always be considered as an option. MGM is targeted word-of-mouth advocacy with a bonus built in for existing customers.

> British Airways ran an MGM campaign among its executive card holders. It used data collected from market research to qualify running the campaign where it explained how many people had wanted to have something to give to others to persuade them to join. The benefit was offered only to new members, not those being asked to recommend new holders.

▶ Media

When evaluating and selecting media, you must establish an allowable cost per sale. This cost will increase if the lifetime value of customers is introduced into the calculations. Other variables to consider in the media plan for recruitment should include:

- size of audience to be reached – the larger the audience, the more viable mass media will be;
- media cost – which has to be weighed against the likelihood of response;
- media availability – even with such a wide range of media available today, you may have to work hard to find the right combination for you;
- media accessibility – do your prospects for recruitment pay enough attention to the medium for it to be a successful recruitment device?
- estimated effectiveness – what is the likely response rate?

◆ the number of stages of communication required to achieve the right response (one stage or multiple, depending on the buying process). The more complex the product or service, the more complex the recruitment process is likely to be. For example, for some industrial equipment products, it may require two or three letters, a catalogue, two or three phone calls and several sales visits.

> The **law of diminishing media returns** occurs in various forms, such as the following:
> ◆ A customer's responsiveness to a particular medium diminishes the more he or she is exposed to it.
> ◆ The more (frequently within a period, total period over which it is used) a particular advertisement is used, the lower the response.
> ◆ Doubling the size of advertisements, the weight of mailing packages or their frequency will less than double response. This is often refered to as the 'square root law', as doubling may lead to a response which is only about 40% higher (the square root of 2 being just over 1.4, or 40% greater than 1).

Multiple media campaigns are usually more cost effective as they are less susceptable to the law of diminishing returns. However, they are more difficult to co-ordinate. There is more chance of their going wrong. For example, if the timing of promotion through one medium slips (e.g. a letter which contains a reference to a television campaign), the effect may be counterproductive.

Media sources can be ranked (from lowest to highest) according to the cost per sale. It is also possible to rank cost effectiveness within individual media such as direct mail (effectiveness of particular lists) and press (by individual publication). This highlights the requirement to source-code all promotions so that their individual performance in customer recruitment can be monitored and ranked over time. A high volume of sales from an advertisement in one particular newspaper may generate many customers. However, they may have no stamina (in other words, the drop-out rate between enquiry and sale may be very high, or they may buy from you only once and never again) compared with those recruited by an identical advertisement in another paper.

In the past, many direct marketers focused on the immediate impact and result of any activity, as opposed to the cumulative impact of several communications. As far as instant results are concerned, high unduplicated (i.e. the same prospect is not hit twice) market coverage will normally outpull high frequency. This is in contrast to the philosophy of general advertisers, who prepare media plans based on reach (the total number of prospects covered) *and* frequency (how often the advertisement appears). However, if you want to focus on customer retention and lifetime value, you need to use both approaches to campaign planning if you want a stable, high-yielding customer base. This principle is illustrated in Fig. 4.1.

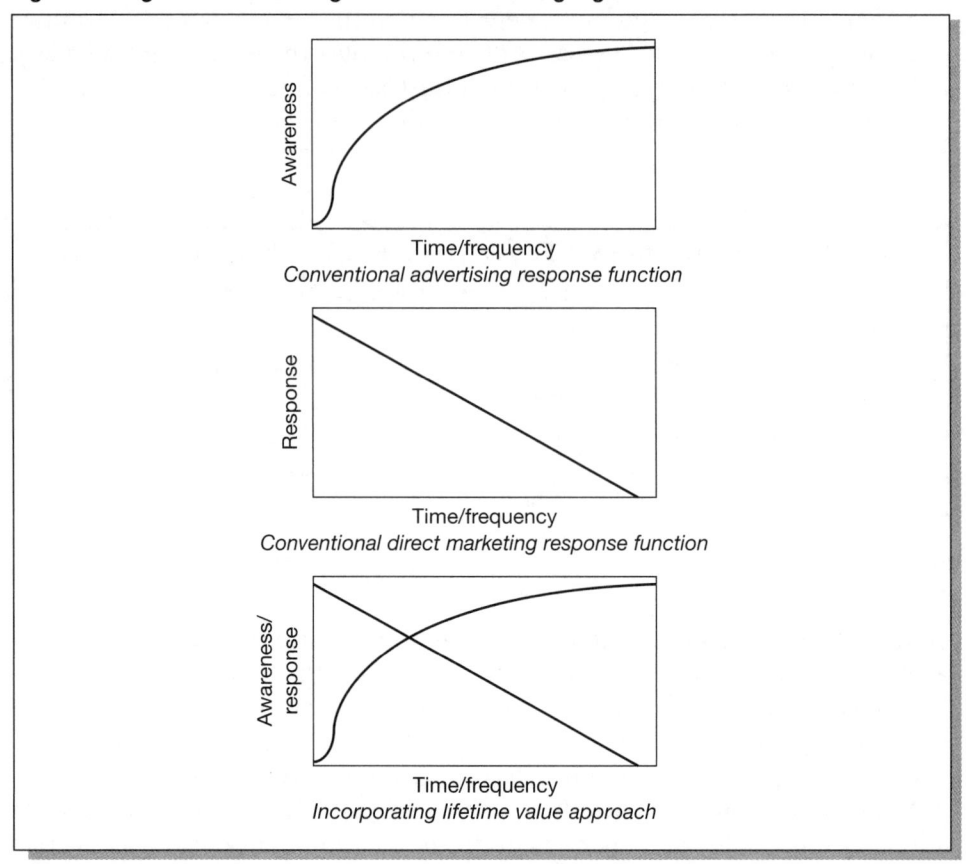

Fig. 4.1 Using media advertising and direct marketing together

Conventional advertising response function (Awareness vs Time/frequency)

Conventional direct marketing response function (Response vs Time/frequency)

Incorporating lifetime value approach (Awareness/response vs Time/frequency)

▶ Communication

Creative treatment and offers made to potential new customers depend on your knowledge of buyer behaviour. Depending on the nature of your company's products or services, you may decide that you need immediate buyers, trial buyers, highly qualified enquirers or loosely qualified enquirers. These decisions will affect the creative treatment, offer and number of stages needed to complete the buying cycle. The creative also depends on the brand personality of the promoted product or service. This determines, for example, whether a communication is product or offer led.

▶ Sales

Once the sale is made, the process of managing and retaining your customer really begins. The obvious step is the need for a communication thanking your customer. Unfortunately, such an old-fashioned, small business norm has not yet permeated many large companies and this simple step is often forgotten.

> **Checklist: acquisition**
>
> Have you set achievable, realistic objectives which will fit with the business's overall needs?
>
> Have you included a mechanism which will enable you to profile your database better in future, and have you made best use of the profiles available to you?
>
> Have you targeted closely enough bearing in mind your objectives and the budget for the campaign?
>
> Can your media supplier give you accurate figures on their profiles? Do they fit as closely as possible to yours?
>
> Does your communication leave the target market with the right messages about your product?
>
> Are your customer services and retention policies strong enough to support the campaign and a possible influx of customers?

▶ Keeping customers – the principle of retention

The purpose of retention strategy is to maximize an individual's profitable lifetime value as a customer. Active customers can usually easily be identified from records of current transactions. The definition of lapsed and inactive customers varies by the average frequency of transaction in the market. To be cost effective, retention strategies have to be planned in some detail and can result in quite complex programmes.

> In merchandise mail order, a lapsed inactive customer might be defined as one who has not ordered for 12 months, an inactive customer as one who has not ordered for 24 months or more. But for goods with longer reordering cycles, these figures might be much higher. If the product is durable and replacement takes place every ten years or so, customers might consider themselves as loyal to a company even if they have not bought for five years. For this reason, companies with long replacement cycle products try to sell lower-value items (service, support, parts, etc.) on a more regular basis. The main reason for this is to generate revenue, but it also works wonders as a way of keeping in touch with customers.

The longer the known lifetime or **potential** lifetime of your customer, the more promotional activities can be undertaken during the customer's life with your company. At the beginning, 'welcoming' activities take place. These are followed by promotions encouraging the customer to upgrade or to buy additional products or services. Finally, as the end of the product's life with the customer approaches (e.g. end of subscription, need to replace equipment), renewal activities are initiated.

▶ Welcome cycle

This is an opportunity to welcome and reassure customers, overcome any cognitive dissonance, build loyalty and gain additional customer information. It also opens up the opportunity of giving your customer initial benefits. Whether a welcome cycle is appropriate will be related to the length of life cycle of the customer.

▶ Up-selling

Given a positive reaction to the product/service, a natural next step would be to promote higher-value products/services. In the case of a normal credit card, it could be a privileged customer gold card, in automobile terms an upmarket model in the range, or in recorded music a boxed set to appeal to a buyer of a single CD/cassette/album. The timing of the offer can be determined by previous customer histories. Often this can be achieved by testing and then applying the test results using statistical analysis applied to the customer database, to give each customer record an individual score which indicates the likelihood of the customer responding to such an offer.

▶ Cross-selling

This is a conscious strategy to switch your customers across product categories. A credit card company could promote a home shopping service or wine club. An automobile company could promote the second car for the family. A book club could promote a music collection. In both up- and cross-selling, loyal customers should be given some incentive to remain loyal.

▶ Renewal

The length of the renewal cycle should be tested to achieve the optimum results for the minimum expenditure. You need to find cost-effective inducements to reward loyal customers for continued patronage. Often a renewal cycle will mean a number of timed, relevant and personal communications before the date of renewal, on the date of renewal and after the date of renewal. Customers who pass the final renewal cycle date become 'lapsed'.

▶ Lapsed customers

Reawakening lapsed customers is usually more cost effective than recruiting totally new customers, unless they have lapsed because of a fundamental problem in the relationship (e.g. product or service quality) or because they have passed out of the target market (e.g. a different life stage, moving out of the relevant area). You may face problems with the quality of the information about lapsed customers. However, because data on lapsed customers is available to you from your database, its value can be tested, so the profitability on promotions to your lapsed customers does not have to be guessed.

▶ Inactive customers

Here, cost effectiveness is a more critical issue. Inactive customers have not bought or responded to a promotion for longer than lapsed customers. Again, however, the answer is to test and compare the results to the acquisition programme in term of cost justification.

> **Checklist: making the most of your direct marketing**
>
> Does your campaign have room for a 'welcome' cycle when loyalty can be built up?
>
> Will the welcome cycle be used to up-sell?
>
> Have you formed alliances with other companies to allow for cross-selling, or does your company have enough interested customers for it to be valuable in an alliance with other companies?
>
> Is your new business section regenerating the database, and are you keeping the customers you recruited?
>
> Do you want to do anything about lapsed and inactive customers? Do you have sufficient budget to regenerate them? Is it cost effective in your business?

Acquisition vs retention

All company sales are made up from two groups, new customers and repeat customers. It is usually – though not always – more cost effective to retain existing customers than attract new customers. Existing customers have known, identified needs which have been satisfied by the company's product. By focusing your marketing strategy on the profitable segments of your customer base, you will normally produce most of the required revenue and increase market share without investing in new customers. Acquisition is more expensive because it takes place in an unidentified universe where much of the campaign falls on hopeless causes. But once you succeed with acquisition, the maintenance of customer loyalty has additional benefits. Loyal customers not only repurchase, they advocate products and services to their friends, pay less attention to competitive brands and often buy product/service line extensions.

> **Warning!**
>
> If you analyze your customers and discover that large numbers of them are unprofitable, and then do everything you can to make them profitable but still have many unprofitable customers left, you may discover that this is due to a poorly targeted acquisition strategy. This is the one time when it is not true that retention is more important than acquisition. In this situation, you must focus strongly on your acquisition policy.

> **In the real world**
>
> The critical issue in retention which direct marketers sometimes skim over is that **customer loyalty** is *not* merely created by cross-selling strategies or customer clubs. Loyalty is a state of mind, which is reinforced by how you manage your customers in the fullest sense, including service, communication and branding.

To develop effective retention strategies, a company needs a thorough understanding of its customers' behaviour and needs. Loyalty is a physical and emotional commitment given by a customer in exchange for their needs being met. You should view your relationship with your customers from their viewpoint. This should help you understand why you are getting your current level of loyalty and how to reduce your customer attrition rate.

> **eg**
>
> MBNA, a loan and credit card company, reduced its annual defection rate from 10% to 5% p.a. and thereby increased its profits by 85%. It achieved this not by introducing a loyalty scheme but by completely overhauling its service delivery system via business process re-engineering techniques. This means that it redesigned its systems and processes for managing customers to meet customers' requirements rather than the functional requirements of different departments. Service quality went up, defections went down and profits soared.

> *Fast-track*
>
> Market research of existing customers is an important contributor to planning retention marketing. If you involve your customer-facing staff, it can be even more effective. Using market research or customer audits as the focus for this gives your staff an understanding of the customer and also of the importance of understanding customers. If you are in a market which allows you to use your staff as field workers for collecting self-completion questionnaires for customer satisfaction research (e.g. retailing, travel and leisure, professional services), you will not only get valuable customer feedback but your staff will also be keen to use the information they have collected.

What creates loyalty?

Your customers' loyalty will grow if you change how you manage your customers so as to meet their product quality, relationship, service, communication and brand needs.

Customers seek:

- convenience and easy access to your products or services;
- appropriate contact and communication with your company;
- 'special' privileged status as a known customer;
- recognition of their history with you;
- effective and fast problem solving;
- appropriate anticipation of their needs;
- a professional, friendly two-way dialogue.

Using information on your customer database, there is no reason why a customer loyalty programme cannot be finely tuned to provide high levels of customer service to the majority of your customers.

Steps in a retention strategy

There are five steps in retention strategy.

▶ Identification

This is the first step – simply to identify and value your best customers against an agreed criterion of profitability. It may be that smaller but regular buyers contribute a greater profit margin and lifetime value than one-time large purchasers.

▶ Analysis

This is a detailed analysis of the profile of your best customers. A thorough profiling and tracking of their purchase histories (frequency – how much, recency – how recently, amount – of what volume or value, and category – what type: usually abbreviated as FRAC) and promotional responses and sources is vital here. It also helps you identify the potential market of similar customers for your acquisition programme. This is sometimes referred to as a direct marketing audit. Many financial institutions have been surprised to learn how many customers and families are multiple purchasers of their products.

▶ Selection

Once each customer's record has been properly analyzed and scored for its likely value to you, it is accessible for selection. The criteria for selection include not only likely profitability but also the customer's accessibility to you (whether by direct marketing or other techniques). At this stage, you should review all your potential contact points with customers for their usefulness in deepening the relationship.

Contact points represent two different targeting opportunities. One type is at a nominal cost to the organization, while the other is paid for. The former opportunities are known as free rides and can include:

- statement stuffers – promotional material in bills, along the lines of most credit card companies or direct print photographic companies;
- product despatch stuffers – promotional material enclosed with products such as mail-order merchandise;
- invoices and account letters – these are also promotional opportunities;
- opening and closing letters;
- catalogues;
- calls from customers;
- point-of-sale or service contact.

▶ Contact strategies

The contact strategy is the type and sequence of promotional steps required to achieve the desired result, e.g. letter followed by telephone call and sales visit. This must reinforce the benefits of repeat purchasing. The aim is to reward customers' decisions to stay loyal and increase purchasing. You may need to combine different media according to their relative strengths, so as to achieve the best effect.

For example, customers who are a long way off from buying (they may have just bought) may need a gentle mail prompt. Customers who are closer to rebuying may merit a telephone call or even a sales visit. But with the cost of keeping a salesperson on the road anything between £50 000 and £100 000, and the cost per visit between £120 and £240, this resource must be deployed carefully. This contrasts with an outbound telephone call at £6–£10 (depending on its length). So you need to assess whether the sales call is likely to be so many times more effective. The answer is that it will be for some customers, not for others. Your task is to find out which, and the best way to do this is to test it.

The idea of putting the customer in a privileged position is common to many contact strategies.

> A number of very large companies, such as British Airways and BT, now use the contact strategy philosophy to determine the contact strategies for many different customer groups, particularly their best customers – thus pushing out the frontiers of customer service.

▶ Testing and evaluation

Whatever stage of the life cycle a customer is at, it is always worth having a continual series of tests to establish optimum timing, frequency, offer and creative treatments. Without these, the profitability of loyalty programmes can be difficult to establish.

▶ Understanding the customer base

Your customer base is your greatest potential market research. It can present your market researchers with an excellent sampling frame, which is why the formal research process should be built into the contact strategy, involving the use of questionnaires and structured telephone interviews. Research can also form part of the customer care programme. If executed properly, it will reinforce the brand and service values you wish to transmit to customers.

> **Checklist: customer retention**
>
> Can you identify your best customers? What percentage of your total customer base are they?
>
> What particular features do they have in common? Can these be found in other customers?
>
> When is the best time to hit them with new services and offers?
>
> Are you communicating with them enough, or too much? Have you researched how they feel about this?
>
> How often do you talk to your customers and listen to their views, or run focus groups? Do you use this information to modify your profiling of best customers?
>
> Are you getting the right information from your customer database? Have you really used the market research element of it? Where are the gaps and what can you do to fill them?

Summary

In the real world
Customer retention can be more important than acquisition as it is usually more cost effective and profitable. However, the two are often closely linked. If you recruit lots of switchers, you will create a retention problem, so you should focus on higher-quality acquisition. If you focus too much resource on retention, you may not spend enough on high-quality customer recruitment. Also, if you make it hard for new customers to come to you, they may talk to existing customers (perhaps in the same family or business) and start to change the latter's attitudes towards you. So acquisition and retention need to be kept in balance.

The communications used in retention vary according to the nature of your business and your marketing objectives. The objective of a retention programme must be to make it worthwhile for your customers to stay with you, which is why a thorough understanding of your customers' behaviour is vital. You will sometimes have to achieve a delicate balance between marginal income and customer irritation. In any retention programme, all possible contact points with your customers must be reviewed, competitive messages must be taken into account, optimal frequency must be tested, and your customers must receive the right products, customer service and quality.

All acquisition and retention strategies and programmes are ultimately driven by the customer database and your customer relationship management strategy. All retention activities are geared to enhance the knowledge the database contains. Every element of the marketing plan should make a clear contribution to acquiring and/or retaining customers. In the next chapter a detailed methodology for developing direct marketing plans is described.

5 planning direct marketing

What makes a good direct marketing plan?

The planning process

Situation analysis

Customer definition – who will buy it?

Financial performance

Reviewing your key resources

Competition

Setting business objectives

Common direct marketing objectives

Strategy options and evaluation

Action plans

The essential skill – what you need in a campaign manager

Financial analysis

Summary

In this chapter we show that direct marketing means more than just planning campaigns – it also means planning long-term relationships with customers. Direct marketing planning is similar to marketing planning, but the emphasis on customer relationships implies a stronger focus on customer acquisition, retention and lifetime values as planning criteria. A strong emphasis on efficiency is also important, as high volumes of customer contacts can be financially disastrous if response or sales rates are low.

What makes a good direct marketing plan?

Direct marketers' strong tactical heritage frequently leads to the idea that many one-off campaigns will produce high response rates. To many direct marketers, a plan is just a string of good promotional ideas. But such a plan is unlikely to lead to long-term success in customer acquisition and retention. A good direct marketing plan is not simply a list of ideas, summary notes from meetings or sets of recommendations. It should be a structured series of initiatives, working to clear and quantified objectives, tightly targeted and (ideally) with the targeting, timing, offer and creative tested beforehand. Where the aim is to manage a group of customers to achieve increased loyalty, these initiatives should be aimed at building and/or reinforcing the relationship with them.

Planning itself is not simply about problem solving, forecasting or making decisions, all of which are day-to-day management functions. Your direct marketing plan should be:

- a written, comprehensive and detailed document, prepared with the input of direct marketing professionals;
- the result of problem solving and decision making to specify the direction of your marketing operation for the quarter, the year or whatever period you are planning for;
- an integral part of your overall marketing and business planning process and not a tactical afterthought.

In the real world

The beauty of a robust plan is that you can follow it and remain focused on your objectives. This is particularly useful if your business is a hectic one, with many frequent, even daily, shifting focuses and priorities. It remains a solid, grounded and rational plan, focused on marketing and sales objectives driving sales, increasing value, etc. A clear plan is also needed for commitment and support from the other areas of the business. It provides clear, measurable objectives for the marketing team. It is also a great basis for briefing suppliers.

High-level plans, such as a yearly marketing plan, may plot out the key campaign periods, with start and end dates assigned and the broad creative positioning and objectives related to each burst of marketing activity. The plan will also be supported by a rationale that explains the principles behind planning and phasing. It should also provide relevant supporting market information.

More detailed plans, such as for each marketing campaign, will require more information, setting out exactly the objectives, budget, timings, requirements, positioning and results expectations. This ensures that the campaign will meet objectives. It provides all the information needed to begin the briefing process. Activities will be quantified and evaluated according to how they contribute to revenue and profit. The plan will have been quantified from the customer perspective, showing how each group of customers is expected to perform in their year of acquisition and over the lifetime of their relationship with you.

The benefits of a good direct marketing plan are that it:

- focuses on objectives;
- identifies relationships between departments or functions that need to be taken into account;
- stimulates creativity;
- allocates resources for their most profitable use;
- creates a benchmark for future decisions;
- improves staff or campaign quality control and deadline performance;
- generates improved supplier performance;
- enables faster rollouts of successful programmes and faster discontinuation of failures;
- saves substantial management time and during implementation stages – it contains all the information in one central place;
- facilitates learning by all involved – they can see and understand where you're going and why.

To achieve the benefits of your marketing plan, it must:

- be easy to understand;
- be precise but detailed to avoid confusion;
- be adaptable to change;
- be realistic in application and goal achievement;
- cover all significant market factors;
- clearly identify responsibilities.

▶ The importance of an executive summary

In companies with many products, operating in many markets and with many types of customer, direct marketing plans are complex. The result is that many people who should read the plan do not. If they do, they may not remember its details. Therefore always include a management summary at the beginning to summarize the key points. A good management summary puts across the dominant themes of the plan forcibly and clearly. It summarizes the objectives, targets, opportunities and threats, resources involved, customers targeted, timings, budgets and expected results and cost per response (CPR) or cost per sale (CPS). It should not, by its nature, go into much detail.

A good management summary means that everyone understands where you are heading. It is also a helpful attachment to briefs to direct marketing agencies (subject to confidentiality).

▶ What expertise is needed?

Direct marketing planning requires a blend of the following types of expertise:

- experience and results of what drives in customer acquisition, retention and lifetime values;
- knowledge of a range of media;
- creative and copy development, especially knowing what works;
- production experience, with a knowledge of the latest techniques and processes;
- systems specialists who understand database marketing and data quality;
- manufacturing and fulfilment;
- understanding of customer service requirements and trends in customer satisfaction;
- buying and negotiating skills, to ensure budgets are used effectively.

▶ The planning process

The main stages in direct marketing planning are similar to those in marketing planning, namely:

- situation analysis (customers, financials, competition and so on);
- setting business objectives;
- identifying, evaluating and choosing strategic options;
- developing action plans;
- financial projections.

▶ Situation analysis

The first step here is defining the products or services to be marketed directly. This process is summarized below.

▶ Product definition – what is it and what benefits does it have?

1. Select the product or service to be promoted – note that this may be a range of products or services because your objective may be to manage a market segment using direct marketing (see 'customer definition' below) rather than just a particular product line.
2. Identify the prime applications for the product(s).
3. Carry out a 'needs and wants' analysis – what do people want from it? This will help to evaluate the benefits, customer profile identification and market segmentation. This supports every aspect of campaign development, but particularly the targeting and the creative approach to be taken.
4. Identify the product or service benefits and USP. All the product features should be expressed in concise benefit statements. Each identified need and want can be stated in terms required of benefits. The same analysis should be carried out for competitive offerings and a comparison undertaken. If a true USP exists, it will provide clear differentiation from the competition.

▶ Customer definition – who will buy it?

Together with product definition goes customer definition. The aim of this is to develop a customer/prospect customer profile. This process is summarized below.

1. Identify the customers you wish to target.
2. Gather data – through research and database analysis – about how they buy.
3. Identify barriers to purchase.
4. Identify what customers consider value to be.
5. Identify which of their needs your products or services satisfy.
6. Identify why prospects you want are not your customers and what might make them yours.
7. Identify which of your existing customers are most 'at risk', why, and which competitors they are most likely to go to or why they might stop buying the product category altogether.

Once the customer profile is developed, you may find that you have different types of people in your target market. By ranking the various product or service benefits against the profiles of different types of customer, you can identify different ways to position the product or service appropriately. The more relevant and tailored the marketing, the more responsive the marketing will be. By recording response rates, you can identify the best performing segments and find more of the same prospects for further marketing. Tracking the behaviour of customers in each segment can illustrate their value to the business. Customers who have purchased recently, buy frequently, have a high monetary value and buy a variety of products are valuable, and by acquiring more of these types of customer you can truly improve the value of your business.

> **Fast-track**
> - To find a good list to market to, compare a sample of the list against your own database. The closer the customer profile, the more likely the list is to produce a good response.
> - Profile your best performing customers (in terms of number of other products they hold, transactions made and how loyal they are) to find out where they live, and by using postcode profiling you can find out more about what kind of person they are. Once you know that, you can choose similar postcodes with the same profile and target more of the same types of people.
> - By profiling your latest customers (acquired, say, in the last six months) you can identify any changes in the types of people buying your product and position any subsequent marketing accordingly.
> - By identifying how customers adopt your product, you can understand what their preferred purchase route is and increase budgets and marketing activity in the best areas. For example, if more people are buying through the Internet than by telephone, you can reduce your use of the telephone and increase the numbers of banner ads you use, trial some offers, and use your URL more heavily on all your advertising.

Your aim is to score customer records for their propensity to purchase. Here standard statistical techniques such as factor analysis or regression analysis are employed. However, each segment identified through such techniques must be accessible cost effectively. Isolating a segment that cannot be located at reasonable cost through existing media options or lists is not much help to you.

Financial performance

The key areas for financial analysis are:

- sales, turnover and profitability;
- product analysis, including unit costing and volumes;
- media effectiveness, assuming response is trackable;
- market performance;
- distribution channel performance;
- promotion and advertising budget effectiveness.

The six main performance measures direct marketers use are as follows:

1 **Customer acquisition costs.** You need to keep down the cost of acquiring customers and know how much allowable marketing cost can be spent to acquire a customer. CPB (cost per booking) budgets/targets need to be pre-defined by finance.

2 **Break-even volumes.** If you know what number of sales are required to break even on campaigns you can plug this into your plan. Marketing costs to acquire new customers need to be recouped over a certain period of time, so your objective will be to retain that customer beyond this point, or bring it forward by increasing their value (credit card companies cross-sell people another product or prompt an increase in spending) and their return on investment (ROI). If you have the luxury of knowing a customer's projected lifetime value, you can assess what the initial investment should be.

3 **Attrition rate.** This measures the rate at which customers are lost. Every company suffers customer losses, either through natural attrition (e.g. deaths, tired products), through poor customer service in the retention phase or because the kind of customer attracted through a particular source had a low propensity to be loyal, perhaps being a 'cherry picker' and always attracted to promotional offers.

4 **Lifetime values (LTV).** It is relatively easy for a sophisticated database with customer transaction histories to be programmed to compute the LTV figures. The higher the LTV, the more valuable the customer. If these customers can be profiled, more of the same can be found to market to.

5 **Profit potential.** This examines what profit might be made by a programme. Products or services with a high profit potential can be prioritized first. It is also crucial to know the time to reach this profit potential.

6 **Resource allocation.** This measures how all your marketing and service resources are deployed with particular customers and the returns from each group of customers. Your resources must be deployed to produce long-term customer loyalty and satisfaction and profit. Only a profitable business will be able to service its customer base effectively and maintain growth through excellence in customer service and quality of products or services. There is little point producing more business if it cannot be serviced well.

These measures must be understood for your business as a whole and for each market segment because they will tell you where you should focus your direct marketing effort.

Reviewing your key resources

You should periodically review the following:

1 database facility – for storage capacity and processing speed;
2 distribution channels – for their efficiency at moving products to customers;
3 fulfilment operation from receipt of order to shipment and customer service procedures;
4 capital available to fund the business;
5 staff expertise in functional areas;

6 quality of the products and/or services;
7 your brand – and the consequent expectations associated with your company's reputation and name.

> **In the real world**
> Being honest about your company's strengths and weaknesses is vital for direct marketing planning. The failure of many direct marketing plans can be traced to lack of a tough review of strengths and weaknesses and to a rose-tinted view of past performance.

Competition

In monitoring the competition, the first step is to determine who competitors are and in what way they are competing. It is important to monitor market share movements, market trends and to gain knowledge of competitors' specific strengths and weaknesses.

Your situation analysis should give you:

- identification of the wants and needs your products/services satisfy;
- customer profiles which can be converted into market segments;
- identification of the distinctive values your company provides to its customers;
- identification of emerging market segments, unsatisfied needs and competitive gaps;
- audit of your communication mix and distribution channels;
- assessment of your company's real ability to service its customers.

Setting business objectives

When you have reviewed your market position and your capabilities thoroughly, you are in a good position to identify a feasible set of direct marketing objectives. Your objectives should be broad enough to maximize the identified market opportunities but narrow enough to ensure your resources can be realistically deployed to achieve them.

Make sure your objectives are sound – they should be SMART:

- Smart;
- Measurable;
- Attainable;
- Realistic;
- Timely.

05 / Planning direct marketing

▶ How do you make sure your objectives are sound?

- ◆ Ensure every objective focuses on results.
- ◆ Quantify every objective (ROI, turnover, % market share, etc.).
- ◆ Where possible have a single theme for the objective.
- ◆ Ensure resources are realistic to achieve the objective.
- ◆ Ensure marketing objectives are directly tied to corporate goals and objectives.

> **In the real world – ranking objectives**
>
> - ◆ Separate objectives that are measured in different ways from each other and be clear about how you'll measure them in practice. Financial objectives will be measured through a combination of product profitability and database analysis. Increasing market awareness might be measured by recall research and quantified.
> - ◆ Rank the financial objectives and then the others, firstly in terms of their contribution to your current financial performance and secondly in terms of their contribution to lifetime value.

Here is an example of campaign objectives and measures.

Objectives of half-price offer	Target	Source of measurement
Sales	50 000 in Q1	Sales – monitored daily against forecast, information taken from bookings system
Cost per sale	£25	Marketing to supply at campaign close, using marketing costs, excluding overheads. Marketing to report on initial response rate, cost per response and cost per sale
Churn	Below 15%	Account closures, from system extract on a weekly basis. Retention team to monitor
LTV	£1200	Finance to measure
Customer profile	Segment A 30%, Segment B 70% of buyers	Customer profile – database marketing to analyze respondents
Customer attitude and behaviour	Response rate to follow-on offers. Attitude questionnaire	Customer insight team to measure in 6 and 12 months

▶ Common direct marketing objectives

▶ Growing market share and volume

Increasing sales volume within a category will grow market share. It is a typical option for companies that live or die on market share, such as packaged consumer goods companies. For many direct marketing companies such as mail-order operations, the same criteria may apply but may be combined with turnover growth, increasing customer cross-selling and upgrading, more frequent purchases and growth of the customer base. Increasing frequency of use is often the objective of loyalty programmes.

▶ Increasing profit

There are three main ways to achieve greater profit:

- **Improving the price and offer.** This is particularly relevant to direct marketers, who have much flexibility in this area because price can be adjusted to the target market segment or even to individuals. By changing the offer, you can increase product price and increase the profit margin.
- **Improving the sales mix.** This can be achieved by discarding less profitable lines. Mail-order companies are quick to delete unprofitable items. Concentrating on tested, proven winners will yield a higher return.
- **Reducing costs.** This can be achieved by combining two offers in one or reducing the quality of promotional material, though in both cases response rates can fall. Marketing costs can be reduced by decreasing print and production costs, negotiating better media rates and tightening up the targeting of leads to direct market. Cutting costs can be dangerous in the longer term because of the risks to impact or to brand image.

▶ Strategy options and evaluation

We have examined the importance of having a robust direct marketing plan and of having clear and measurable objectives. Now let's look at the strategy – the thinking behind the plan.

▶ What now?

Having determined where you wish to go, now's the time to work out how to get there! More formally, strategy is the art of devising a plan, using structured planning methods, to achieve a goal. Any strategy needs to be assessed against the product/service offer, the target market, the marketplace and competition, current distribution channels, media plan and mix, financial situation of the company, internal operational capabilities of the company. Part of the process of strategy formulation is to identify possible blocks to achieving the strategy and then find ways to overcome them.

The following areas need to be covered in the plan's rationale and in the manager's summary to explain and demonstrate the thought processes behind the plan.

- Product strategy – which products should be in your campaigns and which not? Which products must be marketed using direct methods?

- Positioning strategy – how do you want to position your company and your products to each target market? Is there more than one target market or are there many segments? How will this affect your positioning?
- Offer strategy – what is going to make your customers respond to you at the right time?
- Timing strategy – when are the key sales periods and when will your key activity happen? Seasonal influences? New programming or product launches planned? School calendar influences?
- Branding strategy – how will you achieve consistency between your overall brand image and the one you present through direct marketing methods? When are the above-the-line brand campaigns planned for? Integrated marketing communications support each other and tend to uplift response.
- Pricing strategy – how will you ensure that discounts targeted for one market do not bleed into another? You must manage the offers by codes, policing them properly.
- Target market – what are the defining characteristics of the market segments you want to hit and how are you going to apply them to generate lists of customers that match these definitions?
- Sales force and channel strategy – how will your existing methods of managing customers be integrated with your direct marketing methods? Marketing and sales briefings need to take place.
- Communication strategy – how is direct marketing going to build up communication with customers? How will this build-up be sustained by your other marketing communications approaches?
- Fulfilment strategy – how will you ensure that your customers will get the goods and services they have ordered and the correct pricing is applied to the account?
- Competitive strategy – how do you want to use direct marketing to fend off competitive challenges and make holes in your competitors' marketing achievement – whether by aggressive or defensive positioning?
- Acquisition and retention strategy – how do you expect to acquire new customers and then retain them and use retention feedback to shape acquisition communications?
- Database strategy – how will your database support all your direct marketing activities, through data acquisition, maintenance and use?
- Customer service strategy – how will your direct marketing achievements be sustained by how you service customers in other ways?
- Marketing and sales information strategy – how will your customer data be gathered and maintained through a comprehensive approach to marketing data management, affecting all modes of contact with customers?
- Overall strategy – how will all the above activities be co-ordinated to maximum effect?

To prioritize strategies, you may want to build models to forecast the consequences of implementing different strategies.

▶ Action plans

To implement your strategy you need to allocate resources to particular tasks. This is normally done by issuing briefing documents, to creative agencies, printers and list providers. Briefs spell out the detailed actions that need to be implemented for your strategy to succeed. Responsibilities are allocated, expectations outlined, budgets set and timings agreed.

> **Checklist: implementation**
> - Clear objectives for the overall plan and individual campaigns.
> - Assigned responsibilities – what, by whom, by when.
> - Controls in place to monitor progress, plan for errors and document all actions.
> - Clear, concise briefs for all parties involved.

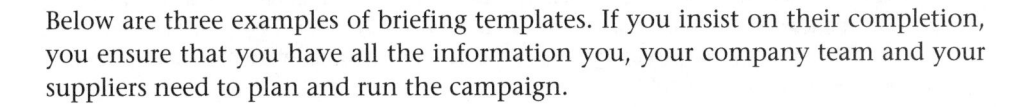

Below are three examples of briefing templates. If you insist on their completion, you ensure that you have all the information you, your company team and your suppliers need to plan and run the campaign.

▶ A media brief template

> **Background**
> - ☐ Information on previous activity and why this activity is taking place. This may contain results from previous campaigns, an overview of brand awareness levels currently from research gathered. You may also wish to reinforce core brand values to ensure focus on them is maintained in this campaign.
>
> **Marketing and campaign objectives**
> - ☐ What are the key deliverables from this campaign and how do they fit into the wider picture?
> - ☐ Are they primarily to drive sales, uplift awareness or support advertising?
> - ☐ Are there any other specific objectives to note?
>
> **Media objectives**
> - ☐ Specific objectives which may influence the channels recommended by the media agency.
>
> **Budget**
> - ☐ Budget should be clearly specified. If it is to cover media, production, etc. then specify this to ensure the resulting plan accommodates the other costs.

Timing and phasing

- ☐ Campaign start and finish, and phasing.
- ☐ You may need to upweight the start of the campaign to establish brand awareness and support any direct marketing.
- ☐ Consideration should be given to the handling of responses generated by media advertising activity.
- ☐ TV (on-air) and radio tend to drive immediate response, so consideration should be given to the opening hours of the call centre if directing people to call in as part of the call to action.
- ☐ Weight of activity should also reflect the budgeted sales volumes, so where there are peaks you may wish to upweight media advertising activity (and spend).

Target audience

- ☐ Who do you want to appeal to? What geo-demographic attributes do they have?
- ☐ Socio-demographic classes, age groups and so on.
- ☐ Existing customers, cold prospects?

Key customer insight

- ☐ Why do you want to target this specific audience?
- ☐ Strengths and strategic rationale – are they likely to be multiple repurchasers? Are they likely to spend more on their credit card? Are they likely to borrow more heavily without greater risk? Are they likely to be more loyal to the brand and therefore produce a stronger return on investment?
- ☐ It's often useful to build up a pen portrait of the kind of person you want to reach – it may be their job type, hobbies, what they read, where they live, the type of residence they occupy, what groceries they buy each week and what newspaper they read.

Regionality

- ☐ National or local coverage.
- ☐ This will be determined partly by the extent of budget available.
- ☐ Are certain areas stronger than others? TV regions are used to break down the country into sections for targeting separately through media.
- ☐ Are there any regional competitive factors which might cause you to uplift, downweight or avoid advertising activity completely?
- ☐ Are there pockets of your target audience in particular areas of the country that you wish to target?

Media strategy

- ☐ Are there particular objectives set out by the business that will influence the strategy?
- ☐ Try to avoid being too prescriptive in this section, so that you receive an objective strategic recommendation, based on your objectives and budget. This is particularly the case when briefing large media planning agencies. Smaller media buyers may request more direction.

Media

- [ ] List in here any mandatory media you want to be included in the plan. The main advertising media are:
  - [ ] TV;
  - [ ] radio;
  - [ ] off-the-page press;
  - [ ] outdoor (posters) – various sheet sizes;
  - [ ] ambient (beer mats, on back of toilet doors, anywhere where you have static media consumption!);
  - [ ] editorials and promotions in magazines.

Creative

- [ ] These guidelines normally stipulate the need to consider the wider brand guidelines to maintain consistency and recognition. However, you must communicate clearly any brand restrictions and what you want to achieve within them. For example, if the campaign must observe guidelines on font, pantone colours, tone of voice and imagery, as long as they are briefed in they will become the foundations of your advertising. But keep the content and positioning of the advertising open to creative interpretation by the agency. From the information in this brief, the agency has all it needs to develop your advertising.

Evaluation

- [ ] It is important to evaluate the success of any advertising so that you know what works and what doesn't. Once you know this you can make a lucid and informed decision on future budget allocation, selecting the best performers.
- [ ] Measurement can be on initial response or on final sale, provided you have reliable tracking.
- [ ] A successful campaign can be measured by tracking recall of the advertising campaign and to measure whether your message has been received and understood. Market research agencies can be employed to do this on your behalf.
- [ ] Hall dips are another way of measuring campaign success. This is where people are invited to attend a session where the components of the advertising campaign are presented and feedback and recall recorded.

Deadlines

- [ ] Be clear about what you want and when.
- [ ] Media plan – first draft with rationale.
- [ ] Media plan – final version (with executive summary perhaps).
- [ ] Activity start and end date.
- [ ] Post-campaign evaluation.

▶ A creative brief template

Background
This contains information that helps the agency to understand why the creative needs developing and anything else which helps them to understand the need for this piece of work. Feel free to attach further information, examples of material you feel inspired by, and additional product information if it's relevant to ensure they have the product knowledge.

Objectives
You may wish to have primary and secondary objectives. Or you may need just one objective. Here's an example:

Primary
☐ To create new sales through use of the telephone number.

Secondary
☐ From customers who are both valuable and loyal to the business.
☐ By encouraging purchases of medium to high value.

Target audience
Who is to receive this direct marketing? Is it certain a newspaper readership profile, people who browse a particular web site, a closed group of prospects of a certain type, or your own customer base?

Key consumer insight
Who are they, what do they look like? Can you include a pen portrait to help the agency visualize who they are? What attributes (geographical, age, income, buying habits, etc.) do they have? Include a geo-demographic profile if you have one. The more detail, the more targeted and tailored the end result and the more relevant it will be.
   The agency must understand the target audience!

Proposition
Firstly, what is the message?
   Are you selling something, or communicating a new service? What is it and do they have to do anything, and by when?
   Be clear about what you want from this communication and chances are the agency will get it right for you first time.
   Secondly, what tone of voice do you wish to use? This varies vastly from the very formal and business address that professional services (law firms, etc.) use to market themselves, to the relaxed, cool style that a product such as Rip-Curl surf wear would use to speak to its youth audience.

Proposition support
This is usually rational information about the features and benefits that enhance your product.
   An example of supporting information that a credit card company might use to drive new subscriptions would be:

☐ 6.9% APR on balance transfers;
☐ standard rate from just 11.9% APR (typical rate 17.9%);

Action plans

- ☐ UK's number one!;
- ☐ no annual fee;
- ☐ FREE price promise;
- ☐ FREE 12 months' extended warranty;
- ☐ FREE purchase cover;
- ☐ FREE Internet delivery protection;
- ☐ FREE additional cards;
- ☐ loyalty points for each time you use your card.

Requirement

What exactly do you want? Give the agency guidelines within which to work, while allowing them creativity to explore a range of executions. As the name suggests, you have employed a creative agency. So avoid being too prescriptive to ensure they are challenged and motivated to produce something strong. The job of a good designer is to challenge you.

For example, if briefing an agency for a set of off-the-page press adverts, you might request them to include certain sizes to fit the titles you have in mind – 25x4 and 20 triple versions, to work with mono and colour. But the content can be left open to interpretation, using the rest of the information you've provided here.

If briefing a direct mail pack, you could ask the agency to consider options other than a classic pack of a letter, brochure and envelope, but consider other approaches for impact and cost efficiency.

Mandatories

This should include anything legal and corporate that must be contained within the marketing piece. This may include terms and conditions, telephone numbers, campaign codes, promotional dates, data-protection wording, registration details. It may also contain guidelines on postal bands and weight restrictions of the pack, postage types, returns addresses, branding guidelines – fonts, pantone references, etc.

Budget/timings

What budget do they have to produce this work? This is often left open and the agency is asked to confirm the costs based on the brief. This can be useful to establish their perception of costs before you determine the cost, but you may need to manage expectations or negotiate if the resulting costs are higher than expected. Of course it can also work in your favour.

Timings should always be clear and achievable. It's useful to specify when you expect to see first scamps, creative, when legal time needs to be built in, and when final artwork should be approved for print. If the job involves printing, you should liaise with the printers to establish the production lead times.

▶ A typical sales centre brief

Campaign
- ☐ What is it?
- ☐ Main components.
- ☐ Include a PDF or illustration for a visual reference or description that can easily identify this marketing piece.

73

Objective
- [ ] Keep simple, clear and concise.
- [ ] Telesales/the contact centre or customer services should be briefed in plain English (no jargon).

Target audience
- [ ] What kind of customers or prospects are we expecting to call or contact us?
- [ ] This may influence the call. If you know in advance what type of person (young married couples, single males, older retired) is likely to call, the call and sell can be better tailored.

Targeting rationale
- [ ] A short explanation of why this target audience has been chosen will help recipients understand objectives. Again try to avoid using marketing jargon as this will complicate the campaign more than necessary and limit understanding.

Message
- [ ] What is the message and call to action – what does the customer have to do to apply or buy? Is there an offer, what pricing is offered?
- [ ] What are the key selling points?

Offer
- [ ] The offer, and restrictions or ties, and when does it expire?

Method
- [ ] What method must the customer or prospect use to respond? What telephone number is being used? Is this set up with an appropriate message and routed through properly? Is this being measured to assess campaign performance?
- [ ] If it's a coupon, where should the voucher be sent and by when? Attach a copy of this for information in case of any queries.
- [ ] Should call agents capture any further information? If a code needs to be captured on screen or on a tally sheet, make sure they have this information to hand.

Timing
- [ ] When will the marketing reach customers and hence when will responses start to arrive? What volumes are expected? Are they in line with budgeted call volumes and is there sufficient staff to take the calls or process the coupons, reply to Internet enquiries, etc.?

Analysis requirements
- [ ] Clear communication of any analysis or reporting that is needed, and how frequently. It's always a good idea to seek written confirmation of this, to make sure it is done and sent as per the brief. Often this gets put to one side when a campaign goes live and the call centre or processing area becomes very busy.

Responses
- [ ] Number of responses.
- [ ] Commencing from when to when?

▶ Briefs, briefs and more briefs

Campaign execution is more likely to fail if your strategy has not been specified properly. This will lead to poor tactical development. A poorly composed creative or media brief means you don't get what you want and this can be time consuming and expensive and lead to inadequate campaign performance. Those you brief include outside suppliers such as research agencies, advertising agencies, list and media owners, printers, mailing houses and computer bureaux, and your own marketing staff and management services (systems/IT, credit scoring, data analysis, telesales, customer service, legal, operations and finance). Don't be afraid to over-brief. Better too much communication than mistakes later.

▶ The essential skill – what you need in a campaign manager

Campaign management is a vital function. It covers tactical planning, control, monitoring and analysis. This role requires strong organizational ability, attention to detail, and the ability to motivate and control internal and external suppliers. Each stage needs double-checking as many kinds of information must be collated, distributed or analyzed. Being able to stand back and review the 'big picture' and identify possible problem areas is vital. It is also important to be able to project the future and to question decisions if in doubt. Anyone who masters this area will be in a much stronger position to develop **workable** strategic plans.

▶ Financial analysis

Once you have drawn up implementation plans and implementation has taken place, the next planning task is to analyze results. Results analysis may include the following:

- response rate (RR%);
- cost per response (CPR);
- response curve;
- conversion rate;
- sales rate;
- repeat orders;
- cost per sale (CPS);
- return on investment;
- merchandise returns and order/service cancellations;
- test results by cell;
- LTV – lifetime value of the customer (calculated much later).

> **Checklist: financial analysis**
>
> Have you got the correct mechanisms in place to monitor financial success?
>
> Can you monitor success over the long term as well as initial success? Will you know which customers stayed with you and how much they bought later on, i.e. their lifetime value?
>
> Has everybody involved in the process agreed success and failure criteria before the campaign rolls out?
>
> What measures are in place if the campaign fails?
>
> How can you learn from the success or failure of the campaign?

Summary

This chapter has covered direct marketing planning. If the direct marketing plan is too detailed, confused over planning terminology, not integrated into the marketing strategy, or lacks the support of line management, it is sure to lead to poor performance. When finalized the plan will provide a clear programme for the use of direct marketing. Concise objectives will be translated into specific operational objectives. Your plan will ensure commitment (if consultation has taken place) and the deployment of resources to the right areas at the right times. If you assign specific responsibilities, detailed schedules and budgets, monitoring of progress is made much easier.

In the next chapter we describe how that critical resource – your customer database – can be built and deployed to support your direct marketing plan.

the customer database

What a customer database is and why direct marketing needs it

How a customer database is used

What has helped database marketing grow so fast?

The strengths of database marketing

The database

Data design

Sources of data

Types of information on the database

Holding the data

Data quality and maintenance

Using the database

Doing it yourself or outsourcing

Summary

What a customer database is and why direct marketing needs it

Direct marketing depends on customer information for its effectiveness. Managing a relationship with your customers over many contacts would simply be impossible were it not for recent developments in information technology, particularly telecommunications and database management.

Direct marketing relies on your creating a bank of information about individual customers (e.g. taken from orders, enquiries, customer service contacts, research questionnaires, external lists). You use this information to analyse your customers' buying and enquiry patterns. This analysis, combined with the opportunity offered by the database to contact individual customers through a variety of media, allows you to achieve a number of objectives:

- designing products to meet the needs of identified customers;
- targeting the marketing of products and services more accurately;
- promoting the benefits of brand loyalty to customers at risk from competition;
- identifying customers most likely to buy new products and services;
- increasing sales effectiveness;
- supporting low-cost alternatives to traditional sales methods;
- making your marketing function more accountable;
- improving the link between advertising and sales promotion, product management and sales channels;
- improving customer care by making all relevant information available at the point of contact between your company and its customers, at any place or time, during service delivery;
- co-ordinating different aspects of marketing as they affect the individual customer, to achieve full direct marketing potential.

How a customer database is used

1. Each actual or potential customer is identified as a record on your marketing database.
2. Each customer record contains information on:
   - identification and access (e.g. name, address, telephone number);
   - other customers associated with this customer (in the family, business, etc.);
   - customer needs and characteristics (demographic and psychographic information about consumers, industry type and decision-making unit information for industrial customers);
   - campaign communications (whether the customer has been exposed to particular marketing communications campaigns);

- customer's past responses to communications which form part of the campaigns;
- customer satisfactions;
- channel and media preferences;
- potential future value of customers;
- past transactions of customers (with you and possibly with competitors).

3 This information is used to identify likely purchasers of particular products and how they should be approached.

4 The information is available to you during the process of each communication with the customer – which may have been initiated by you or the customer. This enables you to decide how to respond to the customer's needs.

5 The database is used to record customers' responses to your marketing initiatives (e.g. marketing communications or sales campaigns).

6 The information is also available for your marketing planning. This enables you to decide:
- which target markets or segments are appropriate for each product or service;
- what marketing mix (price, marketing communications, distribution channel, etc.) is appropriate for each product in each target market.

7 If you are selling many different products to each customer, the database is used to ensure that the approach to the customer is co-ordinated (for example that campaigns for different products do not clash) and consistent, and handled in a way that meets customers' expectations about how you manage data (i.e. any of your staff in contact with the customer, in any channel, can see relevant information about the customer).

8 Your database may eventually replace large-scale quantitative market research for your existing customers, though research will still be required for new products and markets or for changes to your relationship with customers. You devise marketing campaigns so that customers' responses provide the information you need, possibly through questionnaires included in mailings or telemarketing campaigns.

9 You develop systematic processes to handle some key functions of marketing management, in particular analysis and project planning. Analysis must be systematized if it is to handle the vast volume of information generated by database marketing. It ensures that marketing opportunities and threats are identified more or less automatically, and that ways of capturing these opportunities and neutralizing these threats are also recommended. It makes higher quality information on marketing performance available to senior management, allowing them to allocate marketing resources more effectively. It also allows management to identify situations in which direct or interactive marketing is failing. Project planning approaches are used to tighten up the management of campaigns, as database marketing involves a larger number of suppliers and much more complex actions than traditional advertising campaigns.

What has helped database marketing grow so fast?

The growth of database marketing has been facilitated by:

- the powerful processing capability and immense storage capacity of today's computers;
- the way telecommunications technology is being harnessed to make customer and market data available to the wide variety of staff involved in marketing and sales efforts.

Enabling technologies are developing fast. Most technologies, such as those which determine data processing power and speed, memory and storage, are improving at least tenfold every ten years. Speed of access (reading, writing) to stored data is growing more slowly. Communications technology, once slow to evolve, is accelerating. Software, once a barrier, is now easier to use and is more reliable. Application packages (e.g. telemarketing) are more functional and flexible and capable of customization. Application development products have accelerated programmer productivity. End-user computing has created experience and even expertise in handling computers throughout organizations. PC-based systems are available for the small user. Customers are using additional media (e.g. mobile telephony, interactive TV) that allow them to be managed as individuals and, more importantly, to manage their relationships with suppliers.

A wide range of tried and tested database packages are now available for all types and sizes of computing systems. These have been used as the foundation to develop the specific packages required. They include:

- comprehensive customer databases;
- selection management;
- telemarketing (inbound, i.e. call receiving, and outbound, i.e. active calling of customers);
- mail fulfilment systems;
- data analysis and customer profiling;
- connecting different channels and media.

Suppliers of the underlying database software have also made it much easier for systems professionals to adapt this software to their specific marketing use by marketing a wide range of programming 'tools'. Nowadays, even where customers are managed in many locations across the world, systems are available to facilitate this. Companies that experience problems with the development or implementation of direct marketing systems do so because of management problems, such as:

- lack of agreement about the coverage and application of the database, and the related problem of over-specifying the first version of the system so that it costs too much, takes too long to develop and does not deliver benefits early enough;
- lack of understanding that marketing databases succeed only if they are put to use and modified by practical experience – the data will grow and along with it

the knowledge of how to use it, once it is applied. This has been learned over the past ten years, before which it was common to over-specify the database at the outset, making it more complex and difficult to use than necessary;
- lack of attention paid to users' needs – for understanding, training and support during implementation.

These are problems that are common in all areas of business system development. They often occur because of failure to consult with other companies which have been through the experience. A particular risk is of falling into the hands of consultants who over-specify the system because it enlarges their budget. Fortunately, in many countries, there are now enough training courses and professional groups where marketing managers can exchange experiences and avoid these obvious mistakes.

The strengths of database marketing

The use of the customer database builds on the solid foundations of direct marketing, as follows:

- It is **measurable**. Responses to campaigns are measured, enabling the effectiveness of different approaches to be checked.
- It is **testable**. The effectiveness of different elements of the approach – the product, the communications medium, the offer (how the product is packaged to appeal to the customer), the target market, and so on – can be tested. Tests can be carried out quickly, so rapid action can be taken on the results. Test results can be used to forecast sales more precisely, helping manage inventory more effectively.
- It is **selective**. Campaigns can be focused accurately because your communication is with specific customers and can be attuned to their expected value (e.g. more expensive and frequent communications to higher value customers).
- Communications to each customer can easily be **personalized** by including details relevant only to them, drawn from the database.
- It is **flexible** – campaigns can be timed to have their effect exactly when required.

The database

Information about customers and markets is one of your main marketing assets. The information on a customer database has to come from somewhere. Direct marketing involves 'learning by doing' – the process itself provides most of the marketing information it needs. This is because contacts ask for responses. Each response contains information – at least, it should do. It is up to you to make sure that this information is of value.

For example, if a customer responds by calling a freephone number, you may ask questions which:

- qualify the lead for the product or service which is the subject of the campaign;
- provide information that will help in future campaigns.

In this way, database marketing builds up a store of information about individual customers. You need to hold it in the most effective way. Unless it can be turned into profit, it is of no use. So your database marketing system is crucial for organizing the information and making it available.

> **Data use – two key questions: if the answer to either is no, yours is no *marketing* database**
>
> Can you use your database to analyze and segment buyers and enquirers?
>
> Can you use your database to support list generation, lead generation and qualification, direct order fulfilment, direct mail, telemarketing?

> **Question:** What databases hold customer details but are not marketing databases?
>
> **Answer:** Some databases are more likely to be **operations databases**, used for order processing (order taking, delivery, invoicing, etc.) or after-sales service. They record what customers paid, and what they paid for, rather than helping to predict what they might like next! Some data may be derived from marketing databases, used for analysis purposes only. Some are merely 'Christmas card' lists which purport to be a marketing database – these are just lists of names and addresses of people and businesses which are sent things.

▶ Data design

Computers work best with information that is well organized to start with. That is why there is a strong emphasis on the structured collection of data. For example, telemarketing scripts must be designed to get the maximum amount of high-quality information possible from your customers, in a structured form. This allows you to add it to your database without too much further processing. The same applies to the design of forms to be completed by your customers.

Structured information gathering is essential. Unless you observe this discipline from the beginning, problems will emerge later on. To take a simple example, in business marketing, customers' financial year end is usually significant, either because they need to spend pre-allocated budgets or because they are likely to be tightening their belts. So it is sensible to allocate a field on the database for this information and collect it in a structured way.

There is no general formula stating exactly which data should be included in the database. Each database is tailored to the needs of its users. But it is important to avoid the mistake of designing it on the basis of **past** requirements. Some key questions include:

- Is your data structured as efficiently as possible?
- Are you using all cost-effective forms of data collection possible?
- Is there enough room on your database for the envisaged growth in the number of customers and the amount of detail you want to collect about them?
- Are you basing your database on future needs or on a view of the past?

Sources of data

There are two types of data source, internal and external.

> **Internal** or **proprietary** data is data you already hold about your customers, usually arising out of your transaction with them. Your database marketing system should use most of the information you have about customers. This data is one of your company's most valuable assets.
>
> **External** data is data you source from outside, e.g. by renting a list, by exchanging data with another company.

> A **list** is the simplest form of marketing database. It is a set of names and how to contact them (e.g. addresses, telephone numbers).

Data is often organized into lists. A list may be:

- a list which is bought or rented for use in campaigns or in building your database. Clever list buying is the key to many successful database marketing campaigns;
- a list of target customers drawn from your database for a particular campaign. Careful list selection is the key to high response at low cost.

▶ Internal data

Internal data includes:

- customer files;
- order records;
- service reports, complaints, etc.;
- merchandise return records;
- sales force records;
- customer satisfaction data;
- application forms (e.g. for credit, insurance);
- responses to promotions;

- risk/credit data (have they paid on time?);
- market research;
- enquiries;
- warranty cards.

▶ External data

External data includes compiled and direct response lists from sources outside your company. Also included are classificatory data (e.g. census and postcode data, data from credit reference agencies, and their derivations), which can enhance other external and internal data.

▶ Data selection

You should decide which data to put on your database according to its cost and its potential to make you money. Only put data on your database which will help you answer these questions.

- Who are or will be your customers and how can you contact them?
- What will they buy from you or your competitors? How can you motivate them to buy more from you?
- Will they maintain a dialogue with your company and which medium do they prefer to do it through?
- How can they be retained? Do they have any propensity to be loyal to suppliers in your market sector?
- Where can others like them be found?
- When are they most receptive to your communications and when are they most likely to buy from you?

If a data item does not help you answer these questions in a way that clearly leads to revenue defence and/or growth, it should not be included.

▶ Types of information on the database

These may include:

- **customer or prospect**, i.e. information on how to access your customers (e.g. address, telephone number) and on the nature and general behaviour of customers (psychographic and behavioural data);
- **transaction**, i.e. information on commercial transactions between you and the customer, e.g. orders, returns;
- **contact planning and execution data**, i.e. information on what campaigns (tests and rollouts) have been launched, who has responded to them, what the

final results have been in terms of contacts, sales and profits, and also on service contacts and their results;
- **product**, i.e. information on which products have been involved in promotion, who has bought them, when and from where;
- **geo-demographics**, i.e. information about the areas where customers live and the social or business category they belong to.

These types of data are considered in more detail below.

▶ Customer data

If you are marketing to consumers, you might hold these items about customers on your database:

- first name;
- last name;
- title;
- salutation;
- name of spouse;
- address (in meaningful format, three or four lines);
- gender;
- age;
- income;
- marital status;
- number of children;
- names of children;
- length of residence in current abode;
- type of abode and tenure;
- whether recent or anticipated home mover;
- telephone number;
- special markers (VIP customer, do not promote, shareholder, frequent complainer);
- responses to questionnaires;
- customer service history;
- geo-demographic coding.

If you are marketing to businesses, you might hold:

- company name;
- addresses of head office and other relevant sites;
- telephone, fax and telex numbers, possibly mobile and voicemail numbers of key contacts;

Types of information on the database

- e-mail address;
- account number(s);
- names of buyer(s);
- names of contacts and influencers;
- purchasing process;
- links with other companies;
- revenue and profits – size and growth;
- type of company (industrial classification code);
- number of employees;
- site structure;
- responses to questionnaires;
- customer service history.

▶ Transaction data

Past transactions are one of the most important indicators of likely future transactions. So the details of each purchase for each customer must be logged. This includes not only the obvious 'identifying' details (who bought or returned what, when, how, etc.) but also the associated marketing data (at what price, from which promotion).

> The use of **FRAC (Frequency, Recency, Amount and Category)** in direct and interactive marketing is based on years of experience of finding that these variables dominate most explanations of buying behaviour for existing products. Your transaction data must include enough detail to allow FRAC information to be extracted for each customer. It is tempting to summarize purchasing history, but in summarizing it you may lose vital FRAC detail.

In consumer markets, transaction data is usually much more effective as a basis for selection for promotions than geo-demographic variables. However, the widespread availability of geo-demographic data that can be matched to individual customer data means that a consumer products company with limited or no transaction data available can start with a campaign based mainly on geo-demographic data. This will normally be organized in a national file based on the electoral roll enhanced with postal coding and possibly telephone numbers. Census information will usually be used to enhance the file further and provide some of the basis for demographic classification. If you are in this position, your key objective is to learn very quickly which customers respond the best and focus future promotions on them, as promoting to national files is very expensive. To do this, you should start with a test and find out which kinds of customer respond the best, 'score' them and focus future promotions on those with good scores.

> You give customers a **score** by identifying their characteristics which correlate them with their likelihood to respond, buy, etc. This allows you to create a '**scoring module**' or 'directory' for selecting target customers from any larger file. Scores are usually derived from tests. This is based on the idea that when a customer is identified as belonging to a particular group, it can usually be assumed that the customer has the same likelihood as other members of the group of buying a particular product. The score given to a customer in relation to a given product is determined by:
>
> - analysis of all the customer's characteristics;
> - assessment as to whether those characteristics, when they appear in whole groups of customers, make those customers likely to buy.
>
> Once the characteristics that are important have been identified, you can devise a scoring method, to be applied instantly by the computer. This score indicates the likelihood that the customer will buy. This information is combined with campaign objectives to determine a priority for the response.

Your campaign should create transaction data fairly quickly. This transaction data is likely to come to dominate your selection criteria, but geo-demographic data may continue to be useful. The emergence of companies offering comprehensive data services (list validation, data pooling, matching to other files) means that few new users of database marketing have to start from scratch.

▶ Product data

In a one-product company, this raises no problem – each transaction is either a sale or a return. In companies with wide product ranges, product classification may be a problem and a numbering system to suit the requirements of database marketing may have to be adopted. Such a system must allow like products to be grouped easily.

▶ Contact planning and execution data

Documentation of past and present promotions in some detail (right down to which customers were subject to them, and the media and contact strategy used) is essential if you are to measure the effectiveness of your promotions and if your promotional planning is to benefit from analysis of the past. The same applies to details of inbound contacts (contacts arising from customers, whether stimulated by you or initiated by the customer) and service contacts.

▶ Holding the data

Some data must be accessed quickly (e.g. data on customers who have recently received promotions). Other data can be accessible with a longer delay, and some might never be entered into the computer database.

In the real world

Care must be taken about which data is kept for quick access, or the system will drown in useless information. So another characteristic of database marketing systems is the constant check kept on which information is useful and which data is 'nice to know' but not very useful. This latter data can be archived and retrieved if necessary. However, due to the rapid advances in computer storage and retrieval technology, this problem is not as serious as it used to be.

Merging external data with proprietary data, or merging data from different proprietary sources, can be a problem. Special computer programs are normally used to 'deduplicate' data sources. Many companies prefer to use external suppliers to do this work.

> The need for deduplication arises when an individual or company is listed in different ways in different databases (or even in the same one). If the different databases are combined, customers may be listed more than once. The databases or lists must be **'deduplicated'** against each other so that duplicate records are removed, while valuable data (which may be spread over more than one record of the same customer) is not lost.

Deduplication can be computerized. However, some human intervention may be necessary, as the computer can deduplicate only within certain tolerances. Depending on how important deduplication is, the computer may be asked to list entries where duplicate entry is suspected, for manual correction. However, you should bear in mind that the law of diminishing returns applies here. So the costs of further deduplication should be weighed against its benefits. These benefits are:

- savings in costs of duplicated contacts;
- avoiding alienating customers by contacting them more than once for the same reason.

Data quality and maintenance

In the real world

Data does not stay fresh. It becomes stale, as the contacts on which it is based recede into the past. So special exercises are required to check the validity of data and/or update it. This **maintenance** of your database is very important.

Databases **get out of date quickly**. People change addresses and jobs. Companies move, new companies are set up and companies go out of existence. Errors in fulfilment records occur, through commission and omission. This is why audits must be undertaken.

> A **data audit** takes a sample of your customer records and analyzes when the different data items were entered, what their quality is and how accurate they are. Accuracy may be checked by:
> - comparing the data with a source which is known to be accurate;
> - asking the customer (or customer contact staff) to confirm accuracy.

Data quality is measured by the results of the last audit. You can carry out quality checks via testing. Questionnaire mailing can be an effective though costly way of improving data quality, so questionnaires are usually combined with some other promotional initiative.

The quality of the data drawn from your database depends mainly on:

- how up to date your source data is;
- whether it contains the detail needed to access the right individuals (names, addresses, telephone numbers, job titles).

In the real world

If information on your customers' contacts with your company is not entered in your database, you may suffer in two ways:

- You may approach the same customer on successive days (or worse, on the same day) with different messages (or the same message delivered twice). This cannot be avoided – a customer may read an advertisement and receive a mail-shot on the same day. But ensuring different direct approaches are co-ordinated can reduce wastefulness.
- Without a history of contact, you will have no idea where the customer is in the 'buying cycle'. This information is needed to determine when you should write, telephone or schedule a sales visit.

The quality of information depends partly on customer-contact staff (sales, telemarketing, retail branch, etc.) understanding the value of high-quality information and the importance of their feedback in improving its quality. You should take **every** opportunity **to improve data quality**, during every contact with your customer. These contacts may be with sales staff, over the telephone, in showrooms and dealer outlets, on service calls, in shops and at exhibitions, by return of guarantees, via competitions and through past customer records. Lists can be traded with relevant businesses to help here. But the advantage of using your own database is that it consists of people who:

- have done and are doing business with you;
- trust you;
- will therefore respond better to you.

Data quality and maintenance

> A small engineering supplies company wanted to keep better information on its clients in order to be able to service them better and be able to offer them relevant, targeted offers. To ensure the database was kept up to date it needed the support and help of the telesales team. To gain this the company devised several changes to its existing system which saved time. It then asked the staff to capture more data on the customers as they called in than previously, using some of the time saved for them by the changes implemented at the same time. This collaborative approach paid off and the database is now a fully integrated and evolving marketing tool.

▶ External lists

These are often classified into **responsive** and **compiled**. Mail or telephone responsive lists consist of anyone who uses the post or telephone for transactions that could be carried out in some other way, e.g. mail-order customers. Compiled lists are those put together to cover particular kinds of people, e.g. conference attendees, product buyers, small businesses. Lists can be sourced from list brokers who often act as agents for list owners. They may also be sourced from directories and by research.

▶ Techniques for merging and purging data

Merging databases and purging them of errors and duplication saves costs and prevents customers being alienated by being contacted more than once with the same objective. Deduplication of many items may need to be undertaken, so merging and purging of large databases requires sophisticated computer software.

To ensure that you can merge and purge, make sure that:

- all data is entered in standard format;
- matching rules are used which recognize duplicates;
- efficient fulfilment procedures exist, so all transactions are recorded and customers are helped to signal any duplicates or errors (e.g. by asking them to confirm details);
- different ways of selecting customers are available;
- auditing procedures exist.

Software is available to carry out the following:

- the filing of all customers and prospects together with their relevant data (e.g. type and date of purchasing activity);
- merging of bought or rented lists with in-house lists;
- identification and purging of duplicates;
- matching and merging of data which relates to the same customer;
- postcoding of addresses, for ease of access to census data, accuracy of targeting and easier sorting for postal rebates;
- validation of names against relevant official or national standard files, or telephone company directories, to ensure that prospective customers are actually resident at the stated address.

Investment in merge/purge software is often required to set up a useful database. But the investment is well worth it and pays dividends in terms of reduced marketing costs, increased revenue and enhanced customer satisfaction. You can use a bureau to do this, but if you find you have to use a bureau too often, you should consider acquiring the software. However, remember that you need more than software – you also need expertise and time. If you haven't got it, stick with the bureau.

▶ Using the database

Your database gives you a measure of a company's success in moving a prospect through a sales cycle. For example, you could produce a list of customers in a particular market sector with a particular product who have not responded to the last mail-shot on the subject. These could either be followed up more forcefully (e.g. by telephone) or (if there were other priorities) be omitted from a telephone prospecting campaign because lack of response (perhaps after second mailing) demonstrated lack of interest.

The history of your direct contact with customers can be used to calculate the costs and benefits of acquiring particular kinds of customers, not just for the first sale but over their lifetime with you. Thus, if the database shows that customers who buy product X are 50% more likely to buy product Y than other customers, then the benefits of acquiring a customer for X extend beyond the profit made on X. This helps you take a more comprehensive view of the viability of particular campaigns.

▶ Doing it yourself or outsourcing

Many companies prefer to outsource their customer database management. Even companies which have their own very large customer databases may outsource some aspects of customer data management (e.g. for new ventures, additional channels) because they want to focus on using the outputs from the database properly rather than actually managing it, and in new areas of business setting up and managing a database can consume a lot of management time and resources.

▶ Summary

In this chapter we have focused on the central role of the database in direct and interactive marketing. We have examined the raw material of direct marketing – information about customers and your relationship with them – and shown how important it is that this data is chosen and used for its predictive power. This applies particularly to transaction data – always remember your FRAC! We have shown that scoring is the key to using data predictively. We have also emphasized the importance of keeping data fresh, of finding out how fresh it is through audits and testing, and taking every opportunity to update it, i.e. every contact with customers. We have also considered the need to get rid of duplicate records, through merging databases and purging them of duplicates.

In the next chapter we show you how databases are used in practice.

7
who uses the customer database and how?

The start of the story

Which industries are using databases?

The demand for direct and interactive marketing

Summary

The start of the story

Customer databases once tended to be established and developed only through the work of a direct marketing department or section. The database would be used to carry out tactical sales promotions, provide higher-quality leads for a sales force, or support an in-house credit or loyalty card operation. Or it might grow directly from sales force activity, or through the work of a customer service department. Today, virtually every function that has anything to do with customers can use the customer database, for example:

- telemarketing operations – to manage, enter and track customer data, target customers for calls and record their sales rate;
- field sales support – to target customers for campaigns and measure their effectiveness;
- Internet operations/sales – to check customer identity and also to suggest offers to customers when they log on and record response and efficiencies;
- customer service – particularly in companies marketing complex equipment or those in consumer services, where the database is used as the key to managing the full range of service activity, before and after the sale;
- credit collection – where the credit/debit status of the customer is used as a key criterion for relationship management, adding an extra weapon to the credit collector's armoury.

Which industries are using databases?

Direct marketing tends to progress in waves, with particular industries making rapid progress and then undergoing periods of rapid consolidation. This is where the action is likely to be for the next few years.

Power and water utilities

> The **utilities** satisfy some of the basic needs of consumers and organizations – heat, light, power, water, communications.

Their use of customer databases ranges from customer relationship bill inserts explaining the nature and benefits of the service being provided, through targeting high-value users for offers and loyalty programmes, to equipment and maintenance service marketing. The utilities benefit from strong coverage of potential markets – they started with operational databases of practically every household and business in their area. Their strength as marketing entities derives from their regular billing arrangements. However, some utilities have added significantly to their operations. In the UK, Centrica, formerly just a gas utility, now sells financial services and automotive recovery and repair services, as well as a wide range of energy-related products and services. Its customer database is one of the largest and deepest in the UK as a result.

In the real world

Pressure to allow more direct debiting and less frequent communication with customers may reduce the strength of the dialogue utilities have with their customers. Paradoxically, direct debiting has been treated by some as a customer loyalty exercise because it locks in customers. But it also results in much less attention being paid to the supplier, so utilities have been developing aggressive programmes of mailings and telemarketing to defend and develop their customer base.

▶ Financial services

Companies in the **financial sector** provide ways for customers to manage their assets and liabilities (including cash), to conserve them through investment and insurance, to transact and to achieve their desired income and asset profiles over their lifetimes. The sector includes marketers of insurance, pensions, savings and credit, credit and charge cards, banking and mortgage services.

This sector presents some of the greatest opportunities for direct and interactive marketing and has always been one of the biggest users of databases. The underlying growth rate of this sector, relative to the economy, seems assured, notwithstanding short-term problems. The factors driving this include:

- rising incomes (which generate larger absolute amounts of saving);
- more discretion about what to spend, where and the consumer desire to find easy ways to do it;
- increasing longevity and earlier retirement (and the need to fund a longer retirement, with government less keen to fund it);
- uncertain involvement of the state in providing for other eventualities, e.g. sickness, education;
- the risk of longer periods of unemployment;
- awareness (stimulated by suppliers, media comment, government and personal experience) of the need for improved management of personal financial affairs.

Due to the wide competition in the market to satisfy the needs for the above, the search for different ways of developing and then managing relationships with customers other than through the branch network continues. In fact, financial products are available without the presence of a high street branch in the case of First Direct and Egg. These different ways are possible thanks to the development of telecommunications and computing technology – First Direct, Direct Line, Cahoot and Smile are all examples of new companies which have sprung up based on the database approach, combined with telemarketing and the Internet.

However, these new brands do not make much profit and often act as fighting brands for their owners, which are quietly adept at using database approaches to manage customers profitably through more conventional channels.

So the whole sector is moving heavily into true interactive marketing. Many companies have accepted the idea of present and future customer value as a key variable in the acquisition equation. Once the customer is acquired, the central objective is to sell more than just the initial product – a common fault in earlier financial services marketing. Now these companies are aiming to keep customers longer and to raise their average number of '**relationships per customer**', a piece of jargon which puts the focus not on the number of different products sold to each customer but on whether each product relationship endures – this is because switching and early cancellation are endemic in the sector.

Credit cards have been a vital tool for parts of the financial services industry. From a database marketing perspective, they are just a customer identification technology, which happens to facilitate transactions and credit. Smart cards are an emerging addition to the technological portfolio. Cards create postal and electronic traffic and hence opportunities for selling direct. More importantly, they also lead to the creation of a coherent picture of customer behaviour and needs, a prerequisite of true database marketing.

▶ Leisure and travel services

> **The leisure and travel services** sector includes all suppliers of personal transport (rail, air, coach, shipping, car hire, etc.), of accommodation (hotels, timeshare, etc.), of packaged and tailor-made holidays, travel agents, motoring organizations, leisure operators (bingo, gambling clubs, betting shops, theme parks and the like), photographic processors, theatres and cinemas, political parties, charities and publishers.

With so much information about customer behaviour and preferences potentially (and actually, in some cases) available to suppliers, the penetration of even primitive direct marketing into some areas of this sector (e.g. hotels) has been surprisingly slow. This contrasts with other areas (such as airlines, certain holiday companies and cruise operators) where the value of a long-term relationship with customers is well appreciated and exploited through a continuing dialogue, and marketing strategies are based on customer relationships (e.g. frequent-flyer programmes, special sea cruises for previous customers).

This category of expenditure looks robust for the long term, although it has suffered in the short term due to recession and world events like terrorism. The average size of companies is growing through mergers and takeovers. So the potential for database marketing is immense. There are also good cross-selling opportunities within this sector.

However, the low-cost airline model has threatened use of classic database techniques, as these new airlines rely on a strongly product-oriented business model, in which the key concern is to sell by the cheapest channel at the best price. Here, the interactive component (selling first by call centre, then via the Internet) has come to the fore.

▶ Non-profit and public institutions

> **Non-profit institutions** include public sector organizations (e.g. local authorities, educational establishments, government agencies), charities, political parties, professional and trade associations and other pressure groups.

Political parties and charities will see a considerable widening of the use of database marketing in recruiting members and influencing voting. Charities are heavy users of direct mail and understand the characteristics of more generous givers as well as their tendency to give to several different charities – hence list exchanging between them. Trade unions are using database marketing techniques to organize elections. The same applies to many professional bodies and societies. Educational institutions are using their databases of past students (alumni) to raise money as public funding tightens. Many of these types of institution have introduced 'affinity group credit cards' as an additional service to their members. The credit and transaction fees they raise add to their funds, while the database operations are usually facilities-managed by the credit card providers.

Governments are considering ways of using interactive marketing techniques, whether in disseminating information, such as people's rights, or in tax collection (e.g. profiling of likely fraudsters or late payers). E-government is a common phrase. It refers to improving citizen access to government information and services. However, many governments have discovered that direct and interactive marketing techniques need to be complemented by a change in the attitude to relationships between government and citizen – one which is less directive and more responsive, not just in terms of communication but also in terms of the whole public proposition to customers.

▶ Marketers of physical products

> This group includes all companies which have **a physical product to sell**, such as household durables, cars, home improvement products and fast-moving consumer goods, such as food. They have the following attributes:
>
> ◆ the processes of manufacturing and physical distribution, which increase the time and costs involved in adjusting supply to demand. Stocks are present in the system and this creates a strong pressure to find customers for them. However well these companies forecast demand, there will always be this pressure;
>
> ◆ the presence (in many cases) of retailers or distributors between the supplier and the customer, making their own merchandise selection and marketing policies and with (in some cases) a strong hold on customers and customer information.

In general, these suppliers were slow to awaken to the opportunities of database marketing. One exception to this is the motor industry, which uses it to **sustain dialogue after purchase**, and for prospecting. Domestic appliance manufacturers have long tussled with the question of how to maintain a cost-effective dialogue with customers when replacement for a given appliance is typically once every 7–10 years. They usually resort to retail display and occasional media bursts. But most computer suppliers have been working on developing customer loyalty using direct and interactive marketing techniques. Enhanced ability to segment and access particular groups of customers will help them solve this problem. However, they will still need to move away from an advertising emphasis to total database marketing if they are to be able to explore the full potential of their (usually multi-product) relationship with customers. For example, a typical household might have as many as 10 or 15 large and small appliances, many of which could have been sourced from one manufacturer.

Fast-moving consumer goods are a source of much controversy in database marketing circles. Some hold that the contribution of direct marketing is bound to be limited. However, some families may well be spending hundreds of pounds a year on products from a given manufacturer. If cross-product branding is nurtured, these customers become good prospects for database marketing. Their lifetime value is greater than that for many financial products. The potential competitive pay-off to successful database marketing in this area, where the only alternative is massive media spend, is clearly great and has been realized by leading US companies such as Heinz and Procter & Gamble. They have large databases and are sending personalized coupons to their consumers. These are giving such suppliers a good indication of which of their customers are highest value and therefore worth investing in to keep.

Meanwhile, the tactical promotional use of database marketing is receiving more attention from companies in this sector. Many promotions being mounted are single-product promotions which yield consumer lists as a by-product. Many are freephone telephone campaigns.

Here are some examples of incentives to call in (and to buy the product in the first place, of course):

- to find out whether the consumer has won the prize described on the pack;
- to answer questions on the product, receive a coupon and perhaps a prize;
- to listen to a commercial, receive a coupon and a free gift;
- to listen to a pop star's promotional message for a record;
- to have any problems resolved (the Careline approach).

> To encourage brand loyalty and build brand awareness, Lever Fabergé wanted to create a long-term collector scheme for market leader Persil. Lever Fabergé's research revealed that parents and guardians had a strong desire to develop their children's creativity. A high-profile event was needed to launch the scheme and communicate its primary purpose – to take pride in children's creativity. The idea to create Persil 'Big Mummy', the world's largest picture mosaic, was launched to enable parents to bring alive this research-identified desire while building Persil's brand and sales. Accordingly all the imagery and copy was hooked upon this desire, enticing mums and playgroup leaders with the possibility that not only could their children receive a certificate from Guinness World Records but that their image could be the one used for the world's largest picture mosaic.

> Without the support of on-pack promotions, which the campaign was too late to use, the strategy was to use direct marketing to target mums and playgroups. In-store promotions were also run in the aisles of Tesco Extra and the crèches at Safeway stores.
>
> As well as being over double the original target set, 14 755 of the 15 665 pictures came from individuals and groups not already on Lever Fabergé's database, 5713 of which were mums responding to one or more direct promotion. This new intelligence was used to promote Persil's 'Get Creative' scheme.
>
> Every child that took part is now in receipt of an official certificate from Guinness World Records.

▶ Product retailers

> **What are retailers?**
>
> Retail marketing used to be considered very different from the marketing of most of the above sectors. Now they are converging and direct and interactive marketing is helping create this convergence. Retailers are nearly utility companies for some consumers – a source of the basics: food and clothing. They play a key role in financial transactions, representing the destination of most cash. Retailers are used at least as frequently as banks (and some, such as Marks and Spencer, offer a wide range of financial services). They are providers of a service (halfway between leisure and work), but they are also product marketers in their own right, as some of them now have strong brands of their own (e.g. Sainsbury's own-brand Novon).

The main difference between product marketers and multiple retailers is the sheer volume of data about customer needs that they can collect because of frequent and direct contact. This makes them prime candidates for database marketing. Initially slow to take up marketing, let alone database marketing, most large retailers have developed their marketing resources and skills quickly in the past few years. This is partly because of competitive pressure that is internal to the sector, visible in the many mergers, takeovers, extensions of product lines and regional extensions of operations. Retail management is much more aware of the lifetime values of customers and of how database marketing can provide ways of keeping customers. The retail credit card and loyalty scheme give them a strong weapon in their competitive armoury. Retailers already realize the tactical value of these techniques. But they are now understanding their strategic value, as evidenced by the success of loyalty schemes such as the Tesco Clubcard. Members of these schemes are targeted for promotions aimed at getting them to visit more often, broaden their buying range and introduce new members to the scheme.

▶ Mail-order houses

Mail-order houses are one of the largest users of direct mail. Their databases are used for agent recruitment, promotions and also third-party promotions. The use of specialized catalogues is becoming widespread. The question these companies must ask themselves is what their role will be when everyone else becomes a database marketer! In some cases (such as the Next/Grattan merger), the answer has been to help a product retailer go into mail order. Within Littlewoods, the mail-order experience was the starting point for a chain of catalogue stores.

▶ The demand for direct and interactive marketing

The demand for database marketing will continue to be driven by the following factors:

- **Increased fragmentation** of consumer markets, partly as a result of more use of direct and interactive marketing, allowing customers with specific needs to be managed more easily, whetting their appetite for more. This leads to increased ability on the part of suppliers to meet the needs of small groups of consumers, which puts pressure on non-users of direct and interactive marketing to start using these approaches, causing existing users to improve their use, and so on. In many consumer markets, companies find it necessary not only to target their communications more precisely and manage their relationship with customers in a more 'personal' way but also to plan their business using the ever more detailed information accumulated about their customers, and the ever more sophisticated tools available for them to carry out this planning.

- **Further fragmentation** of business markets may also occur, for similar reasons. Other factors putting further pressure on industrial marketers to target their marketing more precisely include the steadily increasing professionalism and knowledge of industrial decision-making units and the pressure that customers' managers are increasingly put under to make more effective use of their time and resources.

- In consumer and industrial markets, **increased awareness** of the absolute and competitive benefits of using computer and communications technology to manage customers. In many markets, companies are keeping a watchful eye on their competitors' attempts to implement particular facets of customer relationship management.

- In all markets, increased emphasis on **'getting closer to the customer'**. In the 1980s, many supposedly marketing-oriented companies were chastened by their marketing experiences. Thinking that the information provided by relatively infrequent and superficial market research gave them good understanding of their customers, some companies were distressed to find that their customers' loyalty was less strong than they supposed, or that they were wrong about the kind of customers they had. In the 1990s, they resolved not to make the same mistake again, though many did. In the new century, many companies have learned from their mistakes and are taking a more steady approach to customer relationship management.

- In many businesses, the presence of an **increasing band of professionals** with direct and interactive marketing or similar backgrounds. These managers are demanding that their companies seize the best that database marketing has to offer, not just in marketing communications but in all marketing.

- In many public sector organizations, **greater sensitivity to the needs of 'customers'** (patients, users, consumers, ratepayers, etc.). This is emerging not only in the 'attitude' training being undertaken by many organizations but also in the kinds of information technology being installed to give better service to 'customers'. Some of them are actively looking to improve communication with their 'customers'. Government pressures have added fuel to this fire, sometimes in the form of tough regulations governing how customers should be managed.
- In charities, political organizations and pressure groups, increased **striving to influence people** and reach them first and/or more effectively. Many charities are expert users of direct marketing in competing for their share of the donor's budget.

> **Checklist: effective use of your direct and interactive marketing techniques**
> - Does it address the increased fragmentation of your customer base, both now and in the future?
> - How does it address the 'new professionals' in purchasing and their demands?
> - Are you continually creative in the way you address your customers?
> - Can you identify your most loyal customers and do you address them differently?
> - Do you regularly try new ideas and approaches to database marketing?
> - Does the tone and message of your database marketing fit with the overall corporate culture?
> - Are you trying to influence your customers or just keep them happy?
> - Does your use of direct and interactive marketing fit with your current corporate objectives and strategies?

▶ The supply of direct and interactive marketing services

The above trends spell radically increased opportunities for companies serving the database marketing market. The leading-edge suppliers in this market form a new group of specialist companies, which work to turn the most advanced technology and marketing concepts into useable marketing systems.

The 'supply-side' factors encouraging increased use of direct and interactive marketing include:

- further advances in computing and telecommunications. These are making it easier and cheaper to hold more complex information about individual customers or users. This information can then be analyzed more comprehensively, accurately and quickly, and analyses can be integrated more immediately into policy. Relationships with your customers can be managed more professionally, using the information held on your database or generated during each step in the relationship.
- relative increases in the costs of other more labour or media-intensive modes of marketing, and relative weakness in performance. In the US, the lack of national and often regional broadcast and printed media and the relative cheapness of classical direct marketing media (post and telephone) may have

been factors in the dramatically higher usage of the latter for marketing purposes than in the UK. In the UK, the situation may never rival that in the US, but the same trend is evident.

Many suppliers are broadening the range of services supplied. Direct marketing agencies are offering fulfilment and database services. Database bureaux are offering mailing and fulfilment services. Virtually all have moved into offering Internet-based services. Thus no company which needs to stay in touch with its customers has the excuse that it does not know how to use direct and interactive marketing.

▶ Summary

The need for mass segmented communication led to the use and development of computerized marketing systems. However, this mass marketing is not to be confused with mass prospecting for new customers. Most direct telemarketing activity takes place between companies and their regular customers. However, as direct marketing professionalism and services have improved, there has been a rapid increase in the use of these approaches in finding new customers. But there is a limit. Success in prospecting depends not just on the effectiveness of prospecting tools but also on successful defence of existing customers by 'incumbents', who can also be presumed to be increasing their professionalism.

In this chapter we have seen how many types of company are using direct and interactive marketing, and what they are doing with it. We have also seen why database marketing continues to grow – mainly because of fragmentation and competitiveness in markets, the need to manage customers better and influence them more strongly, and the improved supply of direct and interactive marketing services.

In the next chapter we examine in more detail how customer databases are applied competitively.

8 the competitive use of the database

Strategic vs tactical use of your database

Identifying opportunities

Quantifying the gain

Quantification

Summary

Strategic vs tactical use of your database

You can use your customer database just to improve your tactics, for example to find customers who are the best prospects for a one-time campaign. But database marketing is more effective when used strategically, to transform the way you do business. Here are some ways you could transform your business using direct marketing.

- Take a more methodical approach to conquest selling, e.g. by regular mailings to competitors' customers, asking for information about needs. This information can then be used to design products and marketing programmes. In consumer markets, data on competitors' customers is readily available from companies which have built proprietary lifestyle and similar databases (e.g. Claritas). Tesco and Sainsbury's have frequently used their in-store loyalty cards to target each other's customers and are now using the Air Miles (Tesco) and Nectar (Sainsbury's) to win each other's customers.
- Take a comprehensive approach to customer retention, with long-term programmes designed to maximize customer lifetime value.
- Make your marketing function more accountable for its expenditure. This has great appeal for finance directors. Marketing results can be traced back to activities and benefits set against costs. Measurability makes it easier to test the effectiveness of different approaches, giving the marketing function the tools to improve results.

> **Warning!**
> Accountability **creates pressures** within marketing. In many companies, the marketing function is not truly accountable for all its policies. It may be accountable in a general sense, but the information may simply not be available to hold it accountable for particular policies. For example, the results of a change in promotional policy or in sales force compensation may not be accurately measurable. Database marketing has changed this to some extent in some companies. Where accountability is strong in a marketing team it leads to greater professionalism in marketing planning, for example, and creates a stronger culture of analyzing what worked in the past. This culture is still missing in many marketing departments.

▶ Cutting field selling costs

In many industries, the field salesperson can make only between two and five calls per day (although in some industries the norm is ten or more). A telemarketer can make between 20 and 50 decision-maker contacts per day. The optimum competitive policy is to use your field sales and telemarketing according to their relative strengths, using a customer database to co-ordinate the two. You can test which works most effectively and profitably in your business and use the results of these tests to motivate the telemarketing and sales teams and to inform the marketing department.

You should use the sales force rather than telemarketing when:

- personal service is considered essential;
- an important new contact is being made;
- a difficult and sensitive problem needs to be solved;
- a complex presentation needs to be made;
- in-depth diagnostic work needs to be carried out;
- the customer's purchasing patterns need to be reinforced or developed (provided the customer's value is high enough for the required investment of time);
- the customer asks for a sales visit.

A telemarketing team working off your customer database can be used for all other calls. Eventually, with appropriate teamwork between your field sales force, the telemarketing team **and the customer** (whose time is also valuable and therefore who wants to be contacted by the most effective means for each call), more complex objectives can be handled by the telemarketing team. The telemarketer may become a full account manager. This approach increases the quantity and quality of contact between the sales force and customers, without increasing the cost. It also provides greater flexibility, enabling the sales effort to be redeployed more quickly to meet competitive challenges. The discipline with which your sales effort is managed can be increased. For example, you can focus your sales force on mounting attacks on competitors whose customers are known to be dissatisfied. For example, an automotive manufacturer could target owners of a competitive make with reliability problems.

▶ Putting an end to neglected customers

> **Warning!**
> Neglected customers are a problem for most businesses. In many industrial product or service markets, small business customers may be neglected. In consumer markets, customers may be isolated households or households with low purchasing frequencies. For both groups, the costs of traditional sales channels may preclude frequent enough contact. The customer may eventually switch to competitive products, assuming that competitors have not fallen into the same trap.

Database marketing can help here. For example, in the small business market for certain types of office equipment (e.g. fax machines, copiers, PCs and telephones), the direct response advertisement and the catalogue, co-ordinated through the customer database, are becoming the industry standard for reaching the customer. Once the prospect has become a customer, database marketing can be used to maintain the dialogue, while supplies and upgrades are bought, until the equipment needs replacing. When it gets near to the normal replacement time the database can be used to track this and it may be worthwhile contacting the customer using a more invasive technique, such as telemarketing, to remind the customer of the need to review their equipment and to offer a further sales call. It could also be done by a mailed offer for upgrading their equipment.

▶ Product launches

Database marketing can be used to improve your relationships with customers. It can be particularly effective in establishing the new customer relationships needed to ensure the success of a product launch. In some companies, the product development function uses market research to determine the features, functions, applications, advantages and benefits required by customers. Much later on, the product emerges and the contribution made by the customers who were researched is forgotten.

Yet in many industrial markets, the most successful innovations are those where potential customers were in close contact with the company from the earliest stage of product conception. Indeed, many successful innovations are actually made by customers. This particularly applies to software applications where some companies rely on their customers to suggest upgrades and fixes. But if the research was driven from the customer database, after the initial product development research a company could use database marketing to contact potential customers for a product and create and sustain a dialogue with them from product conception through to launch. This approach can lead to better designed products and high-quality services and is likely to lead to higher customer satisfaction, as customers involved in this way in the launch of a successful product will feel greater commitment to its supplier.

▶ Building loyalty

For existing products, database marketing provides an ideal way of building loyalty and maximizing revenue. For example, the quality of customer service may be checked by a questionnaire to all customers. This could monitor customer satisfaction and intention to purchase next time. The results of the questionnaire could be used to identify problems and ensure that dissatisfied customers do not become ex-customers. Such a questionnaire could also be used to structure campaigns aimed at managing the replacement cycle. Mailings could be sent just after purchase, halfway through the expected life of the product, and close to replacement decision time.

▶ Alternative sales channels

Many businesses find that their ability to serve their customers' needs is constrained by the cost of accessing them – the cost of the sale. So they are turning to database marketing to solve this supply problem. As we have seen, database marketing can lower the cost of sales, through applications such as telemarketing, mail order, enquiry management and the like. In some industries, e.g. the insurance industry, mail order has taken over many of the traditional functions of the sales representative.

> **eg** Many companies are using auto direct dialling to reduce the costs of handling enquiries and to enable sales staff to focus on the next stage of the sale. Idle enquirers and less interested customers are screened out and given other options, hopefully ensuring that they have got the information they need without incurring the cost of a sales call. In all these examples, the key to success is to match the cost of sales with the value of the customer. One automated test equipment company which chose this route discovered so much of its sales time was being wasted that when it moved to this approach it was able to reduce its staffing throughout Europe (saving millions of pounds); and the remaining staff benefits by being much closer to their (best) customers.

In some companies, whole product divisions are using database marketing as their main process for handling the sale. This applies to the 'supplies' (consumables and user-replaceable parts) divisions of many manufacturers of complex equipment.

▶ Barriers to market entry

If you don't have a good customer database, you may find yourself unable to enter a market if faced with competitors who have high-quality databases and use them effectively. They may have realized that the cost of setting up such a database could make entry difficult or impossible for other contenders. Conversely, possession of a database marketing capability may be the key to entering new markets. Thus, database marketers from other industries (e.g. automobile service associations, retail credit card operators) have used their capability to break into the financial services industry.

> **eg** To some, mainly service, businesses the database has become the company's greatest asset. In a number of cases when a large business has gone bankrupt, the database has been sold off to help cover the debts of the company. After the Internet bubble of the late 1990s burst and some of the companies went bust, their customer databases were sold and recycled. Since more rigorous data protection laws have been passed this is not so easy, but where the customer has stated that they are happy to have their name passed on the name can still be sold as part of a database.

▶ New products and services

Information is a product in its own right – and the information on customer databases is no exception. Strategic alliances between database marketers have been formed. Banks, automobile manufacturers, financial services companies and publishers are in joint venture businesses, pooling the data that each possesses to build a comprehensive picture of their customers. In these markets, a number of services are already being provided, such as:

- ◆ data vending and enhancement;
- ◆ data laundry services, e.g. cleaning up addresses and adding other third-party data to existing customer data;
- ◆ data management – the creation, updating and maintenance of a database.

Telemarketing agencies can be used here, to create a qualified customer information base by starting with cold lists, calling to qualify them and managing sales campaigns through them;
- electronic shopping (e-shopping).

There are now huge multinational businesses which have put together a comprehensive package of services for database marketers, such as:

- creative services;
- credit checking;
- credit card application handling, processing and administration;
- data verification and management;
- data pooling between clients;
- data rental;
- comprehensive geo-demographic consumer classification systems;
- mail services;
- telemarketing;
- household distribution;
- statistical, analytical and consultancy services.

Identifying opportunities

In competitive strategy formulation, database marketing is most frequently used to achieve one or both of the following objectives:

- revenue defence and development (including sale or rental of customer information, subject to conformity with legal requirements);
- cost reduction.

> Where customers are remote and scattered or diffused throughout the population, or the service offered is used by only a small percentage of the market, database marketing may be the most cost-effective way of reaching customers. This is why airlines have taken the discipline seriously. Only 3.5% of the population fly regularly on business. Television advertising informs 96.5% of the population who will never use this service. Database marketing therefore offers a big saving on marketing communications costs.

Many of the changes produced have a short *and* a long-term dimension. For example, telemarketing may produce cost savings and revenue increases which arise relatively quickly through reducing the cost of contacting and selling to customers and by increasing market coverage. However, greater market coverage and reduced cost of coverage may allow you to enter different product markets. You may be able to sell a wider product range to existing customers. These are longer-term gains which also need to be taken into account.

▶ Quantifying the gain

To justify the spend on database development and use you need to identify the revenue and cost changes that result from applying database marketing and quantify them. This can be done in many ways, for example:

- by category of customer;
- by category of product;
- by application introduced (e.g. sales force support, inbound or outbound telemarketing, direct mail);
- by category of change (i.e. whether it is cost saving, revenue defence or growth);
- by time period (short, medium or long term);
- by category of staff, function or marketing channel (e.g. impact on field sales force, sales offices, retail outlets, physical distribution, marketing communication, market research).

Below are some examples of the types of gain you need to quantify.

▶ Cost saving

Field sales force

- Reduction in number needed for given market coverage, perhaps through a more efficient calling pattern and less time spent identifying prospects and obtaining prospect information.
- Reduced staff support required, due to higher quality information available to sales staff.
- Reduced systems support, due to unification of possible variety of support systems.
- Reduced sales force turnover, due to quality of support and consequent higher motivation.
- Possibly broader span of management control and reduced number of reporting levels feasible. This would be due to a better standard of information on activities and effectiveness of field sales staff, leading to lower management costs.

Sales office

- Reduced number of staff required to deal with a given number of customers or support a given number of field sales staff. This would be due to a reduction in the time spent obtaining and collating information and more efficient prospecting systems.
- Reduced costs of handling customer enquiries, due to improved structuring of the response-handling mechanism so that customer enquiries go to the relevant destination more smoothly without passing through irrelevant hands.

- Lower staff turnover, due to higher level of support and consequent improved morale.
- Broader span of control and reduced number of reporting levels feasible, due to better standard of information on activities and effectiveness of office sales staff, leading to lower management costs.
- Reduction in number of branch offices, due to ability to cover market better and more 'remotely'.

Market research

- Lower expenditure on external research, due to higher quality and relevance of information available on customers and prospects.

Marketing and business planning

- Reduced costs of information collection and management, due to availability of higher quality, more relevant and updated information on customers and prospects, leading to a possible reduction in numbers of planning staff or in the planning component of other jobs.

Retail

- Improved site planning, due to the ability to match customer profiles to area profiles more accurately. This might lead to a reduction in the number of outlets to attain given revenue targets.
- Lower surplus inventory, due to the ability to target the marketing of 'sale' merchandise.
- Higher utilization of space, due to the ability to market special in-store events to the database.

Product/brand marketing

- Reduced costs of selling, due to better attunement of existing and new channels – some of which are possible only using database marketing – to customer needs.

Marketing communications

- Lower costs for achieving any given task, due to greater accountability and to improved ability to identify targets for communication and make communication relevant and therefore more effective.

Inventory

- Reduced write-offs, due to reduced frequency of launch of inappropriate products and to earlier termination of dying products.

- General improved forecast ability of marketing campaigns, leading to reduced temporary inventory peaks for given products.

▶ Revenue defending or increasing

Field sales force and sales office

- Higher revenue, due to ability of sales staff to concentrate calling on higher revenue prospects.
- Less lost business and fewer lost customers, due to improved customer care, as database marketing provides better channels for customers to signal needs.
- Enhanced new product revenues, due to improved ability to target customers for new products and eventually greater ease of launching new products.
- Greater ability of sales force to handle broader product portfolio, due to deployment of response-handling system to inform relevant customers prior to the sales call.

Market research

- Greater ability to identify potential for increased revenue among existing customers. This should also include a better understanding of your customers and how they respond which could feed usefully into new product development.

Business and marketing planning

- More coherent plans to address new revenue opportunities, due to higher quality and relevance of information, leading to higher success rate with launch of new products, greater matching of distribution channels to customer needs, etc.

Retail

- Ability to market additional products to existing retail customers, whether at retail or through mail order, due to quality of customer information.
- Higher sales volumes of existing products, due to ability to target promotions.

Marketing communications

- Greater effectiveness of communicating with customers and prospects, leading to higher revenue for given cost.

Product marketing

- Reduced costs of selling, due to better attunement of channels to customer needs, leading to the ability to capture higher market share through lower prices or improved offers.

Inventory

- Lower stock-outs and therefore quicker inflow of revenue and reduced loss of sales to competition, due to improved sales forecasting.

Quantification

This can be carried out as follows.

▶ Target opportunities

> **Action**
> Draw up a list of target opportunities. This is best done in a management workshop, perhaps supplemented by interviews and discussions with colleagues, customer-facing staff and customers.

You'll find that many of the best ideas are usually present in your company and have just been looking for an outlet. They may not have been allowed to emerge because of the way in which policies are planned and implemented. After all, many database marketing applications are the implementation of common-sense ideas through the use of modern information technology. The outcome of this step is a statement of the target opportunities. This provides the focus for the rest of the analysis.

▶ Incremental revenue from database marketing

> **Action**
> Review current marketing plans to identify long-term revenue growth objectives and to clarify the basis for revenue growth plans. One way of ensuring that your plan is customer focused is to gather together any data you have from the customer, such as response rates, any research which is available, and if you have them customer comments and complaints. These are your 'customer metrics'. Once you have assessed this data, look again at your revenue growth objectives and ensure you are focusing on the same things which your customers are saying are important.

Revenue growth plans may be based on factors such as overall market growth, specific marketing strategies (product range, price, distribution, advertising, etc.) or anticipated competitive changes. This analysis will indicate the areas where database marketing may generate revenue growth through improving the effectiveness of policies that are already planned.

▶ Quantification of cost effects

Warning!

Quantifying the cost savings from implementing database marketing before implementation is not easy. It is more difficult if your existing marketing information is not well organized. If you have only recently adhered to the marketing creed, the information to quantify cost effects may have to be estimated. This may require 'reconstruction of figures' (i.e. answering the question 'what if we had done it this way?'), plus pilot studies.

Typically, a comprehensive exercise to gather and analyze cost information is required. It will normally cover every channel of communicating with and distributing products and services to customers, such as sales force, sales offices operating by telephone and mail, retail outlets, media advertising and direct mail. The aim is to quantify costs which may be changed by database marketing approaches.

Action

To do this properly, use interviews, questionnaires and analysis of financial and operating information relating to your channels of communication and distribution. This should be done by market sector and product line as well as for your whole business.

▶ Contact strategies

Action

Document clearly how you contact your customers today. Then identify contact strategy options, using database marketing, and assess:

- the capability of existing channels to support revenue growth targets and the cost of resourcing those channels to achieve them;
- the incremental cost of the database marketing strategy needed to support the revenue growth target.

▶ Revenue and cost review

Action

A summary of marketing activity over the period of the plan should then be prepared. Annotate the summary with findings from your 'customer metrics' exercise and be clear about how the activity relates to your customers and what you know of their behaviour.

This should show the effect on costs and revenues of employing existing methods to achieve targets and compare it with the costs and revenues implied by the use of database marketing. This should show the areas where database marketing is more effective.

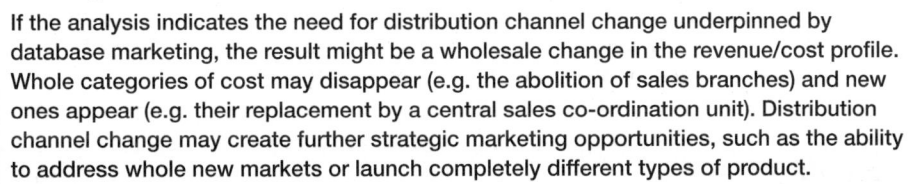

> **Warning!**
> If the analysis indicates the need for distribution channel change underpinned by database marketing, the result might be a wholesale change in the revenue/cost profile. Whole categories of cost may disappear (e.g. the abolition of sales branches) and new ones appear (e.g. their replacement by a central sales co-ordination unit). Distribution channel change may create further strategic marketing opportunities, such as the ability to address whole new markets or launch completely different types of product.

> Egg re-evaluated its route to market and decided to close its telebanking operations and move to a web-based operation. To entice existing customers to switch it offered a much improved rate to anyone who switched their telebanking account for a web one. The company improved its margins year on year and gained customers.

However, the change may be less revolutionary, e.g. the refocusing of a calling sales force on larger customers and the replacement of their efforts by a telemarketing operation.

Points to watch in your strategic assessment include the following:

- Have you assessed opportunities to use database marketing to change how you manage your customer relationships, including restructuring your route to market?
- Are your remaining sales force trained to use the necessary IT, enabling you to reduce back-office support?
- Have you consulted your customers about any proposed change to your relationship with them?
- Have you used your database to reduce your market research budget?
- Are you up to date with the technology required to use your database as a planning tool?
- Have you kept all departments of your company up to date with developments on the database and sold its capabilities in-house?
- Have you created a user group for your database?
- Are your marketing suppliers – particularly your advertising agency – comfortable with the database and its uses? If not, is there an agency within their group who is?
- Have you worked hard to introduce the culture of honest assessment of campaign results?

Database marketing may afford many opportunities for increasing revenue and reducing costs, but unless these opportunities are **firmly built into operating plans as targets**, they are unlikely to be achieved.

> **Warning!**
>
> Make sure you involve every function affected by the introduction of database marketing, as functions outside sales and marketing can determine whether the approach succeeds, e.g. customer service, credit control. If you are changing the interface or working arrangement for the staff who will be using the system, ensure you have fully understood their needs. Often the only way to do this is to spend a couple of days and/or shifts working alongside them and listening to them handle customers.

Summary

In this chapter we have focused on the strategic uses and benefits of database marketing. We've stressed particularly the cost and revenue benefits that flow from planned use of a marketing database. We've also argued that this approach can give you significant competitive advantage. But you must understand that few competitive advantages can be sustained for ever. What you do today, your competitors can imitate tomorrow. This is particularly true of database marketing. The techniques and processes to make database marketing work are becoming widely known. So you need to stay ahead of your competition. Just having your customer database is not enough. Staying ahead of your competitors depends upon the applications supported by the database – the subject of our next chapter.

9 competitive applications of direct and interactive marketing

What types of application are there?

Strategic issues

Data acquisition and development

Maintaining the database

Making applications work

Using management applications

Developing accountability through applications

Supporting decisions

Day-to-day working applications

Sophisticated statistical applications

Phasing in the applications

The fully integrated system and its applications

Stepping through your system

Summary

This chapter shows you how to create cost-effective, competitive and strategically significant applications for your customer database. These applications are the answer to the question 'How can I use computerized customer data to support a significant and profitable dialogue with my customers – now and in the future?'

▶ What types of application are there?

Customer database applications can be split into two categories: customer applications and management applications. A third category, dialogue application, is effectively a combination of the two and forms the basis of many approaches to customer relationship management (CRM).

▶ Customer applications

> **Customer applications** are those uses of the database which involve the creation and maintenance of contacts and relationships with customers.

The main customer applications of a marketing database are:

- direct mail (using the system to select customers to receive relevant mailings);
- response handling and fulfilment (using the system to record your customers' responses and manage the next step in the contact strategy – fulfilment);
- telemarketing (using the telephone to manage your customers, by contacting them or allowing them to contact the company, recording the results of the dialogue and initiating the required next contact);
- dealer, distributor or agent management systems (providing data to them, helping them meet their customers' needs better, monitoring their performance in so doing);
- club or user group marketing (creating an 'inner circle' of your customers, who receive special additional benefits in return for their loyalty);
- customer relationship management – managing customers throughout their period with you, to mutual benefit;
- consumer promotions (e.g. coupon distribution and redemption);
- business promotions (e.g. sales force incentive schemes, competitions);
- credit card management (using the system to recruit credit card customers, record their transactions, invoice them and promote to them);
- targeted branding (using the system to deliver branding messages to individuals identified either as being specially receptive to them or as being at risk from competitive actions);
- data marketing (selling or renting the customer data on the system);
- any other dialogue application, i.e. one which involves a sustained series of communications with a target market.

▶ Management applications

> **Management applications** are those applications which change the way marketing management plan, implement and assess their marketing activities.

Management applications include:

- campaign planning (selecting customers with specific needs and identifying the kind of offers to which they will respond);
- campaign co-ordination (ensuring that campaigns fit into a logical sequence and lead to the establishment of a sensible dialogue with customers, rather than clashing and inconsistent messages);
- project management (managing the delivery of communications and CRM projects);
- campaign performance and marketing mix productivity analysis (identifying which elements of the mix are best for managing different kinds of customers and which campaigns are most successful);
- campaign monitoring (providing interim data on campaign performance so that remedial actions can be taken where necessary).

> **Action and warning**
>
> Which applications you implement should be determined by marketing strategy. They should not be chosen simply because they are possible once the customer database has been created. In fact, it is best to plan the database and applications as an integral proposition. The fact that this is so rarely done gives you a competitive opportunity. If you plan your applications from the outset, you'll get much better results from your database. But if you rush ahead with customer applications and don't pay attention to management applications, your use of your database is likely to be very inefficient.

> **eg** A major retailer with one of the best-known and productive customer loyalty schemes in the business spent large amounts on bringing its data in-house from a bureau. Just before the completion of this project, it discovered that it had no management process for developing strategic use of the database. Rather, it was used whenever the company decided a tactical campaign was necessary. The result was that large groups of loyal users were effectively unmanaged by the company.

> **eg** Another retailer with a similarly strong database discovered that it had no process or software for analyzing its database, other than through guesswork (e.g. 'let's see how many customers behave like X').

> A national utility spent large sums on developing its customer database and direct mail applications, enabling it for the first time to address its target markets with coherent messages. However, it had no system for co-ordinating the work of the many different marketing managers who used the system. The result was high campaign expenditure and clashing of communications, with customers sometimes receiving several conflicting communications in the same week.

In these examples the company had focused on the customer applications, leaving the management applications trailing behind. Much potential profit was lost because it was not able to use the right consumer applications. This in turn was due to failure to develop the right management applications.

▶ Dialogue applications

> A **dialogue** is defined as a structured series of contacts, involving you contacting the customer and the customer responding, giving information, making purchases, etc. The concept of dialogue is central to maximising profit from customer data. A dialogue is more effective than a monologue – a one-way series of contacts with no response – or than a single conversation (a one-off promotional contact).

In a dialogue, you ask your customer questions such as 'When do you intend to buy?', 'When will you next need help?' and 'What other products might interest you?' You effectively program your database system to analyze these responses and the outcome of the analysis is the triggering of future contacts – of a type and timing the customer wants. This is how you develop a dialogue with your customers. The aim of this dialogue is to:

◆ move your customers towards purchase;
◆ keep them satisfied after the purchase;
◆ ensure they buy additional or replacement products later on.

Without this, the result is a one-way flow of promotional literature, most of which is wasted.

Your database system is essential in ensuring that the right communication reaches the right customer at the right time. It selects the initial contacts. It analyzes the customer response pattern. It plans the follow-up. Your aim should be to develop contact strategies and dialogue applications that suit all your target customers and prospects, and to have management applications that ensure that you are able to do this properly.

Strategic issues

Action

Your first step – one that many companies forget to take – is to turn your customer information into a customer database. For example, if you sell to customers directly (e.g. via a field sales force), you are likely to have a reasonably high-quality **customer file** already, and possibly several, containing details about your customers. You will almost certainly have a **transactions file**, showing which customers have bought what and when. Many companies have many such files or databases, one for each business unit, channel and/or product. You need to turn these into a **marketing database**. Remember, a marketing database contains more than just customer records – it also holds details of:

- the marketing and sales campaigns you run;
- the resulting contacts with your customers;
- the outcomes of these contacts.

Warning!

Your customer and transactions files may be hard to convert to a marketing database. You will have to decide whether to merge all your information or keep the source files separate and use them to update a new marketing database on a regular basis. Costs are likely to be high, and issues such as frequency of update from the main database, data quality and data ownership will be prominent.

Your transactions file may contain useful source data on frequency, recency, amount and category. But it may not be stored in the right way so that you can use it to target customers and find out what purchasing histories are associated with high potential for future purchases. Other information which indicates likely customer needs (organisational, psychographic, etc.) may not have been collected methodically or at all. You may need to enhance the database through imported or questionnaire data.

Action

If you have no direct contact with customers, you have three main options in database and application development, which you can pursue simultaneously:

1. Compile, through list purchasing, testing and research, a database of those likely to be buyers of your products.
2. Create marketing applications which by themselves generate the data through direct contacts, often through 'plastic' (credit cards, club membership, promotional entitlement records/cards), clubs, etc.
3. Switch (partially or wholly) to channels of distribution which do involve direct contact.

With indirect sales, critical transactions data (on FRAC) will not be available, except through customer questionnaires or if your bargaining position is strong enough to enable you to extract the data from third parties, e.g. automotive suppliers, or if you can buy it, e.g. from a retailer running a loyalty card.

> **Warning!**
> If you cannot get transactions data, you must find other data which indicates propensity to buy your products. In consumer markets, you may be able to source this data from a lifestyle data supplier. Otherwise, a questionnaire may be the best approach.

> **In the real world**
> The problem of getting the right data can be compounded by the fact that companies often go into database marketing at times of strategic uncertainty. They may not be sure which products they will be marketing to whom over the next few years. This means that it is not easy to determine which data will be needed. If this is your situation, your best strategy may be to start a programme of testing the importance of different variables in explaining buying behaviour for different kinds of products, combined with data reduction (see below) and profiling wherever possible, to simplify the data set, which could otherwise get out of hand.

▶ Data acquisition and development

> A **data acquisition and development strategy** is needed. This strategy determines:
> ◆ which data you need to support your marketing strategies;
> ◆ how sources of data are to be identified, qualified and tested (including different questionnaire programmes);
> ◆ how the data is to be maintained, archived and disposed of when no longer needed.
>
> You need this strategy whether or not you have started with a customer file and whether or not your aim is to sell more to existing customers or to recruit more customers.

> **Data reduction** is the science of finding a few variables to explain a complex set of data, using statistical techniques. For example, you may use a long questionnaire to find out whether your customers are satisfied with their relationship with you, and use statistical techniques to ascertain which questions account for most of the differences between customers. Or you may wish to segment your customers for targeting purposes. Again, you might use a questionnaire on buying attitudes and behaviour and find which questions enable you to divide your customers most neatly into different groups. Data reduction is important because unless you use it, you could find yourself collecting masses of data which proves unwieldy to use.

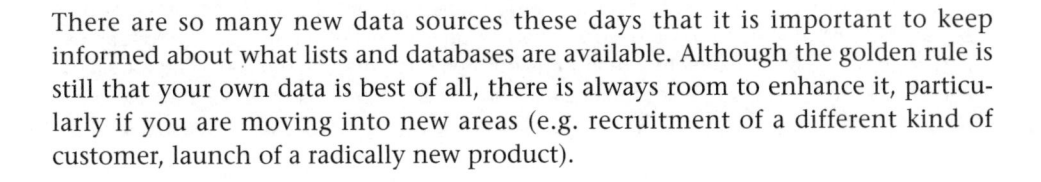

There are so many new data sources these days that it is important to keep informed about what lists and databases are available. Although the golden rule is still that your own data is best of all, there is always room to enhance it, particularly if you are moving into new areas (e.g. recruitment of a different kind of customer, launch of a radically new product).

> **Action**
>
> Though a questionnaire may contain relevant data, the costs of entering it onto the system and analysing it to provide the segmentation you need means that your plan for obtaining, entering and testing the data must be carefully laid out to prevent acquisition of high volumes of information when low volumes would do. An alternative is to build partnerships with non-competing companies to share the information and cost.

> Some database marketing users are investing in **profiling approaches**, to give convenient measures of customer characteristics/susceptibilities. The idea is to develop (usually from an analysis of your existing data) one or more profiles (e.g. of a type of customer the company would like more of). Credit scoring is the 'home' of this kind of work – where it is used to develop profiles of customers that are definitely not wanted! The benefit of this approach is that it provides score cards or directories which can then be applied to any file, provided that the latter contains the variables which the scoring technique uses. For example, in credit scoring, these variables include income levels, home ownership and credit card history. This reduces the volume of testing required and increases the response rates of campaigns. However, campaigns may be required just to bring in the right data.

Maintaining the database

If you have a customer database, you need to maintain it.

> **Warning!**
>
> If the data is not maintained properly, even the most sophisticated applications will founder.

Best practice is that the database should be largely self-maintaining through the applications run on it. But the paradox is that databases which are easiest to update may be the least valuable. If all competitors are in monthly direct dialogue with their customers (e.g. in the credit card market), data on monthly purchasing patterns and repayments is plentiful. Competitive advantage will come not from having data but from turning it into a form that can be used for marketing purposes. Dialogue applications – ones in which you are informing and selling to customers, and they are responding with information and orders – provide the best data but are the most expensive to create and manage.

> **In the real world**
>
> If dialogue is intermittent and conducted through third parties (e.g. cars, domestic appliances), building a database is hard work, involving questionnaires, promotional programmes and so forth. Heavy investment in hand-raising promotion may be required. Once built, it can be used to understand replacement cycles and to target promotions more effectively.

Once the database is in order, it is worth **re-examining objectives** to see whether the database still supports them or justifies **more aggressive** objectives.

> A branded durable goods company which develops a database to target promotions more accurately may discover that some of its customers want to buy mail order from it (they may already be buying from a mail-order company). A small catalogue may be in order, with carefully timed promotions against it. The company may discover that its list is valuable and start to market it. Service contract marketing may prove viable. Related products may be marketed. Having a good marketing database can open up new lines of policy. But all this should be judged against the strategic objectives of the company and the costs of running the database.

Making applications work

In most large companies, the users of the customer database are not just direct and interactive marketing users. The database is used by marketing analysts, sales managers, retail planners, brand managers and so on. The marketing applications they need could be any combination of those mentioned earlier.

Developing the applications plan means aligning database plans with strategic marketing plans. If you have a large number of customers who buy moderate amounts from you but not enough to justify a field sales call, the first applications you are likely to need are direct mail and telemarketing. On the other hand, if you want to use the system to gather information about customers buying your products through retailers, the first applications needed may be high-volume, low-cost coupon processing and questionnaire management.

You can determine which applications you need by:

1 identifying the kinds of contact you have with your customers (pre and post sales) – this is called the contact audit;
2 identifying whether there is a requirement for more frequent or different contact, and what the benefits of these contacts might be;
3 producing a list of possible marketing applications (as detailed earlier, plus any others that are relevant to you);
4 identifying the combination of applications which is most likely to be cost effective, using standard techniques of cost-benefit analysis.

Using management applications

Once the database and its marketing applications are set up, a process is required to make the database work as a management tool.

- **Step 1 – formulate your marketing strategy**, including considering the different ways (channels, products, etc.) of relating to (now known) customers. This is critical to making the database deliver value to general users. The management application should include ways of extracting data about different groups of customers and how your company has performed with each of them. It should also enable you to model the effects of different strategies. If you are following a CRM approach, you need to determine which groups of customer you want to manage, through which channels, with what frequency and depth of interaction.

- **Step 2 – develop a clear view on the kinds of campaign to be run** and whether they will follow particular themes and on the **kinds of interaction you want with your customers** – within and outside campaigns. Develop a structured approach to maximizing learning and effectiveness, minimizing costs and reducing conflict. Different kinds of campaigns and interactions have different pay-offs, use different kinds of data and have different priorities. The further you progress with using your database, the more your campaigns and interactions will increase in sophistication, placing a greater load on marketing, statistical and systems services. Without a proper medium-term plan of action, you may run into bottlenecks or, worse, conflicts. Your management applications should enable you to run simulations of individual campaigns and of several campaigns together. This will help you evaluate different options.

- **Step 3 – co-ordinate your plans to campaign and interact with customers**, to ensure maximum effectiveness and minimum overlap. Make sure that campaigns make sense in terms of the dialogue with individual customers and that interactions take into account campaigns you want to run. A campaign planning and co-ordination application, which shows what campaigns are planned when, and to whom, will help ensure this. In some parts of the 'classic' direct marketing industry, rolling campaign plans – from one to five years' duration – are used. In some companies, the marketing system has a full management process application attached to it. This shows not only what campaigns are planned to be run when but what are the different stages in getting these campaigns to market, i.e. a project management application.

Developing accountability through applications

As soon as you start to use your marketing database to sell to customers, you may run into a series of ownership and accountability problems.

> **Warning!**
> Companies with a territory sales force, regional marketing teams and product or brand managers may find that all these groups want to contact the same (usually the most loyal) customers and claim the benefits of resulting sales.

The solution to this problem is partly political – your senior management must make it clear that the company as a whole owns the data and accountability is therefore **shared**. If anyone asks, 'Who owns the customer?', the answer is 'the customer'. The company as a whole is responsible for managing the relationship. But the effectiveness of the campaigns and interactions managed by different centres of marketing power should be measured and compared. Your database should make performance achievement much clearer. Eventually it should become the foundation for a marketing-mix evaluation application. This shows which elements of the marketing mix are being used cost effectively, by comparing spend with results.

One area where financial evaluation is particularly important is the media mix. Database analysis provides accurate data on media effectiveness. It provides a firm basis for the development of a media usage strategy, overall and for particular markets and segments.

> **Warning!**
> Your financial evaluation may show that **no** media are cost effective for accessing a particular market. You may need to develop new media to access it (e.g. your own newsletter, a customer helpline). The development of a media analysis application (which simply means that the data on media effectiveness must be gathered, through coding of all response vehicles, and analyzed properly) can lead to dramatic savings in advertising budgets.

> **Checklist: using your database effectively**
> Is your marketing strategy developed in consultation with all potential users of the database?
> Does your direct marketing campaign plan lock in with your advertising campaigns and field sales initiatives?
> Will all your campaigns sustain your brand image?
> Have all your campaign plans been 'sold in' to your staff? Will they benefit the whole company?
> Do the timings of your campaigns clash with any other communications going out from your company, such as renewal notices, safety warnings?
> Have you taken all the steps you can to reassure other departments about the database's use and its benefits, including external suppliers such as advertising agencies?

Supporting decisions

The system holding your database must have an executive system/decision support element, which makes manipulation of data for analytical (research, analysis of effectiveness) and policy purposes much easier.

> **Warning!**
> Without this management application, managing the database **can become a nightmare**. It may take you a long time to find out exactly what is on the database or what the results of a particular campaign were. Without fast access to this summary data, bad marketing decisions are likely to be taken – the wrong campaigns will be run, leading to low responses, customer alienation and deterioration of data quality.

Day-to-day working applications

Your database must be **internalized**. That is to say, a clear view must be developed of how it will be used in practice by the many kinds of staff who will want to use it. When your users feel happy about the value of the database, they will be happier about using it more proactively to manage customer relationships.

> **Action**
>
> This requires understanding the perspective of the different users. They must be trained to use it and to feed back information. A reporting process must be developed which incorporates database marketing reports.

You must identify how users can incorporate the database into their traditional disciplines, their planning processes and their day-to-day working, with clear benefit to them. This may mean building a number of simple reporting applications into the system so that it produces the outputs required by different kinds of staff to fulfil their jobs. You may need to combine data from the system with output from your other systems. It may cost more in terms of programming, maintaining data compatibility and sustaining data links, but if it achieves the objective of making the database approach a way of life, it may be worthwhile.

Sophisticated statistical applications

These are not a 'must' at the beginning. The initial benefits of having a customer database are straightforward, i.e. you know what your customers want and what effect your marketing is having on them. However, as experience accumulates, sophistication of use increases and your staff become familiar with management processes. A good 'history' of properly mounted campaigns is accumulated, so carefully and regularly presented reports on these campaigns can really help sell the benefits of using database marketing internally. A good statistical capability becomes essential for understanding the true determinants of effectiveness, e.g. through new ways of segmenting, targeting, and managing contact strategies via scoring.

> **Warning!**
>
> Too much experimentation too early can lead to waste of resources on statistical analysis before the fundamental characteristics and quality of the database are understood. You will best understand how your customers react to your marketing efforts by exposing them to a consistent series of communications, not a few one-off, poorly co-ordinated promotions.

Testing strategies are particularly important for prospecting programmes, in which it is easy to invest a lot of resource for little return. Testing is also vital to establish which contact strategies are right for different customers.

Phasing in the applications

In the real world

How you phase in use of your database depends very much on your company's structure and strategy. Take the example of an integrated company with a structure of local branches/offices in which some marketing and most selling is done, and with a central marketing unit. This company might start with central outbound calling and mailing combined with central response handling and fulfilment. There is low involvement of local sales and marketing staff. Contact strategies may be very simple, scoring may not be used and offers may be just one type per campaign. Later, local outbound telemarketing may be introduced to generate local leads. Then more advanced, central campaigns may be brought in, involving local fulfilment, integrated with central or local response handling but still not as part of a long-term relationship. Campaigns will still be product-based but better co-ordinated.

But this is still not relationship marketing. Eventually, the company may move to fully integrated local and national, fully co-ordinated and planned **'virtual account/relationship management'**. More complex contact strategies will be used, their design driven by a scoring capability. Offers will be much more varied to suit different customer types. For some companies, the ideal will be when the database is used by real account managers, contacting customers on a regular calling cycle, using database marketing disciplines. Campaigns for particular products and services are then treated as a highlight to the relationship, helping focus customer attention on additional benefits.

The fully integrated system and its applications

At the centre of your marketing system is your customer database. If your organization is multibranch or multinational, this database may have central and local elements. Where these are and how they are used depends on the degree of variation between local and central campaigns, the costs of communicating data and of distributing computing equipment to handle local databases. Specialist support staff will need to work with company management to plan and help implement campaigns. Leads generated by the system will need to be passed out to the appropriate channels. Lists of various kinds may be needed to build the database. Further lists are generated from it as the basis for tests and full campaigns. Leads and enquiries from various sources (e.g. mail, telephone, branch customer service) are handled using pre–tested contact strategies and the results placed on the database, which leads to firm orders being placed with the distribution function. Marketing analysis is carried out to show the profitability of different approaches and to allow tactical changes to be made to campaigns currently being undertaken. This is depicted in Fig. 9.1. The figure shows what the system would look like for a business-to-business marketer using the database primarily for a telemarketing and sales support operation, supported by a catalogue.

Fig. 9.1 An example of an integrated system

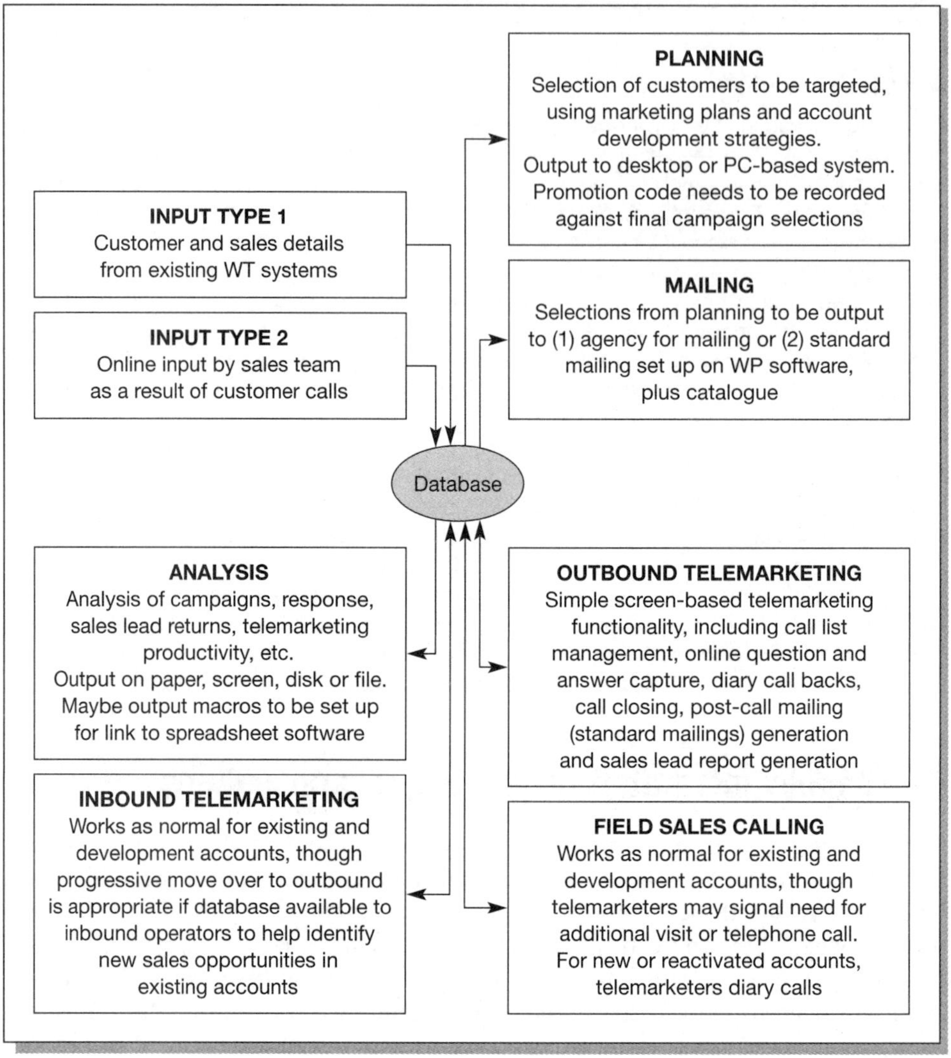

INPUT TYPE 1
Customer and sales details from existing WT systems

INPUT TYPE 2
Online input by sales team as a result of customer calls

PLANNING
Selection of customers to be targeted, using marketing plans and account development strategies.
Output to desktop or PC-based system. Promotion code needs to be recorded against final campaign selections

MAILING
Selections from planning to be output to (1) agency for mailing or (2) standard mailing set up on WP software, plus catalogue

Database

ANALYSIS
Analysis of campaigns, response, sales lead returns, telemarketing productivity, etc.
Output on paper, screen, disk or file. Maybe output macros to be set up for link to spreadsheet software

OUTBOUND TELEMARKETING
Simple screen-based telemarketing functionality, including call list management, online question and answer capture, diary call backs, call closing, post-call mailing (standard mailings) generation and sales lead report generation

INBOUND TELEMARKETING
Works as normal for existing and development accounts, though progressive move over to outbound is appropriate if database available to inbound operators to help identify new sales opportunities in existing accounts

FIELD SALES CALLING
Works as normal for existing and development accounts, though telemarketers may signal need for additional visit or telephone call. For new or reactivated accounts, telemarketers diary calls

Stepping through your system

One of the main justifications for the direct and interactive marketing approach is that it serves the needs of marketing managers who have responsibility for particular groups of customers (or the entire market) or for particular products. These are 'internal customers'. One way to understand how a fully fledged marketing system works to serve the needs of 'internal marketing customers' is to go through the steps by which a campaign is designed and implemented. The channel of distribution being used is a direct sales force.

1. A **marketing plan for a brand, product or sector** is formulated. It identifies the need for one or more marketing campaigns. Preliminary work is carried

out to identify which kinds of campaign are likely to be most successful for the product or sector and which customers should be targeted in them.

2. A **campaign brief** is drawn up, including campaign objectives, targeting, timing, the precise nature of the product or service to be promoted, the offer to be made to the customers, the benefits, how the campaign will help build company brand values, the resources required to implement the campaign, the way in which the campaign's success will be measured and the expected returns. This brief is the basis on which all work is carried out and ultimately executed.

3. The brief is used to derive a **campaign specification**, which is entered into a computerized campaign co-ordination system. This co-ordinates the planning, execution and implementation of all marketing campaigns. It ensures that the approach to customers is co-ordinated and prioritized, taking into account the importance of different target markets, budget availability and the need to avoid clashes. One of its principal outputs is an agreed schedule of campaigns to be run. Without this, databased account management is impossible.

4. A **campaign is designed** to achieve the marketing objectives within the permitted budgets. Data about customers and past campaigns is used to define the target market more closely and to identify which broad kinds of campaign are likely to be most successful for the product or sector.

5. Campaigns are devised to **test the different elements** of the design on statistically significant sample lists extracted from the database. Testing normally covers the main elements of the campaign, i.e. which customers are targeted, which offers they receive, the timing of contacts with them, how they are to be reached and how their responses are to be handled.

6. The test campaigns are **implemented and the results are analyzed** to determine which campaign elements (e.g. media, contact strategies) produced the best results.

7. The detailed design of the **campaign is developed**. As the contact strategy determines a high proportion of the costs of a campaign, contact strategies should be tested thoroughly and prioritized. The tests provide the basis for prioritizing. This occurs in various ways, e.g. by including some customers in the campaign and excluding others, by handling customers in different ways.

8. The **details of the campaign** are agreed and an outbound list is selected. This determines which customers will be contacted in the first step in the contact strategy. The list is selected using a formula derived from analysis of tests.

9. The **main campaign runs**. The customer receives a communication which is part of the campaign. This prompts him to respond, e.g. by coupon or telephone. If the response is to an inbound telemarketing set-up, the operator at the latter finds out which campaign or 'offer' the customer is interested in. The operator, cued by a sequence of on-screen displays, asks the customer a series of questions. These include confirmation of the customer's identity (possibly including telephone number, address and job title), specific needs

concerning the product or service in question, and the customer's needs for further contact. The operator enters the answers into the computer. If the enquiry is by mail, the respondent is contacted by an outbound telemarketing call and a similar process takes place.

10. The **enquiry information** gathered from the customer is matched to the existing customer file (if any) and merged with other information on the database.

11. The computer uses rules derived from tests and agreed with the campaign originator and project manager to prioritize the enquiry according to the likelihood of a customer ordering. These rules are based partly on predetermined campaign profiles (i.e. the kind of customer the company is trying to attract) and may use the **data gathered** during the customer's response.

12. A particular **contact strategy is recommended**, based on the type of product and on the priority.

13. **The fulfilment organisation receives information** indicating, among other things, what kind of letter and additional material should be sent to the customer or, if the product is mail order, what product should be sent.

14. **Local sales offices, sales staff or dealer outlets receive information** about the enquiry on their computers, follow up enquiries and feed back the results of the follow-up to the database.

15. The results of all enquiries and responses are analyzed to provide regular reports on the **effectiveness of activities** and to help improve the effectiveness of future campaigns. Detailed performance data plus expenditure data from financial systems are used to evaluate financial performance and plan new campaigns.

▶ Summary

There are two main types of application for your customer database – customer applications, or what you want to do with customers, and management applications, which help you structure these customer-facing activities and ensure that they take place efficiently. A key issue for both sets of applications is how you aim to acquire, use and maintain your data. We have shown what happens when you leave consideration of applications until after you have built your database.

Database building is a process which doesn't take place overnight. It is a phased activity, which never ends as your data grows and improves the more you use it as your foundation for contacting customers. This was shown through the description of the development of a databased direct marketing campaign.

Having covered all the infrastructural issues involved in setting yourself up for direct and interactive marketing, we now move to the point at which you can start your data collection and analysis – through market research and segmentation.

10
market segmentation and research

Introduction

What is segmentation?

Standard classification methods

Geo-demographic segmentation

Psychographic analysis

Lifestyle questionnaires

Combining sources

Response-based segmentation

How to define segments

Purchasing variables

Modelling

Statistical methods for finding segments

Using market research in direct marketing

Main research techniques direct marketers use

Summary

Introduction

In most markets for consumer goods and services, customers are too numerous to research or understand as individuals. They tend to be researched on a sample basis, to identify what types of consumer exist and what the behaviour of different groups is. We then aggregate this information to make sense of the market.

> Customer research includes:
>
> - **buying behaviour or audit** research – investigating what customers buy, when and how. This is often provided by a few large companies which pay retailers for their data from their tills, repackage it and sell it to the manufacturers. These services are called retail audit;
> - **user and attitude** surveys (U&A) – investigating customers' and prospects' perceptions and attitudes and relating them to their buying decisions. Increasingly U&A is giving way to customer satisfaction surveys that measure levels of satisfaction;
> - **tracking studies** – studying trends in either of the above over time.

This research-based approach to understanding customers is disappearing among intense users of direct marketing because of the amount of response and sales data that they collect about individual customers. However, this can lead to a failure to understand customers' attitudes and perceptions. Eventually their marketing can get out of touch with customers. So wise users of direct marketing continue to research their customers about things that are not revealed by patterns of response and purchase.

What is segmentation?

> **Segmentation** is just a technical term for classifying consumers. To segment customers is merely to group them by shared characteristics. Your aim is to find segments whose members are as similar as possible to each other in some respect (e.g. attitudes, perceptions, buying behaviour, location, responsibility) and as different as possible from members of other segments. You do this because if you find such segments, you can predict their behaviour more accurately, design offers for them more easily and target them more precisely. Getting segmentation right often requires significant research and testing. Some segments will change over time and customers will move between segments.

> **Checklist: consumer market segmentation approaches**
>
> Demographic – age, social class, marital status, number of children.
>
> Socio-economic – occupation, income, assets (e.g. house).
>
> Geographical – location (physical and relative to people with specific socio-economic-demographic characteristics).
>
> General behavioural (shopping, leisure, etc.) – a special case of which is behaviour in relation to product/category (whether or not user, frequency of use, loyalty, etc.).
>
> Psychographic, e.g. extrovert-introvert, optimist-pessimist, planner-improviser, consumer-saver.

Standard classification methods

The most widely used and simple classification is that produced by JICNARS, the Joint Industry Committee for National Readership Surveys. They are called 'social grade definitions' and are as follows:

Grade – status	Typical occupations
A – upper middle	Higher managerial, administrative and professional (e.g. judges, board directors of large companies, very senior civil service administrators)
B – middle	Intermediate managerial, administrative (e.g. lawyers, doctors, lecturers, middle managers, owners of small and medium-sized businesses)
C1 – lower middle	Supervisory, clerical, junior management/administration, etc.
C2 – skilled worker	Skilled manual
D – working	Semi and unskilled workers
E – near subsistence	Pensioners, widows, casual and lowest grade workers, and those at the lowest level of subsistence

The classification gives a rough indication of purchasing power plus behaviour patterns in relation to media. The shortcomings of this simple system are obvious.

> **eg** The media behaviour of students is close to that of group B, while many self-employed businessmen in group B identify themselves quite closely with C2 and have the same media behaviour (*Sun* readers?). However, the system gives you a useful initial classification.

There are moves to update this simple classification to a numerical classification, although the ABC classification is still entrenched and the new classifications have yet to be widely used. The new system is aimed at moving away from the British class system of upper, middle and working class.

Geo-demographic segmentation

Many more sophisticated approaches to segmentation are now used. Several specialist data suppliers have produced advanced socio-demographic classifications, based on a mixture of census, electoral roll, credit and other data. The classifications give up to 50 or more types and data is available down to the lowest postcode level (group of houses – the average number is 15 per postcode).

> **In the real world**
> The main segmentation products are classifications of neighbourhoods rather than individuals. This is because the original source of the data is by area, not individuals, i.e. census enumeration districts. However, companies are increasingly able to supply data on individuals, provided that the data has been gathered according to the terms of the Data Protection Act. So before investing in acquiring this data, always test its usefulness for you. For example, does it improve your response rates?

Neighbourhood classification data falls into three categories:

1 **demographic** – how many people live in a household, their ages, and family structure;
2 **socio-economic** – value of house, income of household, occupations of household members;
3 **physical** – type of dwelling (house or flat), size (e.g. number of rooms).

This has proved particularly useful for direct marketing companies. It allows them to enhance their customer files (which usually cover names, addresses, telephone numbers, response to promotions, and purchases) with other data relatively cheaply and quickly.

> **In the real world**
> Segmentation based on neighbourhood classification systems works on mass-market products, but using it on niche products and services can be misleading and wasteful.

Psychographic analysis

Another development has been that of advanced psychographic analysis, using data on customers' attitudes, interests and opinions. This started with basic psychological categories, but has developed much further. It provides useful categories to use when analysing purchasing behaviour in relation to new products or new channels of distribution. You can also develop categories that are specific to your products and services.

> **In the real world**
> Use this data with care and in conjunction with any other available data such as your own market research and response and sales data. If you can't identify beforehand customers who belong to segments defined using this data, you won't be able to use it for direct marketing targeting.

Lifestyle questionnaires

'Lifestyle' questionnaires are sent out to millions of consumers to gather data on media and buying habits. In exchange for this data, consumers are sometimes sent coupons giving reductions on the kind of products they say they like, or are given the chance to take part in a prize draw. The data is then sold to direct marketing companies, which use it as a promotional list or to enhance their files. The sheer volume and depth of data produced in this way can make it excellent source material for segmentation. It also makes it easier for companies getting started in consumer direct marketing to obtain data on their target markets.

> **In the real world**
>
> Many consumers are becoming wise to these questionnaires and answer them so as to obtain coupons or enter the prize draw, so the information contained in them can be unreliable. Use this kind of data with great care and test the value of the information by running campaigns using this information alongside campaigns using data from other sources.

▶ Combining sources

Many data agencies supply combinations of the main marketing data sets. They started by combining census, postcode and credit data. Now they combine their original data with lifestyle surveys, media surveys (e.g. readership surveys) and shopping data from retail audits to give much greater depth of information on customers of particular types. This combined data also shows companies how to reach customers of particular kinds through published and broadcast media (e.g. for 'hand-raising campaigns' to get prospects to identify themselves, or for branding campaigns to provide a positive context for direct marketing campaigns) and what coupons to distribute in which areas to encourage the purchase of their products through retailers.

▶ Other sources of segmentation data

Some agencies that provide data and analysis also provide forecasts of social, economic and market change. Consumer goods and services companies use forecasts of the impact of changing demographic and social patterns as input for their strategic plans. The factors highlighted include ageing, home-centredness, changing shopping habits, and the growing computer and mobile telecommunications culture. This kind of data is most likely to be useful if you want to look beyond the horizon that current buying data imposes, to what the state of your customers and database will be in a few years.

▶ Response-based segmentation

Direct marketing routinely generates the data needed for market segmentation. Response data includes:

Response-based segmentation

- information your customers give during their response, e.g. questionnaire answers. This includes simple facts about who they are and (if their address was not known beforehand) where they live;
- the fact that they have responded to a particular approach;
- where appropriate, the fact that they have bought and, if you have asked, whether they are satisfied with your company's service or offering.

This data can tell you:

- what products and services your customers have bought and when – and what they have not bought, so by implication what they are most likely to buy in the future, and when they are likely to buy it;
- what kinds of promotion they have responded to, and by implication are likely to respond to in future;
- how they paid (or not) – type and timing, and by implication whether a customer constitutes a credit risk.

Although you might like to customize your entire communication to individual customers – the market segment of one – in practice this is rarely possible (except for **personalization** – addressing the customer by name). Products and offers must normally be designed to meet the needs of groups of customers. You will find it expensive to customize both your communications and your products and services to individuals. Letters must be mailed and advertisements shown such that they reach cost effectively the groups of customers most likely to respond and/or buy. So your aim is to find the best groups – the ones most likely to respond, buy and pay. Years of direct marketing experience have shown that customers' needs are not that varied, so we can confidently expect to be able to group our customers according to their needs.

In some cases, however, the data source used to segment customers is very rich and this enables the owners of this data to offer some tailored offers. This particularly applies to retailers with loyalty cards. The best users of this data have tracked customers' purchasing behaviour and made offers based on this historical data. They also use this understanding when consumers shop online. When they log on for the first time to use the home delivery service, they are asked for demographic data. This is used to bring up a likely list for the shopper to choose from, cutting the time the shopper has to stay online selecting items.

> For a number of years Tesco's loyalty card, the Clubcard, has been collecting information on how the supermarket's customers purchase. This has enabled Tesco to tailor offers to individuals. Using sophisticated systems it sends out voucher and offer packs customized to the shopper's known purchasing habits, including several thousand different combinations of offers each time it mails.

How to define segments

Much segmentation aims at finding variables whose values are associated with each other in different groups of customers, for example:

- finding that people who live in one area have a greater chance of liking a particular product than people who live in another area;
- finding that people who buy product X are more likely to respond to a mailing on product Y than people who buy product Z.

To target as precisely as possible, you may want to find associations between several variables.

Purchasing variables

In direct marketing, the main segmentation variables are purchasing variables. We have already introduced the FRAC variables. Now let's look at them in more detail, along with a few other variables that it is absolutely essential that you track.

Frequency

> **Frequency** is defined as how often the customer buys, typically the figure over the last period, e.g. month or year. Just as important is the **trend** in frequency, i.e. is it rising or falling? Suppose that you have two customers with the same very recent purchasing behaviour, but one's purchasing frequency is rising and the other's is falling. The former is likely to be of more interest to you than the latter, other things being equal.

In the real world

Frequency depends upon how often you promote to a customer. So any analysis of frequency must take into account promotions history. Where customers receive varying numbers of promotions, a better statistic to use might be average frequency of response per promotion, measured for each time period, e.g. last half year, half year before that.

Boden is an upmarket mail-order clothing catalogue which has experienced huge growth over the past ten years. One of key drivers for this growth is that the company mails its catalogue frequently to customers. The catalogue is small and laid out in an easy-to-use style. It is aimed at the ABC1 family market, with ranges for men, women and children. Boden doesn't rely on customers keeping the catalogue, instead it sends it out regularly with different offers. Almost as soon as one offer has run out a new catalogue will be sent with a new offer. If a customer calls in once an offer has run out, the call centre will offer the new offer instead. This has helped the company to build a loyal and responsive customer base.

Purchasing variables

▶ **Recency**

> This measures **when the customer last bought**. Again this depends on promotional factors, i.e. when the last few promotions took place. Other things being equal, more recent purchasers have greater value.

Small changes in recency may be a harbinger of doom – or great success. If you find recency increasing, i.e. your customers are on average waiting longer before rebuying, you must quickly find out which customers this is affecting and why. Are your promotions failing in their objective because of problems with the offer, or have you got a problem with your product or service?

▶ **Amount**

> This measures **how much** the customer bought, usually in value terms. It may be defined for individual products or for your whole product range. This latter definition usually makes sense only if the customer knows that the products come from the same supplier.

The points made about frequency also apply here. For example, a customer could be buying with the same frequency but the average value of purchase might be falling. You need to find out whether this is due to factors you can't control, e.g. the customer's income is falling, or whether it's due to your marketing or product failures.

▶ **Category**

> Category defines the **type of product** bought. The point made above about amount bought per customer applies here. Cross-selling as a concept makes sense – from a measurement point of view – only if the customer knows that the product is coming from the same source, unless you are just using it as a measure of your success in using targeting data.

> In financial services, as companies from different sectors move into each other's territory and the market becomes more competitive, the cost of acquiring new customers is rising. So the key to success is the number of different product relationships maintained, i.e. how many categories the customer is buying. Some companies have successfully launched secondary brands to appeal to different customers and are then able to cross-sell to a wider, new audience.

▶ **Speed of order following promotion**

This can be an important variable.

> **In the real world**
>
> Fast orderers may be very interested in new offers and keen to try them. So it pays to find out the characteristics of fast orderers, profile them using whatever data you have about them, and apply this profile to other data sets to try to find more fast orderers. If fast orderers can be identified only through psychological variables, you may need to use lifestyle questionnaires to identify them.

▶ Mode of payment

Unless all payment is by the same method, the mode of payment can be an important discriminator. Credit card payers may be regarded as safer because there is no risk of default.

▶ Modelling

> Typically, **a model** will cover:
> ◆ which variables are involved, distinguishing between variables that are dependent, i.e. their values are determined within the modelled situation, and those that are independent, i.e. their values are determined outside the modelled situation;
> ◆ how they relate to each other (which ones affect each other, the direction and timing of the relationship).

Modelling involves specifying assumptions about the relationships between the different factors at work in a situation. These include internal factors as well as market factors. For example, you may need to model the relationship between purchasing frequency, income, type of housing, frequency of response to past promotions, and so on.

Often, different models of a situation must be tested. Statistical analysis is used to find out more about how the variables interrelate and which model best explains the behaviour of customers. The model is then used to predict future behaviour, provided that any independent variables can be forecast. In direct marketing, these independent variables may be the ones you control, e.g. price, timing of mailing.

> **In the real world**
>
> We have already encountered one of the best known modelling processes used in direct marketing: 'scoring'. Initially derived from credit markets, the aim was to give customers a score according to their likelihood of default (e.g. on credit card payments). A number of variables are normally analyzed, such as past credit record (in particular whether any previous defaulting took place), court judgements against customers (if any), type of housing, mode of house possession (rent, mortgage, etc.), possession of a bank account, and so on. A customer is allocated a better score the better the values of the individual variables. This scoring approach is the foundation for much direct marketing modelling. In some sectors, such as direct insurance, a company's scoring module is considered the source of competitive advantage. Get customer scoring right and you'll lose less money through bad debt.

Statistical methods for finding segments

Once, market segmentation was a matter of creative guesswork, based on deep experience of the market. Tables of data would be examined in detail to find links in behaviour. Today, statistical methodologies can do most segmentation work automatically. Some methods produce transparent results, meaning that you can see why the segment behaves as it does, but others are less transparent (so-called 'black-box', for obvious reasons). The details of these techniques would take a whole textbook to explain.

> **In the real world**
> Here we content ourselves with one simple rule: if a technique helps you identify that a particular group of consumers is good, e.g. has a high response rate, buys a lot, but you cannot in practice select that group as a target (e.g. because you can't predict who will be members of that group or find a group that is quite similar to the group you've identified), then the result is not very useful for direct marketing purposes. But if you can target the group in practice, then target it again and again, because the more you concentrate your efforts on that segment, the stronger your presence will become, and although you may find yourself subject to the law of diminishing returns, you'll be putting up a barrier to entry which your competitors will find tough to overcome.

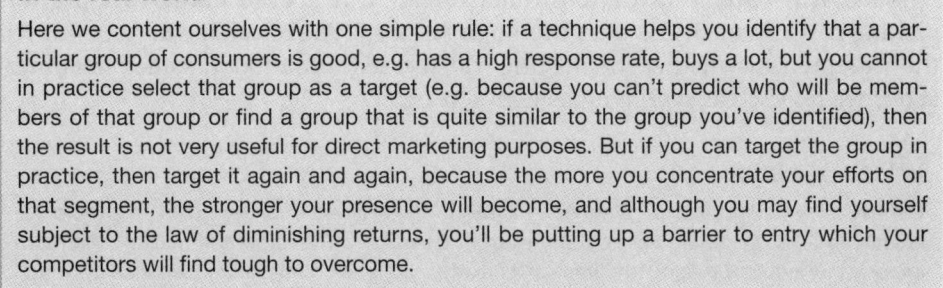

Using market research in direct marketing

Compared with traditional methods of marketing consumer goods and services, direct marketing has not used marketing research enough. The question for direct marketers is whether market research can add to their understanding of customers, given the rich data provided by their customer databases. Research should be used to find the link between information on your database and the emotions behind customer behaviour. Qualitative groups, possibly using a viewing facility so all personnel using the database can attend, will bring to life the reports and statistics produced by the database. They may also produce ideas about campaign design – who to target, with which products and service, and with what offer and creative.

Groups are also an excellent vehicle if your campaigns start to become less successful. They will tell you why. Look for a researcher who is experienced in the use and techniques of direct marketing and they will be able to help use the findings constructively around the business.

Why some direct marketers do not use market research

There are several reasons why some direct marketers have been slow to use market research. The direct marketing industry used to be dominated by many small entrepreneurs who knew how to make quick money out of a mailing. They had lots of good product ideas. They did not really care why a product sold or what customer needs they satisfied. All they wanted to know was whether the product sold. If it sold, they went on selling it. If it did not sell, they tried another. Direct mail entrepreneurs succeeded because of their ability to act quickly, based on their judgement of a product's saleability. They moved from one product to another at great speed. Long-term planning and the idea of customer acquisition were largely foreign to them.

With such a mentality dominating, research is seen as a cost rather than as an investment which can lead to higher response rates, fewer test failures and less waste of resources. Given the low costs of setting up a simple direct mailing operation, the costs of research looked high compared with the profit to be obtained on a single mailing. Without the perspective of customer acquisition and development, it is hard to justify customer research. It is even harder when a test mailing costs so much less than thorough research. The research will not even tell the entrepreneur whether the mailing will succeed. Even today, some direct marketers see research as synonymous with testing.

> **In the real world**
>
> Usually only longer range planners research their direct marketing as it should be researched and these are very often the larger operators. The larger the mailing, the more important it is to get it right first time, particularly if there is no relevant experience on which to base the test concepts. If the test is the wrong test, you may be sacrificing large potential profits if you do not research the test concepts properly. So, for your largest campaigns, don't go ahead without at least a few focus groups.

▶ Why direct marketers are starting to use research

The new wave of direct marketers is composed partly of companies that formerly marketed entirely by brand marketing techniques, which are very research-intensive. They have always wanted to know not just **whether** a concept worked but **why** it worked. The largest of these companies are also concerned about their public image and the standards of customer care that they achieve. Their degree of success in these areas is normally measured using market research techniques. So they would no more launch a major direct marketing campaign without researching the concept than they would launch an advertising campaign or a new product without research.

▶ Where research can be used

There are a number of areas where you can use research, as follows:

◆ **Product/concept testing** – to get an idea of the viability and acceptability of a new product or concept before investing money in producing it and test marketing it.

◆ **Product features** – to find out which product features are important to customers and what advantages and benefits they provide.

- **Creative guidance** – to direct the creative effort by obtaining a current reading on the market. This enables you to understand whether its message is being understood, whether it is using the correct wording, whether consumers have hidden objections or whether opportunities are being missed.
- **Missing features** – to uncover hidden emotions and feelings behind customer response.
- **Purchasing channel** – to understand which channel consumers would rather use to buy goods. This could be via the telephone, the web or face to face. This will also look at the level of service the customer will expect when purchasing from you, for example will they tolerate a voice-activated system if using the phone, are they prepared to go so far with an online purchase then expect human contact?

So research, by creating a true understanding of the awareness, attitude and interests of customers, can help to focus testing programmes and avoid some test failures.

Some questions to ask yourself when deciding how to use research in direct marketing are:

- Are you launching a totally new product or service? If so, do you understand **why** customers might buy it?
- Is your modelling data available, provable and reliable?
- Do you understand the reasons for the response rates you are getting to your campaigns?
- Will it help you and your colleagues to get closer to your customers and understand what motivates them?
- Have you ensured your customer service is right for the offer and your customers?
- Are you convinced that your creative execution will motivate your customers?

▶ Understanding customers

The results of your tests and full campaigns will give you a lot of information about who responds and to what degree they respond. However, **why** customers respond in a certain way can only be inferred. Why customers do **not** respond is hard to infer as they have given no additional data except the fact that they did not respond.

Lack of response may be due to:

- poor product;
- poor offer design – customers may have wanted the general concept but not the way it was embodied in the offer;
- poor targeting;
- competitors providing better offers;
- poor company image – consumers liked the offer but didn't trust you as a supplier because your image was poor or non-existent.

A research programme can uncover these reasons.

Main research techniques direct marketers use

> **Group discussions** are commonly used as a pre-testing technique. They are usually externally moderated by a research professional and cover a range of pre-decided topics. The results of this research are presented and then usually argued over in order to establish what are the implications for campaign design and relationship management.

Group discussions are used for many more purposes, including:

- basic need studies for new product idea generation;
- new product idea or concept exploration;
- product positioning studies;
- advertising and communication studies;
- background studies on consumers' frames of reference;
- establishing the vocabulary consumers use, as a preliminary stage in questionnaire development;
- determination of attitudes and behaviour.

> **Depth interviews** are usually used to find out why individuals buy various products and what buying, owning and using means to them. The interview can last anything from a few minutes to two hours or more. This method can uncover basic pre-dispositions, e.g. why a consumer does not order through the post. People's attitudes can be explored and their cause, intensity and implications can be uncovered.

If the subject is sensitive, personal or complex, depth interviews can be better than group discussions. This applies particularly in business marketing, where topics being researched may include complex buying procedures. The other reason it works better than groups is that recruiting specific individuals for groups can be difficult and an in-depth interview at their offices is generally far easier to organize.

> **Mail questionnaires** are just that – questionnaires that are mailed to customers for them to complete by themselves. It is wise to include a stamped addressed envelope. An incentive such as a free draw will often help response rates but may slightly bias the results.

Mail questionnaires are used widely in direct marketing, usually when you want a large enough sample to derive a statistically valid result. They are also used to gain additional information about customers already on a database. If qualitative information is required, this can be elicited through more detailed questions about why they respond in particular ways to particular questions. Some responses may be triggers for action for you, e.g. when a customer indicates an immediate need or raises a customer service problem.

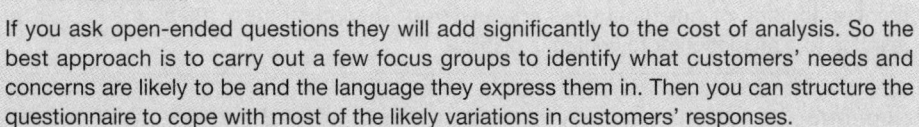

Main research techniques direct marketers use

> **In the real world**
>
> If you ask open-ended questions they will add significantly to the cost of analysis. So the best approach is to carry out a few focus groups to identify what customers' needs and concerns are likely to be and the language they express them in. Then you can structure the questionnaire to cope with most of the likely variations in customers' responses.

Mail questionnaires have these advantages:

- They are more economical and convenient than personal interviews.
- They avoid interviewer bias.
- They give people time to consider their answers.
- They can be anonymous.

They have these disadvantages:

- The questions need to be very straightforward if the response is to be valid.
- Answers must be taken as final.
- Respondents see the whole questionnaire before answering it.
- It is impossible to be sure that the right person answers it.
- They sometimes throw up more questions than you started with as you analyze the data. If this is the case consider holding some focus groups to ensure you fully understand the results.

The main problem with mail questionnaires is non-response and the consequent likelihood that non-responders will be different from responders. The higher the response rate, the more valid the result. But the only way to check this is by chasing up a sample of responders.

> **Checklist: how to encourage response**
>
> Using a covering letter explaining what the survey is doing, how the respondent's name was selected, and why he or she should reply.
>
> Telling the respondent the benefits of replying.
>
> Explaining why the survey is important.
>
> Enclosing a stamped addressed or business reply envelope.
>
> Giving a premium for responding, such as a free prize draw.
>
> Following up on any issues raised by respondents.

> **In the real world**
>
> When you get your research results, a great way to have them analyzed is by using a specialist market research data processing agency. Ideally, you should consult them before you design your research strategy. They can advise you on questionnaire design, sampling and how best to analyze and use the results. Off-the-shelf analysis packages cannot offer the depth of knowledge of a reputable research data processing agency and can take a very long time to use, as you have to input the data then use the analysis tools.

> **Telephone questionnaires** are used in similar contexts to mail questionnaires, with the notable addition of questionnaires administered when customers telephone in, e.g. to respond to a promotion or to contact a helpline.

Telephone surveys are normally more accurate than mail surveys. They combine many of the advantages of mail questionnaires and in-depth interviews. Their strengths are:

- they are one to one;
- the consumer cannot see the whole questionnaire;
- any problems of understanding can be dealt with;
- careful scripting helps avoid interview bias;
- computerized routing of questionnaires allows for complex patterns of behaviour to be captured;
- response rates are higher – customers can be called until they reply;
- costs are lower than personal interviews;
- the telephone is a way of life to business;
- speed – telephones get higher priority than post and the results are available immediately.

Their disadvantages are that:

- some consumers object to the approach;
- the call is at your convenience and not the customer's. This can produce a negative response from the customer. For this reason telephone is often not the best medium for customer satisfaction work. However, if you have a long questionnaire to administer, you can overcome this problem by scheduling the call at a time agreed with the respondent;
- the costs of setting up a telephone questionnaire can be high;
- calling costs are higher than postal costs;
- it is a voice medium only, so customers' reactions cannot be seen.

▶ Using market research in post-testing

Post-testing, which uses the same techniques as pre-testing, is used to find out why things went as they did. Typical questions include:

- Why do particular kinds of consumers order or not order a catalogue or a product?
- Why are members cancelling?
- Why is the conversion rate low or high?

Summary

Market segmentation is the essence of direct marketing. But not all the data used in direct marketing arises from campaigns. Market research has got a particularly valuable role to play in backing up the customer data and in exploring areas that cannot be covered by customer data. It is also vital if you are to use direct marketing to position your products or services – the subject of our next chapter.

11 making the right offer

The definition of an offer

Components of the offer

Are new products required?

Pricing the direct marketing offer

Promotional offers

Distributional channels in direct marketing

Summary

In direct marketing, the product or service is promoted through an offer. Knowing **which** offer is the most effective is what direct marketers strive for.

The definition of an offer

An offer is defined as 'the total proposition made to the customer'. This means the physical product you are selling, the positioning, format and of course pricing. The most effective proposition is personal and relevant. It encourages the customer to respond, often by a certain date – ideally as soon as possible. The direct marketing contact is usually short – the telephone call is received, the letter read, the advertisement seen, for anything from a few seconds to a few minutes. So a call to action must be clear and stand out.

The offer is usually used to close a sale once awareness has been created or increased by other means, e.g. advertising. Think of brand advertising as getting the ball and players on the pitch and direct marketing as using the offer to strike the ball into the back of the net.

To keep customers interested in your product, you should rotate your offers regularly to avoid the 'wallpaper effect'. For example, if a furniture store is always offering interest-free credit and half-price furniture, after some time no one notices it. To avoid this effect you must keep the message and offer fresh. You can do this by giving different, maybe seasonal reasons to buy, by using a range of different limited offers or by refreshing the advertising.

In each offer you need to satisfy needs and add extra value to be effective.

In the real world

In banking, marketing is mostly via various customer communications – booklets, posters, the bank staff, the chequebook, welcome letters and statements. The offer provides information and uses additional products and services (surround benefits) and USPs to reinforce purchase decisions and add value.

In acquisition, retailers use offers which combine rational and emotional reasons to visit them (low prices, biggest range in the UK, late-night opening hours, voted Britain's best loved electrical retailer) with booster offers as a call to action (offer must end Sunday, 50% off everything this Thursday only, etc.).

In the car market the physical product – e.g. an estate car – or in banking a service definition – e.g. money transmission service – is not enough to make a person choose your product. It must compete with somebody else's products and their offers. So you must differentiate your offer from the competition. This is where the brand comes in.

The symbolic association that is formed between your company and product in the customer's mind is very powerful – a symbol or trademark can give your product additional status. It may be a logo, such as the prancing horse of Ferrari or the black horse of Lloyds Bank, or sometimes it is a strap-line and a logo combined: 'BMW – the ultimate driving machine' or 'Abbey National – because

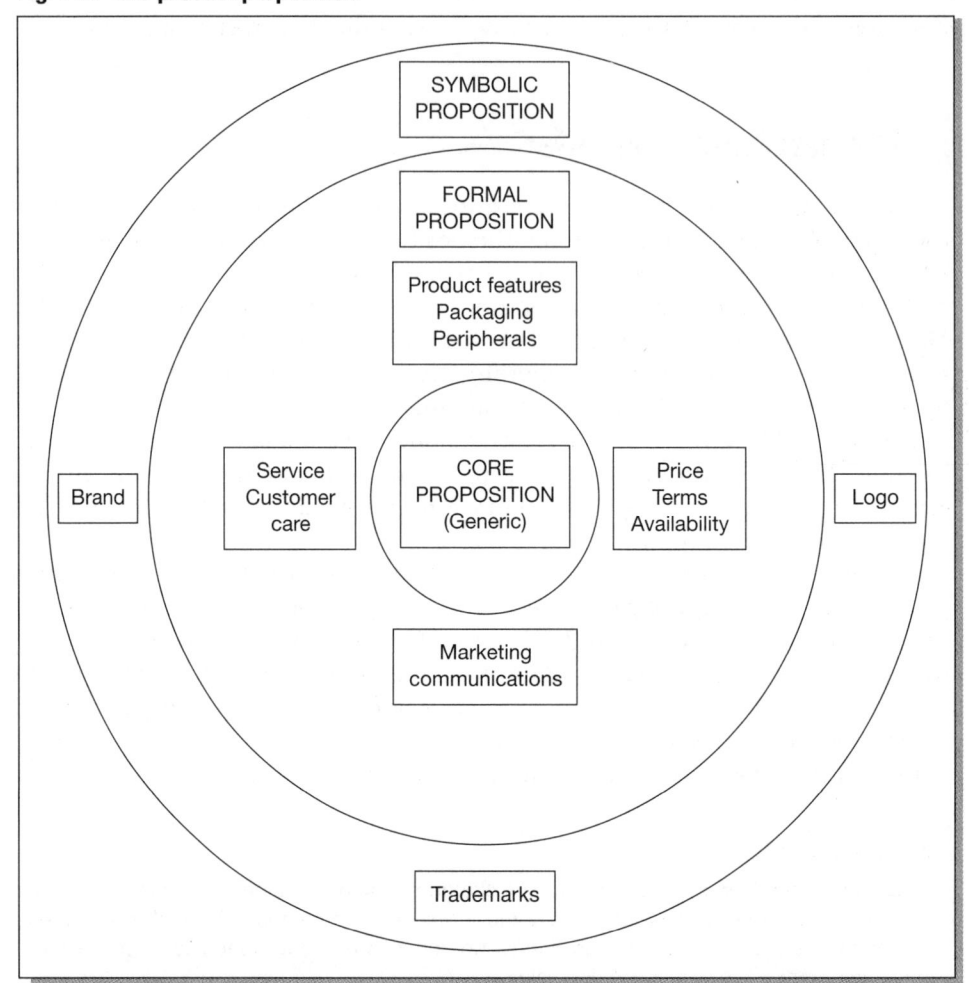

Fig. 11.1 The product proposition

```
                    SYMBOLIC
                   PROPOSITION

                    FORMAL
                  PROPOSITION

              Product features
                 Packaging
                 Peripherals

         Service          CORE            Price
 Brand   Customer     PROPOSITION         Terms          Logo
          care          (Generic)      Availability

                    Marketing
                  communications

                    Trademarks
```

life is complicated enough'. Ultimately it is, or should be, a fully integrated set of ideas about a company and its products summarized in a memorable proposition. Mention Virgin, BMW, Sky digital and people will say 'leading brand', 'leading car manufacturer', 'leading digital TV provider'.

The different levels of the offer are summarized in Fig. 11.1.

▶ Components of the offer

▶ Core proposition

This is an abstract benefit, e.g. peace of mind, fear reduction, status. It is your key business or product and key message. For example, Sky digital, UK's favourite digital TV provider, British Airways, the world's favourite airline.

▶ Formal proposition

This turns the core proposition into functional benefits, e.g. lower price, stronger packaging, better credit terms. These are the nuts and bolts that support the core proposition and which differentiate your product from the others. They include:

Product features	Number of channels, breadth of programming, flights per day, worldwide destinations for example
Packaging	Visual – corporate identity
	Content – packaging of offering: value pack, premium movie or sports packs, economy or premium tickets, discounts, last-minute deals
Peripherals	Interactive content, menus on board, lounge access, facilities for business travellers
Service	Online flight information, one-stop booking line
Customer care	24-hour customer care, freephone calls, technical help desk
Price	Lowest price, entry-level packages
Terms	Terms of the offer, eligibility, close date, restrictions, conditions
Availability	As part of offer, 'while stocks last', offer period, and so on
Marketing communications	Look and feel, tone of voice, paper stock, font, etc. all contribute to the overall positioning of the offer

▶ Symbolic proposition

The brand values convert the generic benefit and the functional attributes of the product into a specific and hopefully unique set of brand benefits, which might be considered into a logo, strap-line and/or trademark.

Brand	This will shape the appearance and tone of voice of your communications for integration and consistency
Trademark	This can be used to add further confidence and status to the company brand
Logo	This helps punctuate and support the offer. It adds instant recognition and promotes confidence in the communication and offer

In the real world

There is one final element – **customer service**. Whether you are supplying a product or a service, you must provide customer service. If your brand promises much but your service delivery fails, your brand itself will be questioned by your customers.

▶ Is the product right for the offer?

You must choose the right product and the right offer. To help you do this, ask yourself the following questions:

- Which marketing channels are best to communicate the offer?
- Is any product modification required?
- Do you need new products?
- How should you develop them?
- Which marketing channels are best to communicate the offer?

Some products are suited to some forms of direct marketing and not to others. For instance, packaged consumer goods (e.g. grocery foods) use door-drop sampling to good effect, to encourage trial of their goods at home and repeat purchase. But direct mailing is also used to distribute coupons, customer recruitment questionnaires and information packs to prospects. Heinz, Unilever and Procter & Gamble are the leading exponents of this kind of direct marketing. Airlines now use e-marketing campaigns rather than direct mail to communicate last-minute flight offers, to prompt rapid and often spontaneous purchase.

> **In the real world**
>
> Almost all financial service providers make intense use of broad-brush direct marketing to reach large numbers of customers at low cost. For some, it is their main marketing channel (e.g. direct motor insurers). Financial services are intangible and less frequently purchased (annually at most and for some products only once or twice in a lifetime), so mass marketing is a low-cost way to reach a large audience many times. This ensures that when the customer does buy, the company is on the customer's list. The company needs to be in the right place at the right time. Airline flights have rapidly changing availability and the market is highly competitive and quickly affected by climatic, political and international factors. So they are best marketed through a rapidly updated direct marketing channel such as e-mail marketing.

You also need to consider whether and how customers are prepared to receive messages from you, communicate with you and buy from you.

▶ Is any product modification required?

Often, **some** product modification is required. Thus, if mail is used to distribute the product, the product must conform to postal regulations and may need to fit weight/price bands. Changes may need to be made to other mix elements. Price, for instance, may need to be reduced to make the offer more attractive. Promotional offers can be added. Service may need to be improved, e.g. faster delivery.

Quality improvements aimed at increasing, say, a product's functional performance allow you to use response-lifting words such as 'new', 'improved', 'better', etc. This is frequently the main message used by washing powder companies and toiletry manufacturers.

Feature improvements or additions may increase your product's versatility, safety or convenience. Again these changes give copywriters the chance to lift response and possibly create a USP.

Style improvements to enhance the aesthetic appeal of the product can create product uniqueness and allow fresh visual treatment in promotional material.

Are new products required?

All marketers need 'new' products, if only because old products eventually die a natural death. New products are always needed. The key issues facing the direct marketer are:

- When will the need arise?
- What will be the source for new product ideas?
- How should their potential be evaluated?
- How should their potential be tested?
- Which test results indicate that rollout is desirable?
- What effect will new products have on existing products?

Pricing the direct marketing offer

You have more scope to be creative with pricing tests using direct marketing than with advertising media where you have to advertise a national price. This is because you can target pre-defined and similar sets of people with different offers covertly and compare the effects. However, you must ensure that you have set up measurement processes to enable you to do this, e.g. different telephone numbers for respondents or different codes for the customer to quote.

In the real world

In a pricing test, you must keep other things equal. So the target audience should be from the same data sources and the communication, call to action and activity timings should be identical. The difference in response and/or sales will then show the effect of the pricing. Proper planning (perhaps with some research) is needed to identify the best prices to test.

Promotional offers

By 'offer', most direct marketers mean response and purchase incentives that may be short term and are normally extrinsic to the brand – they are not a permanent feature of the brand itself. They include:

- basic offers;
- free trial;
- extra merchandise free, e.g. two for one;
- end of stock offer;
- free gift offers, including mystery gift when you order, order now, etc.;
- discount offers, including temporary ones;
- easy terms – more time to pay, low-cost credit, no or small deposit;
- sale offers;
- sample offers;
- time limit offers;
- guarantee offers, including money-back;
- build up the sale offers;
- competition offers;
- club and continuity offers.

None of these is an intrinsic element of the product. All can be made or withdrawn without affecting the basic product. They are offers which give additional incentives to buy the basic product. They are loosely referred to as offers, but it makes more sense to think of them as boosters or motivators, i.e. additional incentives to buy your product or service.

eg Procter & Gamble, which owns the Pampers nappy brand, links its web site for parents with posted offers. After a parent provides their postal address through the web site, they receive regular money-off coupons for new products. This allows Procter & Gamble to promote new products and helps build loyalty in a competitive market.

Consider how and why such techniques work. This requires a different classification of offers:

- product;
- money;
- service;
- time.

This classification suggests that prospects can be motivated by, for example:

- the basic product;
- more of the basic product;
- money now;
- money at a future date;
- product-related service;
- service now;

- time saving;
- time in the future.

It is important to understand which customers will be motivated in these different ways and why. Consider prize draw offers. These usually offer very large cash prizes to very few 'lucky winners' (and smaller value merchandise prizes to a larger number of less lucky winners). Who will be attracted by such an incentive? It is reasonable to assume that these schemes will attract those who covet the big prize and believe that they have a reasonable chance of winning it. However, by spreading the cash value of, say, £100 000 among 100 000 customers by giving them £1 off their purchase, you can attract a very different prospect, already interested in the product but needing a small incentive to switch brands.

A discount off the retail price (say half price) can increase response to an offer by as much as 100%. This may be worthwhile if your gross margins are high enough and if you don't thereby attract customers who leave you as soon as the offer disappears.

In the real world

To analyze the success of promotional offers, you need to check the subsequent customer life cycle, not just the initial response. You can do this by taking a sample of respondents from each offer and measuring their response rate, conversion to a sale or booking, customer behaviour (other products or services purchased, spending patterns) and attrition (when they close their account or switch brands). For the health of your business, it's important to measure the whole effect to avoid a strong initial campaign response followed by low long-term sales and a declining customer base.

Distribution channels in direct marketing

Direct marketing is not just direct distribution, although many products that are marketed directly are also distributed directly. You can contact the customer in one way and get the product or service to them in another. For example, you can mail them with an offer, which they can collect in a retail store or which they can call to respond to. Direct marketing focuses on building relationships at any location. These relationships can be forged and developed in the home and via direct response media, but direct communication can also be used to encourage retail traffic and purchasing.

Marks and Spencer and Selfridges invite their regular (e.g. account or card) customers to special shopping evenings where customers can shop and at the same time enjoy a glass of wine, some snacks and even live music. Such events add value for their customers and of course build relationships while prompting additional sales and word-of-mouth advertising. These events constitute an integral part of the total proposition, i.e. the offer (e.g. to take out a store card). Special sales preview days and discounts for 'privileged' customers are another example.

11 / Making the right offer

So, you should consider distribution channels, particularly retail channels, as part of the offer strategy. You add value by making products available when and where customers want them. The above incentives may be more effective than lower prices, easier payment terms or product offers such as 20% more for the same price, as they make the customer feel special. You are giving something back, but it is probably much less costly for the business and more personal than a 'money off' deal.

In the real world

In recent years we have become aware of the dangers of short-term promotions. They can erode brand loyalty through damage to brand values and may only bring forward tomorrow's sale to today, with no overall increase in sales. Since everyone is using similar techniques, short-term promotions have no long-term effect on brand share. They are viewed instead as the price to be paid to stay in the market – a defensive rather than an offensive tool. It is far better to combine branding to grow market share and brand loyalty with tactical offers to encourage repeat purchases. This combination is powerful.

Action

You should integrate incentives early on in planning and view them as brand-enhancing rather than brand-eroding incentives for your customers to purchase and keep purchasing your brand. You should see the offer as the **total proposition** rather than as an individual element, and seek ways of developing integrated offer strategies. Do it at the creative stage in developing your campaigns. The ideas offered in this chapter provide the framework for such an approach.

Warning: an offer won't work unless you've sorted out your strategy!

Make sure you have answered these questions:

- Is your product right for the market you have in mind?
- Will direct marketing work within your marketing strategy?
- What modification or changes need to be made to your strategy if direct marketing is to work?
- Are your customer care policies strong enough to support a direct marketing campaign?
- What effect will using direct marketing have on your existing channels of distribution?

Suppose that a company markets high-quality porcelain china collectables, mainly figurines. Its market is BC women aged 30–55. Media to be used are middle-market press and direct mail. Response is one-stage coupon/telephone response with flexible payment methods. Fulfilment is direct by post within 28 days of receipt of the order. Previously, response had been achieved with a premium offer of a pocket history of the great porcelain manufacturers. A new approach is sought. Consider these questions:

1. **What/where is the generic offer, i.e. the core benefit or service?**

    To answer this, some research is needed. Suppose that research indicates three basic motives for purchase of china collectables: aesthetic value, investment value and status value. Suppose, too, that the figurines are purchased for aesthetic reasons. They beautify the home and are a pleasure to look at. They are not bought for investment reasons and customers do not regard them as showing indications of social status. So the generic offer is the **aesthetic value** of the physical product. Incentives to respond are best related to this primary purchase motivation. **Price** is likely to be less important than a promotional incentive, which adds aesthetic value to the offer. Place incentives can be viewed in terms of media, i.e. where the **offer** is seen and in terms of channels of distribution, i.e. where and how the offer is made available – in this case in the home through postal distribution.

2. **What physical evidence does the prospect need?**

    Clearly physical evidence is crucial. The prospect must be able to see the quality and aesthetic appeal of the offer. Dimensions, proportions, design, colour, detail – all these need to be clear. Above all, the advertisements must add value to the offer, featuring the products' aesthetic characteristics. Ideally, the prospect should be able to see, handle and even keep the product before purchasing. Should the response incentive therefore be, say, 28 days' free trial or simply the name and address of the nearest retail stockist (if this applies)? What about a premium offer, say a miniature replica with each order? Or would a product-related premium work better, say a full-colour print of the figurine in equally tasteful design?

3. **How will branding affect the offer?**

    China collectables tend either to be branded with a manufacturer's name, e.g. Wedgwood, or with the marketer's brand name, e.g. Compton & Woodhouse, or both. Which should be given most prominence? Which branding device is likely to work best – name or logo? Such questions reflect creative concerns and are an important part of the offer strategy. But we also need to think about pricing considerations. If price is not an incentive, what about payment terms? If a free trial is the incentive, it will need to be supported by a 'send no money now' offer. When will the customer be invoiced – on despatch or receipt of the item? These are important considerations that are heavily influenced by branding decisions. The offer strategy must support the branding, not conflict with it.

    Place considerations centre on media. Media make the product available either to specific market segments – direct mail does this particularly well – or to broader target markets, depending on the media vehicles chosen. Will the media affect the message, particularly the brand values? How will brand values be affected?

4. **How can the service delivery system be used to add value to the offer?**

    The service delivery system starts with the message 'Have you made it easy for customers to reply?' and ends the first cycle with product fulfilment and customer care. Each point in the system is an opportunity to enhance the quality of the offer. Provision of alternative response vehicles, mail, telephone, even fax, alternative payment methods, alternative delivery points, etc. – all of these add value through the service delivery system. Opportunities to enhance the offer arise in the following areas:

    - product inspection, availability and returns;
    - payment methods, payments processing, refunds;
    - premium availability and despatch;
    - efficient media planning, retail alternatives, postal delivery;
    - faster delivery, better customer care, advice bureaux.

Summary

This chapter started by saying that the best offer you can make to your customers is **to satisfy their needs**. To do this you must base your offer strategy firmly on your product, which is at the heart of the offer, outwards towards the service delivery system. In this way, you arrive at the total proposition you wish to make. This in turn gives you the basis of your product positioning strategy.

We have shown that this offer-building process can incorporate all the marketing mix elements. Indeed, your core benefit may be in one of these mix elements, e.g. swifter delivery (consider Next Directory, for which next-day delivery is a central feature of the product offer).

We have shown that direct marketers have relied on extrinsic offers, often of a temporary nature, to bring forward the purchase decision and to strengthen their proposition over and above other choices in the market. Such offers are very similar to classic consumer goods offers, e.g. price promotions, premium incentives, competitions.

direct mail 12

Targeting

Components of a mailing

Who uses direct mail?

Quality and the law

The brief for a direct mail campaign

Formats

Making your mailing more effective

The creative

Managing a direct mail campaign

Summary

> **Direct mail** is defined as personally addressed communications sent through the postal service.

Direct mail has three main uses:

1 As a prime medium – a self-contained vehicle for selling a product or service, promoting an event, etc.
2 With other media, to support or follow up other activities.
3 As support to a channel – before the sale (e.g. to provide leads) or after the sale (e.g. to follow up a sales call).

▶ Targeting

As with all direct marketing media, targeting is critical in direct mail. In a mail campaign, unlike with telephone marketing and some other media, the response cannot be instantly adjusted at the moment of interaction with the customer. It is no use finding out after the event whether the customer is the right one and whether the form of communication is right for that customer. Though the cost of each communication seems low, the costs of a large campaign are not. Hence the importance of testing.

> **Warning!**
> Misdirected mailings waste print and postage and alienate customers. A balance must therefore be struck between the suitability of a list and the cost of editing it. This is one reason why lists based on your existing customer data are usually the best.

In a direct mail campaign, you must be very clear what action your customer is expected to take as a result of receiving the communication. **You won't be there when the letter is opened to tell them what to do!** Your customers' motivation in taking the required step must also be understood. Don't forget that for your customer, **response equals effort** – the effort of cutting out, completing and posting, or picking up the telephone and dialling, or logging onto the Internet, or visiting your branch. Your mail pack design must take these issues into account. The message and any call to action needs to be as simple and clear as possible.

> **Reminder – response equals budget too!**
> The likely response rate and the value of each response determine how much can be spent on the mail pack. The cost of handling responses must be within budget, so gather as much information on likely response and likely marketing costs before you make your final decision on volume, pack type and lead management costs.

Components of a mailing

The letter

Consider the letter as part of a sales call:

> **Checklist: making the most of your direct marketing**
>
> | | |
> |---|---|
> | The outer envelope | Knock on the door |
> | The letter | Sales pitch |
> | The brochure | Product or service demonstration |
> | Samples and testimonials | Reassurance providers |
> | Order form and reply envelope | The close |

> **Warning!**
> Just as you would not ask a salesperson just to show his product without speaking, you should rarely send a brochure without a letter. However, some very successful campaigns have been conducted without letters (or, for that matter, without brochures). There is no general rule except that what works, works, and this can be discovered only by testing.

Letters are deceptively simple. Because you write letters yourself, you might be tempted to approach direct mail letter writing casually. This can be a mistake. A letter has fewer ways of attracting and retaining your reader's attention than other media, but it has a good chance of being read. So effort invested in writing it brings rewards. All the rules for writing copy apply to letters. The key rules are as follows:

1 Promise a benefit as early as possible in the letter and then say more about it and why it's so good and special. Use your customers' language and relate it to the benefits they can expect to get from it. A bold or coloured headline can be used to increase the impact of this key benefit.

2 Tell your customers exactly what they're going to get if they take up your offer and tell them what they'll miss if they don't.

3 Back up what you say with evidence, endorsements, testimonials and rational appeals.

4 Tell, tell and tell again – introduce the benefits you're offering, describe them and summarize them at the end.

5 Get the customer to act – now. And tell them what they'll miss if they don't.

These are 'tried and tested' formulae which direct marketers have used for years. But don't confuse them with brash over-selling. The way to avoid this is found in Rule 1 – use the customers' language, not yours. Hence the importance of research and concept testing.

▶ The brochure

The brochure complements the letter. If the letter is your salesperson, the brochure is your product or service demonstration. Your brochure should demonstrate your product or service and turn the letter into pictures. If possible, your product should be shown yielding the benefits claimed for it. Support your claims by a full and logical story, guarantees and testimonials.

▶ The catalogue

The well-used catalogue indicates a solid relationship with your customer. It is a permanent representative in your customer's office or home, selling all the year round without additional costs of following up. It also supports other channels. It can help your salesperson to sell the full range of products and services without having to explain them all. To do this, your catalogue must be a direct response vehicle – more than a listing of product, features and prices. It must create the desire to buy and be as readable and productive as any other piece of marketing material. You can distribute your catalogue in various ways – by mail, at exhibitions, handed out by sales staff, at shop counters, and so on.

▶ Order forms

Order forms may be part of a brochure, catalogue or letter, whether separate or detachable. The order form is your salesperson's close, but the salesperson is not there. So make it as easy as possible to complete. It should look valuable, be reply paid, with the customer's details already entered and with clear instructions on how to complete it. It could be a freephone number with easy ordering instructions. This gives you the opportunity to check customer details, confirm stock availability and delivery dates, and to cross-sell.

> **Warning!**
> When using telephone order-takers try to avoid too many questions before the order is made. Customers ring to order, not give numerous personal details which they consider irrelevant or which they believe you already have.

> **In the real world**
> Using a freephone number encourages response. However, it can attract people you don't want, such as hoax callers, complainants and so on. So it may be more cost effective to use a local-rate number.

▶ The envelope

The envelope encourages your customer to see whether there is useful information contained in it. This usually means over-printing and using paper of high-quality appearance. Matching graphics on the envelope, letter and brochure can help make it stand out.

▶ One-piece mailers

One-piece mailers are used to reduce costs or to provide ways of giving more material to your customer within a cost budget. They may attract a low response, but this can be made up for by the higher coverage obtained within a given budget.

> **eg** One-piece mailers are used by many holiday companies. For example, they send postcards at recognized booking times, reminding potential clients what a great time they had last year.

▶ Enclosures

Many enclosures have been tried, with great success. They include gifts, testimonials and imaginative ways of showing the product in use, samples, guides or other items of enduring value. As a general rule, the more pieces in a mail pack, the better – provided that they all reinforce the central offer.

> **eg** The Consumers Association has found that an **11-piece pack** gets the most response from cold files, i.e. of customers with no previous history of contact with the association. In the United States, up to **32** pieces have been used with great success. Remember, the more pieces in the pack, the greater the chance that one will strike a chord with the prospect.

▶ Who uses direct mail?

The traditional heavy users of consumer direct mail are mail-order companies, insurance companies, consumer credit companies, book clubs, charities and magazines. In recent years, they have been joined by credit card companies, retailers, airlines, government departments, political parties, motor manufacturers and dealers, and banks. In the business-to-business arena, most suppliers of goods and services now include direct mail as an essential element in their marketing mix.

The advantages of direct mail are as follows:

1. It is possible to target highly specifically.
2. It is personal and confidential.
3. It is more competitively secret.
4. The message can be highly specific, enabling you to dovetail it closely with messages put out through the less targeted media, such as television or the national press.
5. Even in the lowest cost postage bracket, a lot of space is available in which to communicate.
6. A variety of formats and materials can be used.

7 There are many opportunities to introduce novelty (e.g. by different formats and types of enclosure).

8 Mailings can be scheduled to arrive within a fairly well-defined period.

9 Testing is relatively easy.

10 The response vehicle can be defined so as to ensure that your customers know exactly what to do when they receive the mailing.

11 Properly planned, it can be much more cost effective per reply than most other media.

> **Warning – direct mail has some inherent disadvantages**
>
> Direct mail has some specific weaknesses:
>
> 1 It is not appropriate to all markets. For example, the mail of senior managers of large companies is usually intercepted by secretaries and any mailings not considered relevant may be rejected.
>
> 2 It does not suit all objectives. For some products, your customers may not trust direct mail, preferring to visit a retail outlet to gather information. In this case, it may be better to use direct mail to stimulate customers to visit particular retail outlets.
>
> 3 It cannot be used in isolation to build a brand.
>
> 4 Some customers are sceptical of direct mail.

> **Warning – you can make direct mail fail if you don't use it properly**
>
> Here's how you can make it fail:
>
> ◆ **Emphasize short-term response rather than relationship building.** Now that so many companies are committed to a relationship management approach, this approach is less common. But many companies still decide to 'do a mailing' to bring in some leads. They rent a list, design and despatch the mailing, and never work out whether the targeting was accurate. The opportunity for learning and improving is lost, as is the opportunity to build a customer database.
>
> ◆ **Use it tactically.** Even if you have a good customer database, you may be tempted to use direct mail entirely tactically, just to generate leads. You may miss opportunities for building loyalty, developing a catalogue operation, selling additional products and services, cross-selling and researching your customers.
>
> ◆ **Don't integrate your contacts with the rest of your company's customer contact efforts.** For example, letters may be going out at the same time that sales or service people are due to call.
>
> ◆ **Choose your own messages** and don't worry about the other messages your company is sending out or what branding you're trying to achieve. This is a great way to confuse customers.

▶ Quality and the law

Given the risks to quality standards that might be incurred with such high volumes of mailing, the British Royal Mail works closely with direct mail users and agencies to ensure quality standards.

▶ Mailsort

To encourage the growth in direct mail and to counter criticisms about the efficiency of its services (in particular unreliable delivery dates, which made it difficult for direct mailers to know when their mailings reached customers), in 1989 the British Post Office introduced Mailsort, a new rebate scheme for bulk mailings.

▶ The Direct Mail Services Standards Board (DMSSB)

This was set up 'to help achieve and maintain the highest standards of practice and conduct in the provision of direct mail services and in the use of direct mail generally'. It operates a Recognition Scheme under which recognized companies are closely scrutinized by the board. They also undertake to observe certain codes of practice and only to work for clients who do so. Recognized agencies must pay the appropriate levy to the Advertising Standards Board of Finance and, where relevant, subscribe to the Mailing Preference Service. One of the problems this initiative faces is the rising number of in-house mailings, carried out directly by clients and not involving agencies.

The board's work includes liaising with industry bodies, such as the regulatory bodies in the financial services industry. It also monitors agency samples, picking up problems such as unspecified delivery dates for cash-with-order offers, insufficient prize draw rules and breaches of the Sale of Goods Act. The DMSSB also monitors letterbox leaflet distributions. It works closely with the Advertising Standards Authority and Trading Standards Department where appropriate. The DMSSB also publishes guidance notes covering specific legislation and giving general advice on the preparation of direct mail.

▶ The law

The British Code of Advertising Practice and the British Code of Sales Promotion Practice have been drawn up to protect consumers and suppliers. Provided that all suppliers observe these codes, consumers will not receive offers which break the law or mislead them, and suppliers will not have to face unexpectedly high costs by being forced to comply with terms of an offer which were not properly worked out or by having to defend their actions in the courts.

> **Warning!**
> The main areas where problems occur are:
> - prize draws and competitions;
> - misleading or exaggerated claims;
> - guarantees;
> - delivery times;
> - appeals to fear.

▶ Sector-specific requirements

Various sectors have specific rules about what can be claimed in copy. These are usually industries that are regulated for other purposes. Examples of regulated industries include financial services, utilities, telecommunications and public transport. Generally, these industries have rules about what you can and cannot say to customers, and possibly even about how you should contact them.

▶ The Data Protection Act

This was not developed solely to regulate direct mail but it has significant implications. The Information Commissioner has already issued a number of rulings relating specifically to the use of personal data by the direct marketing industry. The Act states specifically that personal data shall be:

1 **obtained and processed fairly and lawfully**. This means that people who give data should know why they give it and should not be deceived into giving it;
2 **held for one or more specified purposes**. In other words, it is not legal to collect data without a specified purpose;
3 **disclosed only for the purpose held**. For example, data collected for the purposes of checking creditworthiness should not be disclosed for the purpose of marketing products. So if the intention is to use it for both, the individual from whom it is being collected should be told so at the time of collection;
4 **adequate, relevant and not excessive**. In other words, if you collect data, you should be able to justify every element of it in terms of improving your ability to meet customer needs;
5 **accurate and updated**. It is not enough to collect it and continue to use it, even if it becomes outdated. You should ensure that you budget for updating – often very expensive;
6 **retained only as long as necessary for the stated purpose or purposes**. Provided you are using the data as a foundation for building a relationship with the customer, this should not pose a problem. But it would be illegal to collect the information, use it once and then keep it in case it could be sold;
7 **accessible to individuals at reasonable intervals and without undue delay or cost**. It must also be corrected or erased as appropriate. A charge for access to personal data has been fixed by the Registrar;
8 **appropriately secured against unauthorized access, alteration, disclosure or destruction and against accidental loss or destruction**. These are common-sense provisions.

Note that now data protection applies to communication with business individuals as well as consumers and will come to apply to paper records as well as to computerized data. However, a very good rule is to always seek permission from customers about what data you hold, how you want to use it and which channels you use to contact them, using the data.

▶ The Mailing Preference Service (MPS)

> The aim of **the MPS** is to 'promote with the general public the direct marketing industry in the United Kingdom by providing facilities for the consumer to exercise a choice in regard to the receipt of direct mail'. The emphasis is very much on encouraging the continued growth of direct mail by ensuring that customer alienation is minimized.

With the MPS, consumers may add their name, free of charge, to the register of those not wishing to receive unsolicited direct mail. Many add their names in several different formats, according to the formats they are addressed by, so there are many duplicates on the list. The MPS is paid for by the subscribing companies, which include users, agencies, bureaux and list brokers.

To maintain quality standards, many bureaux and list brokers are insisting that client lists going into deduplication are MPS-cleaned beforehand.

▶ The brief for a direct mail campaign

This is not radically different from any other direct marketing brief. It should cover:

- business objectives;
- marketing objectives;
- customers in the target market – who they are, how they behave, what they buy, how they are normally communicated with, what their needs are, how much they know about the product on offer and the company supplying it. This should include any market research that is available;
- what response is required, e.g. a complete sale, a lead;
- the features, benefits and USP of your product or service, and how these match customers' needs;
- the positioning and brand image of your product;
- the offer;
- what the rest of the market is doing – direct competitors, indirect competitors and suppliers of products and services that are in some way similar to the product in question, retailers, etc.;
- your previous record with the product – sales, marketing campaigns and their results;
- what other marketing actions are planned for the product and for your other products;
- what might be learned from the campaign;
- what should be tested;
- how responses will be handled;

- the schedule;
- the budget.

Formats

As mentioned earlier, a big advantage of direct mail is the variety of formats that can be used. The classic format is the following:

- the 'outer' or, more fully, the 'outer envelope', with the recipient's address and often over-printed with an additional message. However, over-printing can cause customers to think that the mailing is 'just junk mail' to be thrown away. It must therefore be used judiciously;
- the letter itself, personalized if possible;
- a brochure, referred to in the letter;
- the order form;
- a flyer (for some other product or service, or for an additional offer within the offer);
- an envelope for the reply (usually a business reply envelope – a BRE – or a Freepost envelope).

> **Action**
> You could include non-competing companies' flyers to help cover the cost of the mailing, but beware of diluting impact. So test first!

Making your mailing more effective

Ways of doing this include:

- involvement devices – stamps, tokens, rub-offs, sealed envelopes, jigsaws, keys;
- specialized devices which form an integral part of the print medium, e.g. attention grabbers, pop-ups, tip-ons, die cuts;
- product samples (e.g. of furniture coverings or other fabrics);
- a second or 'publisher's' letter;
- closed-face envelopes;
- invitation formats – implying a special privilege;
- simulated telegrams;
- personalization – not just in the letter but on other items as well. Some printers can now personalize catalogues. One stationer's letter asks: *'You have not bought toner cartridges for three months, are we too expensive? Turn to page 15 and take a further 25% off the sale price'*;

- testimonials;
- guarantees;
- free trial and cancellation;
- money-back offers;
- reassurance about your reliability.

The creative

There is no formula for a perfect direct mail pack, but there are many 'rules' which have helped make packs which pull better. So, if you can't afford first-line agencies or top creative consultancies, or if you use in-house resources, here are some guidelines.

> **In the real world**
> Some of the best mailing pieces succeed because they are unusual. However, there is a degree of consensus about the kind of mailing that will usually work – provided that targeting has been accurate, timing is right and the offer is appropriate to the target market.

▶ Calling to action

The aim of a letter is to get action.

- The envelope must make your customer open it.
- The letter must make your customer refer to the brochure.
- The brochure must make your customer find and fill in the order form or call you.

So your words must be powerful. But additional incentives may be required – discounts for early applications, free entry to prize draws, and the like. Some argue that incentives should always be closely related to the offer being made, on the grounds that irrelevant incentives devalue the offer. However, irrelevant offers do pull responses – the latest cheap electronic gadget often works. As with all the points below, what form of words and what incentive works for the target market and product in question is best established by testing. But to make sure that your copy pulls responses, it should repeatedly ask for and spur to action, with cut-off dates, reasons to act and reminders of benefits at the point of asking.

A vital point is won if the offer is packaged to create a favourable first impression. What 'favourable' means depends on the market and product. In some markets, an envelope that 'screams' at the customer to be opened may be the right impression to create. In other markets, only a business-like and formal letter may create the right first impression.

> **Action**
> Use market research to test ideas. Suggest a succession of ideas at one time. Then use the favourably received ones one after the other, in a succession of mailings.

A call to action 'out of the blue' often fails. You must lead your customer towards the call in a convincing way. Take your customer through the classic advertising cycle of attention, interest, desire, conviction and action.

▶ Benefits

> **Benefits** are what your product or service does for the individual customer, by satisfying the customer's objectives.

But for customers to understand that the product will meet their objectives, your copy must be written in their language. For example, if you are selling a washing machine, don't express the benefit of trouble-free and cost-efficient washing in terms of the pence per minute or likely need for service calls. These are not factors to which customers relate. Their objectives are freedom from trouble and low cost.

> **Warning!**
> It is tempting to extol the features (the description of the product or service's technical characteristics) and advantages or functions of the product (what it does) rather than its benefits. This is especially so if not enough is known about customers (which makes it difficult to know their objectives and hence the benefits).

▶ Consistency and quality

> **Remember**
> The tone, style and copy of the entire pack should be consistent with your company branding.

This is a matter of principle, the value of which is difficult to prove by testing. A powerful creative execution entirely inconsistent with your company's brand might create a very high response. But the question is, would too many such promotions lead to the value of your brand falling? Response might begin to drop. The vast majority of companies with strongly branded offerings insist on complete consistency with branding across all marketing communications media. Presumably this is not due just to a few smart marketing consultants!

The same point applies to consistency with product and target customer. 'Cheap' creative can sell quality products, but testing is likely to show that 'quality' creative would pull even better.

▶ Using personal data

Increasing numbers of direct mail users are working with their own customer database. This enables them to incorporate personal details about the customer in the letter copy. For example, a letter might say:

'... When you bought your washing machine from us five years ago you returned us a questionnaire that indicated that you would be likely to replace your machine after five years. Five years have now passed, so we would like to offer you a very special trade-in price for your old machine...'

This might lead the customer to wonder how on earth you managed to remember what the questionnaire response was five years ago. The customer might also be slightly worried that information that they thought was used for market research has now been used to encourage replacement.

> **In the real world**
> A more subtle approach would be to use the data to target the customer in question and make a trade-in offer, without actually reminding the customer about the data. The rule is that in the body of the letter, customer data should be used only where the recipient would expect you to have and use it. **This applies even if the customer gave you the information directly in the first place.**

▶ The appeal

All direct mail packs appeal to the customer to respond in some way. There are various ways to make the appeal stronger – by appealing to logic, the rational appeal, to the emotions, e.g. guilt, humour and so on. Whatever the basis of the appeal, it must involve your customer. It must talk personally to your customer, not impersonally. Where relevant, it should aim to solve your customer's problem.

▶ Clarity and uniqueness

> **Warning!**
> Copywriters easily get carried away with nice phrases that are bound to appeal to customers and with fulsome praise of the product or service. However, your mail pack aims to make an offer and get your customer to respond to it. Therefore the offer should be obvious at a glance. The proposition should be clear, precise and concise. One understandable, clear benefit should dominate. A memorable reason for buying should dominate.

Express the benefit of your offer uniquely. So many of the 'magic words' of direct marketing have been used so often that they can no longer be relied upon to achieve the effect by themselves. These words include new, news, now, at last, announcing, introducing, for the first time, breakthrough, new kind of, first ever, how to, advice on, why, you, surprising, remarkable, save, improved, offer, bargain, opportunity, discount and, of course, FREE! The exclamation mark has also been overused!!!!!!!!!

One way to make a big impact is for your communication to start with a unique benefit or offer and say why it is important to the customer and why it is impossible to do without it. Of course, any claims to this effect should be backed with examples and testimonials. Conviction should be built in by guarantees, testimonials, research figures, scientific or independent proof, sales figures and examples of experience of other people or other markets. Facts and figures should be specific.

The above notwithstanding, most direct marketers believe that all possible benefits should be mentioned in the copy. It gives the customer additional reasons to buy, even after the main benefit has been correctly emphasized. It also ensures that those not 'captured' by the main benefit are captured by a subsidiary one. However good your targeting, you can't always be sure that every customer selected to receive the promotion will respond to the major benefit being promoted.

▶ Honesty

Perhaps because a letter is printed and because it can be taken at its own pace, consumers tend to believe direct mail.

> **In the real world**
> It's not hard to write copy which customers find unbelievable. So every effort should be made to make the communication true, believable and sincere. Make customers feel you are honest and know what you are talking about. Obvious obstacles should be admitted to and potential objections dealt with. Attention should be seized not with gimmicks but with news of benefits or offers. News or interesting information is a solid basis for gaining attention.

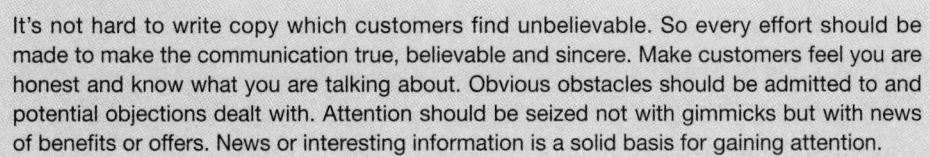

▶ Transferability and synergy

A direct mail pack may be part of a wider campaign, extending over published and broadcast media. It therefore helps if the creative idea used in the brochure can be extended over all elements of the campaign. This creative 'synergy' can make a campaign much more powerful, as each element reminds the consumer of all the elements. Direct Line's Red Phone is a good example of this.

> **Action**
> Transferability also works in a more practical way. A given piece of print may be usable in many ways. For example, a brochure might also be usable as a magazine insert, for household distribution, parcel enclosures, directories, take-ones, distribution by staff and so on.

▶ Copy length

The golden rule is: use as much copy as is needed. The more the letter is trying to qualify customers, the more information needs to be given to your customers to allow this qualification to take place. You don't want people to respond if the product or service isn't right for them. You'll get a high return rate and/or high customer dissatisfaction. A leading direct marketing consultant once wrote a 12-page letter to promote a speech he was giving and filled the (large) auditorium. The letter made sure that recipients knew what they were coming to hear.

However, the golden rule is normally to keep the letter concise and short. This is especially true for letters selling services and subscriptions.

▶ Copy style

You should follow standard rules of good writing and technical layout. Sentences should be kept short. One paragraph should lead clearly on to the next. Long copy should be broken up by sub-headings. You can make copier easier and more interesting to read by indentations, handwriting, underlining, sub-headings and highlighting. Bullet points and tables are also useful ways to keep the letter easy to read. The use of pictures and imagery is another way to break up the letter content and maximize impact. Using the back of the letter is another way of optimizing selling space, spreading out the content and creating impact.

When using imagery, all pictures should be captioned and the axes on all charts should be properly labelled. The copy should also flow logically. To make sure that the reader carries on reading, use carrying phrases to continue the flow. These can include:

- 'but that isn't all ...'
- 'there is one more thing ...'
- 'now – here is the best part ...'
- 'here is all you have to do ...'
- 'more important than that ...'
- 'you'll also receive ...'
- 'so that is why ...'

Carrying tricks should also be used, such as questions at the paragraph end, pages ending halfway through a paragraph or at a tantalizing point.

Your pictures or graphics should demonstrate the experiencing of benefits, or even better make your customers feel they are already getting the benefits. They should be easy to absorb, without tricky effects. Show people, to engender interest. Of course, the pictures should reflect the copy and, if possible, tell a full and logical story.

▶ Additional items

Apart from the brochure and order form that usually accompany a letter, other items can be used to reinforce the message. These include testimonial facsimiles, gifts (e.g. pens, rulers), ways of showing the product in use, samples and enduring information (e.g. 'A quick guide to X, maps', calendars, telephone numbers).

▶ Managing a direct mail campaign

There are four main streams of work or processes, which overlap:

1 generating ideas for the format of the mailing (the offer and its creative expression), starting with the briefing of the agency or creative team;
2 determining who should receive the mailing and when (the targeting and timing), starting with the briefing of the list broker and/or the database manager;
3 sending the letters via the mailing house and the Post Office. Preparation for this starts as soon as the general format, timing and volume of the mailing are determined;
4 response handling and fulfilment – the completion of what you promised to your customers.

However, because a direct mail campaign involves so many elements and decisions, there are many campaign management points that need to be dealt with in detail.

▶ Paper stock

The weight and quality of paper must be determined. Weight is important because it affects the mailing weight and therefore the cost. It also determines the quality of the printed stock and so the impression it creates. Lighter weights of paper tend to feel 'flimsy' (an exception to this is letters which arrive by Airmail which are expected to be lighter). Also, the type of paper used (weight, kind of coating) affects what can be printed on it. However, the demands of the direct mail industry have stimulated a high degree of product innovation and paper can be finished, treated and so on to accomplish virtually any task. The only exception is that no one has yet invented weightless, high-quality bond paper.

> **In the real world**
> Any special paper requirements should be specified as soon as possible. These include any pre-printing, special sizes, gloss, embossing and the like. This is because these factors may affect the kind of machinery the paper can pass through at a later stage of processing. For example, embossing can cause problems with high-speed laser printers, and lazering cannot be printed onto shiny, slippy surfaces.

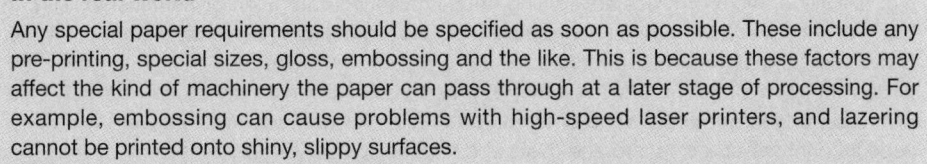

▶ Letter volume

At the early stages of campaign development, it may not be clear exactly how many mail packs are going to be sent. This is because the systems and targeting side of the campaign runs partly in parallel with the creative side. Thus, the target customer type may have been specified, but more work may be needed to establish how many of the target customer type are on your database. Or list development work may still be taking place, perhaps in consultation with list brokers or list vendors. So at an early stage, requirements may have to be specified in bands, e.g. between 30 000 and 40 000 packs. In some cases, there may be a target sales level. If you are certain about expected response rates (perhaps because you have tested properly), the mailing volume will be known. But if you are uncertain, a quick test may be necessary before rollout volumes are finalized.

In order to provide flexibility to increase volumes if necessary, always brief your printer with both scenarios. This will allow the printer to plan for a contingency and order the paper. If volumes increase, so will the need for additional press time and space, and more paper.

▶ Testing

Direct marketing thrives on testing, in particular of target markets, offers and creative. These all affect the volume and character of a mailing. Provided you have planned your campaign properly, you should have time to order the print volumes required for the rollout mailing.

▶ Stock levels and ordering

> **Action**
>
> For the initial mailing and the fulfilment to take place smoothly, the sizes and locations of stocks of different elements of the mail pack should always be specified.

> **In the real world**
>
> Different elements of the mail pack (e.g. the envelope, letter and brochure) may arrive from different suppliers at different times. Stocks for the initial mailing are likely to be held by a mailing house, stocks for fulfilment are likely to be held by the fulfilment house. The stocks required for the initial mailing depend upon the volumes of outbound mailings required and the scheduling of the making-up of the mail pack. For fulfilment, the volumes of mailings required will depend upon the timing of the customer contacts that stimulate the response, e.g. television, radio or press advertising, a telemarketing campaign or an initial mailing. If high volumes are being moved very quickly, the stock should all be ready before the start. But some campaigns could continue for up to a year, with response trickling in over the period. In such a case, a print volume optimizing calculation might be carried out. This involves working out what is the optimum batch size for printing and storage, taking into account print set-up costs, storage costs and finance costs. Also, response packs might be made up in small batches, particularly if there are many variations, because the work might be manual.

Specify very clearly when suppliers are required to deliver and to where, and when the stock will first be used. Also, as postal delivery schemes such as Mailsort give extended delivery times for lower prices, determine your campaign timing in the light of these opportunities, as long as they are consistent with meeting your marketing needs.

Print ordering should take into account the lead times of suppliers. Most direct marketing users operate with one or more printers with which they have a continuing relationship. The user has an updated statement of supply lead times for different kinds of work. For really large and complex mailings requiring specialized printing and/or inserting machinery, the timing of the mailing itself may be determined by the availability of these machines, of which there might be only a few in the country.

▶ Letter copy management

A direct mail letter is very different in status from a brochure. To the recipient a brochure is usually clearly advertising copy. But a letter is from a named individual, who can expect to receive many direct replies, i.e. through other than the suggested response route. These replies may be letters or telephone calls.

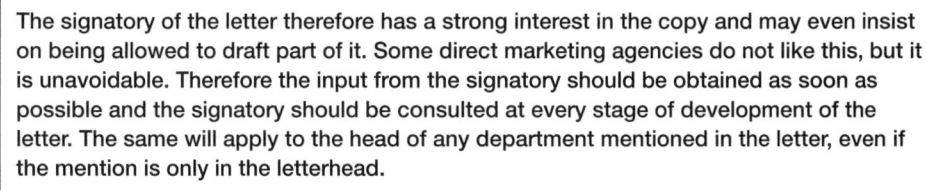

> **Warning!**
> The signatory of the letter therefore has a strong interest in the copy and may even insist on being allowed to draft part of it. Some direct marketing agencies do not like this, but it is unavoidable. Therefore the input from the signatory should be obtained as soon as possible and the signatory should be consulted at every stage of development of the letter. The same will apply to the head of any department mentioned in the letter, even if the mention is only in the letterhead.

All this means that you must be absolutely clear about who is writing, who is contributing to the letter and who will be the signatory. Finally, the type of letterhead to be used and the form in which the signature is to be supplied to the printer must also be specified (e.g. digitized).

▶ Pack management

> **Action**
> The pack may consist of a number of elements. You must design them not just to relate to each other but more simply to fit together!

> **Warning!**
> You must avoid the situation where your mailing campaign reaches a late stage of development only for you to discover that your pack items do not fit into the chosen envelope.

This is why preparation of a pack dummy is needed as soon as decisions about pack contents have been taken. This also confirms that the pack will fit within the chosen weight band, to achieve target postal costs. Postal costs can account for up to 50% of the cost of a mailing, so it is obviously important to design the pack according to postal weight bands. If machine enclosing is to be used, all folds and items need to be checked for this.

If your pack is complex, and particularly if it has a number of variations, every element of the pack should be coded. Each pack variation should also have a code. This not only makes print ordering and accounting easier but also makes holding records easier. When performance statistics are reviewed, it can be extremely cumbersome to have to refer to every element and pack variation by name. Of course, every different response vehicle should be clearly coded, allowing response variations by pack type to be measured.

> **Action**
>
> Pack management is a task in its own right, superimposed on managing the development and printing of the individual items. So clear responsibility for getting the pack right (in all its variations) must be allocated and each variation is signed off appropriately. This includes any later variations which might be added.

As the pack may involve many other people (e.g. mailing and fulfilment houses, sales staff, customer service staff), make sure that copies of the pack are available to these as early as possible. This avoids the obvious problems that can occur when someone involved in a campaign in any way does not have a copy of the pack to hand when their time to act comes. The worst example of this is where a customer calls in to a sales office to enquire about an offer contained in the pack and the person answering doesn't have the faintest idea which pack the customer is referring to. Finally, to prevent confusion, have a clear procedure for disposing of old stock of the pack and its components.

▶ Order forms

The order or response form is the most important part of the mailing. (The same applies to catalogues and other media, so what is said about these forms applies to all uses of order or response forms.) In many cases, the form is detachable from the carrying medium. This applies even if it has to be cut out from a magazine – it may be left lying around until the customer decides to fill it in. So the form must be viewed as a medium in its own right. It must clearly state what the customer is asked to do and what they will get in return. The reverse also applies – the medium carrying the form must make sense in the absence of the form. At the very least, the customer should be told how to obtain further copies of the form.

> **Action**
>
> The form should be easy to complete and easily understood when complete. Testing is always recommended – with the target type of consumer and not merely 'someone in the office'. Freepost is always a good idea for order forms. Faxed order forms are also favoured, especially when related to office supplies, since fax machines are normally situated in the office.

> **Action**
>
> If you already know the customer's name and address and are using a direct medium to reach them (e.g. direct mail), print the customer's name and address on the form. This ensures that database cleaning takes place automatically if the customer's address is incorrect. It also saves the customer's time and ensures that there are no problems with legibility. If the customer has an account number, this should be included on the form as it reduces keying-in time. You can also use personalized barcodes to ease order entry.

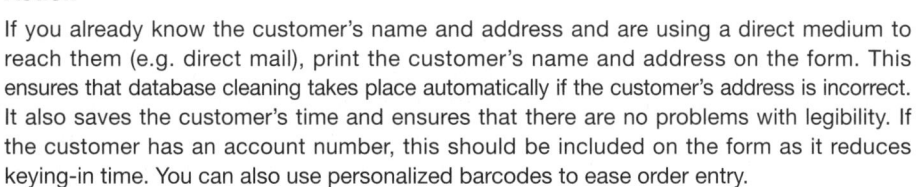

It is good practice to pay for your customer's reply. If the customer is ordering or is asking for more details, postage costs should be absorbable from the sale or expected sale.

▶ Envelopes

In many cases, companies make their envelopes stand out by using bright colours, catchy headers, die cuts and so on. Advanced printing and packing technologies permit the envelope to be an integral part of the mailing by utilizing the space with a message or in fact making the envelope part of a one-piece mailing (self-mailer). At the other extreme is the simple transparent wrap, allowing your customer to see at least some of the content of the mailing directly. This is used most frequently with directly mailed publications and catalogues.

> **Action**
>
> However tempting it is to use all these modern variations, envelope choice should be made in the same way as with every element of the mailing, i.e. in accordance with the objectives of the mailing (and each piece within it) and its tone. Thus, a platinum charge card offer to high-flying businessmen should be enclosed in a standard, high-quality envelope, in keeping with their formal business correspondence, to portray an image of quality, seriousness, efficiency, for the discerning reader. Harrods Bank is a good example of this type of positioning. On the other hand, an offer of three free issues of a gardening magazine targeted at gardening enthusiasts can be much more informal and fun. It can therefore carry an overprinted strong message to this effect.

Unless the mailing is very low volume, you should aim to have your mailings machine-enclosed. Keeping the envelope standard size will minimize production problems and achieve discounts on postal costs to reduce your overall pack cost and subsequent cost per response. Use of an address window depends on the kind of letter to be used. If it is to be personalized, a window is likely to be less off-putting than where the letter is addressed to 'Dear Occupier'. If a window is used, alignment of the address in the finished pack must be checked.

> **Warning!**
>
> If a bulky promotional item is to be included, ensure that the mailing cannot be mistaken for, say, a dangerous object, and that the pack can be posted through a normal letterbox. The latter also applies to business mailings, as many deliveries to smaller companies have to go through a letterbox.

The envelope should normally have a return address for undelivered mailings. For a high-quality mailing, this should be printed in a conservative style and be used discreetly so that it doesn't indicate that it is a mass mailing.

Choice of mailing class depends on budget and also on the tone to be established by the envelope, though the Mailsort types are not normally noticed or understood by the recipient. A well-planned campaign will allow for time for mailing to be decreased to Mailsort 2 or 3 to achieve postal cost savings. Again this will help reduce the overall campaign cost, substantially.

▶ Summary

Direct mail is a deceptively simple medium. In its simplest form – an envelope, letter and reply device – it looks as simple as writing a personal letter. But it can be a powerful message conveyer. To make it work, you need to follow the essential rules laid out in this chapter – in targeting, formats, creative, print and production, response handling and fulfilment. You also need to comply with certain standards. So it's quite a technical business. For this reason, you need to plan your direct mail campaigns carefully, test them wherever possible, execute them with due control and precision, and evaluate them objectively when they are finished. This is not a job for the enthusiastic amateur. If you don't have the expertise in-house, don't hesitate to use an agency – there are plenty around and they'll be only too happy to compete for your business.

We can't guarantee that if you follow all these guidelines you'll have the best mailing campaign there ever was, but you will avoid the obvious errors made by so many of your predecessors. You'll also be ready to take on an even more complex area – telemarketing, the subject of our next chapter.

13 telemarketing

What is telemarketing?

Strengths and weaknesses

Why customers may like telemarketing

Key concepts in telemarketing

Functions performed

Telemarketing objectives

Contact centres

The technology of telemarketing

Productivity ratios

Additional targets and ratios for inbound telemarketing

The important measures for inbound and outbound telemarketing

The importance of feedback

Setting targets

Call guides

What is telemarketing?

> **Telemarketing** means using the telephone as a properly managed part of the marketing, sales and service mix. It differs from telephone selling, which aims to get sales over the telephone. Teleselling is usually used as a stand-alone strategy rather than an integrated element of the marketing mix.

In business-to-business marketing, telemarketing has been used for many years. In consumer marketing, teleselling is becoming less common and many companies now use telemarketing as one of their main ways of managing customers. At the other extreme from teleselling is full account management via the telephone, or telemanagement. This is a more cost-effective way of managing customers than a field sales force.

Many businesses and consumers find teleselling a nuisance. Consumers have ready excuses to deal with poorly targeted calls. *'I've got one already'* or *'we had it done last year'* are the most common. In business, such calls may be barred by secretaries, acting on their managers' instructions. Telemanagement is at the other extreme. The relationship with your customer is established, so your telemarketers won't be barred.

The difference between telemarketing and teleselling

Telemarketing	Telephone selling
Controlled message	Individual communication
Uses structured scripts	Operator's own methods
Variety of objectives	Objective to sell product or service
All results collected and analyzed	Measurement haphazard – only sales
All parameters testable – list, offer, script, etc.	Impossible to test elements
Possible to plan and integrate with all other media	Usually stand-alone, with some mail follow-up
No commission paid usually	Commission paid, sometimes only commission

Telemarketing is a discipline in the fullest sense of the word. Highly trained staff use telecommunications equipment and networks to achieve your marketing objectives by carrying out a controlled dialogue with your customers, who need the benefits you provide. These staff are supported by systems which allow you to manage the workflow, measure it and follow through the outcome of the dialogue. Customers calling your company are identified by their telephone number, and this plus other data is used to route the call to the right telemarketing agent, who proposes the right offer. In its most advanced form, the dialogue between customer and company can be switched between telephone and the Worldwide Web or Interactive TV, or combine them simultaneously.

In the real world

Telemarketing requires systematic management, measurement and control of every aspect of its operation. Without this, you could not know the relationship between the inputs and outputs of your telemarketing operation. This information is essential to achieve effectiveness. So, when you are considering the introduction of telemarketing, make sure that you are open to a re-evaluation of your entire process for managing your customers.

Telemarketing is still growing. Costs of contacting and managing customers by other means (e.g. the field sales force) are rising. More and more is being learned about why and when customers are happy to do business over the telephone, and how to put this knowledge to work. Customers find the telephone a cost-effective way of learning about and buying your products and services. However, the costs of running big telemarketing operations are coming under scrutiny. Many companies are moving their contact centres to developing countries or persuading their customers to use even lower cost channels, such as the Worldwide Web.

Strengths and weaknesses

Compared with other direct marketing media, telemarketing has the following strengths and weaknesses:

Strengths	Weaknesses
Immediacy: high impact, personal contact	**High unit cost per call**: but low cost per customer and per sale if well targeted
Two-way medium: interactive, active qualification, information can be checked	**Risk of lack of commitment (verbal only)**: needs good follow-up
Flexible: variety of approaches, different scripts, answers questions/objections	**Easily abused**: pressure sensitive, so requires careful control
Accurate and controllable: easy to target, result from each call, testable in low volumes	**Single dimension**: voice only, no pictures, no written commitment
Can optimize contact: selling up or across ranges, setting up appointments, update list during call, market feedback	**Must be effectively integrated with other marketing strategies**: difficult to use in isolation

Why customers may like telemarketing

Your customers find the telephone one of the best ways of conducting their relationship with you because:

- **It saves their time.** They do not have to handle the formality of a sales visit or travel to see the product.
- **It allows them to feel they control the relationship.** They can tell you when it is convenient to call and can call you when convenient to them. They can terminate the call when they want.

- **It gives them information when they need it.** They may find it frustrating to wait for information to come in the post or during a field sales visit. They can call you and you can respond immediately or quite soon after.
- **It gives them a direct dialogue with your company.** This gives them confidence in the relationship.

Toll-free calling

An important element of telemarketing is the toll-free number. This allows you rather than your customer to pay for the call. Call costs can be shared, with customers paying only for the local element. The very fact that you have set up dedicated phone lines and are paying for all or part of the call ensures that you are properly organized to take the call because you don't want to waste your money. However, the main cost of handling a call is not the phone bill but the cost of running a contact centre.

Many companies prefer to use in-house telemarketing facilities rather than agencies. This is because with a 'live' call taking place with customers, it is felt to be important that the caller is a true representative of your company, often with access to your information systems and so able to check customer status, inventory position, etc. Agencies have responded to this by offering 'in-house' teams – effectively a facility-managed telemarketing. Meanwhile, agencies are popular for response handling (e.g. receiving calls asking for further specific information or a brochure) and market research.

Key concepts in telemarketing

The dialogue principle

Telemarketing is best employed as an aspect of customer relationship management. A key principle of CRM is the need for you to be in constant dialogue with your customers. This ensures that your customers' needs are being met and that the information on your database is kept fresh. In a dialogue, information flows both ways. Your telemarketer becomes committed to a dialogue with customers. This dialogue lasts as long as the customer remains your customer. It will consist of a series of 'conversations', conducted over the telephone. Letters, brochures and other material confirm or add to what is said. A sales visit or visit to a showroom takes place where necessary.

In the real world

The objective of telemarketing is to achieve a managed dialogue, consisting of a progressive series of conversations focused on your customers' needs. Each conversation is targeted to achieve specific sales cycle objectives – gathering information, presenting options, and so on. Build this idea into your communications and sales planning, and develop measures of success which monitor the progressive deepening of the relationship with your telemanaged customers.

Conversations should have specific objectives in terms of conveying information and/or moving your customer forward one or more stages in the buying cycle. Some calls should be outbound, reflecting proactive management of the dialogue, but inbound calling is a key part of relationship building. It is the way many customers want to access you.

> **In the real world**
>
> To maintain the cost effectiveness of the approach, calls should not be made at the convenience of the telemarketer. They are either scheduled to your customer's convenience or programmed by support staff or systems to maximize the effectiveness of the day's workflow.

▶ The need to plan

Telemarketing requires detailed planning. Whether or not a precise script is used, each call must be under control and planned. Telemarketing differs from telephone selling in that every call is measured and the results analyzed. This enables the different elements of telemarketing to be measured and tested in the same way as with direct mail – the list, the script, the offer, the timing and so on. Telemarketing also needs to be tested in competition with other media and with different combinations of media in the contact strategy.

> **Fast-track**
>
> The management of a telemarketing campaign must be very precise, including careful control of costs (e.g. operator time, list selection), through budgeting and planning of campaigns. Quality must be monitored very carefully. It is easy to target a telemarketing campaign to produce a specific number of appointments for the sales force, only to discover that the quality of appointments is very low.

So, telemarketing must be measured as part of the overall contact strategy, which is designed to yield more sales and profit, not just appointments. The customer database must therefore be set up to allow tracking of the effectiveness of every contact medium from beginning to end of the sales cycle.

▶ Functions performed

Telemarketing can perform any of these functions:

- call reception;
- enquiry handling;
- enquiry qualification;
- customer (market) research;
- product research;

- list cleaning/enhancement;
- complaint handling;
- information dissemination;
- order taking;
- cross/up-selling;
- lead generation;
- servicing marginal accounts;
- progress chasing;
- account management/development;
- after-sales customer care.

Telemarketing objectives

Telemarketing helps achieve many objectives. They include the following:

- **Call handling:** answering customer calls on any matter, whether enquiries about products, requests for service, handling complaints or problems.
- **Moving towards a sale:** lead generation, appointment creation, order taking, seeking or closing, selling up or cross-selling, converting non-sales-related inbound or outbound calls into sales opportunities.
- **Cold calling:** normally as part of a campaign or following up a mail-shot. Don't forget to check the list with the Telephone Preference Service (TPS) before calling, this is now law.
- **Building loyalty:** by meeting needs and by just listening and remaining in contact; by following up a mail-shot; by asking what they thought of X product, brochure, etc.
- **Enquiry screening:** obtaining information to confirm whether a customer is a prospect for a product or how serious a particular problem is.
- **Customer and market research:** gathering information to use in making business decisions. This includes screening of lists of customers or prospects to be used in particular marketing campaigns.

> **In the real world**
> If a market research agency is conducting this type of work they are unlikely to give you addresses as this is against the code of practice for market researchers.

- **Delivering customized advice:** by anticipating what your customers need to know and briefing your telemarketers so that they can help.
- **Account management:** improving the quality of account management, so certain groups of customers benefit from a better relationship with you. This

may include finding new purchasers within existing accounts, preventing competitive inroads into customers, and reactivating lapsed customers.
- **New business:** identifying and developing new customers and new markets, extending coverage of existing markets or launching a new product or service.
- **Quality:** improving the effectiveness, professionalism and economics of the sales force and other channels.
- **Customer care:** improving customer service and satisfaction. Many customer care departments are using the telephone to speed up the complaint-answering procedure. Stena Line, the ferry service, has been using this method to great effect.

> **Checklist: using telemarketing in your business**
>
> Have you trained your telemarketing team sufficiently to close a sale?
>
> Are they confident enough to cold call?
>
> Have you screened your list with the TPS before starting to call to comply with data protection rules?
>
> Will the cold call create strong lists to hold on your database?
>
> Are you building loyalty with the most valuable clients or just the easiest to handle on the telephone?
>
> Does the market research agency you are using have a direct marketing/telemarketing arm which will pass the contacts to you – provided that it is collected under Data Protection rather than Market Research Society rules?
>
> Are your telemarketing team up to date with all the products in your portfolio and will they be skilled enough to spot a cross-selling opportunity?
>
> Will they identify new business opportunities?
>
> Is your customer care/relations department using telemarketing yet? If not, is there a valid reason which you may not have considered?

Contact centres

Contact centres are usually highly automated, with on-screen scripting, often online access to inventory systems to check availability, and the ability to key in orders or book service calls on the spot. Such centres can be particularly effective for handling telephone responses to mass mailings or broadcast and published media campaigns, or for handling customers who call in often for service reasons (e.g. bank balance checking, booking service calls). Many companies that manage their customers on the web can now browse collaboratively with those customers and push different screens at them to help them.

The technology of telemarketing

The progress of telemarketing has been facilitated by the development of telecommunications and computing technology. The systems and equipment used in telemarketing are of two main kinds: telecommunications-based and computer-based. The exact computer and telecommunications requirements will depend on the type of business and the nature of the company's existing systems that need to be linked to the telemarketing operation. Increasingly, telecommunications network operators are offering intelligence built into their networks, taking some of the call-routing work away from the contact centre.

> **In the real world**
>
> Telemarketers' workstations need various support systems. Where possible, involve your in-house telecommunications and computer specialists in this project. They can advise on design and ordering of the systems and help with implementation and testing.

▶ Telephony

The telephony requirements are usually provided via an automatic call distributor (ACD) or through computer-integrated telephony which can fully emulate all the features of ACD.

> An **ACD** is an independent unit which allows calls to be distributed between call receivers on a variety of programmed bases. It also allows the telemarketing manager to monitor each telemarketer's inbound and outbound telephone usage (since it provides call-handling statistics).

ACD statistics help in monitoring telemarketers against their targets. ACD systems enable the telemarketing manager to listen to and record any conversation at any time. The telemarketers can also record their own conversations. They can then use these recordings to improve their technique.

The ACD directs calls automatically, for example:

- to distribute workloads evenly;
- to give valued customers preferential treatment;
- to ensure that the right person handles each caller (based upon skills, product knowledge, etc.);
- to direct particular calls to telemarketers with special expertise;
- to promote personal relationships with customers.

All this requires either issuing different telephone numbers for different needs or true digital telephone networks. The latter allow ACDs to identify the number of the inbound caller so that the call can be routed to that customer's account manager, whose screen will then automatically display the customer's details. This is through a feature called 'calling line identification'. If several telephone numbers are used for the centre (e.g. for different products or different marketing campaigns), the 'dialled number identification service' allows the ACD to determine which number was dialled and to allocate the call to the relevant telemarketer(s).

Where a high volume of outbound calling is required, the 'automatic dialling' feature can be used. This operates by automatically dialling the next customer number as soon as a telemarketer has finished the previous call. An advanced version of this is 'predictive dialling'. This dials many more calls than the telemarketer can handle, predicting that only some of them will be answered. Obviously this makes sense in consumer marketing and not in business-to-business marketing. Only calls that are answered are distributed to telemarketers.

> **eg** Liverpool City Council has decided against automatic dialling after research showed it to be unpopular with customers and offputting for many. Instead it has used sequential numbers for each one of its services and publicized the numbers heavily. It allows customers to ring the service they want straight away without having to put themselves through to the right department.

▶ Lines

A telemarketing operation needs enough inbound capacity too. Here, you need to decide whether lines should be toll-free. There is a strong argument for toll-free, if you can afford it. A strong customer-oriented message is emitted if you allow the caller to call you at your expense. It also acts as a strong incentive for you to make the best use of the call (and of the customer's time waiting to be answered or being answered).

> **Fast-track**
> The number of inbound lines must be kept under review. Customer research and ACD traffic statistics indicate whether customers feel they have to wait often for a free line, and if so, how long.

▶ Computer-based systems

There are a number of standard and 'tailorable' computer systems that can be used to support a telemarketing operation. The benefits of computer-based systems are that they:

- provide online scripts or call guides so that telemarketers are steered to cover all the required points in a structured way;
- store information about customers and dialogues with them. This takes place as the telemarketers are talking with customers and is especially effective if call guides are being used. The information can then be used either within the conversation, to trigger decisions about next steps in the sales cycle, or in a future conversation, to enable the telemarketer to 'remember' customer details;
- act as a diarying tool for customer callbacks within a sales cycle;
- prompt fulfilment, by providing a feed to an automatic literature fulfilment process, or even directly to a product distribution system, which in turn can be attached to a stock control system.

▶ Relationship with the main database

Telemarketing works best when based on a comprehensive customer database. This should be borne in mind when choosing the system to support your operation. Some users of telemarketing support it via a central database, on which they hold their entire customer information set, thus integrating the approach to the market. They use this database to feed information to telemarketing systems, which in turn feed new information back to the central corporate database (see Fig. 13.1).

▶ Telemarketing packages

These packages are sold under the generic title of telemarketing, call centre or contact centre systems and run on anything from a personal computer to a mainframe. Some perform only telemarketing functions. Others offer a whole range of extra functions such as territory planning, direct mail and sales accounting. Almost all have some form of database management facility linking the different functions.

The four main areas covered by most computerized telemarketing systems are:

- information management;
- call management;
- fulfilment;
- performance analysis.

▶ Information management

Current information about each customer, such as name, address, telephone number, is held on the system's database along with details of all previous contacts (e.g. name of operator, which literature was sent, quotations sent, purchases

Fig. 13.1 A simple view of a telemarketing system configuration

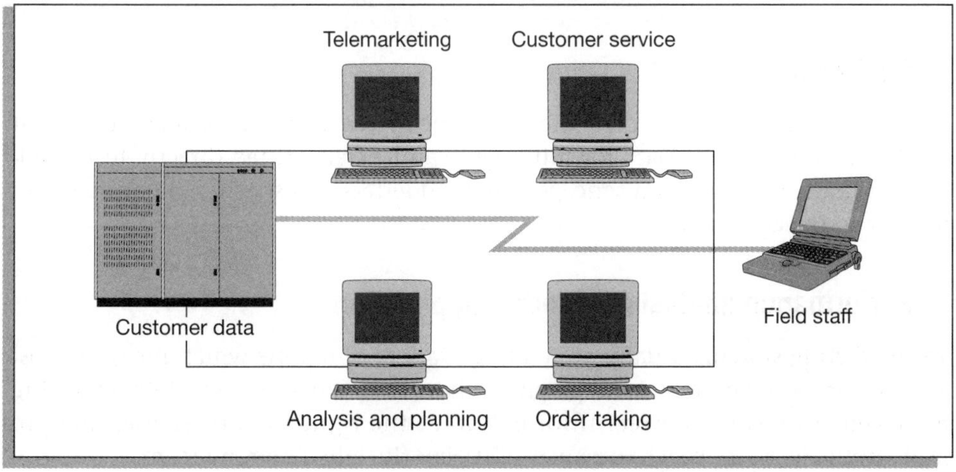

made) and information gathered during the needs analysis carried out by the telemarketers. Each telemarketer can access records from their own list of designated customers by name or telephone number. Lists can also be put together using a variety of marketing criteria such as time of last contact, location or interest shown in a particular product.

▶ Call management

The telemarketing system manages calls by the use of lists, such as an initial campaign list. Once the first call to each customer is made, the system's diary facility takes over. This facility allows your telemarketers to set their own call-back time, as well as providing an automatic scheduling facility for calls which are initially engaged or do not answer.

On most systems, calls are managed via interactive call guides. These start with a needs analysis to ensure that the required information is gathered from each customer in a structured and consistent manner. The facility to use call guides, scripts or prompts is offered on most telemarketing systems.

Telemarketers' screens prompt them with what to say to customers. The system can be programmed with (if necessary) complex logic so that the telemarketer is steered to the relevant part of the guide depending on what the customer has said in reply. This process is called decision tree prompting. Telemarketers key in these replies from the customer directly onto the screen and a record is therefore kept for later use, either during that call or in subsequent calls. Telemarketers have access to other call guides, including those which are product-specific or for objection handling. They should be able to access any information on the system (customer information on the database, information from previous calls, information from this call).

> ### Fast-track
> The level of flexibility for call guide construction, length, decision tree branching and cross-referencing varies between systems. The more expensive systems offer more choice. Take the costs and benefits of greater flexibility into account in your purchasing decision.

▶ Fulfilment

Personalized letters can be generated by some systems, either for local fulfilment or via a mailing house. Data for fulfilment can be transmitted directly to the fulfilment house so that it can send personalized letters and specific literature pieces directly to the customer.

▶ Performance analysis and other applications

Telemarketing systems usually offer a large variety of reports which measure most aspects of performance and productivity. This ensures that telemarketing management has the correct information at the right time to enable them to lead, motivate, train, coach, organize and plan the telemarketing team.

There are a number of other systems applications, such as:

- processing pro-forma and customized letters to customers;
- communicating with other parts of the organization via electronic mail;
- preparing standard (or tailored) quotations and contracts;
- general word-processing applications.

Note that many contact centres have several roles – outbound and inbound call management, and customer service. 'Selling on service', i.e. selling when a customer calls for service, has proved quite successful for some companies, provided it is approached sensitively.

Productivity ratios

In telemarketing, the old management sayings '*You get what you inspect, not what you expect*' and '*If you can't measure it, you can't manage it*' apply with a vengeance. Telemarketing works with a number of targets and ratios. The following are some of the main ones for outbound telemarketing.

Dials

If telemarketers are not trying to speak to customers often enough, every hour, every day, every week and every month, few of the purposes of telemarketing can be achieved. So each telemarketer **must** be set a target number of dials per day.

Decision maker contacts (DMCs)

A DMC is defined as making contact with the person who can make the decision to buy (not his or her secretary, spouse, etc.). A target is required for DMCs per period and the ratio between dials and DMCs. Achieving the target ratio of DMCs per day (or week) is important for two main reasons:

- it ensures that resources are geared correctly and effectively towards the level of customer coverage that is demanded by the telemarketers' role;
- measuring the number of **decision makers** contacted ensures that your telemarketers are getting through to the right person in the family or customer organization.

The level of these targets depends on target decision makers' habits and telemarketers' skills. If the results fall below an acceptable level (less than one in five may make the job frustrating and selling rather expensive), the reasons for this must be established. These could include:

- **telemarketer's attitude**. If there is a high level of 'busy' tone or 'not available' dial results for a particular telemarketer, there may be an attitude problem. If

so, the telemarketer may be backing down at the customer's switchboard. Fear can lead a telemarketer to fake dial records. This can be checked by comparing the telemarketer's own notes with ACD records;
- **market factors**. Competitors having tied up the market, products not right, previous problems in relationships with the company, all these are beyond the telemarketer's control and should have been investigated earlier.

> **In the real world**
> The telemarketer should not be the victim of poor marketing planning.

▶ Decisions and contracts sent

Measuring the ratio of:

- DMCs to customer decisions (end of the sales cycle, for good or ill);
- DMCs to number of confirmed purchases

gives the information needed to drive:

- **up** the number of calls that are active sales presentations or closes;
- **down** the number of follow-up calls per sales cycle.

These measures show where telemarketers need coaching to close sales.

> **Warning!**
> New or tired telemarketers fear rejection. This leads them to avoid pushing customers to make a decision one way or the other. This makes each sale more expensive and can irritate customers if a telemarketer won't take 'no' for an answer.

▶ Orders returned

To ensure customers are not being pushed into decisions on the phone so that unwanted orders are sent out followed by unproductive chasing calls, you should measure the difference between orders and returns. This indicates the quality of the sale.

▶ Detailed ratios

Various more detailed ratios can be used to fine tune telemarketing, e.g.:

- sales revenue per order;
- sales revenue per customer;
- future value generated per operator;
- DMCs vs brochures/literature sent;
- brochures/literature sent vs revenue received;

- revenue per DMC;
- number of orders per DMC;
- product demonstrations per DMC;
- revenue per product demonstration.

Many others can be used. Which ones are right depends upon the type of product sold and the type of customer. Your statistics should be measured for each telemarketer over longer and shorter time periods, to facilitate skills development and encourage personal endeavour.

Additional targets and ratios for inbound telemarketing

Many of the above ratios also apply to inbound telemarketing, except that DMCs as a target in its right does not apply (the caller is presumed to be interested). Therefore all other ratios are per caller rather than per decision maker contact. Other ratios include:

- time to answer;
- number of calls answered;
- time taken to deal with each call satisfactorily.

The importance of a good call queuing system cannot be overemphasized. This indicates to the telemarketing manager how many calls are on hold and tells the customer that the call will be answered shortly.

Other important measures for inbound and outbound telemarketing

Two other main areas need specific attention.

▶ Absolute performance, e.g. total sales

It is this, compared with the cost of the telemarketing operation, that determines its viability. It is also likely to be the basis for performance comparisons and their derivative – sales competitions.

▶ Quality of customer dialogue

This is as important as absolute performance. But it is more difficult to measure because it is qualitative. To measure this quality, your telemarketing manager must listen regularly to calls.

This is measured by listening to live calls or by using a tape recorder so that the calls can be listened to later. In both cases your telemarketers should be informed at all times of exactly what is going on and the reasons. They should also be given clear quality criteria and shown how to improve quality. They should be encouraged to listen on their own to their tapes, particularly after difficult or successful calls, to understand and learn from what happened. Note that laws on telephone privacy and equipment failures are two sources of problems with this approach.

The importance of feedback

To help improve the skills of your staff, and to motivate them, your sales management process should include:

- setting performance targets (quantitative and qualitative);
- measuring performance against these targets;
- feeding back the results positively to that member of staff.

Setting targets

Setting realistic targets can help ensure that your telemarketers meet their overall objectives. This allows achievement and relative progress to be measured. It also allows your telemarketers to see this progress and to be motivated accordingly. You must set targets for quality, not just quantity. High quantitative targets may cause the quality of calls to drop. So targets should be based on experience. If you have just started using telemarketing, you should obtain advice about what performance levels are reasonable and have been achieved in similar industries using telemarketing for similar purposes.

Typical telemarketing target areas include:

- number of dials;
- number of decision-maker contacts;
- number of hours at the workstation;
- number of sales made (or other absolute measurement);
- volume and value of sales made;
- product mix sold.

In the real world

Normal target-setting rules apply. Targets should:

1. be realistic;
2. be reviewed regularly;
3. reflect the company's strategic direction.

Targets should also be adjusted as telemarketing experience grows, i.e. increased. The learning curve is steep. Initial productivity is often low as telemarketers and customers are learning. As customers get used to the approach, as your telemarketers gain more experience, and as the relationship between the two deepens, productivity should rise steeply. A key productivity measurement is the 'telemarketing phone hour', the number of hours telemarketers spend at their workstations dealing with customers over the telephone in any one day. The phone hour is not just how long the telemarketer spends actually talking on the phone. It includes time spent preparing for a call and time spent immediately afterwards on matters related specifically to that call. It does not include lunch time, tea time, any breaks, meetings, training, etc.

Factors affecting what you can achieve include:

- complexity of product/service being sold;
- value of product/service being sold;
- stage of evolution of telemarketing in your company;
- level of awareness the customer has of your company and/or the product or service.

Variations in the above areas lead to different call structures – call guides are different and calls will last for different lengths of time. These need to be built into each telemarketer's objectives. Their productivity is then tracked throughout each campaign and compared with their objectives, for control and bonus purposes.

Call guides

The call guide in telemarketing is the equivalent of the copy in direct mail. It can be written in a completely scripted form, giving the telemarketer no choice of form of words, or it can be written as a series of prompts to explore topics. In all cases, a prior stage to writing the call guide is setting out the 'decision tree' or logic of the conversation. This states the sequence that the conversation is intended to take and also any branching that depends upon the answers given by your customer. Just as different forms of copy are tested in direct mail, so different decision trees and call guides can be tested. Call guides can be presented on paper or they can be programmed into a computerized system. Most computerized telemarketing systems allow programming of customized call guides. The call guide allows telemarketers to navigate their way through the call. It gives prompts and support at every stage. This includes prompting on product benefits and prices. It also provides possible answers to tricky objections.

The management benefits of call guides include:

- providing the telemarketer with a structured dialogue, ensuring that all possible points are covered;
- easing the training process, as telemarketers use call guides to help them sell new products;

- giving telemarketers confidence and professionalism quickly, so increasing the productivity of telemarketing;
- standardization and adherence to specific marketing approaches without loss of techniques or skills. This in turn allows true testing with complete validity of results.

Benefits of the call guide for the telemarketer include:

- a chance to listen attentively to the customer without worrying about what to say next;
- clear signs to the telemarketer of their exact position within a call, regardless of the number of seemingly similar calls made before that particular one. This applies even when a customer takes a different tack during a call. A telemarketer can be 'side-tracked' by the customer (to mutual benefit) without losing the thread. This ensures the objective of the call is met;
- the opportunity to close more business as a result of a more thorough sales approach;
- the availability of detailed product information allowing them to answer many of the customer's questions there and then;
- the ability to enter answers to relevant questions speedily via the same screen as the call guide and store those answers automatically on the database for future use.

> **Fast-track**
>
> Your telemarketers should always be in control of the situation, which is where call guides come in. Create a different guide set for each possible situation. This includes having specific product or service benefits in each set. Call guide sets should be modular. In this way, duplication is minimized and flexibility maximized. A wide product portfolio can be managed more easily too.
>
> The modular approach requires logical links and signposts between modules to help telemarketers chart the most productive path between them during a conversation. If call guides are computerized, logical links can be hidden.

The most advanced computerized systems incorporate expertise, so your system can analyze the results of past conversations and learn from them which modules and links work best, i.e. what is the best path through a conversation for customers of particular kinds who give particular responses. Whatever the sophistication of your approach to call guides, each call guide set should allow your telemarketers to:

- identify and reach the decision maker;
- accept detours the customer wants;
- determine the decision maker's needs and identify opportunities;
- offer solutions;

- handle questions and objections effectively;
- keep the door open at the end of the call.

When creating a call guide you should include:

- the products on offer, their features, advantages and benefits;
- likely customer needs and how to identify them;
- how the products solve customers' problems and which solution is most appropriate to which problem;
- likely competitive products and companies that will be encountered, and good arguments against them;
- and so on.

Promoting the telephone number

With inbound telemarketing, you must ensure your customers know which number they are supposed to call. Most large companies can be contacted on any one of several numbers. But if your telemarketing operation is to work properly, the right number must be promoted. In a campaign where the first medium used is press or direct mail, this should raise no problem. The number can be strongly promoted, often on or near a mail coupon, where your customer will usually look for details of how to respond. With radio or television, the situation is slightly different.

> **In the real world**
> In television advertising, the telephone number is all too often added as a quick afterthought to a campaign which is not designed primarily to generate a direct response. In such cases, the response is usually very low. The advertisement does not lead up to the telephone number, thus maximizing its impact. It is very visibly an afterthought and attracts little attention.

Here are a few rules for the use of telephone numbers in television advertising:

- The number should be clearly visible on the screen for at least five or six seconds.
- The number must be spoken too, as part of the call to action. Since people mostly watch television advertisements in the evening, it is vital for the number to be available when the advertisement is shown, and probably 24 hours. The call to action must stress 'now' and '24 hours'.
- The number must be highly visible. It must be at least one inch high and with a strong enough background colour to make it stand out (important if it is shown against anything other than a simple background).
- If the call is freephone, the advertisement should emphasize this.
- The commercial should explain what will happen when the respondent calls (e.g. they receive more information, enter a prize draw).

Of course, it goes without saying that the number should be a memorable one.

With radio, it can be even more difficult to ensure that the number is heard and then remembered. Many people have a stronger visual memory than an aural memory. The key here is repetition and grouping of numbers in a memorable way. For example, 0207-213-1415 could be promoted as 02-072-13-14-15, even though this does not correspond to the exchange code grouping.

▶ Automated response and premium rate use

You can now make revenue directly from the telephone. By using a premium rate number, you can ask consumers to call in and receive a promotional message. The call is charged at much higher than the normal rate and the advertiser receives a share of the call revenue. You should use this only where research shows that it will not prejudice your relationship with the customer. Many companies now have a block on their employees using these premium rate numbers (which often promote dubious services!).

▶ The Telephone Preference Service

This is the equivalent of the Mailing Preference Service. Sponsored by the Direct Marketing Association, it is a 'do not telephone' file of people who have requested no telephone contact without prior consent. This service will eventually improve the image of outbound telemarketing as unrestricted teleselling becomes harder.

▶ Summary

There is no doubt that telemarketing is one of the most powerful media you can use. With the costs of telephone time and systems and equipment in decline, and database software so much better, you can now confidently plan to 'telemanage your customers'.

As we emphasized at the beginning of this chapter, powerful though telemarketing is, it can't convey every message. Telemarketing works best in combination with other media. We've already looked at direct mail. Now let's look at some ways in which different media can be used to manage customers.

14 customer relationship management (CRM)

Managing the relationship in stages

Why CRM is important

A model of CRM

Summary

Customer relationship management (CRM)

As with many management fashions, relationship marketing, customer relationship marketing and customer relationship management are terms that many managers or marketers use but define in different ways. The set of ideas that we use to improve customer management has passed through different phases, including:

- customer relationship marketing, which included a strong focus on the customer;
- customer relationship management, which was supposed to remedy the alleged neglect of other functions' contribution to the management of customer relationships;
- enterprise relationship management, which adds the supply chain dimension;
- E-CRM, electronic customer relationship management, which adds the focus of e-business.

Despite these changes, the main focus of the activities described by these changing definitions has remained the same, namely *the use of a wide range of marketing, sales, communication, service and customer care approaches to:*

- identify a company's named individual customers;
- create a relationship between the company and its customers that stretches over many transactions; and
- manage that relationship to the benefit of the customers and the company.

However, this is a little lacking in feeling. In marketing, a good way to define a concept or technique is in terms of what we want our customers to think or feel as a result of us using it, one we could even explain to customers. So a company could describe relationship marketing to its customers as below.

CRM is how we:

- find you;
- get to know you;
- keep in touch with you;
- try to ensure that you get what you want from us in every aspect of our dealings with you;
- check that you are getting what we promised you

...subject of course to it being worthwhile to us as well.

In the late 1990s, CRM became a heady fashion among managers of marketing, service and information technology, and even among general managers. This was despite strong evidence that many consumers did not want to be managed in relationships, and that in industrial markets, many big buyers used their relationships with suppliers to extract maximum value while returning minimum value. We are therefore cautious about over-using the word relationship – we use it only where we feel that it is justified. Customers can be managed in many ways. CRM is just one way of doing it. In many situations, we prefer to use the term customer management (CM) because it does not imply a particular model of customer management.

14 / Customer relationship management (CRM)

▶ Managing the relationship in stages

In markets in which buyers and sellers do experience benefits from developing relationships, these are rarely simple relationships in which a customer is 100% loyal to one company or to another. Most relationships develop in stages, with customers sampling different products and often remaining 'switchers' or 'multi-sourcers' – buying from several companies. To help companies manage this situation, we have developed a simple model of relationship development. Many companies have used it to understand their customers better and to develop policies for improving the relationship. We summarize the relationship as a series of stages and then identify how many customers are at each stage and what takes them to the next stage. Here are the main stages along with some problems companies have in managing them.

Stage	Definition	Typical problems and opportunities
Targeting	When the customer is targeted as being an appropriate customer for the company, and induced to 'join'	Targeting is not precise enough. So, if the company tries to cross-sell to all its existing customers, irrespective of their suitability, cross-selling can be a loss-making activity. Very large numbers of customers are targeted, using a variety of approaches – direct mail, off the page, TV. This leads to overlapping coverage and wasted promotional budgets. At worst, if the activities of different product managers are not co-ordinated, the same person may be targeted in for several different products at the same time, with the same names being rented more than once.
Enquiry management	The customer is in the process of joining	Usually a very short stage, but critical. In many cases, failure to manage enquiries properly leads to many customers being lost before they join. In fact this stage is the main prospect-gathering stage. By capturing prospects in a database and maybe issuing information, you can convert this interest to sales by targeting these hot leads. Care should be taken to set customers' expectations for future treatment. They can often be dis-appointed and the relationship damaged before you start.
Welcoming	After the customer has joined, depending on the complexity of the product or service, it is important to ensure that the customer is 'securely on board', e.g. knows whom to contact if there are problems, knows how to use the product or service	This is also often a very short stage, yet it is clear from what happens when a customer has problems or makes a claim that they often do not know whom to call or what to do. For decisions involving significant outlays, customers may need to be reassured that they have made the correct decision, and given the opportunity to say whether they felt they could have been handled better during the buying cycle.

Getting to know	This is a crucial period, when both sides exchange information with each other. Additional customer needs may become apparent, and the customer's profile of use of the product or service becomes known. More is also learned about the customer's honesty, ability to pay, etc.	Many companies assume that this stage does not exist and that their customers go straight into a mature state of account management. Yet if we take the example of financial services, the early cancellation that applies to many types of insurance policy and loans indicates that this is clearly not so. We cannot expect that no customers will cancel early, but we can expect to be able, through data analysis, to identify customers most likely to and implement preventative action. Experience in insurance and banking shows that if we try, we will have some success. Analysis from other industries with long-term relationships with customers indicates that communications behaviour, brand attitudes and satisfaction with the category are good predictors of loyalty. Strong preferences can be formed quite early on in the relationship, e.g. if they respond to your communications, rate your brand highly and are satisfied with how you have arranged their portfolio of products or services, they will be more likely to stay with you.
Customer development	The relationship is now being managed securely, with additional needs being identified in time and met where feasible	This is the ideal state, though quite a few customers never reach it and often dip into the next stage or remain in the previous stage for a long time. This is best detected by short questionnaires which can be administered by mail, telephone or by sales staff.
Managing problems	The customer has such severe problems that special attention is needed to ensure that they return safely to account management. If this attention is not given, the customer is so dissatisfied that divorce is imminent. If the customer does leave, they will usually, after a cooling-off period, be ready for 'winback'	This stage is defined in terms of what the supplier should do, but of course the need for it is often missed and the customer goes straight into pre-divorce, e.g. after a mishandled service event or a change in the customer's need which remains undetected. If a company does not handle the initial problem well and the customer

14 / Customer relationship management (CRM)

✓			
			considers leaving, companies often fail to recognize that this is happening. Surprisingly, many companies give up here, and even pride themselves that they make it easy for customers to cancel. If the reason for cancellation or termination of the relationship was a change in circumstances or a move by the customer out of the category, brand loyalty may be intact, and in some cases enhanced, if the supplier made termination easy.
	Winback	Sometimes the relationship ended because of high price or the wrong product, so winback can be initiated when these issues are resolved. Winback is hardest if the customer left due to poor service, unless the competitors' service is even worse!	The targeting of winback campaigns is made difficult because many companies are poor at defining and identifying lost customers and because they have no reliable customer database.

We would like to see some recognition that:

1 customers don't simply move from being 'prospects' to 100% 'loyal customers' and then to 'lost customers';
2 stages of the relationship can be identified and managed; and
3 data can be used to manage this activity.

Why CRM is important

CRM is important because acquiring customers is usually much more expensive than keeping them. To put this into perspective, on average it costs five times more to recruit a new customer than it does to keep an existing one.

In direct marketing this can actually be quantified and in other marketing environments, estimates show the same. The benefits of CRM can be shown through accounting techniques that reveal:

◆ costs of acquiring customers;
◆ changes in the number of customers;
◆ changes in what each customer is buying.

The benefits of CRM are usually in one or more of these areas:

1 improved customer retention and loyalty – customers stay longer, buy more, more often, i.e. increased *long-term value*;
2 higher customer profitability, not just because each customer buys more but because of:
    ◆ lower costs of recruiting customers, and no need to recruit so many to maintain a steady volume of business;
    ◆ reduced cost of sales, as existing customers are usually more responsive.

However, acquiring the wrong customers and keeping them is often very damaging. Focusing on customer retention as a top business priority can be damaging if most customers are not profitable. In many industries, such as banking, general insurance and utilities, and also in many business-to-business situations, a high proportion of customers are unprofitable because the cost to serve them is much higher than the value derived from them. In such situations, customer management techniques can be used to reduce costs to serve and possibly even to get rid of unprofitable customers and concentrate on your profitable ones.

Customers usually want these things from companies:

◆ When I enquire about the product, give advice to me promptly and courteously and do the things that you say you will do when you say you will do them.
◆ Be timely and relevant in your contacts with me.
◆ Make it easy for me to contact you.
◆ Make it easy for me to buy the product I want at a competitive price. I want the product to be complete and working, and if the product is being delivered, for it to be delivered in specification, on time and in full.
◆ Use the data I give you properly and ethically and in ways that benefit me, and make sure you can access it when I am in contact with you.
◆ After the sale, don't pester me, but keep in touch if there is something to say. More importantly, if I have a problem or ask for support, please give it promptly and courteously. Trust me and live up to your promises.

Meeting these needs requires:

◆ good manufacturing/operations and distribution;
◆ properly recruited, trained and motivated staff;
◆ robust enquiry, welcoming, sales and complaints handling processes and measurement systems;
◆ good information technology, so that the company can recognize customers and provide relevant offers, information and advice.

If your proposition matches customers' needs and you are friendly and professional in the way you deal with customers at all stages, the benefits can be massive. If you align your customer management with customer needs, you will:

- hold on to customers longer;
- maintain or even improve profits from existing customers;
- improve your share of your customers' purchases;
- get more referred business – this is the most effective way to acquire new customers too.

A model of CRM

QCi, a specialist CRM consulting company, has developed a straightforward way of representing what doing CRM involves (see Fig. 14.1). Rather than describe CRM as a high-level concept, it describes it simply as a list of management activities, which put together result in customers being managed better. We describe it below.

Fig. 14.1 QCi's model of customer management

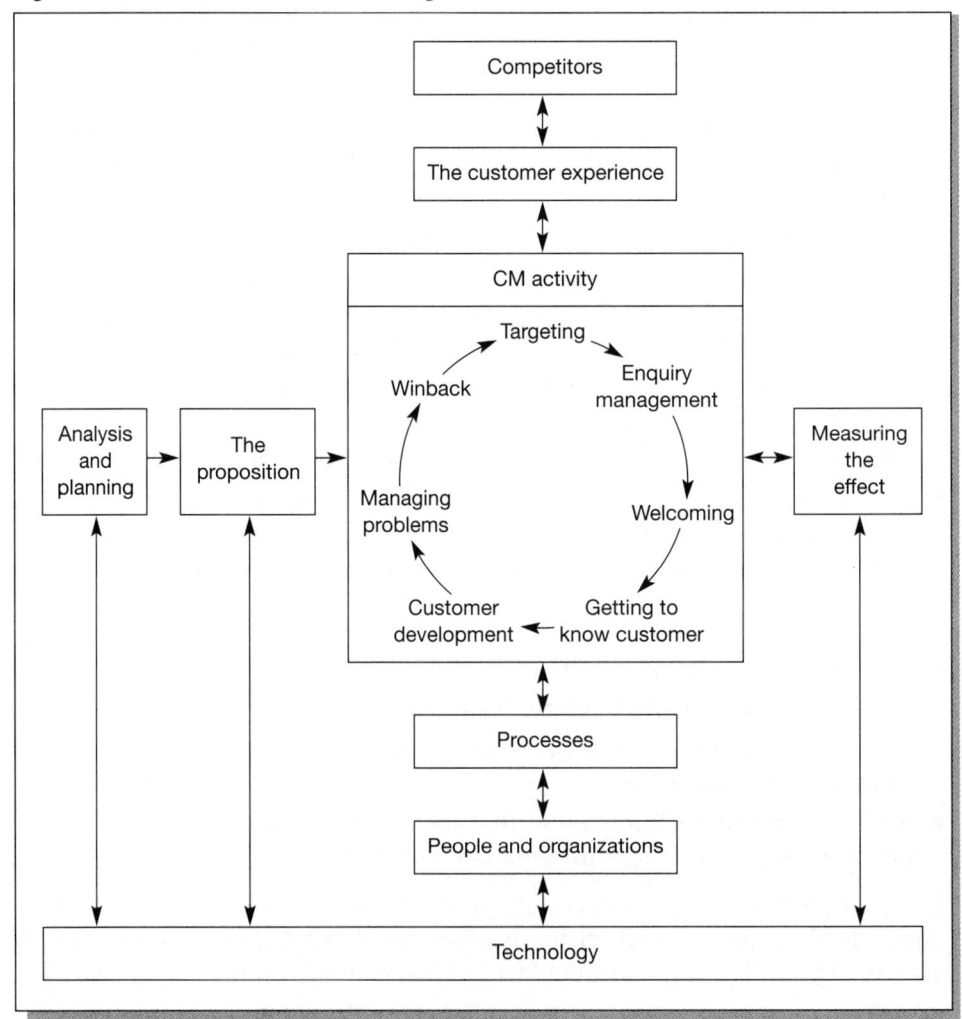

▶ Analysis and planning

Customer management starts with understanding the value, behaviour and attitudes of different customers and customer groups. Once these are understood, the company can plan cost-effective acquisition, retention and development of customers.

▶ The proposition

The understanding of customers derived from analysis and research will help the company identify groups or segments of customers who should be managed. The next step is to define the proposition to each of the segments and plan the appropriate value-based offers. This is done through focused 'needs' research, mapped against the values and behaviours discovered during analysis. The proposition is normally defined in terms of brand, price, service, transactional interactions, relationship, logistics, product. For each element of the proposition a service standard is defined in terms that can be measured. It must involve all functions within the operation that impact on the proposition and customer experience – it cannot successfully be developed by marketing and imposed on the organization. The proposition must then be communicated effectively to both customers and the people responsible for delivering it.

▶ Customer management activity

This is the delivery of customer management. Plans and objectives, based on the retention, acquisition, penetration and efficiency findings of the analysis, and the needs of the customer groups, lead to activity throughout the customer life-cycle from prospect, through new customer and on into mature customer. This involves day-to-day working practices of marketing, sales and service support functions in:

- targeting acquisition and retention activity;
- handling enquiries;
- support for new and upgrading customers;
- getting to know customers and how they want to be managed;
- account management (service, billing, technical support, field, third-party telephone);
- identifying and managing dissatisfaction;
- winning back lost customers.

▶ People and organization

People deliver the activity. Companies should identify and develop required competencies. Leaders should create and support customer management objectives, within an organizational structure that facilitates good customer management.

Clear, understandable customer management objectives should be linked to overall business goals and employee satisfaction. Suppliers should also support the organization with the skills not available internally.

▶ Measuring the effect

Companies should measure how people, processes, profitability, proposition delivery, channel performance and customer activity (e.g. campaigns) support achievement of the company vision and objectives. Identifying performance relative to plan allows a company to refine and redefine plans and activity.

▶ Understanding customers' experiences

CRM is about managing customers. So companies need to ask customers:

- How well are we doing?
- What can we improve?
- What do competitors do better than us?

... for each experience they have with us, especially the ones that they consider most important.

▶ Information and technology

Information and technology underpin the whole model. Information needs to be collected, stored and used in a way that supports the strategy, the way people work and the way customers want to access the organization. Technology needs to be used to enhance the way customers are managed (from analysis to data at point of contact) and enabled.

▶ Summary

In plain English, CRM could be described by a company to it's customers as how we:

- find you
- get to know you
- keep in touch with you
- give you what you want every time we deal with you
- check that you are getting what we promised you

CRM is about injecting the personal touch back into the way companies deal with customers. It means aligning systems, customer-facing staff, marketing communications and the complaints/customer care department must put the customer first.

It's critical for the success of companies to get CRM right, and promote growth by loyalty, advocacy and repeat sales.

electronic and broadcast media

Tess Moffett

Broadcast media

Interactive media developments

Interactive TV developments

Mobile marketing technology

Key success factors

E-mail marketing

New developments

Recently, direct marketing has been transformed by the rapid growth of new types of electronic and broadcast media. As well as tried and tested direct marketing techniques, such as direct mail, database and telemarketing, marketers are now embracing the capabilities of online advertising, e-mail, interactive TV and SMS (short messaging service) or text marketing to target consumers.

Today's consumers have more choices than ever before on where they gather information about products and decide what to buy, and then on how and where they make the purchase. Thus consumers can find out about new products via TV, radio, press and online advertising, can gather information and compare prices immediately online or on interactive TV, and then purchase online via the web or digital TV, or from a catalogue or contact centre or in a store. Marketers must learn how to use the most appropriate tools and techniques to influence the consumer.

▶ Broadcast media

Broadcast media such as radio and television have traditionally been used to raise awareness among consumers of new products and services. However, the way they are being used is undergoing significant change. The growth of cable and satellite television means that subscribers have a wide choice of channels and can opt for specific interests, such as sport, cookery, science and history. For the marketer, this provides a new opportunity. In the UK, they can now raise awareness of new products and services through around 7 million Sky digital homes in addition to terrestrial TV homes. Tailoring audiences is also easier. Niche audiences can be targeted more closely by advertising on specialist channels, e.g. insurance companies targeting women would choose Living TV. Furthermore, by including web site addresses in the advertisement, consumers can be directed to additional information on the products or brands featured. They can register for newsletters or for coupons, or can purchase the product straight after they see the advertisement.

In the UK, television viewers are also familiar with Teletext services that are integrated with their TV set. Despite the firm presence of the Internet, this service is still popular, being accessible to almost all homes and very simple to use. Travel and financial services companies continue to advertise heavily on Teletext, with offers which can be followed up on mainly by calling the featured telephone number, and increasingly by accessing the company's web site. Teletext is now available online, incorporating the tried and tested formula but with enhanced content.

▶ Interactive media developments

When companies began to include interactive media in their marketing mix, they started by creating product web sites, which they tended to use in the same way as offline press advertising, i.e. for publishing information. However, this relied upon users knowing the address, or URL, of the web site in order to find the information they were looking for. Marketers therefore started positioning advertising for their site at the top of other popular web sites. These included search engines such as Yahoo.com, where users could click straight through to the site in question. This is known as banner advertising and is one of the most widely used types of advertising on the Internet.

A major advantage of banner advertising (and other online ad formats) is that the marketer can track exactly how many users have clicked through from the banner ad to the web site. These can be related back to timescales and therefore campaign measurement is possible. 'Click-through rates' can be tracked for placing the same advertising on different sites, so you can monitor banner ad performance when targeting different audiences with tailored messages, according to the site the advertisement was placed.

In the real world

Care should be taken to monitor not only the number of click-throughs (or the 'hit rate') but also the resulting sales. There is little point in looking at purely the number of impressions alone, as without the conversion rate it will give you only half of the campaign performance.

▶ Online advertising formats

There are several advertising dimensions available on web sites defined in Pixels which denotes the size:

- the banner ad: this usually measures 468 wide × 60 high pixels and appears at the top of a web site;
- the small skyscraper: this usually measures 120 wide × 240 high pixels and appears as a side panel in the web site;
- the skyscraper: this usually measures 120 wide × 600 high pixels and also appears as a side panel in the web site;
- the large rectangle: this usually measures 360 wide × 300 high pixels and appears in the centre of the web site.
- the button ad: typically 200 × 200 pixels and appears as a pop-up advert in a web site. This is a more intrusive form of advertising so is becoming less effective as popularity grows.

But which online advertising format brings the best results? As with press advertising, larger ads are more effective, but there is obviously a trade-off to be made between the increased revenue and the additional costs of creating and placing a larger ad online. There may be diminishing returns.

▶ Online advertising technology

In addition to the size of the advertisement, marketers can choose whether they use images, with GIF or JPEG files, or newer technology that enables a richer quality of content such as Flash and Shockwave. Audio and video also help to enhance and enrich the experience and help advertising to stand out. There is a trade-off between the cost of using more sophisticated technology and the expected benefits, but as users become more accustomed to rich media in web sites, their expectations from advertisers are also increasing.

▶ Positioning the online ad

There are three main options to consider when deciding where to position advertising on the web site:

- on the page, as part of another web site;
- as a pop-up ad, which appears on top of another web site page;
- as an interstitial, which appears as the user moves from page to page.

▶ Creating content for the online ad

It is important for marketers to recognize the capabilities of the online environment and to design the content of advertising accordingly. For example, banner ads with complex messages, pictures and fast animations can often be considered too busy. This is particularly the case if the brand is relatively unknown – the user may be deterred from clicking through to the web site. Users also need to be guided to where they should click to receive more information. Many banners have no 'click here' instruction, leaving users confused as to the purpose of the advertising.

▶ Maintaining brand values online

Good online advertising also exploits a company's offline brand values and translates them online so that the banner is immediately recognisable. You need a good fit between a company's characteristics and how it is portrayed both online and offline. Beware of succumbing to the enhanced graphics capabilities of the web just because they are available. For example, a conservative insurance company with brand values of trust, reliability and tradition would risk damaging its offline brand if in its online advertising it used graphics, colours and animations that were considered too bold and modern and could offend its existing customer base. Focus on your chosen brand tone and voice and maintain it throughout your whole marketing mix. E-marketing is merely an extension of your classic and more traditional channels.

▶ Web site selection considerations

Marketers should research the web sites on which they would like to advertise, not only to ensure that they target the appropriate user but also to ensure that the site has a good balance between content and advertising. Footfall is also a key consideration. The more traffic to the site, the more users will be exposed to your message. It's possible to negotiate marketing costs based on click-throughs, i.e. not on a fixed marketing cost, thereby focusing the owners of the medium on helping you improve response rather than just creating presence.

Interactive TV developments

Interactive television enables digital TV viewers to become involved in their viewing. It's more than just TV. Involvement takes many forms, but the main features include:

- access to the Internet;
- use of real-time shopping services;
- interactive guides to television programmes;
- online betting;
- game playing;
- choice of camera angles to view programmes (especially sports);
- additional information about products and services;
- online voting for views on different issues.

Benefits of interactive TV

Interactive TV provides consumers with additional choice. It gives them options to personalize what they watch and the opportunity to give feedback, and so puts them in control. It also enables consumers to react immediately to something they have seen. So if they see a product that they like, they can undertake further research and buy the product without leaving their armchair. Unlike using a PC to access the Internet, consumers are used to watching TV and using remote controls, so the inconvenience is minimized and fear of technology is reduced.

Marketing opportunities enabled by interactive TV

Major brands have already been experimenting with interactive TV, particularly the consumer products and services sector, where impulse purchases or additional information are key to the success of the product. Shopping channels on digital TV use interactive TV as an extension to their product sales process, so the viewer presses the red button for more information on the product. The key to interactive TV is to exploit customers' desire for information with the physical action of a response to advertising they have seen.

In the real world

Procter & Gamble's Pantene questionnaire on NTL digital TV led through to a micro-site, and its Pampers campaign on Sky digital led the viewer through to information tailored to the child's age group. Users provided information about themselves, enabling them to access additional content. This helped advertisers to improve their targeting and measure the effectiveness of their marketing more accurately. As interactive TV enables immediate response to advertising, the success of campaigns can also be gauged more quickly.

Interactive TV has been more successful in the UK than in other parts of Europe because of the consolidated nature of the broadcasting industry.

Although the medium is not as mature as the Internet and therefore not yet as widely used in the marketing mix, in the longer term it will provide additional ways to reach out to the consumer with compelling, personalized offers. Already we are seeing impressive results. Sky digital, the main UK interactive TV broadcaster, reports that in 2002:

- 76% of its game players play games for longer than ten minutes;
- over 180 000 betting accounts have been opened via the TV prompting repeat bets;
- 372 000 mobile phone products have been downloaded since May 2002;
- 17 million people are registered e-mail users through the TV set;
- over 2.4 million votes have been cast on Sky News Active.

Case studies to demonstrate some interactive advertising campaigns and their results include Panadol ActiFast, Butlins holidays and Rimmel cosmetics.

Fig. 15.1 Interactive TV promotion for Panadol

▶ Panadol ActiFast case study

Figure 15.1 shows some of the screens used in this campaign. Its results were:

- 0.2% response rate in female 25–44 target audience;
- high spontaneous recall of brand;
- 68% of those interacting agreed that the advert was better than that of competing products;
- strap-line spontaneously mentioned by 34% of interactive users, compared with just 10% of the control group;
- 68% of those interacting stated that Panadol would be their future purchase preference for pain relief, compared with the control group's 38%.

Fig. 15.2 Interactive TV promotion for Butlins

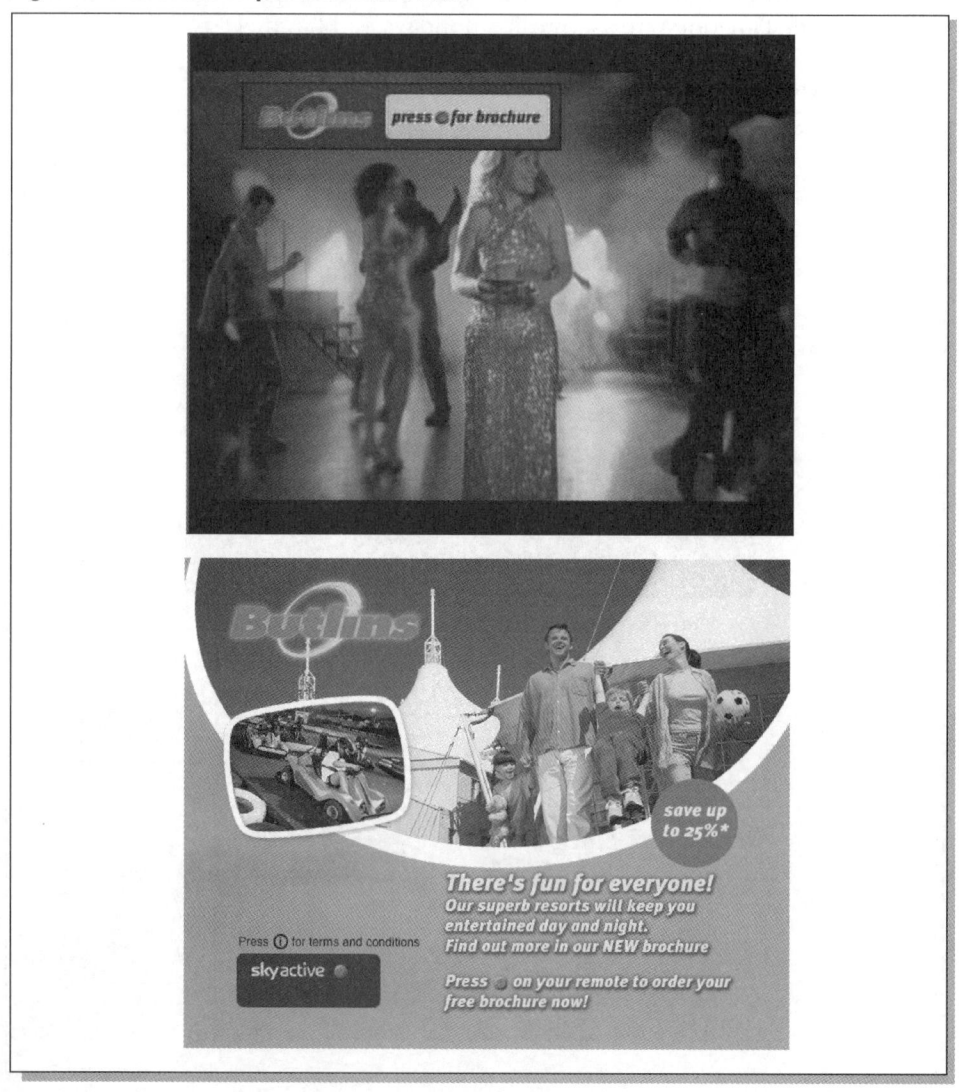

Interactive TV developments

▶ Butlins case study

Figure 15.2 shows some of the screens used in this campaign. Its results were:

- simple, cost-effective interactive site;
- over 10 000 brochure requests;
- 37% of cost per response of TV/phone including creative;
- interactive TV response channel added to advertising throughout year.

▶ Rimmel case study

Figure 15.3 shows the screens for this campaign. Here the brief was to:

- raise awareness among women aged 16–44;
- attract new users;
- distribute over 50 000 lipsticks.

The solution:

- Extend traditional TV campaign with one-scene 'Mini DAL'.
- Accessed via interactive ads and Sky Active banners.

Fig. 15.3 Interactive TV promotion for Rimmel

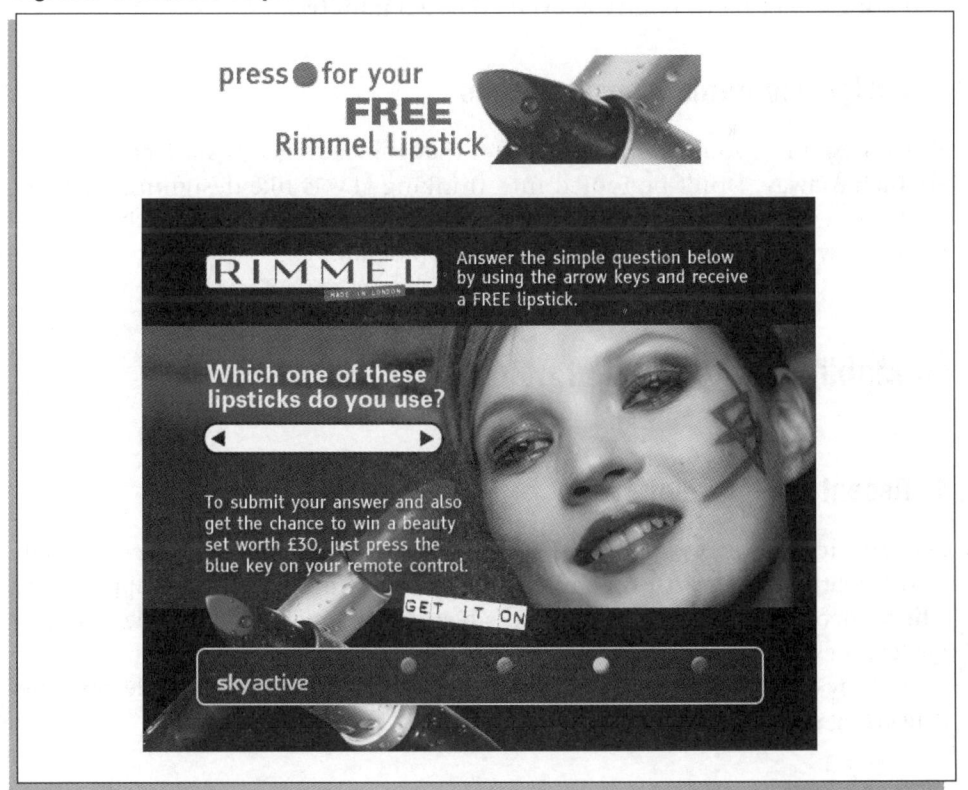

Key campaign results:

- response rate of over 3.2%;
- over 52 000 samples sent out;
- names and addresses retained by Rimmel as future marketing database.

▶ Measurement and accountability

The following key performance indicators and measurement tools are used to assess the success of an interactive TV campaign:

- Online respondents – who are they? Details can be captured from a set-top box and profiled to obtain geo-demographic information.
- Names and addresses of those who opt.
- Data files (XML or Excel) passed to fulfilment house.

Reporting includes:

- access point – channel or banner;
- time of interaction;
- time spent interacting.

Reporting can be daily, hourly or even every ten minutes.

▶ Design and format considerations

When designing your interface consider that the audience is six feet away, not six inches away. Don't be fooled into thinking iTV is like designing for a PC. Consider what you can realistically achieve in a two-three minute break. The customer will want to resume watching their programme.

▶ Mobile marketing technology

▶ Recent SMS developments

Pervasive technology is gradually becoming part of the marketing mix, especially in the youth market, with the rapid update of short message service applications which enable companies to deliver an advertising element to a mobile customer via text message.

SMS messaging is being used widely for marketing. Uses include revenue-generating services such as:

- up-to-the-minute results during major sporting events;
- casting votes, especially during reality TV shows such as *Big Brother*;
- daily horoscopes;
- weather reports;
- local cinema guides.

Many companies are using this technology to offer free prompts for things such as sport news and entertainment gossip. This allows them to ask consumers to sign up for a service and then ties their brand in with the medium. For example, Carlsberg used the World Cup to engage subscribers to its free service and got World Cup recognition immediately.

With the introduction of handsets with additional functionality, such as media phones with high-speed access, mobile phone companies are launching new multimedia services enabling users to download games, images information services and ring-tones. Although these presents new opportunities to marketers, success will depend largely on the uptake of next-generation mobile phones. It will also depend on whether users continue to upgrade their phone as technology moves on.

▶ Benefits of SMS marketing

By its very nature SMS (or text) mobile marketing is:

- **immediate**. It gains a rapid response, which allows brand managers and direct marketers to know quickly how successful their campaign has been. It also lends a certain urgency to the message as it is such a personal and responsive medium;
- **personal**. This message gets right through to the target customer's handset. This means it is important to get buy-in from the consumer. However, once consumers have agreed to receive text promotions, they are likely to react quickly. The medium also lends itself to viral campaigns. Messages will often be received when the consumer is in a group, prompting them to talk about the message instantly. Messages are easy to forward;
- **cost-effective to deliver.** The technology used to deliver these messages is straightforward and the situations surrounding a campaign are generally controllable. You rarely have to reschedule a text campaign in the same way that a TV campaign might need to be (e.g. because of a change in programming).

With well-designed campaigns it can be highly engaging and effective, but for this it must be:

- fun and familiar (billions of text messages are sent daily);
- interactive (the opportunity for two-way dialogue is there);
- viral (people forward messages).

Key success factors

Don't underestimate:

- the impact of **timely** campaigns (e.g. Night Fly Pub World Cup Campaigns – 123% return on investment);
- the impact of the **location** variable;
- the potential for **conversational** campaigns;
- the potential for **multiple message** campaigns;
- the **viral** nature of the medium;
- the importance of high-quality **opt-in** from customers;
- the importance of simple **opt-out clauses and clear communication** of the promoter's name.

In the real world

Too much SMS mobile marketing can result in SMS going the same way as Internet banner advertising. So take care not to bombard people, overpromise or underdeliver.

Risks

Like any marketing channel it is important to consider the medium, message and the person you're targeting. Try to avoid:

- fake or very limited offers, or prizes nobody wants – these will not impress;
- campaigns aimed at closed user groups – these can be difficult to target and manage and can be difficult to integrate with other media;
- poor privacy practice – this may lead to heavy regulation; legislation is already under way for controlling SMS spamming (bombarding people with unwelcome messages).

Note too that:

- rate cards are not well established, so try to focus on proven market responses and on the cost per response;
- some companies are using randomly generated mobile numbers to bombard customers. Regulators are monitoring these and are likely to fine guilty parties;
- industry associations are publishing codes of practice to restrict spamming and safeguard user privacy.

Measurement and accountability

The main measures in SMS marketing are:

- messages sent;
- messages delivered;

- response rates (who responded to the call to action?);
- conversion rates (who then went on to purchase?);
- recall (did people remember receiving the SMS?);
- appeal (the propensity to recommend or forward the service to others);
- brand impact (impact on the opinion of the brand).

▶ The state of SMS as a medium

While this channel is still quite immature, the following results have been observed from SMS marketing campaigns in 2002:

- SMS marketing messages have proven most effective as part of an integrated CRM campaign from a mobile network provider.
- From the same provider, SMS marketing has accounted for nearly four times the number of messages sent to customers than e-mail marketing, due to its direct nature and linked medium.
- Multiple-message campaigns are particularly effective.
- Lower impact was achieved for single-message campaigns.
- The more interaction during the message, the better the result.
- 10–20% of respondents provided comments, service suggestions or conversational messages – managing this data should be considered before the campaign commences.
- Well-executed SMS has a positive effect on the brand if your brand is right for an SMS campaign. Campaigns that work best are those with a high youth content and which have a strong tie to a particular interest, such as sport or entertainment.
- Nearly half of recipients said they would follow up their message, e.g. by viewing the ad, visiting the web site or calling back.

▶ E-mail marketing

E-mail marketing is a cost-effective way of reaching consumers with targeted messages. It can be used to build awareness of new products and services, inform consumers via newsletters, and cross and up-sell by providing special offers and promotions. Indeed, after a customer has purchased a product from a web site, they expect to receive information confirming their purchase and shipping via e-mail, and increasingly use e-mail for customer service queries.

Permission-based e-mail can be very effective, and marketers can either build their own lists as consumers opt in to receive information, or buy in lists from third parties. E-mail campaigns and response rates can also be measured and tracked effectively. However, consumers tend to have a negative perception of unsolicited e-mails, so take care to ensure relevancy.

Some Internet service providers provide bulk e-mail functionality to prevent companies bombarding consumers with this type of e-mail, or spam. Bulk e-mails are sent to a separate file in the user's in-box from e-mails sent by individuals and as such are often left unopened or can be blocked from a user's in-box completely. It is therefore important for the consumer to be able to recognize the e-mail sender's identity in the header and be reassured that the e-mail is from a company with which they have a relationship, so that they are happy to open the e-mail and read its contents. Even with permission-based e-mail, consumers can react negatively if they receive e-mails too frequently. Marketers should therefore gauge consumer feedback on the appropriate frequency with which they should send e-mails.

As with traditional mail-based direct marketing, e-mail marketing depends on the accuracy of the contact details in the list, and when consumers change job or Internet service provider, their e-mail addresses invariably change as a result. It is therefore important that consumers are actively encouraged (through online forms, for example) to keep companies updated when they change their contact details.

▶ E-mail marketing requires tough data management

Effective e-mail marketing is as much about data as it is about transmission and good creative. Managing the data complexities of today's sophisticated direct mail programmes can be complicated enough, but when cycle times are reduced to hours rather than days or weeks, these challenges are intensified.

▶ Costs of e-mail marketing

E-mail has a clear edge over direct mail both in terms of cost and response rates, so it has an immediate appeal to marketers. Traditional direct mail costs between 40p and £1 per item. This compares with a cost of between 1p and 5p per item for e-mail. Response rates are better too, with direct e-mail campaigns to permission-based audiences typically generating between three and ten times more responses than traditional direct mail.

In the US, e-mail marketing has been gaining so much in popularity that some analysts are suggesting there has been a significant drop in the level of direct mail as a result. In the UK, e-mail marketing is still relatively new but growing rapidly, partly due to the cost-conscious environment. However, companies which are trying it out are often finding they have severe technical and data challenges to overcome before they can really make a success of it.

▶ Systems requirements

Given the ease with which we all now send and receive e-mails, it is understandable why many companies assume they can embark on an e-mail marketing programme using their existing IT infrastructure. But sending out bulk e-mail campaigns, and handling and tracking responses effectively, is a very different matter to managing low-level e-mail traffic between individuals.

Primarily, you need to have the ability to send out high-volume batches of e-mails and track how many people opened the message and which links they clicked on. This detailed level of tracking can help predict likely volume of inbound responses and provides multiple opportunities to refine the campaign creative and get better results. You can even use different kinds of creative treatment for the same link in the same e-mail and test which one was more effective by tracking which one more people clicked on. Users of the most advanced software that integrates web and telephony can see a solution when customers are having problems contacting them via the web and need to move to the telephone. 'Call-me-back' functions are becoming popular on some web sites, particularly in the travel industry, and these can be incorporated easily into outbound e-mail campaigns.

Once the responses start coming in, you need to be able to send a reply to the customer straight away and then route the message through to the relevant sales/marketing/service departments for action. It's going to be important to be able to close the loop and meet the customer's expectations about the time frame in which you get back to them. You also need to make sure you can negotiate the preference management and data protection minefield without any false steps, especially in the light of new EU directives heralding stricter legislation on commercial e-mail.

▶ You need to respond too!

Companies' failure to respond to e-mails can have a very negative effect on customer attitudes to the company and their propensity to buy. To give an example of how things can go wrong: in a typical e-mail campaign, up to 2% of people will hit the reply button and respond directly to the e-mail (rather than doing what you expect them to do and clicking on the links or response mechanisms you have directed them to in the e-mail). This means that in a mailing to 100 000 there may be 2000 ad-hoc replies to handle over a very short period of time. People expect e-mail to be an immediate channel, so a delayed response or no response at all is unacceptable and will do serious damage to the brand. An automated response as a holding device is ok, as long as the customer understands when someone will get back to them with a proper response and as long as the company delivers on the promise. Ideally, they would get a personalized response that takes account of any previous dealings with the company (in the case of existing customers) and provides a relevant answer to any queries. All of this is entirely possible, but it takes a sophisticated e-mail data management system with infrastructures optimized to handle high volumes. Many companies are just not geared up for this at the moment.

It has taken around 20 years for most companies to get to grips with mail and telephone. Even the most advanced practitioners readily admit that they still experience problems that have their origin in data. Deduplication may no longer be as difficult as it was, but in sectors experiencing rapid changes to their customer base (usually because of mergers and acquisitions, or because of frequent entry into new products and/or new markets), problems still abound. In the e-world, matching and deduplication is made harder by the use of multiple addresses, possibly unconnected to a physical name and address. However, these problems can be resolved by applying simple database marketing techniques – the development of a clear data strategy and good quality standards applying to particular fields (from names and e-mail addresses to interests and media preferences). Certainly companies that ask their customers to state e-mail preferences (frequency of contact, subject matter, etc.) are getting good results. However, many of us have been on the receiving end of less responsible practitioners. Ask anyone who has not logged onto their (usually several) web-based e-mail addresses for a week or two how many unsolicited e-mails they have received (often from far-off countries, offering weird and wonderful products and services). Some ISPs seem to be better than others at shielding their customers from this kind of abuse, but in the interests of privacy alone, serious tightening up in this area would be well advised.

The rapid turnaround of an e-mail campaign puts the spotlight on database management capability. Even today, it can still take between one and three months for some companies to get a traditional direct mail campaign out of the door, and some marketing databases are still updated only on a weekly or even monthly basis. This is way too slow in the online world. The power of e-mail is that it is theoretically possible to get feedback on a campaign instantly, and refine the message and the creative treatment in a matter of hours. Subsequent waves may be going out the next day or the next week, so it is important to close the loop on unsubscribe/opt-out requests before the next one goes out.

▶ Internal problems and the outsourcing option

In-house marketers are keen to exploit this new channel, but internal IT departments can be slow to respond and many of today's e-mail programs are not sophisticated enough to meet the needs and preferences of the rapidly evolving online customer. As a result, e-mail campaigns often do not even have classic direct mail disciplines applied to them. Sometimes this is because it is almost too easy to send out an e-mail campaign, so multiple departments, or regional offices within an organization, may be sending out e-mails with little central control over branding and contact strategy. As this is all still fairly new, few companies have few rules and processes covering how both outbound and inbound e-mail should be handled, and even fewer have a data strategy in place to handle the additional data generated. In many cases, existing marketing databases are not set up to even hold e-mail addresses and while they might hold opt-in/opt-out data for customers, are unable to differentiate by channel, i.e. offer the customer the option to be contacted by e-mail but not by mail or phone.

Some of the other issues that need to be addressed are:

◆ being able to manage bounces (from incorrect addresses) effectively (by using the information to clean the database);
◆ being able to send out multi-part e-mails (combining HTML with plain text so that the recipient's browser can display the message appropriately);
◆ including an automated and customer-friendly unsubscribe option which you are able to act on quickly.

Given the complexities, outsourcing is an option well worth considering, particularly at the outset. The cost to an individual company of setting up the kind of infrastructure required may be prohibitive and there are a number of specialist suppliers that offer competitive rates for an outsourced service. As this is a relatively new medium, companies would be well advised to draw on external expertise to get their e-mail program off the ground and gain a better understanding of what's involved.

A number of e-mail marketing suppliers can deliver sophisticated personalization. They will also have an existing large-scale technical infrastructure optimized for e-mail (which would probably take a minimum of three months, at considerable cost, to set up in house). Where this kind of expertise can be coupled with traditional skills in direct mail campaign planning and data management, you have the ideal combination. Once equipped, you can send high volumes of e-mails, with multiple waves/segments and track responses at a very detailed level. The technology available will even allow you to send messages in multiple character sets for regional or global campaigns.

E-mail data management issues are more complex than with classic direct mail. The database needs to manage individual customer-based opt-ins and stated preference codes in real time. These opt-in/outs and preferences can change much more frequently than in the offline world.

▶ Who chooses what is sent – the customer or you?

A key question is whether to put the customer in control of their preference management, i.e. provide an online facility where they can review and edit their personal details and contact preferences. As maintaining preferences online means that customers will be able to view some or all of their data, customers will be more aware of the quality of data held about them. With the flexibility of the medium, it is worthwhile considering making preference choices more granular, i.e. not just asking customers to opt in or opt out but consulting them about what kinds of products, services or content they are interested in receiving information on, how often they would like to be contacted, etc.

This approach is not without its pitfalls, however. If individuals transact through different sites or divisions belonging to the same company, it will be evident to them if data about them is not co-ordinated across different access routes and channels, so a single view of customer preferences across brands and channels becomes even more important. Customers may keep their preferences under review, switching them on and off for different purposes, so there is increased complexity in terms of managing the opt-in/opt-out data. The reason it is worth taking on these challenges, however, is that online preference management has the potential to improve targeting and minimize blanket opt-outs. As customers can choose the kinds of products or content areas they are interested in and even how often they want to be contacted, they feel in control and consequently more receptive to receiving further e-mail communications.

Companies not moving up the e-mail learning curve fast enough and offering more sophisticated preference options will find that more and more recipients just opt out completely. We have already seen this in the US where companies inundated consumer in-boxes with little differentiation or preference management. The result is a significant drop in response, and many users have cancelled their registration for e-mail lists. Over-use not only leads to diminishing returns but also damages the brand.

Personalization is also essential for minimizing opt-outs. Here again some of the specialist providers can help you get this right from the outset. You set up the business rules and the software will personalize the e-mail message content for each customer based on their preferences, interests and segment or profile. Message content, including images, paragraphs, words and links, can be assembled based on stored data such as customer age group, past purchase history and even data returned at run time from external applications such as credit status. In principle this is not difficult to achieve – the technology certainly exists – but it may be problematic for internal marketing departments to co-ordinate their agency, data bureaux and internal systems providers to bring together the various sources of data to be able to make it happen.

With the uptake of broadband services gathering pace, it is likely that richer media will increasingly become the norm. This adds further complexity but is an excellent opportunity to maintain high response levels and opt-in rates, particularly if you have a technology-literate or younger customer base. In order to be able to deliver and track audio and video elements in e-mails, you need an even more powerful infrastructure and it is probably not going to be cost effective for an individual company to make the kind of investment required unless it is core to their business. With access to the right technology, however, you can achieve high levels of rich media personalization even when accessed by large numbers at peak click-through times, and can track consumers' interaction with these rich media components whether they are sent as attachments in the e-mail or as links.

The fact is, though, that whether through improved systems integration, content personalization, data management or rich media micro-sites, personalization is essential to protect the medium for the company and for marketers in general. If every message is relevant and different, if the consumer receives only messages that they are interested in, or special offers just for them, they will open the message and read on. If these offers are exclusive to the medium, e.g. special rates or fares not available over other channels, opt-out rates are typically very low.

Most customers will respond positively to receiving e-mails if they are asked permission and feel favourably about the brand. In fact, consumers are generally enthusiastic about the medium as a convenient way to exchange information with the companies they deal with, but this enthusiasm may be short-lived. This is an opportunity to redress some of the excesses of direct mail that have alienated many customers. E-mail can easily be abused, but if used only with permission, and if the technology and data are managed effectively to create timely, relevant communications, most consumers will welcome it and response rates will remain high.

▶ E-mail conclusions

So for most companies, some form of external support is required. External suppliers take many forms, however, and it is important to choose the ones that can provide the right kind of service. Among the contenders are the creative agencies, but a good creative solution will fail if the agency doesn't have sufficient technical experience in this area. Then there are the new media agencies which understand the technology but may not be skilled enough in direct marketing and data management to carry out effective end-to-end campaigns. They will also typically operate in isolation and will not connect the e-mail activities with other customer contact channels.

The conclusion: in this brave new world, direct marketers should not miss this opportunity for precision targeting and personalized communication with customers. However, traditional direct marketing disciplines must be applied to e-mail marketing programmes and one shouldn't underestimate the complexity of some of the data management and technology issues involved. In the short term at least, using an external supplier can help meet the challenge and get the best results from the medium. To enhance rather than damage the brand, you need the process and the technology to handle responses efficiently and see them through to fulfilment.

▶ New developments

In recent years, other interactive media have emerged, including self-service applications using kiosks, as used by the major airlines including British Airways. These self-check-in facilities through its kiosks enable travellers to check in without needing to wait in a queue. E-ticketing, which is the order of tickets over the Internet, is also used widely and allows travellers to book travel by e-mail and turn up at check-in without the need for paper tickets, just ID. Kiosks are being used for a variety of marketing applications, and this is expected to increase still further. Boots the Chemist for example uses in-store kiosks to provide product offers, information and loyalty point statements to its Advantage Card loyalty scheme members.

Wireless marketing to mobile is also becoming more widespread. It uses the principle that response and conversion rates increase if people are ready to buy, especially if they are **where** they can buy. With wireless marketing, you can make offers that are relevant in time and space. You can prompt impulse purchases and achieve instant fulfilment. Consumers can receive and use discounts for shopping in certain stores. The person receiving a message with a discount attached can pop into the nearest branch of the retailer and show their mobile phone screen to redeem their money off.

The mobile is becoming a means of payment. Customers can carry out transactions by exchanging messages. Suppliers can tell customers about what's in store or in the catalogue and what stock is available. Just as they can purchase over the

Internet by registering payment details and address with certain online retailers, customers can now buy through their mobile phone. This works best with small-value goods such as books, DVDs or CDs. SMS marketing combined with the ability to purchase through the handset is a powerful sales and marketing tool, as it provides spontaneity.

Small-value transactions are being tested in charity donation campaigns, e.g. in combined SMS and DRTV campaigns, involving an SMS message sent to mobile phones with the option to 'press SEND to donate £4 now'. In horse racing, betting companies send SMS messages to mobile phones a few hours before the race to encourage last-minute bets. This approach will prompt an explosion in small-value bets due to its accessibility to consumers. This approach is also being applied to all other areas of betting, e.g. on hit songs reaching the top of the chart, on which team or individual will score next in a football match.

> **Checklist: e- and broadcast media**
> - Do you know which channels, TV/ radio programmes and web sites your target customers are most likely to use?
> - Do you know what your brand values are and have you translated them correctly online?
> - Is your online advertising easy for your consumers to understand, with simple, compelling messages?
> - Do you track your click-through rates and e-mail response rates to gauge the effectiveness of your campaigns against cost?
> - Do you know how frequently your customers like to be contacted?
> - Are you keeping informed on the latest interactive marketing developments relevant for your organization?

Summary

- Look and Feel – new media channels offer truly integrated marketing opportunities, but should be treated as an extension of your core marketing plans with the same brand identity and core values.
- Clear and Simple – internet IDTV sites should be user friendly and easy to navigate. So make your home page clear and remember the importance of traditional direct marketing values:
- Clear call to action
- Strong benefit led copy
- Product selling product
- Sympathy and Empathy – text and e-mail messaging are highly personal and therefore intrusive media. Use with care and consider the person you're targeting.
- Measurement and Improvement – identify what campaigns work by making them measurable.
- Remember – new media marketing is the same as traditional below the line marketing, just new and delivered in a different way – on screen rather than on page.

16 lots more ways to contact customers

Targeting – always the key factor

Press

Inserts

Tip-ons

Leaflet distribution and free newspapers

Coupons

Designing press or managing response advertising

Television

Shopping channels

Catalogues – offline and online

Exhibitions

Sales seminars and other company-sponsored special events

The range of media you can use to contact the customer is evolving constantly. Your most successful campaigns will combine different media to deliver those elements of the message that are most suited for each medium and for which each medium is the most cost effective.

The media you can use in direct marketing are:

- broadcast media – television (including Teletext) in all its distribution modes – terrestial, satellite and cable, interactive TV – radio, fax, cinema;
- publications – newspapers, magazines, journals, owned media such as newsletters, customer newsletters you issue yourself or issued by other companies but open to your use, e.g. newsletters for credit card holders or airline customers;
- distributed media – door-to-door leaflets, catalogues, free newspapers, within customer communications, invoices, bills to your own customer database and to other third party's customers;
- display media – exhibitions, posters, outdoor bill board advertising, point-of sale advertising;
- personal media – sales offices and sales forces;
- new media – Internet ads, viral e-mail marketing, SMS and MMS text messaging, interactive TV.

In the real world

You can combine these media too. At an exhibition, posters will be on display and your sales staff will be in attendance. These media can also be combined into a sequence of contacts (the **contact strategy**) in an **integrated media** campaign (see Chapter 22).

▶ Targeting – always the key factor

Whatever media you choose, targeting is key. The closer the fit of the target market to your customer base, the higher the likely response to further campaigns. By profiling your existing customer base to understand it, and by finding your best customers, you can find more prospects of the same type, with the same attributes. Once you have this information you can make an informed choice about two things:

- who they are;
- where they are.

▶ Who they are

This refers to whether they are male, female, old or young, their social or geo-demographic class, their life stage, leisure activities, interests, hobbies, values, priorities and so on. Much of this information can be collected from simply asking your customers, but if you can't contact them directly or a questionnaire isn't appropriate, suppliers of customer data and modelling tools can help you.

▶ Where they are

Once you have built up a pen portrait of your customers – and this is very useful to do – you can use the same techniques to map out other areas – postcodes or even regions – with the same characteristics. While analysing your present customers, you may also discover certain common aspects, such as 70% may be readers of a mid-market daily newspaper, 60% may listen to early morning radio while in the car, 80% may have children aged between 0–10. These attributes will determine your targeting strategy. It will tell you how to reach your target customers, through which media, at what time of day. It may even help you to determine your message, as you will understand them and what makes them tick better.

Some media can be personally addressed or distributed so that they are restricted to particular types of customers. A catalogue can be sent to named customers, distributed house to house to areas of known average characteristics, as well as being given to anyone who wishes to take one. A magazine may have a subscription list of people with known characteristics (because of the details included on the subscription application), but it may also be available through retailers. Broadcast media are also more targeted than ever. You can reach private subscription groups (closed user groups) and different types of people by advertising at different times of the day and alongside different programming. Exhibition attendees can be invited individually and their attendance logged on your database, so you can see how effective the exhibition has been in generating sales. So don't lose any opportunity to target individuals and record results on your database. And use this information to determine your next target strategy.

Most media – often working in conjunction with independent commercial agencies – have developed audience or readership membership systems, enabling marketers to get a much more precise measurement of the audience they are reaching. This has been reinforced by the rising cost of media advertising and the need for more controlled, measurable and accountable budget spend.

Many companies regularly compare the pulling power of all media. This does not imply that the different media are always in competition. The best direct marketing campaigns usually combine different media. Each medium is asked to do a specific job. In some cases, the campaign is sequenced by medium, with the first contact being by, say, published media and followed up by direct mail or telemarketing. In other cases, different media will be used to generate the first response. This is because different kinds of consumer respond better to different kinds of media. Some are more mail-responsive, others telephone-responsive, yet others media-responsive.

In the real world

Irrespective of addressability and audience measurement, many companies have experimented with adding a response element to their existing advertising. Some of the issues involved in telephone response have already been discussed. But executed properly, a direct response element can dramatically increase the effectiveness of media advertising and also help companies at the early stage of database building.

Press

The volume and type of use of direct response varies greatly by type of published medium. The more targeted the circulation, the higher the proportion of advertising which aims for a direct response. Thus, magazines aimed at investors, managers of small companies or companies in particular industries tend to have a higher proportion of direct response advertising than magazines aimed at enthusiasts of a particular sport or holiday magazines. In the latter case, the audience is less targeted, but also the products and services concerned are more likely to be available through retail outlets. In the former case, the aim is often to generate leads for a sales office.

Some common ad formats, used in accordance with the campaign objectives and budget, are:

- double page spreads (DPS);
- ful-page ads;
- fractionals – 25 × 4, 7 × 7 and so on – this is the mm depth × number of columns;
- repeats – usually smaller ads but on many pages for cumulative impact;
- mono (black and white) – cheap and functional;
- two or three-colour – for some stand-out;
- colour – more expensive but with more impact.

> While targeted circulation means better response rates, and the greater the circulation volume, the higher the response, some tried and tested editions work better than others. This is due to lifestyle factors. The weekly or weekend supplements of national newspapers (Sunday or weekday) have proved successful in attracting direct response advertising. Catching the viewer at rest and at ease means weekend supplements are read in more depth and by more readers. This improves response rates. In many ways weekend editions and their supplements are similar to magazines like the *Radio Times* (weekly) and *Readers' Digest* (monthly). They have a longer coffee table life, are therefore seen more than once and not just in passing. Well over half the advertising in some of these magazines carries coupons. Use of these media by direct marketers has made a great contribution to their financial success. This in turn has caused more and more publishers to enter this and related markets (e.g. women's magazines), contributing to media proliferation and audience fragmentation.

Inserts

The main users of nationally distributed inserts include insurance suppliers, specialist mail-order companies (general merchandise, fashion, publishers), photographic laboratories, credit card companies and financial services companies and telecoms suppliers. Inserts combine many of the advantages of direct mail pieces with the advantages of press advertising. This is an example of what is called **through-the-line** advertising.

The insertion process is increasingly complex and rapid, requiring high-speed production runs and different combinations of inserts. This enables the testing of different creative propositions. Also, where regional or local editions of a publication are produced, or production batches are allocated to different areas, inserting can be varied by region and area, even down to individual distribution depots or publication wholesalers. Less sophisticated insertion machinery can be used to insert leaflets in every copy of particular editions, e.g. for local papers. As a last resort, manual insertion can be used. So don't ignore inserts in your media mix, particularly for media with highly targeted circulations.

> **In the real world**
> Inserts and press advertising can be a good way of running a tactical or short-term campaign as direct mail lead times can be very long.

You can also distribute coupon books. Known as free-standing inserts, these are widely used by retail stores, banks, charities and consumer goods manufacturers. A free-standing insert takes its name from the idea that it is almost a publication in its own right, with coupons and possibly promotional articles from many suppliers grouped into one binding. This reduces the 'confetti' problem so often experienced when the reader picks up the paper or magazine – leaflets fall out like confetti. An alternative approach here is to group inserts into envelopes, which can be produced by normal direct mail processes.

Common insert formats are:

- loose – A4, A5 and any finished size in between, used in newspapers and magazines;
- bound-in – stitched into the spine of a magazine to keep it attached;
- thread-through – the insert is stitched through the spine so one page appears once, then a few pages later the other half appears;
- cover-wrapped inserts – insert is placed in the outer cellophane cover of a magazine;
- colour/mono – both used, though colour has more stand-out;
- folded/flat – both used, according to information, content required;
- die-cut – edges are cut into a shape for improved stand-out and impact.

Although inserts are less targetable than direct mail, their delivery cost is a fraction of the cost of postal delivery. Depending on volumes they can be as little as 1p each. As testing requires no additional technical planning other than keeping to the predetermined specifications of the title, you can try many different formats and identify which and in what title they are most efficient. If you need to increase your reach (the total number of individuals you talk to by any media), volume can quickly be up-weighted or other titles chosen. This can be a better way to extend reach than to rely on an additional media such as direct mail, which is both time consuming and more expensive.

> **In the real world**
>
> If using a multitude of publications and newspapers in your media insert campaign, measuring the response rate of each different title is ideal but tough. A separate campaign/source code, unique indicator or telephone number can be pre-printed onto each insert run to distinguish each title and/or format. However, the use of these indicators will be determined by your data capture and reporting system's back-end. It is important to consider their capture when planning your campaign to achieve measurable results.

The advantages of inserts are that:

- you can use different sizes and formats – different paper sizes and weights, ways of folding, etc.;
- respondents can reply easily, e.g. tearing out coupon. Inserts can be perforated, but display advertisements can't;
- you can test copy and product variations easily and more cheaply than the cost of a split-run advertisement;
- you get more space than with display advertising;
- you can advertise in media which traditionally do not advertise or greatly restrict the amount of advertising;
- they are tactile. Even if they fall on the floor, they usually have to be picked up (except in the shop), hence the saying, '*An ad in the hand is worth two in the mag*'.

▶ Tip-ons

Inserts can be of three kinds, loose, bound-in or gummed on.

> **Tip-ons** are cards which are gummed onto the magazine advertisement to which they relate. They often consist of a coupon in the form of a postcard, or information on a credit card-sized card. When they are made of card, they allow the customer to respond without using an envelope.

Tip-ons stand out from the page, making it more likely that they will attract your customer's attention. However, tip-ons are much higher cost than a conventional leaflet or display advertisement, so their use should be carefully tested if possible. It is usually advisable to test the straight insert or display advertisement first, so that the tip-on can be tested for addition to volume or quality of response. Tip-ons can also be used to deliver small folded leaflets to customers. Some tip-ons are not response vehicles but enduring information (e.g. useful telephone numbers, store location maps).

> **Action**
>
> Even if the tip-on is the coupon, always include response methods on the advertisement itself, in case the tip-on is detached.

Leaflet distribution and free newspapers

In many ways closely related to inserts, leaflet distribution has also increased greatly in targetability and cost effectiveness in recent years. Leaflet distribution companies have worked closely with major providers of geographic data on social, economic and marketing characteristics of consumers to provide packages that allow you to target leaflets down to individual postcode areas or even smaller areas.

The rise of leaflet distribution has been closely associated with the rise of free local newspapers. In fact, leaflets that were once distributed separately are now often distributed as inserts in free newspapers. The existence of a local free newspaper distribution system has created a whole new approach to selective distribution of leaflets.

The main benefits of free newspaper distribution are as follows:

- **Coverage and penetration**. Most households receive a free newspaper, and some several. In fact, free newspapers risk being a victim of their own success, in that overlapping coverage can be a problem, with some households receiving three or four newspapers a week.
- **Flexibility**. They are delivered weekly so that the timing of distribution can be more or less exactly matched to client needs.
- **Targeting**. In addition to offering distribution according to postcode areas, some offer distribution by housing type. Because local areas are known well by the distributors, the right kind of housing can be selected.
- **Reliability**. Circulation is controlled and accounted for locally. Monitoring is carried out independently and therefore trusted by advertisers.
- **Credibility**. Free local newspapers are viewed by consumers as a highly credible source of information, and leaflets included in them benefit from this status.
- **Service**. Because leaflets provide an important element of a free newspaper's income, the client service is good.
- **Cost effectiveness**. Leafleting by free newspapers is cheap.

Of course, not all leaflet distribution is direct response. It is commonly used by retailers to stimulate visits to their local stores. They frequently include coupons and special offers.

Coupons

Warning!
Your coupons may not be redeemed against your product (malredemption). This is usually caused by poor targeting – too many people receiving the coupon who don't buy your product. Still, most coupon users view them as an essential part of their communications mix.

Coupons have benefited considerably from the use of direct marketing and direct distribution techniques, which enable you to get coupons to exactly those customers who will use them properly, e.g. take up an invitation to try your product, or get a reward for loyalty or multiple purchasing. The combination of coupons into freestanding inserts may reduce the accuracy of targeting but makes an immense difference to the cost of coupon delivery.

> ### Fast-track
> Some coupons have personalized bar codes so that it is clear precisely which consumer has redeemed them. This information is then used as the basis for targeting future promotions. If your product is sold through third-party retailers, send your coupons direct to your customers, bar-code them and have them scanned when they are presented back to you by the retailers, to check who's taking them up.

Designing press or magazine response advertising

Most of the rules of good copy writing apply to display advertising. However, there are some important differences.

▶ The wow! factor

> ### In the real world
> The first aim of a direct response is to get the reader to stop and read before turning the page. If you don't make sure that your advertisement does this, your response rate is likely to be very low.

Your advertisement is doing the same job as a direct mail envelope or the first words of a telemarketing call. As the header demonstrates, you need stand-out to catch attention. For this reason, arresting graphics or pictures or extremely large and bold headings are often used. These may include challenging statements of the kind you would never include in a direct mail letter.

> ### In the real world
> Your advertisement aims to get readers to respond, so your whole advertisement should lead to the response device. If a coupon is included, your copy should refer to it and lead the reader to it. Some advertisers prefer not to include coupons because they believe a coupon might damage the tone of the advertisement (e.g. for a very high-quality car, domestic appliance or furniture). In this case, the address must be prominent and the information the reader needs to send or call in should be clearly stated. If telephone is the main response device, tell the reader what will happen when they call (e.g. they will be asked their address for sending an information pack).

▶ Size matters

The size and positioning of your advert is critical. There is evidence that response tends to increase roughly as the square root of the size of the advertisement. For example, double the size will bring in only 40% more response (the square root of 2 is 1.41). Full-page advertising must be powerful for it to stop the reader turning over the page, so many advertisers prefer to go for smaller sizes so that the advertisement is present while an article is being read. However, this can raise problems if the article is not appropriate (e.g. an article targeted at men beside an advertisement targeted at women).

> **Warning!**
> Editorial policy may not permit pre-planning of advertisement placement (although editors are becoming more customer-oriented, understanding that to keep advertising revenue flowing in, they must show flexibility).

▶ Timing

For daily newspapers, daily variations in readership are important. For products aimed at the business-to-business market, insertion on Saturday is less likely to produce response. Avoiding holiday periods may also be appropriate. However, consumer products and services are often better advertised during holiday periods, when consumers have more time to consider taking up offers.

An additional issue is frequency of placement. Unlike with direct mail, you can get reduced prices for multiple insertions. Multiple insertions have an attrition rate – response can die off quite quickly. For a product or service which is advertised regularly, you should test 'drip' advertising – frequent, regular and perhaps small advertisements – against 'burst' advertising – infrequent multiple insertions in close succession. You should also test insertion in one medium versus insertion in several media (again on a drip versus burst basis).

> **In the real world**
> If you run a direct mail campaign at the same time as an advertisement campaign, you can expect the response rate to be significantly higher.

▶ Television

For the direct marketer, the major advantages of television are that:

- nearly every home has one (and in some countries most homes have two or more);
- many people spend a lot of hours watching TV;
- programming provides segmented advertising opportunities.

The disadvantages are:

- it is usually expensive to use as a direct response media;
- timescales and expertise are involved in producing TV advertising;
- it is challenging to tell the consumer how to respond during the few seconds available (hence the use of free and memorable phone numbers or web site URLs for more information);
- it can be difficult to find out exactly who in the family has been watching what.

> **Action**
> The proliferation of TV media is causing many TV companies to work hard to attract direct response clients. Some offer payment by results (PI or per item) schemes where you pay a small amount for airtime and a royalty per item sold. This allows low-budget advertisers to test the medium. Find out if this facility is one you can use.

Telephone numbers in commercials are becoming more common and viewers are growing more accustomed to phoning these numbers. A special case of this is the charity appeal, where consumers phone in and donate using their credit card number. Premium-rate calling can be used in the same way. Other examples of direct response include the viewer poll.

In the UK, one of the major barriers to direct response use of TV has been the shortage of airtime. The near monopoly situation of the ITV companies has driven up the price of airtime to astronomical levels. In the US, where airtime is much more freely available, much longer advertisements, demonstrating the product and giving testimonials and full details of special offers and how to order, can be mounted cost effectively. A direct response advertisement on the TV in the US is scripted in a similar way to a direct mail letter, with the additional power of the moving image to make sales by calling for the order 'face to face'. This approach is also used widely by the home shopping channels aired into satellite and cable TV homes.

In many countries, direct response TV advertising is very successful. Examples include not just the US but also France, Australia, and Hong Kong. DRTV, as it has come to be known, works differently from normal TV advertising. Normal rules of TV buying (coverage, frequency, etc.) are suspended in favour of profitability measures. The higher the profit, the more often the advertisement is shown.

> **In the real world**
> In DRTV, no plans are made to gain specific audience ratings. Rollout of a campaign is determined entirely by profitability. Advertisements are specially targeted to appear in low-interest programmes, when consumers are likely to take more interest in the commercial than in the programme and when they are less likely to worry about missing part of the programme when they take time out to note the details or even make the telephone call. Programming is changed at very short notice, according to which items sell the best.

For similar reasons, DRTV is less likely to be successful during the busy hours of the day and week and more likely to succeed in the late evening, early morning and weekends (the 'bored' hours). For cost reasons, commercials tend to be shown at off-peak viewing hours. They are much longer too, ranging between one and two minutes and including several repeats of the phone number. Of course, it goes without saying that DRTV requires 24-hour inbound telemarketing facilities.

The high cost of UK airtime has also created a barrier for some advertisers. Charities, which are major users of other direct marketing media, cannot afford to advertise on TV to a mass audience due to the costs of doing so. However, they are starting to use much more tightly targeted media such as digital satellite and cable TV, using powerful, thought-provoking and heart-tugging advertising which generates good response to offset the initial high costs. The response from targeted audiences, particularly the health and female channels, tend to work well.

> **In the real world**
>
> Charities often make a strong appeal to the emotions. These may be quite distressing to some recipients (e.g. pictures of starving children and mistreated animals), but they work. In the UK, charities are not allowed to use such images on television. In countries where they are (e.g. Australia), television response advertising has proved more effective.

Where subscription is required, the ability to access the list of subscribers by different media can be a strong asset (provided that collection of the data has been carried out in accordance with local legislation, e.g. Data Protection Act).

Shopping channels

These channels, such as QVC, consist entirely of editorial that sells. The presenter discusses the product, often with a group of prospects or customers. Programming is changed to maximize revenue per second. Programming is up to 24 hours a day and coverage is continental. The best products for this approach are ones which might be of use to many types of people but where it is difficult to segment in ways that other media could use for targeting, e.g. teeth whitener!

Catalogues – offline and online

Catalogues are one of the oldest direct marketing media, in both consumer and business-to-business marketing. The most conspicuous consumer catalogue marketers have been traditional mail-order suppliers, benefiting from considerable economies of scale in purchasing and stockholding, but the number of major players has fallen steadily over the years.

In business-to-business marketing, virtually any supplier of a wide range of products has a catalogue, in particular suppliers of frequently ordered lower-value items (e.g. components, office supplies, consumables). There have been successful new entrants in the consumer world, particularly in the fashion business. However, they are moving towards e-commerce – a more cost-effective route to market. Increasingly stores are offering Internet shopping, albeit with a more limited product range, as demand increases for online shopping.

Catalogues, whether on or offline are 'the perpetual mail shot' or the 'ever-attendant sales person', because they are there all the time, asking your customer to place an order. You can combine other media with the catalogue to achieve maximum effectiveness. In business to business, telemarketing is often used to prospect for customers for the catalogue and then to stimulate catalogue holders to buy more. Mail-shots are used to prompt repeat orders, particularly for special offers. Inbound telephone is used to take orders.

Fast-track

Your main aim should be to place your catalogue where it is most likely to generate orders. Even the best-designed catalogue, in the hands of the person who will shelve it or use it to develop ideas about what to buy from other companies or shops, is useless.

Because catalogues are expensive to produce, experienced catalogue operators test the effect of extending their market very carefully before distributing catalogues to a new segment. In consumer markets, applicants for catalogues may be screened carefully, catalogues which have generated no orders may occasionally be requested back by the supplier.

Consumer catalogue marketers are therefore past masters of segmenting markets according to propensity to buy, sizes and types of orders placed, credit worthiness and payment habits. They keep detailed records of customer habits and develop 'scoring systems' to enable them to predict the likelihood of payment defaults, high merchandise return ratios, or low ordering, based on an individual's location and personal characteristics. Many of the techniques of the wider direct marketing industry have their origins in the practices of catalogue marketers.

The major advantages of a catalogue are as follows:

- Particularly with business-to-business marketing, a catalogue is less vulnerable to competitive activity – once your customer is used to ordering from one catalogue, they are less likely to switch to another. Also, sales are unaffected by circulation shortfalls in print media.
- The cost effectiveness of the operation improves in line with the growth in your customer file. If recruitment of customers can be predicted, then sales can. Although new customers may be less likely to order, their order rate should still be predictable. The more experience a customer has (provided the experience is satisfactory), the higher that customer's order rate is likely to be.
- A catalogue has a longer life than most other direct response media and therefore encourages repeat purchase. Catalogues are treated like magazines or, even better, as reference books.

- Catalogues are a useful testing ground for new products and concepts. Catalogue space is not free, but it is not as costly as a dedicated mail-shot. A catalogue has high fixed costs but low marginal costs. The cost of including one more product is low. Of course, every product should bear its full cost of inclusion over its life cycle. A corollary of this is that your catalogue can be used to promote a range of items, none of which could be cost effectively promoted individually.
- Catalogues can be treated like published media, with scope for inserts, articles and the like. This can make your customer keep the catalogue even longer and refer to it more often. In this respect your catalogue can be treated as a customer service, containing all the information a customer needs to do business with you and use your products and services.
- Because catalogues have a relatively stable customer base who are responsive to promotions, seasonal workloads can be smoothed out by the use of well-tried incentives to order early and order extra.
- Customers are encouraged to consolidate orders and therefore to order ahead.

▶ Designing your catalogue

Once the catalogue is in the hands of the right buyer, it can start its work. Its success in this is determined by merchandise range and presentation. The main conflict, which exists in virtually all distribution channels, is the conflict between breadth of merchandise range and focus.

> **Warning!**
>
> In a catalogue, this conflict emerges in the decision about how many products to feature on each page. Too many will prevent the creative staff (graphic and copy) drawing attention to every item, too few and the turnover per page will not be high enough. The same applies to the overall size of the catalogue. The best and most successful catalogues are usually a compromise between these two pressures. There is no simple recipe.

The best advice is that every part of each page, every page, every section, the catalogue itself and the wrapper, enclosed letter, other enclosures and order form should all be treated like a direct mail-shot, but economically, because there is far less space per product. If your customers are interested enough, they will buy from a straight listing of products, but this will deter customers who are not interested or who are unfamiliar with the merchandise. Direct mail experience indicates that long copy is required to capture interest and properly qualify the customer. In catalogue marketing, the unqualified customer who orders is the customer who returns the merchandise. However, the copy can be less 'aggressive' than in a direct mail piece or a media advertisement. This is because the reader's attention is already secured and the reader is expecting to be given useful information about the product in your photograph.

Fast-track

The catalogue is the carrier of your brand and must therefore convey this brand on every page. This should guide the layout, the copy and the photography.

The best-selling pages in a catalogue are nearly always the back cover, page three, page two, followed by early right-hand pages through to the middle of the book. This is where the big sellers are likely to be and where the profitable items should be. The best items should also be given more space, as the return is likely to be proportionate to the space used. There are diminishing returns, of course.

Photographs must highlight the main selling points of the product, e.g. looks or usefulness. However, they should not exaggerate the product's size or attractiveness – a sure way to get high return rates. Crowding a photograph with many others makes it less likely that your customer will appreciate what the product really looks like.

Traditional catalogues used to group products within product categories rather than according to customer needs. Today, increasing numbers of catalogues are grouped according to related ideas, e.g. products that could be used on holiday, products for home entertainment, furniture for particular kinds of room instead of types of furniture. This is how some (but not all) customers think about products. Of course, both kinds of catalogue may be needed to cater for different buying styles.

There is a lot of evidence available on what print is most readable. Because a catalogue has so much print in it, good practice would suggest that the print style should be researched and tested for readability. This includes the size of type, the background colour, breadth and length of paragraphs.

▶ The catalogue product

Very few products cannot be sold via a catalogue. But whether your product can be sold **profitably** in a catalogue is another matter. Will your product sell via catalogue?

- Is it the kind of product that target customers are likely to want to buy from a catalogue?
- Does it have a price that customers will want to buy it at?
- Can it be properly presented in a catalogue (copy, pictures, etc.)?
- Is it orderable by mail? If it has to be completely tailored, ordering by mail would be too complex.
- Is it shippable, without great likelihood of damage?
- Does it have the right image for the catalogue?

If your product has a price advantage, it should be strongly emphasized or it will be lost in the welter of price and product information.

Exhibitions

Exhibitions are a hybrid medium. Some exhibitions are like broadcast media advertising. The aim is merely to put products on show to a large number of customers and excite their interest. Many national consumer exhibitions are of this kind. There may be a direct marketing component. You can ask consumers showing interest to give their name and address to stand staff. These can then be distributed to local dealers for follow-up, or customers may receive a mail-shot to sustain their interest and trigger a visit to an outlet where they can buy.

Increasingly, especially in business to business, exhibitions are used as an integral part of the contact strategy. Prospective or existing customers are targeted through your database or rented lists. They are invited to the exhibition and perhaps asked to confirm their attendance. An appointment with stand staff may even be booked. After the exhibition, depending on the success of the visit, there may be a follow-up contact (sales force, telephone or mail).

You should use exhibitions when:

- sales calls are expensive and you want to get many customers visiting you rather than you visiting them;
- you want to attract new customers and the exhibition has proven quality of attendance. In this respect, the exhibition functions like a rented list;
- complex concepts are being demonstrated, so instead of individual demonstrations having to be mounted all over the country, many customers can see the demonstration in one location.

Sales seminars and other company-sponsored special events

These include the following:

- the straightforward sales seminar, where a concept is described and perhaps audio-visual techniques are used to demonstrate it in action;
- the physical demonstration of the product, often held in your sales office or at the factory;
- awareness and training events, where your aim is to educate customers so that they can appreciate the value of your company offering. This is the 'soft sell' approach;
- entertainment, e.g. visits to sporting and cultural events. Here your aim is to reward your customer for loyalty and to further cement the relationship.

All these have much in common with exhibitions from a direct marketing viewpoint. The difference is that, being sponsored by you, all those attending must be invited by you or your business partners (very common in business-to-business marketing). To ensure the right quality of attendee, direct marketing is the medium most commonly used to market such events. In some cases, this direct marketing takes the form of personal invitations from your management and sales staff.

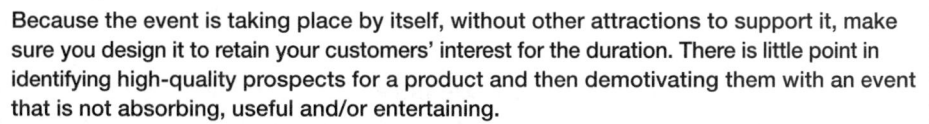

> **Warning!**
> Because the event is taking place by itself, without other attractions to support it, make sure you design it to retain your customers' interest for the duration. There is little point in identifying high-quality prospects for a product and then demotivating them with an event that is not absorbing, useful and/or entertaining.

▶ The sales force

Most sales managers would not be happy to call the sales force a direct medium. But a sales force satisfies (or can satisfy) all the criteria for being a direct medium, in that:

- it is directly addressable;
- the costs and results of each contact can be measured;
- tests can be carried out on the frequency, depth and type of contact.

In many respects, the sales force is like telemarketing because contacts are made directly by human beings. For your sales force to work as a direct medium, you need the strong control over activity rates that characterizes telemarketing. So some types of sales force cannot be considered in direct marketing terms, e.g. a major account sales force, selling complex and large technical products, where several calls are required to carry out diagnostic and negotiating work before a sale is made and much preparatory work is required between calls. At the other extreme, for sales staff selling relatively simple products and calling on large numbers of customers every day, carrying out a quick check on requirements before closing the sale, direct marketing disciplines can be valuable. In fact, these kinds of sales force are increasingly working in harness with other direct marketing media, specifically direct mail and telemarketing.

▶ Sales promotion

Sales promotion gives customers reasons to react in the desired way towards a product or service that go beyond the basic benefits of the product or service. Sales promotion focuses on triggering the action, on motivating the prospect to take the critical step of responding. The simplest example of sales promotion in direct marketing is the premium – the gift sent to customers who respond or order. But there are many other ways of motivating customers to buy using sales promotion. Many of them are associated with close dates. The aim of most direct marketing campaigns is to sell or get response within a defined period. So customers most be motivated to act as soon as possible and certainly within the campaign period. The speed of response is important because the impact of most campaigns fades with time.

Examples of sales promotion techniques which can be used with direct marketing include:

- free samples of the product (although related to the product benefit, it does not change it in any way);
- offers of more of the product for a given price;
- joint promotions, e.g. discounts off other products;
- coupons and cash refund offers;
- trading stamps and additional credit card or similar promotional points;
- loyalty point schemes;
- sweepstake/lotteries (subject to the law);
- free trial or demonstration.

Posters

Posters are not normally a good response medium. This is because when people see them, they are in no position to respond. However, as radio advertising has shown, mobile phones can provide a valuable response channel even for the most mobile customers! Certain kinds of poster do afford some prospect of response, in particular static transport advertising (e.g. in rail stations and other places where people have to wait). However, in general, if posters are used with direct marketing, it is as back-up to the campaign, to reinforce awareness or branding.

Public relations

Public relations aims to improve communication and understanding between your company and those you need to influence. In marketing campaigns, this need is focused on:

- **media relations** – where the aim is to create a positive climate towards your company by influencing the influencers, i.e. those who talk to the market through the media. This can be particularly valuable during a major direct marketing campaign;
- **customer relations** – direct liaison with your customers in contexts other than immediate sales or service. This is particularly important with large customers in business-to-business markets. Strengthened relations at a time when a major direct marketing campaign is launched can considerably increase the response rate and also minimize any problems caused by poor targeting or errors on the

database. Conversely, if customers are selected for a campaign and your database does not hold details on those experiencing customer service problems, you risk targeting customers who are not only unlikely to buy but who also may be further alienated by being targeted when their relationship with you is weak.

E-mail and the Internet

The Internet provides marketers with the ability to interact with people far more. Its main benefits to the direct marketer include the complementary use besides other more classic direct marketing methods to supply further information. It also provides a platform for information on benefits and services for any new potential prospects and a means to apply online or request more information, ask questions or register online. It can be refreshed regularly and cheaply, which can be far more efficient than updating a catalogue. Banner ads can be placed on complementary sites to attract your chosen target audience to your site to increase response to tactical offers, as well as e-mail marketing to raise awareness of your campaigns and offers.

The Internet, due to its progressive and innovative nature, lends itself well to similar approaches. Therefore creativity and interactivity are key to achieving and maintaining cut-through in this highly competitive medium.

Short messaging service (SMS)

SMS is the written text service which is sent from mobile to mobile and also, though less widely used, from PC to mobile and from digital TV set-top box to mobile. This is often called 'message to mobile'. As this channel is fairly new, it has the benefit of increased cut-through and impact on its audience who may still be receiving marketing through SMS for the first time. With SMS comes the promise of personal and local marketing that is both interactive and immediate. However, because this is an incredibly personal channel, care should be taken to ensure the message is targeted to the right person, at the right time, with the right offer, or else the message can be lost and damage done. Results have shown that the more interaction you have with the receiver, and the more value you add, the better the response. We cover this in detail in the next chapter.

In the real world

SMS communication should never be used as a stand-alone campaign. The media space is simply not robust enough to communicate on its own. However, the combined impact of brand activity and a strong timely offer through SMS can have a big impact. Mobile will enhance but not replace traditional marketing functions.

MMS

Multi-media messaging (MMS) is being rolled out across the UK and is available on all major networks. It comprises SMS but with pictures and sounds to enhance the message. This will revolutionalize mobile marketing. Customers will be able to receive still images, short, moving images with sound and more text to help get your message across better. However, care must be taken to ensure the message is still relevent and targeted. MMS is predicted to rival the success story of SMS, although penetration will be low initially. Colour handsets are widely available and many manufacturers soon expect to sell only colour handsets. These are as significant to the mobile marketplace as the shift from black and white TVs to colour was for the broadcasting industry.

Third generation (3G mobile phone services)

The next generation of mobile services is expected to further revolutionalize the mobile market over the coming year. By 2003 five government licences had been issued in the UK. 3G will enable mobile operators to deliver multi-media interactive services, for example short movie clips, pop video and music downloads, downloadable games, in addition to a much broader range of multi-media content – share prices, directions, weather, and so on. Services like these combined with new mobile payment solutions will effectively turn the mobile into a shop and wallet, making instant purchases possible.

Summary

This chapter has demonstrated the immense variety of media that you can use in direct marketing. However, this very variety can be direct marketing's own enemy if these different media are not planned and managed properly – the subject of the next few chapters.

17 the creative side

What does 'creative' mean in direct marketing?

Creative and action

How can you create creativity?

Direct marketing vs advertising creativity

Developing the creative strategy

The creative brief

Summary

In this chapter we explain the role that creativity plays in direct marketing by providing the images, symbols and phrases that make your brand recognized, whichever medium you decide to use to contact customers or targets. We show that creativity is required not just in how you show your messages but also in what message you want to convey. We explain that good briefing is the key to obtaining relevant, cost-effective and timely creative.

What does 'creative' mean in direct marketing?

Put two creative people together and three different views of creativity will emerge! Direct marketers often disagree about the meaning of 'creative' and about the role of creativity in direct marketing. Some see little or no place for it because tried and trusted methods work. However, in the increasingly competitive world, creativity is often vital to stay ahead of the rest. Yet new ideas and creative approaches – the next big thing – can often be a challenge to produce.

Most direct marketers have experience of media advertising and are exposed to its traditions and to the learning from new media. Marketing through many channels using many different media is now very common. Much marketing thinking has shifted to longer-term brand values rather than short-term sales, but this requires creative ideas that shape, sustain and develop those values.

> **'Creative'** is often applied to ideas which are original or stimulate the imagination. In direct marketing, it's best to define creative as 'ideas that work to achieve their objectives'.

Originality of ideas often means reworking a familiar idea in an unfamiliar way or context. This is demonstrated well by looking at the Swedish vodka company Absolut, which developed a creative and effective campaign using various media. It featured the bottle as the centrepiece, as a work of art, with scenes changing beyond the bottle – the Absolut effect. Press, outdoor, TV and radio advertising remained true to the brand. The constantly refreshed creative executions pushed Absolut to the top of the category, conveying a strong message that it is a fresh, young, trendy, edgy vodka – a premium, quality brand. The campaign has been highly successful in increasing Absolut's recognition, brand strength and market share.

Tango provides another good example. Tango is an orange drink brand that has been successfully rebranded as a powerful drink sensation with the 'you know when you've been tangoed' campaign. Creativity was pivotal to success in a competitive soft drinks market where most marketing was conservative. The company used a variety of abstract situations and exploited the PR generated from the adverts to increase sales.

> **In the real world**
> While these examples demonstrate the power of creativity, care should be taken that the concept is not too abstract. If it is, consumers may not understand the campaign and therefore won't react with the required behaviour. Your aim is to stimulate the consumer's imagination, not the creator's. Beware of ideas that appeal to their creators but leave their targets cold.

It may help you to think of creativity as 'the process which produces the **relevant unexpected**' – the juxtaposition of familiar and unfamiliar images in a way which has relevance to the customer. Not too much direct response advertising fits this definition. Too much of it looks too familiar to create any sense of excitement by arousing the imagination. The trick is to combine the creative brand element with the rational sales message.

▶ Familiarity and creativity do mix

Creative ideas must be relevant, but they don't need to be unexpected. Customers loyal to your product, brand or advertising will be comforted by familiar messages, and even seek them out. They like to find them in familiar places. Still, your advertisement must stand out on the page and differentiate itself from the competition, especially for customers who don't know you or your product. Faithful customers will spot the familiar name as readily as they spot their own in the telephone directory.

> **In the real world**
>
> Creativity and targeting go together. A familiar message works with regular customers – if it is relevant. Some degree of surprise may be required if the target audience are prospects, but make your message relevant and clear to convert that interest to sales.

▶ Creativity and action

However creative your campaign, remember that your message must also be seen, understood and acted upon. These are the key stages in 'hierarchy of effects' models of the communication process.

> **Hierarchy of effects** models of communication analyze the consumer's reaction to a marketing communication in terms of successive stages, usually starting with attention or awareness and ending with purchase. The most widely used is AIDCA – Attention, Interest, Desire, Conviction, Action.

AIDCA suggests that consumers need to see and have beliefs about your product before buying it. Communication influences these 'receiver effects' as in Fig. 17.1. This suggests that seeing, believing and buying are a function of:

- your customer's perception of the source of the message, particularly the credibility of the source (both you and the medium you use);
- how your message affects your customer;
- how the media you use shape the message (through their different physical characteristics, for example);
- the nature of your customer's world.

Fig. 17.1 The communication process

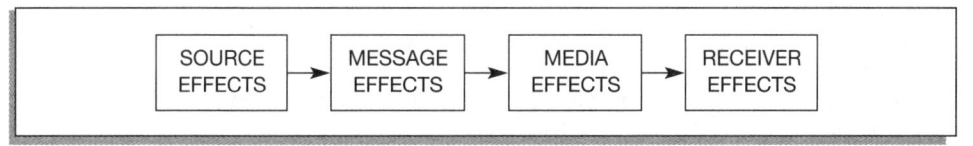

SOURCE EFFECTS → MESSAGE EFFECTS → MEDIA EFFECTS → RECEIVER EFFECTS

Creativity should not be judged by message design alone. Creative ideas must work, i.e. obtain the result you want: change or reinforcement of behaviour, e.g. purchase, brand switching, increased frequency of purchase, etc.

How can you create creativity?

There has been much research on why some individuals out-perform others in creativity but little conclusive evidence that one set of factors matters more than another.

> **In the real world**
>
> The ability to associate does seem to make a difference, i.e. the ability to think laterally rather than vertically. This is done by:
> - combining related ideas (e.g. a chair that warms you);
> - adding unrelated features (e.g. speaking video recorder);
> - taking away problem features (e.g. bulk), creating associations with unrelated products or benefits (e.g. a credit card and charity);
> - making things simpler (e.g. buying motor insurance over the telephone);
> - substituting (e.g. the 'eau' Perrier campaign);
> - switching (e.g. the Dr Barnado's child abuse with old-age faces campaign).
>
> So you can use techniques aimed to stimulate creativity.

Lateral thinking and brainstorming are just two of many techniques used to help groups produce new ideas. You can also try using techniques designed to help groups get away from the constraints imposed by their current thought patterns. This can involve including people from other areas of the business and other companies in your brainstorm, holding sessions off site, involving fun group activities and so on, to break down barriers and also the habit of thinking in set ways.

Whatever techniques you use to produce creative ideas, creativity is above all about ideas that work. Direct marketing is ultimately about making a sale, so care should always be taken to focus each time on balancing the creative versus the response and sales rate, and of course the cost per sale. Whether your ideas are visual, original, clever or aesthetically pleasing, they must achieve your objective.

17 / The creative side

> **In the real world**
>
> When responding to a creative brief, creative agencies frequently present communications that are technically challenging and expensive to print and produce. While creative and interesting packs with freebies included, crazy folding, die-cut envelopes, special inks, funky finishes and so on may result in award-winning campaigns and good PR for the agency, the focus needs to be fixed on cost of the pack, projected response and sale, and ultimately the cost per sale. The creative brief therefore needs to be very clear on cost per pack or overall budget and objectives to help manage this at the start of the creative process.

▶ Direct marketing vs advertising creativity

Your media advertising usually aims to create awareness and brand images. Your direct marketing communications usually aim to make a sale. Your direct marketing can build on foundations laid by image advertising. However, much direct marketing is unsupported by image advertising. It does the whole job – creating awareness, interest, desire, conviction **and** action, all in one piece. But because the main requirement is to make a sale, it tends to be action-oriented at the expense of brand values.

> **Warning!**
>
> Don't allow all your thoughts to go into offers and response devices rather than the longer-term objective of building your brand. You will allow a creative vacuum to emerge between awareness and action, and your direct marketing will become less effective. The key stage in AIDCA is conviction, i.e. building your customer's beliefs about your brand. Once they are established, the desired action is likely to follow.

The beliefs you should be interested in are customers' estimates that if they do what you want them to (buy, reply, etc.), they will derive benefit from doing so. For example, 'If I send off for a Queen Elizabeth, the Queen Mother commemorative plate, it will arrive in 28 days and I will own a piece of history that I will want to pass to my children one day.'

> **Action**
>
> Aim to form beliefs – they are essential for any form of marketing communication to succeed. Use ideas to build lasting beliefs about your brand. Don't just use offer strategies to raise response levels. Once the person is emotionally engaged, not just rationally, and has bought into your product, they are far more likely to purchase.

Your success in creating belief depends on:

- being single-minded about the kind of brief you are trying to form (your single-minded proposition will be at the heart of the creative brief);
- how often and how strongly you reinforce it.

In the real world

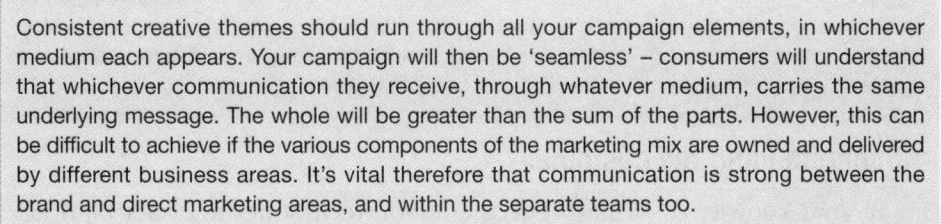

Consistent creative themes should run through all your campaign elements, in whichever medium each appears. Your campaign will then be 'seamless' – consumers will understand that whichever communication they receive, through whatever medium, carries the same underlying message. The whole will be greater than the sum of the parts. However, this can be difficult to achieve if the various components of the marketing mix are owned and delivered by different business areas. It's vital therefore that communication is strong between the brand and direct marketing areas, and within the separate teams too.

There are few examples of such a consistent approach in direct marketing. This is because clients tend not to think this way and agencies tend to take the client's approach. But the 'big idea' that characterizes most successful advertising campaigns – the mental bridge between the product's features and the consumer's perception of the product's benefits – is a target for every direct marketing campaign. Successful examples include Direct Line (red telephone), Orange (orange box), Virgin (red handwritten Virgin signature).

The success of Direct Line's red telephone campaign, in a market where brand loyalty is low, price competition fierce and brand switching very frequent, is a goal for every direct marketer to aim for. In direct response television advertising, the telephone is a highly flexible branding device. It can appear in every medium. It can change its shape, size and speed of movement to identify with different types of cars and therefore with different target groups. It can be used to suggest that the company is more dynamic, bigger or cheaper than its competitors. It is also used to improve response, of course. Moreover, as the company moved into other types of personal insurance, e.g. house contents, the red telephone was used to stimulate home-related images, by changing its shape to that of a house, for instance. The red telephone is a simple idea. Carried through all advertising, and adapting to circumstances, this simple little branding device plays a strategic role in the communications programme. The effect is powerful because there is a big creative idea behind the little red telephone.

▶ Developing the creative strategy

The seven basic steps in developing a creative communications strategy are:

- identify and understand your customer;
- know your product's strengths and weaknesses;
- assess your competition;
- position your product;
- develop the customer benefits;
- communicate the message;
- build a dialogue with your customers.

> **In the real world**
>
> Don't insist on taking these steps in strict order. Do it interactively. Try starting with step seven in order to proceed to step one. Lead generation programmes first establish a dialogue (step seven) in order to identify the prospect/customer (step one).

▶ Understanding the customer

Use all your knowledge of market segmentation techniques to understand who customers are, what they think and perceive, how to reach them, through which media, and how they buy. Information and emotion play important roles. How much information do they need? What kind of message are they likely to respond to? How persuasive must the message be?

▶ Knowing the product's strengths and weaknesses

Your product's strengths will build its USP. But some strengths are more important than others. A car may be high on comfort, speed, economy and safety, but it would not make sense to give all these strengths equal weight in the message. You need to concentrate upon the product's and/or your company's main strengths to achieve clear product differentiation. For Volvo it is safety, for Ferrari it is motor racing heritage.

> **In the real world**
>
> Don't forget your weaknesses. Try to eliminate them from the message or turn them into a strength. In Bill Bernbach's advertisements for the Volkswagen Beetle, the copy said 'noisy', 'ugly' and 'slow'. It sold millions of Beetles!

▶ Assessing your competition

Competitive analysis is central to positioning strategy. You need to decide whether you should make references to competition in your message. In the UK, clear guidelines forbid 'knocking copy', but justifiable competitive comparisons are permitted. This can be particularly powerful when there are many competitors with similar product specifications. The customer just needs to know 'what makes your product so different?'. Competitive advertising is used to good effect by credit card companies and by banks to illustrate rate tables.

▶ Positioning your product

Everything in your communication strategy should support your positioning strategy. This consistency should run through all your media and message components for a sustained period. This ensures that each component supports the effect of the others and helps to make the most of your advertising and marketing spend. Results prove that when a fully integrated campaign with TV (and often radio activity) is running, there is a significant, often dramatic effect on response rates. By running brand and direct marketing together with shared branding and positioning, you get more bang for your buck.

▶ Developing consumer benefits

Consumers want to hear about benefits – immediately. Hence the maxim, 'get the main benefit in the headline'. This idea has stimulated much of the best copy, including many 'How to ...' headlines, such as:

- How to improve your memory.
- How to burn off body fat hour by hour.
- How to make your second million.
- How to double your power to learn.
- How to make a fortune in mail order.
- How to win friends and influence people.
- How to get more for your money at ...

The hardest task is to turn the product feature into a genuine benefit – in short, 'sell the sizzle, not the steak'. A technique that identifies genuine benefits, not features, is called FAB analysis: Features, Advantages, Benefits.

▶ How to do a FAB analysis

- List the features – what your product or service consists of, is made of, etc.
- Express these as advantages – what the features mean it can do or what can be done with it.
- Convert the advantages into benefits – how the customer's needs are satisfied by these advantages, expressed in your customer's language.

For instance, a washing machine has a built-in spinner (feature), which means it takes up less room in the kitchen (advantage), which means there is now room for the dog's eating bowl (benefit). Notice the phrase 'which means'. In searching for the benefit, keep asking yourself 'which means?' until you get to something the customer would say about how your product or service helps them meet their objectives.

Most products have several features and therefore several benefits. The way a given feature benefits each customer depends upon that customer's needs, so one feature can produce a variety of benefits. The benefit of the above washing machine to a non-dog owner may be that there is also room for a dishwasher. A feature may produce many benefits, only the most important of which should be stressed in the advertising.

> **In the real world**
>
> You can only find out which are the most important benefits by research. Ask customers which benefits matter most. You can also develop different types of copy, highlighting different types of benefit. You can see, from response rates, which benefit appeals to which type of customer. You may also want to find out what the barriers are to people buying your product so that you can turn these concerns into a positive in your marketing communications instead. For example, research may uncover that purchase price is deterring people from buying your goods, so by including a monthly direct debit scheme or hire purchase agreement and telling people about it, you may knock down this barrier. Listen to your customers and give them what they want.

▶ Communicating the message

This refers to what your words and pictures should say and show and to how they should be combined. This raises several important direct response issues:

- **Length of copy**. It used to be argued that long copy out-pulled short copy, that long headlines could often beat short ones. However, as the competitive nature of advertising nowadays means fighting for someone's attention, direct response ads tend to work well with shorter copy and briefer headlines. People tend to skim-read advertising, so punchy bullet points, short paragraphs and the use of images to punctuate an area of copy are all good ways to break it up into manageable chunks. If in doubt, test!

- **Number of pieces**. How many pieces? Again, a general rule is the more the better. Each piece is a selling opportunity – the more selling opportunities the better. However, there comes a point where saturation occurs. So response should be monitored on all communications to detect when this occurs. For example, Sky digital avoids using a press advert and a media insert in the same edition of magazines or newspapers. Care is taken to avoid the two channels clashing, as the effect on response does not outweigh the cost of both media. However, a positive effect can be seen when direct marketing is used in tandem with TV and radio advertising. During heavy brand activity, response and conversion rates increase as the digital TV category interest is being moved in Sky's favour.

- **Personalization**. This is normally a good idea because it is flattering to be mentioned by name. But it is important to get the right name and not to overdo it. More importantly, personalization should mean relevant, personal details, not necessarily repetition of your customer's name. With laser printing you can personalize many details in one pass through the printer. For example, insurance mailings often feature age, renewal date, maturity value, surrender value, and so on. With lasering advancements it's possible to use different inks for personalized areas for stand-out if required. It is also possible to use personalization as part of the creative for extra impact.

- **Mood and tone**. This can be crucial to response. But the mood you create depends on the target. Established customers like to be treated gently, but prospects may need a harder sell. Some customers need to be cajoled, pushed and even threatened. Others need to be given an incentive to respond. The nature of the product also determines the tone. Thus, Harrods positions itself as a prestigious retailer to an upper-income target market and to the tourist market, so the company communicates in very formal English and in a sophisticated, traditional manner. Legal practices use a more formal, efficient and business-like manner that mimics their products and services. Virgin uses a friendly, informal and often cheeky tone that appeals to its target market and to its positioning as a company that challenges convention.

▶ Building the dialogue

Communication means interaction: a two-way process. A dialogue is the simplest form of communication, therefore it should start as soon as possible. Headlines which pose questions immediately involve the prospect, as do all involvement devices, e.g. 'yes/no' envelopes. Reply coupons which say 'yes, I do wish to receive my introductory copy of X', also use the dialogue-building technique. Marketing via SMS text messages relies on the principles of dialogue to engage the audience and cut through with messages. Results show that where you are asking the recipient to do something, reply to a question, tell you their favourite film/music/artist, etc., they are more likely to accept the message positively and respond. To engage the subject is to involve them and this is much less annoying and intrusive.

> **In the real world**
>
> When in dialogue with your target audience it is vital to talk to them in the right way. Using an inappropriate medium, tone and formality can do more harm than good. By trying too hard to sound 'cool' when talking to a youth audience you run the risk of sounding out of touch, old fashioned and even parental. Similarly, communicating funeral services by SMS is not altogether appropriate. It's important to consider the whole communication first.

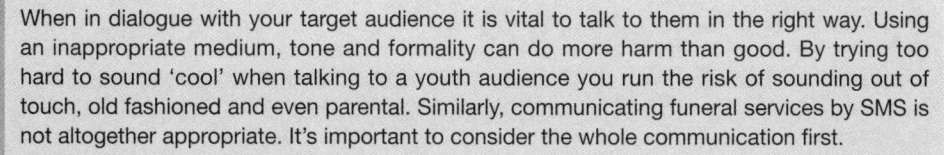

▶ The creative brief

There are seven Ws of the brief which goes to the (usually agency) team asked to produce the creative approach:

- Who? (the source of the message) says.
- What? (the message) to.
- Whom? (the target audience).
- When? (timing).
- Where? (media).
- Why? (reasons for consumer purchase).
- With what effect? (desired objectives).

You should then translate these seven Ws into a structured communications brief, examples of which can be found in Chapter 5.

▶ Summary

This chapter began with an examination of the word 'creative'. The best interpretation is 'ideas that work to achieve their objectives'. These ideas are more likely to work if they are relevant to the target audience. Beyond being relevant they must be communicated effectively. This depends not just on the brilliance of the idea but also on effective marketing and communications programmes.

17 / The creative side

Ideas must work either to make a sale or to produce behaviour that leads to a sale. Often direct marketing communications work without the support of image advertising. This means that creative ideas must sustain the whole process in the conviction or belief stage. Without a strong conviction that the product will satisfy your consumer's need, you won't get the right response. Ideally a big idea should be sought and executed throughout the campaign. This big idea could also be a branding device.

Effective direct marketing creative strategy depends on a carefully written creative brief. This brief should provide all the relevant market background data, isolate the main thought and provide convincing rational and emotional support for the main thought.

18 production and fulfilment in direct mail

Production

The start – artwork

Typsetting

Reproduction/make-up

Mailing

Developments in direct mail technology

Understanding Mailsort

Fulfilment

Fulfilment tasks

Fulfilment steps

The management of handling

Summary

In this chapter we show that a good direct marketing plan, backed up by well-designed campaigns, is no use unless you get it to the market through production and fulfilment. This involves a series of activities, ranging from graphic design and typesetting, through to printing, stock management and despatch. For example, mailings can and often do go wrong because failures in planning, briefing or communication are translated into material which is poorly designed, badly printed, sent out at the wrong time or to the wrong people.

Production

Production is the process by which print material is produced ready for outbound mailing and fulfilment. Once, when direct marketing was dominated by direct mail, the term 'production' accurately described the production process for all direct marketing. Now, with telemarketing, e-marketing and SMS marketing in the game, the term should be qualified by adding the word 'print' before it.

In the real world
Direct marketers need expertise in print production. Production costs account for a large proportion of total direct mail costs – as much as half the budget. So it's important to understand how the costs add up and how to manage them. In this chapter we outline some of the main production tasks, including some details of particular production techniques, but these change rapidly. If you are new in direct marketing, find out more by asking to spend time at a printers to see print and production techniques in action.

The start – artwork

It often makes sense to produce the artwork in conjunction with input from the printer from the start. We've mentioned already about the importance of keeping the focus on costs, and this is particularly the case when producing the marketing material. If the creative agency liaises with the printer from the design stage, the print matter can be designed to take advantage of cost-effective formats, mail discounts from using standard sizes and pack weights, four-colour processes, and so on. The printer is the expert in the latest production techniques. These are developing constantly so it's well worth taking advantage of his knowledge. By being flexible about the job and open to his recommendations, you may be able to produce material that is printed much more cheaply. If savings can be made on print and production, they can be used to produce more volume.

The first step in production is preparing the artwork, or the copy and illustrations. The 'artwork' is the subject to be printed. It is produced by a creative agency or specialist graphic art agency/studios and should be signed off by the client (and if necessary the client's legal department). Once the artwork is approved, it is 'locked' together and sent as a file to the printers. It can be sent either on a disc (usually a CDRom) or via ISDN. This is like sending an e-mail but an ISDN link can enable vast files to be sent and downloaded quickly.

> **In the real world**
>
> Involve your printer as early as possible in the job. Encourage your design agency to talk to the printer direct to explore a range of formats to find the most suitable and efficient design. To minimize problems later on, include any mandatory printing specifications, such as using corporate pantone colours, certain finishes, fonts, paper weight constraints on the creative brief so the printer and designer know what limitations to work within.

▶ Colour and reproduction

All colours used in print, whether to produce the copy or imagery, can be made from four colours: cyan, magenta, yellow and black. By using tiny dots these four colours are not visible separately, so any colour can be made up. If a single colour of one of these is needed, say black, only a one-colour process is used. This is the cheapest print process. A four-colour process is needed for a mix of more than one colour (i.e. blue and yellow are needed to make green). Where specific colours are needed and the breakdown of four colours is not vivid or sharp enough it may be necessary to use special inks, or pantones. There are hundreds of colours available, all pre-mixed to be printed on their own, without the combination of another colour. For some greens, special inks are often used. This is because the four-colour process of combining green and blue and black using dots can sometimes look murky or dull. If the desired effect is acid green, a special colour is required for this. This means going from a four-colour process to a five-colour process (cyan, magenta, black, yellow and acid green). This is more expensive, and an extra part of the printer is needed for the additional ink well. This may affect which printer it is produced on.

When using the four-colour process it is important that the inks are lined up well to avoid a halo or shadow effect over the images or words. This is often seen in colour newspaper print where the 'fit' is not accurate and there is a halo of pink (magenta), yellow or blue (cyan) around the words or pictures. To avoid this it's important that the proof is checked thoroughly, using an eyeglass to magnify the dots to check this before the job is printed.

Another influence on cost is whether the job is to be printed on both sides, and if so, how many colours are required on each side. If the material is to be printed both sides with four-colour this is called 4/4. Or 4 back 4. If it is to be printed on one side only it's described as 4/0. Or 4 back 0. If it's to be printed in four-colour one side but in black and white on the back, then it's 4/1. Or 4 back 1. And so on. All these factors influence the quality of reproduction but also eventual cost so all considerations should be made during the design stage.

▶ Typesetting

Every typeface (or font) has a different effect. Choice is normally determined by the company's brand guidelines, which ensure that its communications look the same. Legibility is of course critical, though it is surprising how much type is not terribly legible. This may be, for example, because type designed to emphasize a few characters or words has been used for an entire piece. It may also be because white copy is used on a dark background, so clarity is lost if type size is small. In this case the white font should be made bigger. Similarly, type meant for body text may be ineffective when used to headline.

Different fonts may be used to good effect. Capitals, different colours, different weight of fonts can all be used to make a sub-title stand out from the body copy. However, care must be taken to avoid cluttering the page with a variety of fonts, sizes, types, colour, etc. or impact will be lost and the overall effect will be messy.

> **In the real world**
> Remember you will do best by adopting a clear style that endures over time. A clear communication style becomes recognized by your customers and supports branding. If your company has an existing typeface for its communication, check whether it is acceptable to deviate from the style.

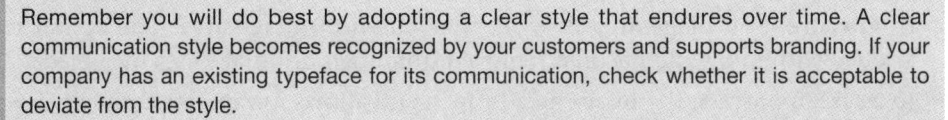

Most typesetting is now computerized, although some type (e.g. large headlines) is still set by hand. This does not mean that typesetting is an unskilled job. Software has removed some of the unskilled work, but skill is still required to produce excellent work. Image manipulation techniques allow images to be rotated, sized, reversed, overlaid with effects and repositioned. Manual assembly of page elements is now much less widespread. Publishing software enables composition and layout to be carried out more quickly, so the finished material can be checked with clients more quickly. Laser and ink-jet printers allow signatures, text and formats to be stored, allowing every communication to be customized and large numbers of variations to be created around basic themes.

> **In the real world**
> Digitized images can be stored and transmitted, making libraries of print images easier to manage and reducing communication problems between artwork and printing organizations. Image banks are also available and accessed through the Internet, bringing the world of images to your desktop. Having these on hand helps to speed up the design process instead of waiting for a transparency to arrive in the post. This enables faster response to market needs.

Reproduction/make-up

Once all the elements of the job to be reproduced have been converted to printable images, they are assembled into the correct position and fixed. The complete job is then sent 'to repro' (or for reproduction). This means they are sent to the nominated reproduction house for plate making. The plates are the copper plates needed for the later printing process to work from. A variety of processes have been developed to go straight from artwork to plate.

▶ Printing processes

Most printing processes convert the required design into a printing image carrier. This has an image area that receives and transfers ink to the material being printed. The exception to this is laser printing, where toner is transferred from an electrostatically charged drum to the paper. Printers often refer to the printing image carrier as a plate or cylinder. Here are a few of the techniques used at this stage:

- In **letterpress**, the image area is physically higher than the non-image area. A roller carrying ink is rolled across the surface and the ink is transferred directly to the material being printed.
- **Flexography** is similar to this, except that the ink is less viscous.
- In **gravure**, the image area is lower than the non-image area. The carrier is flooded with ink, which is then removed from the non-image area by a blade.
- In a **screen** process, the image area is open and allows ink to pass through. The non-image area is closed.
- In **lithography**, the difference between the image and non-image areas is based on the fact that ink and water do not mix easily. Materials that are ink-receptive are used for the image area, while water-receptive materials are used for the non-image area.
- **Offset** printers use an intermediate roller between the plate and the printing roller.

Once the finished material is printed it then needs to reach the target audience. For a direct mailing the printed elements need to be put together, personalized, mail-sorted and delivered to the mailing house. For items that don't require personalization, such as media inserts, it is necessary to despatch them to the individual magazines and newspapers for insertion.

The amount of planning you need to do depends on the remit and capability of your printer. However, it is also necessary to make sure that your printer is well briefed in advance, to ensure the correct postage is used, that they have the correct delivery instructions and deadlines, and that any specific delivery or personalization instructions are carried out.

▶ Mailing

▶ Choosing the mailing house

The mailing house is usually chosen based on volume, as follows:

Hand enclosing houses	Very small volume packs
Cut sheet houses	Medium-size volume packs
Continuous houses	Large volume packs

You must choose the correct mailing house as this has a big effect on costs. This is an area where print management and direct mail agencies are useful partners as they specialize in tendering to the marketplace and advising on cost-cutting ideas to help reduce the pieces price.

Mailing houses can offer additional services such as:

- docket reconciliation – confirmation of mailing quantities and dates of despatch to the postal service;
- suppression of names in files – they can run programs such as deceased programs, in which they identify and extract deceased files found in the data. Mailing houses will also search for any discrepancies in data and flag to the client;
- data capture – if you have a response device such as BREs (business reply envelopes) to manage or telephone numbers to call, the mailing house can usually manage this area for the client.

Developments in direct mail technology

The direct mail industry is focusing strongly on multiple-version mailing pieces. This is because marketers are using increasingly focused lists. So the development of the print industry is being led by the need to target marketing more efficiently and in a more personalized way. Many industries (e.g. travel) are using digital techniques to maximize their information stored within their databases.

▶ Data processing

There are various processing formats for data, depending on your objectives.

Objective	Action
Create personalization and valediction	Converts data from upper case to title case and generates appropriate salutation and valediction. Success depends on how data is supplied. Ideally each element should be supplied as a separate field, such as: Title – Mr, Mrs, Lord, etc. First name or initials – Nick, N.D. Surname – White End title – MBE, BSc Salutation – Dear Mr White Valediction – Yours sincerely Name as appears in address – Mr N D White, MBE
Create default	Where, for example, gender is not known, the client should specify a default, i.e. Dear – Customer, Reader, Sir/Madam, etc.

✓	Run against PAF – Post Office Address File (Address-It)	Uses Royal Mail Postal Address File (PAF) to validate and (if required) correct and supply postcodes to help maximize mail-sort. It also allocates delivery point suffixes (two-digit code that identifies delivery location) for customer barcoding
	Dedupe (match-it largely for businesses)	Merges files and removes duplicate names. May be run against one or more files. Dedupe can be performed at several levels: ♦ individual – which looks for a specific name, i.e. 'Mr Nick White MBE'; ♦ family – which looks for surname, i.e 'White' so all 'Whites' living at an address would be identified; ♦ household – looks for all records at address regardless of name, so Nick White and Richard White will be matched if they live at the same address; ♦ business contact (Match-It) works to find an individual company; ♦ Match-It also works on identifying a whole household.
	Suppress	Various criteria may be given for selecting specific records from a main file. For example, if the selection is to suppress a pack being sent, i.e. for seed packs to be pulled out, or to identify a random person in every ten, or to select a particular number of packs targeted to a particular region, these can be predetermined up-front and planned in for selection and sampling to occur.
	Mail-sort (Sort-It)	This sorts the data to the level required for postal requirements, including discounts, which are available where the direct mail packs have been sorted, as the post office can easily distribute the mailing with no additional sorting effort. Various levels are available: ♦ mail-sort level – for mailing; ♦ walk-sort level – for door drops, hand-delivered mailings; ♦ press-stream; ♦ it also involves printing individual barcodes on each item as a unique identifier, and reports are produced with bag labels so they can be simply passed to the post office ready to go.
	Generate barcode	This can be used either for mail-sorting (customer barcoding), which improves post handling and results in higher discount, or for customer response handling back-end. It is a unique identifier that can be matched back to the original mailing list to identify the data source and can be scanned in for instant name and address details.

Understanding Mailsort

Mailsort is designed for high-volume mailings with the customer performing part of the Royal Mail sorting process in return for a pricing discount.

Mailsort levels are:

- Mailsort 120 – applicable to Mailsort 1 and 2 – addresses must be OCR/machine readable or barcoded.
- Mailsort 700 – applicable to Mailsort 1, 2 and 3 – addresses must be barcoded.
- Mailsort 1400 – applicable to Mailsort 1, 2 and 3 – barcodes or OCR fonts not necessary but further discount given for OCR-readable addresses.

Mailsort services are:

- Mailsort 1 – for letters and packets targeted for delivery the next working day after the day of posting.
- Mailsort 2 – for letters and packets targeted for delivery within three working days after the day of posting.
- Mailsort 3 – for letters and packets targeted for delivery within seven working days (but also with a deferred delivery option) after the day of posting.

A working day for collection is defined as Monday to Friday throughout the year excluding public holidays. A working day for delivery purposes is defined as Monday to Saturday throughout the year for Mailsort 1 and 2, and Monday to Friday for Mailsort 3, in both cases excluding bank holidays.

Mailsort criteria

The minimum number of items which can be sent in any single Mailsort mailing is **4000 letters or 1000 packets**. At least 90% of the addresses on letters must be fully and accurately postcoded in each Mailsort posting.

Letters are defined as:

- C5+ (240mm × 165mm) or less;
- not more than 6mm (¼ inch) thick;
- items larger than C5+ size but not more than 6mm thick and weighing less than 60g.

Packets are defined as:

- larger than C5+ size (240mm × 165mm);
- any item weighing more than 60g but not more than 2kg;
- or are more than 6mm (¼ inch) thick.

Fulfilment

Once the sorting and mailing has been done, fulfilment represents the practical completion of the direct marketing cycle once the marketing communications have taken place.

In the real world

The best planned campaign, with the cleverest offer, the most brilliant creative and the most professional targeting and timing, will come to nothing unless it is handled well at this stage.

In theory, fulfilment starts when a customer first responds to a campaign, i.e. after the first contact between your customer and you. The **first contact** may be via direct mail, outbound telemarketing, a television or press advertisement, a leaflet, or any other medium. The customer then responds, whether by telephone, mail or even a call into a showroom. The handling of this first response, whether by processing coupons, receiving telephone calls or directing customers to the right counter or display, is called **response handling**. The next step is that you give the customer something – a brochure, a catalogue, or the product itself. This latter step is **fulfilment**.

▶ Timing

From a management point of view, dealing with fulfilment differs very little from managing delivery in the two direct media which dominate initial contacts – mail and telephone. The main difference is **timing**. An initial mailing can be scheduled to take place within a defined period, taking advantage of postal rebates and allowing workers and machinery to be optimally scheduled. Handling a mail or a telephone response (processing coupons or receiving a call, sending a pack in return and in some cases making a telephone call) takes place when the customer decides to respond. With campaigns that are repeats in markets you know well, timing of response can be predicted fairly well. But in new markets or with new products, prediction is harder.

▶ Volumes

The other major difference is in **volumes** – outbound mail and telephone campaigns usually involve larger numbers of customers than the responses. But when your first customer contact is a media advertisement, response is likely to be high volume and involve collecting a lot of basic data about the respondent.

Action

Many handling houses cover both initial mailings and fulfilment. This has the advantage that you need to brief only one company, which does not have to find out from you or another supplier about outbound volumes and timings. If you think this sounds a small point, you should understand that half of the problems that occur in campaigns are caused by poor communication between client and supplier, or between suppliers. So consider the advantages of one-stop shopping.

Fulfilment tasks

Here, we focus on the handling of direct mail fulfilment. The main steps in fulfilment are:

- **providing a communication point** – somewhere where customers can phone or write to make contact;
- **recording the response**, by creating or updating the database. Errors here can cause packs to be sent to the wrong address, and wrong packs sent to customers;
- **processing the order** (anything from an acknowledgement letter, through a brochure to a complex pack of several inserts, and of course a product);
- **warehousing literature and/or goods** (receiving deliveries, warehousing, picking, packing and despatching). Delays here, particularly in despatching, can create lots of customer queries. You won't be happy with your suppliers because of the damage to your image;
- **inventory control**, so both you and the handling house know precisely how much is in stock at any time, and when re-ordering should take place. Lack of control here can also lead to high levels of pilferage and other forms of stock wastage;
- **financial control** – this includes reconciling customer payments (credit card and cash) with despatches and returns, invoicing and credit control. Errors here can lead to campaigns failing to meet financial targets. They can also lead to financial problems for the handling house, which may be debited with any errors;
- **returns handling** – receipt, quality check, repacking and/or rewarehousing or disposal;
- **customer query handling** – failure to handle your customers' queries properly and promptly can lead to high levels of dissatisfaction, cancellation of orders and damage to your image;
- **reporting and forecasting response**, shipment and returns data. Errors here can cause stock to run out or surpluses of stock to be created. They may also cause campaigns to go on for too long or too little (if the aim is to bring in a target absolute number of responses).

> **Warning!**
> Unless all these steps are fully catered for from the outset of the campaign, you may end up with a **high-profile mistake** communicated to all your customers.

Fulfilment steps

How all these capabilities are put to work is best seen by following the fulfilment process. This is described below. It may not be exactly like this in all handling houses, but it will be similar.

▶ The brief

You brief your handling house, specifying exactly what is to be done when. Brief them as early as possible so they are able to provide sufficient resource and a robust data-capture facility. Consider sending it in draft form, before final numbers are specified. You may still be doing some work on targeting and response rate forecasting. A draft brief gives your handling house time to respond and point out problems or opportunities.

▶ The response

In response to the brief (and, where necessary, having finalized the brief from the draft version), your handling house issues a quote, usually on a per item basis, with a fixed charge to cover overheads and set-up costs. It is also good practice for the handling house to add to its quote its understanding of the project plan, i.e. when items will be arriving from print suppliers, who is responsible for producing what, when action is likely to be required. It is also useful for it to understand the job so that in its response to your brief it may comment on and recommend features to enhance and simplify the call to action. Simple improvements in the customer-facing copy and instructions, etc. can really help to improve the fulfilment process later.

▶ Preparation

If the quote is accepted, the handling house makes preparations to run its part of the campaign. Likely response levels are forecast and work schedules devised to cope with them. Machine and warehousing capacity is allocated. Postal and telecommunication arrangements are made (including Freepost and freephone numbers). Temporary staff are recruited and permanent workers allocated.

▶ Implementation

The campaign starts and responses come in. Mailbags are received, opened, sorted (by client or promotion, hence the importance of properly coded and clearly labelled envelopes), envelopes are arranged for feeding into opening machines. Order forms are checked for completeness. Applications and orders are checked against order forms. Payments are checked for validity (e.g. cheque signatures, dates, wording and amounts). Items to be queried with customers are batched up for inspection, while responses that pass these checks are batched up for data entry. In the telephone room, calls are answered and details entered for processing. Inventory is checked. Numbers are reported to ensure that stocks will be sufficient. Payments are sorted, verified, totalled, reconciled and banked in the client account daily. Payments for stock-out items are held pending availability of stock.

Details of orders are entered onto the computer. This includes not only information about the order and the customer's name and address but also other information about customers that may have been collected by questionnaire.

Stock is allocated to individual customers (this may have taken place online with inbound telemarketing). Where relevant, existing information about customers is accessed, e.g. past payment records, to check whether the order can be processed or whether it should be queried.

Using the order information, consolidated picking lists are created for mail-order companies. Where the fulfilment is in the form of more information, in a pack which is built from several items, each selected to match the customer's need, data is created for transmission to the relevant inserting and labelling machinery.

Stock is released from storage (valuable items may require supervisory signatures). Picking machinery may be used. Items are packed and held pending despatch, via post or a distribution company.

▶ The management of handling

You need to be confident that the handling house you choose is able to perform the required tasks, at the right time, within the agreed budget. For this reason, you may wish to develop a close relationship with just a few handling houses (perhaps only one). This enables you to develop in-depth knowledge of your handling house's capabilities. It also allows the two of you to align systems and procedures. For example, your campaign briefing process must give the handling house the right instructions early enough for it to prepare to handle the campaign (secure additional staff, schedule machinery and storage, etc.).

> **In the real world**
>
> Handling houses tend to be process driven and may not perform a fundamental duty if you have forgotten to put it on the brief. Work with them and encourage them to be proactive in identifying omissions and opportunities.

▶ Handling capabilities

From the point of view of the handling house, meeting your requirements depends upon a wide range of factors, some of which are listed below. If you are considering carrying out your own fulfilment, you should weigh up whether you have these capacities and whether you are prepared to dedicate resources to such activities. Remember that an independent handling house achieves great economies of scale by handling fulfilment for many clients. Expensive machinery, staff and space are not left idle for long periods.

▶ Size

The house must be of the right size for your job. If the job is very large, the house must have the right storage facilities, staff and equipment to handle your job, or at least be able to demonstrate its ability to subcontract some of the work reliably. Conversely, if your job is small, the large handling house must have the right processes for handling smaller jobs. Size also affects whether the handling house can cope with the inevitable late deliveries, overloads and rush jobs.

▶ Condition of premises and equipment

The premises and equipment must be clean and well maintained, to ensure that there are no problems with deterioration of stock or damage to material while it is being processed by the equipment. The premises should also be secure and fire-safe. Anti-fraud/theft measures should be in place such as audit trails and secure despatch to ensure the fulfilment material goes where it should.

▶ People

Firstly, there must be enough staff to handle the job. They must be of the right specializations and know the type of work and their processes well. Too high a staff turnover, particularly among management, may mean lack of familiarity with procedures, and consequent errors. Proper personnel management procedures need to be in place, for recruiting and managing them. This includes payment, training and motivation systems and quality procedures. Supervision should be careful and professional, with regular checks being carried out where appropriate. Staff should be well looked after, with staff welfare facilities and appropriate benefits. Clients have many problems with handling houses that are due to poor personnel management and very low pay levels. Avoid such companies by finding out who they are from other users.

▶ Account management

The relationship between you and the handling house depends critically on the quality of account management. This depends partly on the house's processes, partly on the quality of the account manager – the person responsible for managing all relationships between your company and the house. The best way of checking this is to ask to see completed process documentation, management systems and reference clients. Note that if the house has high staff turnover, account management quality is likely to be low, and you won't be able to rely on your account manager knowing how you like to work and what your processes and systems are.

▶ Processes and systems

The handling house must have clear processes and systems for handling all jobs, from quotation through to agreement to a schedule, to signing off work as it goes through different stages. Computer reports should be routinely available on where any project stands and the numbers of items/customers processed when the fulfilment goes live. These processes and systems should fulfil all customer requirements in the quality sense of the word. Ask for a list of current clients.

▶ Client conflict

You need to decide whether it matters to you if the house is also handling competitors' campaigns. The risk is that they will find out what you are planning to do. Even if 'Chinese walls' are claimed to exist, discovering plans can happen by chance (e.g. the competitive client is in the warehouse and spots some of your merchandise). So think about any possible client conflict.

▶ Performance

Make sure your handling house has a good track record of delivery of projects on time, to high-quality standards, on budget.

▶ The equipment

Fulfilment is the factory of direct marketing – it requires a lot of equipment. The equipment used in handling is listed below. Only the largest handling houses have all of this, but most houses would have most items.

▶ Computing equipment

- Data-capture equipment, enabling data about responses to be captured and transferred to storage. This includes terminals for keying in data from coupons or from telephone calls, and scanning equipment (barcode and optical character readers) for capturing coded, written and typed data. As the technology becomes more robust, voice recognition equipment will become common, particularly for processing orders from catalogues.
- The computer itself (processor, storage, software, etc.) for processing the information keyed in and matching it (where appropriate) to pre-existing customer records. Desktop publishing software may be used on some microcomputers, to compose copy and layout.
- Networking equipment and software, for **secure** transfer of data around the handling house and between the handling house and your computer.
- Data-output machinery. This includes printers of all kinds (impact, ink-jet and lasers). Laser printers range from small correspondence printers to printers for desktop publishing and high-speed laser printers for personalizing mass correspondence. Other technology used here includes plastic card embossers with magnetic stripe encoding, and barcoding printers.

▶ Print machinery

This ranges from small office offset equipment to full four-colour machinery.

▶ Telemarketing systems

These are used for inbound telephone fulfilment and can range from a single answering machine to a 1000-line fully automated system, including digitized voice response.

▶ Materials storage and handling equipment

On major campaigns tens or even hundreds of thousands, and sometimes millions, of items need to be sent out to customers. All this material needs to be stored securely (so that it does not deteriorate and can be handled by machines without problems) and accessibly (so that it can be located quickly and transferred to where it is going to be processed, packed and despatched). Proper storage and materials moving equipment is therefore required.

▶ Addressing and labelling equipment

This includes electronic and mechanical addressing and labelling systems, e.g. ink-jet systems (for printing directly onto envelopes) and automatic labelling machines that accept names and addresses in computer printout format (up to four across), then guillotine to label size and affix to envelopes. For very low-volume mailings, it may still be necessary to type individual labels. Cheshire machines are used for high-volume labelling.

▶ Finishing, packing and wrapping equipment

Machines are required to finish the print items and fold and insert them. Equipment is also needed to shrink wrap, band and strap items together. These must be able to handle many different sizes and weights. Finishing equipment includes bursters, trimmers and collators.

▶ Weighing and calibrating equipment

This includes electronic and mechanical scales for all purposes, measuring weights from fractions of a gram up to a fully loaded pallet. Also required are electronic counting machines to assess postal costs.

▶ Print design equipment

Some handling houses are involved in producing some elements of the mail pack. Those that are need a studio, dark-room and design equipment.

▶ Summary

In this chapter we have covered some of the key elements of production and fulfilment. It should give you the clear idea that these are areas where quality is critical, as the best designed campaign can fail if it is not implemented properly. You should select suppliers of these services with the same care as your other suppliers. It does not pay to cut corners. Big houses may be more expensive, but they are usually better managed and pay a lot of attention to quality. However, word-of-mouth recommendation, from a number of clients, is the ultimate test.

Of course, it's no use demanding high standards of campaign management if yours are not up to scratch. In our next chapter we show you what high-standard campaign management looks like.

managing the hit

The campaign process

Campaign planning

Campaign development

The offer

Creative

Promotional action

Implementing targeting

Campaign management processes

Quality in campaign management

The management process for progressing a campaign

Staffing

Summary

A quality, high-volume, properly managed campaign can take up to three or four months to plan and get ready for launch. Very large companies, with millions of customers, may need to do a lot of database analysis, market analysis and planning, and even simulation of campaigns. At the other extreme, a tactical campaign, particularly one involving new media, may be planned in one day and completed by the next.

You may need to design and test complex contact strategies to ensure the effect on the customer is an effective and balanced one. In such cases, lead time can be six months or more. Faster tactical campaigns do, of course, run and with good results. Mounting a campaign too quickly usually leads to quality problems, sometimes in targeting or creative, and frequently in back-end support and fulfilment.

▶ The campaign process

Developing and implementing a campaign involves the following sequence:

- Planning:
    - What are the key objectives?
    - How are they to be met?
    - Will it require a single or series of campaigns?
    - Who is to be targeted?
    - What product features and benefits are required to meet your objectives?
    - What are the timings and their influence on the above?
- Development – when the details of each campaign are determined.
- Implementation – when each campaign is run.
- Evaluation – when the results of each campaign are analyzed.

▶ Campaign planning

Your marketing plan should give you clear overall objectives, strategies and targets. You now need to translate them into direct marketing actions. The first step is to summarize intentions in the form of a campaign brief. Many companies use their own templates or formats to ensure that all the relevant information is communicated. The brief describes what the target market is, when it is to be promoted to, with what offer and product and how, to meet what objectives and as part of what strategies. We have included examples of briefs in Chapter 5.

You can refine and add to a brief as you get more information which may influence timings, proposition and so on. It's good practice and labour-saving to prepare the brief early and circulate it to those involved (within your business and among agencies) early on, even if only as a draft. This way all involved will understand your objectives and rationale. This will help to avoid clashes with other projects, data problems and resource bottlenecks. It also helps with getting buy-in and co-operation.

19 / Managing the hit

In the real world

Check that your brief does the following:
- Does it help organize thinking?
- Will it guide implementers?
- Does it communicate the essence of the campaign to your company and to your suppliers?
- Is it the supporting document for more detailed forms covering different aspects of the campaign?

▶ Campaign development

This is when all your campaign details (targeting, including lists, timing, offer, creative, etc.) are determined, using agencies where appropriate. Getting details right at this stage ensures that your campaign runs smoothly once it is launched. You must be absolutely sure of your objectives and rationale at this stage, to avoid confusing yourself and others later.

Action
- Make sure all suppliers are working well, to a common plan, and communicating progress.
- Build a team with external and internal suppliers, including, for example, in-house print, telemarketing, finance, database marketing, risk and so on.
- Brief all your suppliers – internal and external – together where possible.
- Encourage them to work together.

▶ Campaign implementation

Your campaign is running. Here, you need to ensure that campaign logistics are running smoothly (e.g. mailings going out on time, responses being handled properly) and that interim results are analyzed to see whether any details need changing. This stage may be controlled through your customer database system and possibly managed through your management information system. You must set up your measurement approach beforehand, so you can see results as they come in and assess performance. Otherwise you may miss problems, or even brilliant results which you can build on.

▶ Campaign evaluation

After the campaign has run, you need to find out what worked and what did not. Here, your main activity is analysis of response rates by different categories (media, market segment, timing of response). However, you need to check that the statistics were correctly measured, to avoid false conclusions.

Now let's look at these stages in more detail.

Campaign planning

Setting campaign objectives

Your first step in relating the campaign process to the marketing plan is to determine which marketing plan objectives can be achieved through direct marketing. Here are some likely objectives and the campaign strategies that might help achieve them.

Objective	Examples of how
Gaining more business from existing customers	◆ Identifying, from purchasing data, whether there are gaps in your product and service range/variants, then creating relevant products and services and promoting them. ◆ Promoting existing products and services to customers on your database. ◆ Creating new relationships with existing customers, tying them more closely to you and increasing customer loyalty. ◆ Developing loyalty programmes, which allow customers to develop a closer relationship with you. ◆ Identifying your customers' requirements for levels of service, developing and promoting the required level of service, and following up afterwards to ensure that good service is remembered and poor service compensated for, to achieve higher levels of customer satisfaction and loyalty. ◆ Identifying competitive threats to particular customers, developing stronger incentives for these customers and promoting them heavily.
Increase your customer base	◆ Developing profiles of existing valuable customers, applying these profiles to selected external lists, and promoting relevant products to customers so identified, and offering relevant relationships. ◆ Re-awakening past customers by identifying them, determining their needs, developing and promoting offers which meet these needs. ◆ Gathering prospect data from people who have contacted your company, capturing this and using this to market to these clearly warm prospects. ◆ Identifying gaps in the market and targeting competitive customers with a stronger and more compelling proposition.
Reducing promotional costs	◆ Examining current methods of communicating with customers and seeking to achieve the same effect through direct communication. ◆ Analysis of your present cost per response to reduce cost of marcomms in line with targets. ◆ Testing the effect of different formats, messages and offers to achieve similar esponse with a reduced marcomms (marketing communications) cost.
Positioning and branding	◆ Every direct marketing campaign should support the creation of positioning and branding (master and sub-brands) with all customers. You should maintain strict standards in relation to the types of offer promoted and their creative presentation. ◆ By co-ordinating direct marketing activity in terms of timing, you can optimize awareness and translate it into sales.

> **Fast-track**
>
> Your objectives are an essential part of the brief to your agencies. Specify them clearly and in quantified form. Check that your agencies understand them. The more they understand and are accountable for results, the better they will understand their role and the more responsible they become.

Keep campaign objectives simple and specific. If you aim to recruit good new customers, all your campaign objectives should relate to this. The meaning of 'good new customer' should be specified, as should the number of them you want. Objectives which are too complex lead to weak campaigns.

▶ Justifying the campaign

In your planning documentation, justify the campaign in terms of the main marketing objectives it supports (e.g. the need to increase sales of a particular product or to capitalize on a growth trend). The statement should be as specific as possible, particularly in terms of:

- the type of customer involved;
- the attitudes and behaviour you are trying to influence;
- the influence of timing of customer behaviour on timing of campaign (e.g. when they are most likely to buy).

This provides the key to campaign co-ordination, as well as to setting clear, quantifiable campaign objectives.

▶ Relationship objectives

You may want to create a relationship with your customers that transcends individual campaigns. This resembles how a salesperson develops a relationship with customers that transcends the individual sale. You need some measure of the progress of the relationship, for example, the number of customers of a specified value or greater that you have recruited onto your database through the campaigns.

Various themes can be developed during a relationship. Here is an example of development of a theme.

> *Stage 1* Recruit a set of customers (new or existing) into a new relationship.
> *Stage 2* Promote to them an offer which is relevant to the relationship.
> *Stage 3* Promote second and further offers to them (up-selling, cross-selling).
> *Stage 4* Develop further offers based upon a study of those with the greatest take-up (more cross-selling).
> *Stage 5* Enrol customers in member-get-member programmes.
> *Stage 6* Develop offers which group products together.

The development of a relationship can be over a short period (say six months) or over several years. In practice, long-term relationships should be composed of a series of short, feasible steps, paid for all along the way by the take-up of offers. Here is a way of viewing the development of the relationship.

Recruitment	Attract totally new customers.
Competitor acquisition	Make conquest sales from those who do not use your product but use competitive products (i.e. Sky digital targeting cable homes areas).
Optimization	Cross-sell or up-sell new products to push up usage and revenue per unit/user.
Activation	Get existing customers who don't use your product actively to start using it (i.e. targeting dormant credit card accounts) and bring forward their next purchases.

These strategies can be expressed in terms of the classic product-market matrix shown in Fig. 19.1. Earliest results may come from existing customers (they have already demonstrated that they need the product). The slowest results often come from totally new customers. It may be possible to attract some totally new customers as your sequence of campaigns begins, but achieving significant numbers (and getting them to stay with you) may involve a stronger effort.

▶ Campaign objectives and measurement

Direct marketing requires quantified objectives. These should come from the quantified objectives of your marketing plan. If these are not quantified (at all or in enough detail), you must still quantify your direct marketing objectives. Include in your campaign plan details of how performance against objectives will be measured, e.g. through responses, actual sales or research measurements. Your quantification should include:

◆ target levels of achievement;
◆ dates by which the achievement is to be reached.

For longer-term campaigns or a sequence of campaigns, where you may wish to change objectives along the way, include interim measures to show whether you are achieving targets, and dates for taking these measures.

Fig. 19.1 The classic product-market matrix

		Markets	
		Existing	New
Products	Existing	Market penetration	Product development
	New	Market development	Diversification

Campaign development

> **Campaign development** is the heartland of direct marketing. It covers targeting and timing, combined into contact strategies using particular media, the offer and the creative.

Targeting

Your targeting should be as specific as possible. With a clear statement of your marketing objectives and strategies, you should be able to identify the customer types who form the target market for the campaign. Good targeting is a creative process, split into two separate and very different issues:

- who the campaign is aimed at;
- how to find them and gain access to them.

Who?

Creativity is required in answering the 'who' question, to determine the different customer types who fit into the target market definition. Use your knowledge of customers to build a picture of the different types of person who form your target market. For example, the target market for a very high-contribution executive pension plan might include directors of very profitable small businesses, directors of big companies, and so on. Your customer database should enable you to turn each of these definitions into different selections. Then different, relevant promotional actions can be developed for each customer type.

If your database has been built over several years of promotions, you can use another kind of creativity – the statistical. Many statistical techniques are available to identify clusters or segments of customers who are similar in one or more ways. It is sensible to start your search for segments in these areas:

Type of segmentation	Typical variables used
Transaction/purchase behaviour	Usage of particular products
	Their revenue
	Their loyalty – length of customer relationship
Socio-demographic or economic	Geo-demographic location – where they live
	Household income
	Marital status
	Residential status (detached, semi, rented)
	With/without children
	Interests/leisure pursuits

Note that the more sophisticated your segmentation, the harder it can be to identify specific customers who are members of a particular segment.

The higher the quality of your data, and the more clearly you identify profiles or segments, the more you can rely on this approach for creative targeting. Also, you will have fewer problems in finding and gaining access to identified groups.

The **number** of customers in your campaign target market should be determined by your quantified campaign objectives. You may be targeting **all** customers in a particular geographical market who fit a particular definition. Or quantified sales objectives will lead through expected response and sales rates to a target number to be contacted. If response or final sales rates are difficult to forecast, test them. If you have a proper marketing and campaign planning framework, you'll be able to build in time to test.

▶ Timing

Timing can be split into two elements:

- **macro-timing** – when the campaign should be run. It takes into account other campaigns you might be running and your target customers' needs;
- **micro-timing** – when each element of your campaign's contact strategy should be run. It takes into account the timing of other elements of the campaign and what is known about the likely receptiveness of customers at different periods.

Macro-timing is often determined by the greater sales forecast plan and illustrated in your wider marketing plan. The main factors that influence timings are:

- sales forecasts – when should the budget be focused, when are the big sales numbers expected?;
- brand activity – when the main advertising campaigns planned will take place. When awareness is being driven, your direct marketing should be integrated with it;
- products – when new or modified products are available for sale;
- seasonal influences – seasons, bank and children's holidays, tax year and so on will affect demand for your product;
- capability and resources – when your company has the time and money to dedicate to the campaign;
- hit rate – how many times you hit the customer/prospect. This can be monthly or quarterly, but take into account previous mailings to avoid bombarding customers.

An important element in the justification for any campaign is why it should run at the proposed time. A specific issue is frequency of mailing to good customers. You should control this, but also test it across different products. Evidence from many sectors shows that there is almost no limit to the number of times a loyal customer can be mailed. However, one condition applies to this: Every mailing must be good quality, relevant and consistent with other mailings.

The same applies to telephone calls, particularly in industrial markets. No calls must be idle. They must all be of benefit to both you and your customer.

If you have no policy on frequency, develop one and keep it under review in the light of experience. Testing and customer research are required to monitor response and attitudes under different mailing frequencies. If you are selling many products and each sale requires more than one contact (e.g. an initial letter followed by a mail pack, which produces the order), the risk of over-contacting is even greater. Frequency should be established by testing (for response) combined with research (to ensure no customer alienation).

Micro-timing should be based on your in-depth knowledge of customers' receptiveness to different types of communication and how different media work together. Information on this will come largely from past campaigns and from agencies, if they have experience in similar markets. Here are some guidelines:

- Media inserts are often uplifted by TV and radio brand advertising.
- Media inserts should not be used in the same title less than six weeks apart to avoid wear-out.
- Door drops may be more effective when rested for three months.
- Press advertising should be placed no more than once in the same title to maintain response.
- Direct mail should be sent to the same person no more than every three months to maintain response.
- Chaser packs should follow within 10–14 days.
- SMS sales messages achieve greater results when done in two parts and chased up by a follow-up message. A third message is too much.

▶ The offer

The offer is not just a description of the product. It combines one or more propositions with incentive(s) to try the proposition. More than one proposition may be promoted in a campaign. The areas to explore for propositions include:

- product characteristics – performance, quality of service, reliability, variety of functions;
- market factors – types of customer, market share, exclusivity;
- ways of using the product – to save time, to make more profit, to treat;
- surprising facts about the product, users or usage (used by celebrities, for example);
- price characteristics – value for money, money-back guarantee, discounts;
- image – top quality, good value, friendly, reliable;
- needs-satisfying – physical, status etc.;
- company – nationality, energy, direction, customer-orientation;
- drawbacks of non-use – what the customer loses or misses by not buying;

- competitive comparison – product, company;
- newsworthiness – recent changes, anniversaries, topical events, new facilities.

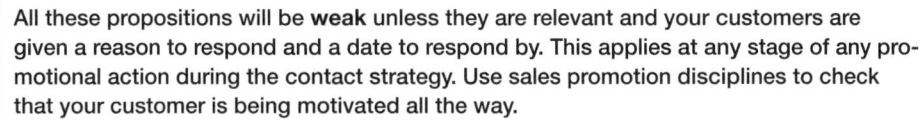

> **Warning!**
> All these propositions will be **weak** unless they are relevant and your customers are given a reason to respond and a date to respond by. This applies at any stage of any promotional action during the contact strategy. Use sales promotion disciplines to check that your customer is being motivated all the way.

There are many ways of generating response through the offer. For a high-quality response, the offer should be related to the product or service. For example, a free electronic gadget may give a high response, but the end result may not be good. However, if your targeting is accurate (i.e. those receiving the promotion are the right ones and in the market now), it may be sensible to push up the response by a non-related offer. The offer most relevant to the product is one that adds value to the product or is just more of the product (e.g. half price or two for one), with the 'call to action' being a limit on the period of availability of the offer in terms of time or quantity.

Test to discover which offer is the best. If there is no time to test, examine the results of past offers for similar campaigns (similar products, media and target markets). Some customers are mail-responsive, others telephone-responsive. Certain kinds of customers respond to certain kinds of offer, others to other kinds of offer.

Creative

In all forms of marketing communication, the creative element – the expression of the campaign in words (printed, broadcast or telemarketing scripts) and pictures – is always the most obvious and so tends to attract most management interest. It is certainly important, but so are the other, maybe less glamorous factors such as leads and offer.

> **In the real world**
> Poor creative development is one of the main reasons for delayed campaigns and last-minute rushes. Worse, the scope for confusing customers through the form of the offer is also great. Creative usually goes wrong because of poor briefing, lack of standards applied to each medium (e.g. copy style, typeface), lack of understanding of the target customer, and poor communication between client and agency (e.g. no version control).

Consistency in creative standards is essential. This means much more than standards for displaying the corporate logo. You should have clear standards on the layout of print, the look of pictures, the tone of copy, paper weight and stock and so on.

This need not impose a grey uniformity on your campaigns. But if you aim to develop a long-term relationship between the customer and your whole company (as represented by your master brand), the master brand must come through every presentation. Each sub-brand must have a clear relationship with the master brand. Rules for relating the two in every medium must be stated.

Problems arise with the creative with:

- imprecise or too generalized a description of the target market – irrelevant, no real hook;
- inadequate specification of how the buying process takes place – muddled CTA, drop-off will occur from order to purchase;
- lack of clarity on desired tone, proposition, and branding – inappropriate, irrelevant;
- inclusion of too many objectives for the medium being used – too confusing, no key message;
- not putting every item of creative through the proper approvals process – inconsistency, legal issues likely, wrong information, back-end fulfilment problems;
- inconsistency of message and tone with the particular medium being used – stand-out reduced, brand damage, inefficient campaign costs.

Different media can sustain different degrees of complexity of message. For example, in a mailing several pieces can be included, with different objectives, provided they are clearly from you and have something in common. This is because customers tend to look at each enclosure, so each may have separate messages. But each enclosure should be single-minded. The same does not apply to television or radio, where the same approach would confuse customers.

Promotional actions

The promotional actions used for a campaign should be as simple as possible and based on what the company **knows** works for customers in the target market. Any really new approach should be tested before it is rolled out, to manage any likely risk of it not working.

> **Checklist: each promotional step**
>
> ☐ The objectives – what should happen to customers who are the target of the campaign, e.g. be informed or persuaded, give information, identify themselves as being in the target market, i.e. hand-raising, buy a product.
> ☐ How customers should respond (e.g. fill in a questionnaire and send it, buy a product and give proof of purchase, phone and book, book online).
> ☐ How the promotional action will achieve this (e.g. description of mail pack or advertisement, in particular the response device, if any) and the strength necessary.
> ☐ How many customers are expected to respond in different ways.

Keep the number of promotional steps to a minimum. However, you may need more than one step. For example, you want to recruit new customers, you may want to use media advertising or external lists with a straightforward letter and small leaflet to identify prospects, followed up with a more expensive mail pack to those who have confirmed that they are in the target market. This might achieve a more effective contact (in terms of final results versus costs) than sending an expensive pack to the external list.

Implementing targeting

You may find that your first draft campaign plan aims at too many different segments. This can lead to high promotional costs and poor results. So segments should be prioritized and combined where possible to reduce the complexity of the campaign. Through testing or experience with past campaigns, you should be able to identify rates of trade-off between response rates (and sales rates) and campaign coverage. Too high a response rate and too much contribution per promotional contact may mean that the campaign is too small (because you tend to get very high response rates with small segments that exactly fit the target market). If the opposite occurs, the campaign may be too big.

Sizing the selection

The process for determining campaign size should go as follows:

- **Segment.** Break down your target market into target segments.
- **Costs and benefits.** Identify the likely cost and benefits of promoting to each target segment. Distinguish fixed costs from variable costs, and also the effect that more precise targeting and targeted offer design will have on your response rates. If the benefit to you cannot be stated in profit terms but the promotion is essential for strategic reasons, an 'alternative cost' measure can be used. This measures what it would have cost to promote to the customer using the next best method. The implication here is that the difference is being saved.
- **Lists.** If your target market is not well represented on your database, consult with your database administration or list brokers about which lists should be used. Consult your agency about which advertising media to use. Identify your best customers and their attributes and apply the same selections to other lists or media to pick the best likely prospects. You may want to test target other segments that your research tells you might also be responsive if the positioning of your product can be modified.

> **In the real world**
>
> An example might be tailoring your PC software from 'cutting-edge technology and cool', which targets the early adopter and 15–25 male PC user, to 'easy to use, help desk on call 24 hours a day' to target the late adopting parents and 'silver surfer' generation.
> Another example is mobile positioning with 'funky facias, cheap SMS rates to mail all your mates' to target the school kids, to 'stay in touch, peace of mind, your family always a call away' if positioning to the middle-aged and retired market.

▶ Database analysis

If large numbers of your target market are on the database, experiment with selections until:

- several target segments have been identified as not overlapping or differing significantly in the kind of offer that can be made to them;
- a simple selection criterion will suffice because more complex selection criteria do not give target segments of sufficient size for a cost-effective promotion.

▶ Selections

Define the segments for final selection purposes. Plot out their key attributes and differentiators to maintain focus on positioning and message.

▶ Measurement

Specify all the criteria by which success of the campaign will be measured. For direct mail, the following matrix may be used as a template. There are many sections in here which cover volume, anticipated response, costs and resulting cost per response and bookings. This matrix may be tailored to suit your specific business needs and per campaign, but it's a good idea to keep all aspects of the campaign together in the same place to get a clear view on results as you progress through the response curve.

▶ List usage

In choosing a list, follow these basic golden rules:

1 **Your own database will give better results than external lists.** It is based on fact, not assumption.
2 **The best external lists will have customers that resemble your existing customers.** They may have many of your existing customers on them, but screen or deduplicate them to remove them before using such an external list, so as not to antagonize your present customers.
3 **A responders' or prospect database list pulls better than non-responders** (e.g. compiled). A list of customers with proven histories of buying from a medium (mail, telephone, off the page) pulls best of all for that medium.

▶ Mail-order lists

Mail-order purchase lists include fashion, gardening, household, book/record clubs, magazine subscriptions, holidays, investment/insurance, gifts and self-improvement. If a list is not available, try inserts in a publication that reaches your target. Choose a publication which defines a strong affinity (e.g. a members' publication).

▶ Responder lists

Lists of responders but not purchasers (enquirers who didn't buy, also known as prospects, controlled circulation publication requests, exhibition attendees, lifestyle databases compiled from returned questionnaires) are usually less responsive but give you better ability to target.

▶ Compiled lists

Leads from your own databases are a valuable asset, though many companies fail to follow up those who respond but do not buy. Do all you can to capture your prospects and re-use them. Leads that are compiled by a lifestyle database company tend to be higher cost but more responsive than those profiled just on geo-demographic data as the person has filled in a questionnaire and the data is gathered in response to a particular question or series of questions. To enhance geo-demographic data, you need to use profiling models which are based on your best customers to home in on your best targets.

In the business-to-business market, data of this type is gathered from many sources, such as attendees at conferences and exhibitions. As such lists are often compiled as part of a general data-gathering exercise rather than to find good prospects, their usefulness for direct marketing purposes may be low.

▶ Deciding on lists

To make a decision about lists, you need information about the source and how it was collected, and the type of offer from which the list was derived. The source may be a mail promotion, SMS or Internet promotion, from enquiries about magazine editorial, from circulation or membership. You may need a list broker's working knowledge of the list and the selections available.

You need to know:

- frequency (how often list members buy/respond), recency (when they last did so), amount (how much they bought) and category (what type of product they bought) of purchase;
- date of expiry, if the list is subscription expiries (this shows they have at least bought at some time in the past);
- who the most recent purchasers are ('hot-line');
- how often the list is mailed to – the best are usually mailed most often because they work and because list members like receiving and responding;
- when and where it was sourced, and when it was last cleaned.

> **Warning!**
>
> Although externally provided data may be valuable, if you have a customer database, be selective about what information you buy. Always test the usefulness of additional data, whether it is new names and addresses or additional information on customers you already have on file. Deduplicate and carry out spot-checks for poor spelling and data in the wrong fields. A mailing addressed to Mr Deep-Sea Diver instead of Mr Brown may be funny but not for the customer. It does nothing for your credibility and your brand.

> **In the real world**
>
> A test is valuable and useful only if it provides you with a statistically valid cell of responders that can be analyzed. Typically the market standard bases the minimum sample size on that needed for 50 sales/responses, so according to your anticipated response rate (use your standard response as a guide) you can calculate the mailing volume needed to test. For example:
>
> 5% is the average response rate for your direct mailings so:
>
> 1000 mail packs × 5% = 50 responses, therefore 1000 is your minimum mailing test cell size.

Most lists are available for rental only and only with a high degree of security. Lists will also have seeds (usually members of staff from the owners or their agencies) on them to ensure that you do not misuse the list. You may be asked for samples of mailings by list owners. Plan your list usage well in time, to ensure the right coverage and quality for the right price. Allow time for the various data-processing operations needed before you can use a list.

Allow time for testing each list. To test a list, the volume needs to be large enough to test it against other sources of data to check that the variance in the result is due to the list. The recommended size of a list test cell is 5–10k for first-time test, 25–50k to validate. If the list is too small, a sample of the list should not be tested – test the whole list.

▶ Campaign management processes

▶ In-house work

In direct marketing, much of the work in delivering campaigns is done in-house. This can surprise companies which are used to communicating with their customers mostly through media advertising (television, radio, press, etc.). Large users of direct marketing have to manage relationships between many people. They include:

- specialist direct marketers;
- internal 'customers' (such as product and brand managers, sales management, store operations management);

- systems staff (for the customer and other databases);
- a wide network of suppliers (direct marketing agencies, print production, tele-marketing agencies, mailing and fulfilment houses, etc.).

It's important to ensure that the many people involved in direct marketing work together and produce quality campaigns and implement them in a quality manner.

Quality in campaign management

If you are or aim to be a serious direct marketing user, try to be methodical about the planning and execution of campaigns, to ensure high quality.

> **Warning!**
> Lack of quality leads to:
> - lost market share;
> - low response and high campaign costs.

Causes of quality problems

Here are some examples of problems and what they lead to.

Problem	Result
Late, incomplete briefing by the 'client'	Hurried campaign development cycles, poor targeting, rushed printing, unclear instructions, and the inevitable consequences of poor material or the wrong material being sent to customers, or responses being handled badly.
Too aggressive objectives relating to size of database	High volumes of low-quality customer data being brought onto the database. This in turn leads to high mis-targeting and returns rates, and high costs of database maintenance relative to financial returns.
Lack of analysis of past results	Poor targeting and wrong media choice.
Lack of communication with those at the 'coal face' (e.g. call centre, field sales staff, branch workers)	Systems being developed which are cumbersome and difficult to use. It also leads to applications being developed in the wrong order (e.g. direct mail instead of telemarketing). This is because unless those who work at the coal face do their bit in 'closing the sales loop', even the best laid campaign plans will not be realized. For example, a mail shot which produces a 20% response rate is no use if sales people are too busy to follow up the leads or do not understand what they are supposed to do with them.

The solution to these problems lies in using project management disciplines. Direct marketing usually involves running many campaigns a year. Each of these campaigns is a project. The problem with managing these projects is that each differs from the others. To manage this kind of work, project management techniques are required. These are designed to progress complex projects through teams of people working on them. These processes include the following.

▶ The project file

You need a comprehensive project file for each campaign. It includes the relevant marketing plan details, forms for briefing all suppliers, the project timetable, sign-off authorities, criteria and codes for selections, descriptions and codes for all promotional material, forecast returns and actual results. A master copy of this file should be held by your campaign manager and duplicates by all parties involved. Examples of campaign briefing formats and completion instructions are included at the end of this chapter.

▶ Project planning software

This is used to schedule the tasks required to deliver campaigns and reschedule them where slips occur. It is also used to identify bottlenecks. It produces status reports and enables us to identify accountabilities for failures. However, you can do this manually through using a simple spreadsheet template. This allows you to sort tasks according to their type, accountability, budget, etc. See Fig. 19.2 for a simple spreadsheet template.

▶ Targeting and scheduling processes

You need processes for targeting and scheduling campaigns. These reduce clashes and increase the effectiveness of targeting. The processes range from consensus to directive. The consensus approach may be through a team of all interested parties. The directive approach may be through a database directorate having authority to determine campaign sequencing. In both cases, your in-depth understanding of the database and past campaign results should be deployed in determining which campaigns go forward.

▶ Communication

You need structured processes for communicating campaign status to all parties involved. In their most advanced form, these processes are computerized. In most cases, this is done via e-mail where exchange of notes, briefs, extracts from the campaign database, campaign matrices and so on can be communicated widely, and quickly. In more advanced companies, all those involved in a campaign have direct access to relevant parts of a computerized campaign project file on the shared server.

Quality in campaign management

Fig. 19.2 A simple campaign project plan spreadsheet template

P = planned, R = revised plan   = done

Task name	No.	Resource	Budget	2	3	4	5	6	7	8	9	10	11	12	13	14	15	16	17	18	19	20	21	Comment
Define target markets	1.01																							
Analyze database	1.02				P																			
Brief research	1.03																							
Research customer needs	1.04				P	P																		
Workshop	1.05						P																	
Quantify objectives	1.06						P																	
Define plan	1.07						P	P																
Define contact strategy	1.08							P	P															
Brief print	1.09								P															
Brief script	1.10								P															
Select test list	2.01								P															
Prepare test mailing	2.02								P	P														
Prepare test telemarketing script	2.03								P	P														
Send test mailing	2.04										P	P												
Follow up calls	2.05										P	P	P	P										
Follow up sales visits	2.06											P	P	P										
Compile results	2.07														P									
Evaluate	2.08														P									
Finalize list	3.01															P								
Modify script	3.02															P								
Send mailing	3.03																P	P	P	P				
Follow up calls	3.04																	P	P	P	P			
Follow up sales visits	3.05																		P	P	P	P		
Compile results	3.06																							P
Evaluate	3.07																							P

▶ Training

Your staff must receive the training they need to develop the skills their position requires. Typically, a specialist group of database/direct marketers, acting as both a consultant and a technical expert with authority to decide, needs training in:

- basic consultative skills – listening, communicating, influencing, interactive skills (meetings), contracting (fixing agreements);
- how to put together projects that will meet customer needs, and manage the projects through.

▶ The management process for progressing a campaign

Many direct marketers have to design and deliver campaigns without any management process. Some are given as guidance a list of 'stages of campaign development' (see Fig. 19.3). This was fine in the days when direct marketing consisted of the odd tactical campaign. Today, when direct marketing has become central to the strategic marketing of many companies, it is not good enough. Your process should specify clearly:

Fig. 19.3 Stages of campaign development

Briefing/planning	**Mail**
Campaign confirmed	Creative agreed
Agency brief	Approve pack dummy
Proposition agreed	Lists ordered
Concept agreed	Final copy approved
Contact strategy agreed	Mailing/fulfilment houses briefed
Media brief produced	Print production schedule issued
Confirm media plan	Approve artwork
Receive media details	Artwork ready for print
Issue media details to suppliers	Laser proof approved
Systems team briefed by direct marketers	Sign off live pack
Systems programme produced	First mailing
Internal lists ordered	First fulfilment
Lists produced	
External lists ordered	**Inbound telemarketing**
External lists delivered	Brief telemarketing agency/group
Go/no go	Scripts agreed for testing
Check campaign logistics	Operator briefing
Brief internal staff (hq/regions/branches)	Systems test
Campaign live	Scripts revised after testing
Campaign ends	Scripts live
Evaluate results	
	Outbound telemarketing
Advertising	Brief telemarketing agency/group
Creative agreed	Scripts agreed for testing
Copy approved	Operator briefing
Artwork approved	Systems test
Copy despatched	Scripts revised after testing
Advertisements appear	Scripts live

- the steps involved in developing and delivering a campaign, and who is responsible for them;
- a specification of the data and communication requirements to support the flow of work, and who is responsible for providing and communicating the information.

▶ Cross-campaign planning and co-ordination

Unless all your marketing communication is based on direct marketing, you need to co-ordinate direct marketing with other marketing communications. Campaign planning and co-ordination is not theoretically complex. It is just a question of making sure that campaigns deliver messages whose content and timing is co-ordinated and which contribute to the development of the company's brand(s). This means co-ordinating every aspect of campaign development.

▶ Co-ordinating targeting, contact strategies – media and timing

Co-ordination within direct marketing is mainly a question of selections (or lists) and timing their use. In companies whose main marketing channel is direct, such as mail, and which have good customer databases, co-ordinating selections is the key activity. It is so important that some companies treat access to the database as the key marketing decision. Brand managers and sales managers are required to submit their briefs to the database manager. The database manager's job is then to determine who are the best prospects for the campaign in question and when they should be addressed, taking into account targeting, timing and offers of other campaigns, as well as strategic priorities and degree of selectivity of campaigns.

> **In the real world**
>
> In some companies, the database manager suggests which campaigns should be run and what contact strategies they should use. From being a manager of the database, the database manager becomes the initiator of campaign ideas. This is because, through analysis of the database, the campaigns that should be run can be identified. The database manager plays the customer-advocate, with customers speaking through the database on the basis of what campaigns they have responded to and what campaigns are missing.

▶ Offer co-ordination

If your company needs direct marketing to push several products at the same time, co-ordinating can be difficult. Direct marketers live with the constant possibility of clashes in timing. However, the earlier the warning about the need to promote a particular product, the more time you get to develop ways of presenting products through offers – hence the importance of having the bigger picture and maintaining a marketing plan and communications with senior marketing management.

If products differ greatly in their nature and target market, co-ordination is not a problem. But if products are similar, with overlapping target markets, ways of positioning products relative to each other must be developed. You need time to test how far target markets actually do overlap, so that non-overlapping segments can be identified and promoted to differently.

> **In the real world**
> Offer co-ordination demands a deep understanding of target markets and product benefits. The secret of offer co-ordination lies in early briefing on product benefits, clear and early-stated views on target markets, and early warning of campaign timings. So make sure this happens in your company, not just through your own efforts but through a formal process.

▶ Organizing co-ordination

Many companies organize by committee. Briefs are collated and submitted to a campaign co-ordination committee. Big direct marketing users such as credit card companies need this centrally co-ordinated process to manage their many inserts, statement messages and cold recruitment campaigns. Briefs and rationale are discussed, campaigns are prioritized and slotted together using different selection criteria. In other companies, a planning department receives all briefs and allocates them a budget and timing slot. Whatever approach is used, the most important achievement is getting briefs submitted well in time. The output of the planning process must be properly communicated, so that the whole team knows what it must do when.

▶ Campaign statuses

Because it takes time to decide if and when a campaign should run, a campaign can have different statuses, from being a gleam of an idea of a product manager to the finished product. Here are the kinds of statuses your process needs:

- **Provisional** – you have identified the campaign as needing consideration, but have not yet submitted it for formal consideration by the campaign co-ordination process. Normally, a deadline for such consideration should be set. The campaign proposal should contain an outline brief, timing and suggested budget.
- **Submitted** – you have submitted the campaign for consideration through the campaign co-ordination process, with the brief and timing firmed up. Again, a deadline for approval or otherwise should be set.
- **Approved** – the campaign has been approved by your campaign co-ordination process, with timings for development, launch and close agreed.
- **Budgeted** – although an outline budget should be considered when a campaign is at earlier stages, final budgeting should not take place until quotes are received from suppliers. There is no point in getting detailed quotes before the campaign is approved because this wastes suppliers' time and may slow down

other projects. Your outline budget should be based on experience with earlier campaigns. An outline budget also stops you wasting suppliers' time if the requirement turns out to be infeasible within the outline budget.

- **Under development** – you have started serious work on the campaign, your suppliers have been briefed, and money is being spent.
- **Live** – the campaign has hit the market.
- **Completed** – the campaign is completed. No further actions in the market will be taken.
- **Closed** – the results of the campaign have been analyzed and properly documented.

The above are 'operational' statuses. They describe where your project stands in its normal process of development. However, things do not always run so smoothly. Campaigns may be cancelled, deferred or even absorbed into other campaigns. So four further statuses are needed, as follows:

- **Current** – the campaign is at one of the above statuses and progressing normally.
- **Cancelled** – your campaign will not go ahead. This may be determined at any stage until the campaign is live. Records of the work done for the campaign should be kept as they may be needed later.
- **Deferred** – the campaign is put off until later. No new timing has been specified and it will require resubmission through the co-ordination process.
- **Absorbed** – the campaign has been absorbed into another campaign (perhaps after a delay).

> **Warning!**
> The above four statuses are 'management statuses'. Changing a management status has important resource implications and may have legal or contractual implications with suppliers. For example, cancelling a campaign may create a risk of breach of contract with suppliers.

If these statuses are used, it becomes much easier to manage campaign co-ordination and resource allocation processes. The whole team, including suppliers, will know at any one time what campaigns are being considered, planned, worked upon and finished.

Staffing

One neglected aspect of direct marketing management is recognition of the different roles that are needed to ensure that campaigns are delivered properly. Some have already been discussed implicitly – the campaign manager, the manager responsible for co-ordination. But there are other roles:

- **Initiation or origination** – coming up with the ideas for campaigns.
- **Workload control** – ensuring that the resources of the team, including suppliers, are adequate to meet the demands upon them, and that work is scheduled so as to optimize use of these resources.
- **Campaign administration** – ensuring that all campaigns are well documented and communicated, and that everyone in the team meets their deadlines.
- **Delivery** – actually doing the job of bringing the campaign to market.
- **Sponsoring** – providing the funds.
- **Being the internal customer** – the person benefiting from the campaign, typically a product, service or sales manager.

In some companies, these roles are combined in the direct marketing manager. But in large companies doing lots of direct marketing, the roles are often split. The most underrated of all these functions is campaign administration. Although quite a junior person can fulfil this role, good campaign administrators are worth their weight in gold.

All the above may seem a little top-heavy for the small company. However, there is no reason to suppose that the small user of direct marketing will face fewer problems in managing direct marketing than the larger user. Indeed, the small user may have one person doing **all** the marketing. With a few adjustments, all the foregoing can be used to manage any kind of marketing campaign, whether an advertising campaign, a sales force campaign, a product launch or a sales promotion.

▶ Managing resources

A large marketing department also requires a production process. This is seen particularly in agencies rather than clients, and involves viewing the department as a sort of jobbing workshop, through which campaign work progresses. Each 'job' requires certain resources to progress it, and each resource is required for a certain amount of time. If all campaigns are organized using the kind of status descriptions used above, it should be relatively simple to organize production planning. The main question is how much each campaign takes of the different resources available. These might include account managers, direct marketing specialists, print specialists, database and systems people, media planners and so on.

The production planning process reviews forward workload with these aims:

- to check that the workload required of each resource is feasible;
- where the workload of any individual or department is temporarily too high, to arrange for the redeployment of resource or the hiring of external resource on a temporary basis;
- where the workload of any resource is permanently too high, to arrange permanent redeployment or increased resource;
- where budgetary constraints prevent resource readjustment, to recommend that work be deferred or ended.

The planning horizon depends on the average period from the time a campaign is identified as likely to run to the time it goes live – its gestation period. The planning period should be at least double the gestation period.

▶ Information requirements

All planning information should be collated periodically, typically every few weeks. The following information is required:

- the status of all projects under gestation or live;
- the likely loadings of all these projects on different members of staff and agencies;
- likely bottlenecks.

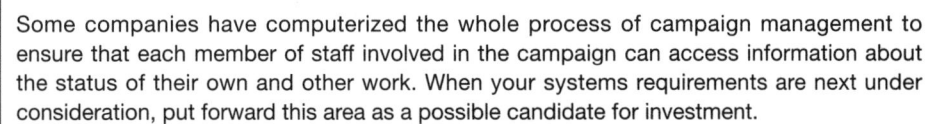

> **Action**
> Some companies have computerized the whole process of campaign management to ensure that each member of staff involved in the campaign can access information about the status of their own and other work. When your systems requirements are next under consideration, put forward this area as a possible candidate for investment.

▶ Summary

All that we have described above is no more than common sense. The problem is that most direct marketers find it hard to make the time for good management – they are frequently too busy! However, planning more effectively and investing time in advance will save you time and make campaign delivery and management much easier. The importance of quality and value is recognized far more these days, so focusing on customer contacts, their relationships with you and their value to the business is critical to your success as a marketer, and also for the business.

Quality also depends partly on testing campaigns, to make sure they're right for the market. After all, everything changes, so a critical aspect of good direct marketing management is making time for testing. Let's see what you have to do to test campaigns properly, in our next chapter.

20 testing in direct and interactive marketing

- What is testing and why should you test?
- Specifying testing
- The objective of testing
- The aims of statistics – to generalize
- Narrowing down what is to be tested
- Sampling and interface
- Distributions
- Testing differences
- Sampling methods
- Test matrices
- Split runs and other ways of varying sample treatment
- The control group
- Response rates vs sales rates
- Advanced statistics
- Summary

What is testing and why should you test?

Your key to direct marketing success is to discover what works and to repeat it. Testing helps you discover what works and what doesn't. It helps you to repeat successes and avoid costly failures. There are three main kinds of test:

- on a sample of the target market, before full rollout, e.g. to test whether targeting and media are right;
- within a full campaign, e.g. customers receive different offers or packs and you discover which works best;
- on a sample of the customer base, to test whether your campaigns and other customer-focused actions achieve the results you want in terms of recruiting, retaining and developing customers. These other actions might include changes in the channels or media by which you manage customers.

> **Action**
> Try to combine both of the first two kinds of test – test before your full campaign and during it. You may not have time for the first, so at least do the second so you know what will work best next time.
> Always have tests in place for the third kind of test, as this is what shows your finance director that all the effort was worthwhile.

Specifying testing

You can test:

- media – by which media you contact your customers;
- lists – whether your own or external;
- offers – the core offer and also the promotional offers that motivate customers to buy – now!;
- contact strategy – the promotional steps that make up your campaign (for example, does mail followed by telemarketing work better than straight telemarketing?);
- creative – how each offer is expressed;
- pack composition – how many offers, how they are enclosed, etc.;
- customer management strategies – whether what you do increases the net value of customers to your company.

In all your briefs, you should specify clearly what should be tested and what you are trying to learn by testing (sometimes more than just 'which pulls best?', e.g. what sales targets you should set for future campaigns, your hypotheses about particular segments).

The objective of testing

The starting point for all testing is to identify what questions you want answered, for instance:

- Do older people respond better than younger people?
- Do richer people respond better than poorer people?
- Do people who have seen and remembered a television advertisement respond better than those who haven't?
- Is product X a better basis for an offer than product Y?
- Does the level of education of customers affect their response?
- Is it possible to get more net value from customers?
- Do customers who are easy to recruit turn out to have higher attrition rates?

Action

Don't test without hypotheses that you **need** to have checked. Testing can be expensive. Variations in copy cost money. Including a group of people in the test to see whether they will respond costs money if they turn out to be low responders. So justify your need in terms of:

- your marketing objectives in respect of the target market;
- the likely benefits of testing set against the costs.

Define your test needs in measurable ways. For example:

- define in quantifiable ways the terms you use ('level of education', 'younger', 'poorer');
- ensure that data that supports the quantifying criteria you use will be available (e.g. because it is already on the database or because it will be gathered as part of the campaign, perhaps through a questionnaire).

eg

The loyalty card Nectar launched with a huge integrated media programme including extensive direct marketing. It invited customers to register on the web site or by telephone. The take-up was so huge – in excess of 10 million in the first two months – that its web site went down and the call centre jammed. It is hard for any company to gear up for the demand Nectar experienced. The problem also gained publicity – good news if you take the view that no publicity is bad publicity then this may also have been a positive. Nectar's problem was that it could not test the uptake of the card among the customers of its business partners.

Warning!

Definitions and quantifiability are central to testing. If you haven't got an agreed definition of a factor to be measured, or if it can't be quantified in practice, you can't test whether it is important.

A question formulated in a form you can test is called a **hypothesis**. Thus, a computer company might want to test the hypothesis that at least 5% of its existing customers who ordered more than £3000 of supplies from it in the previous 12 months would take up an offer of one box of computer paper free with every ten boxes if ordered before a given date.

The aim of statistics – to generalize

Once you have agreed what needs to be tested, the next question is how to test it. The simple answer is: try it out on different groups. So how should you choose the groups?

The main use of statistics is to summarize the characteristics of a population (e.g. customers in a particular target market). The population might be a past, present or future population. For the latter, the description is a forecast. In direct marketing, your aim is to use the characteristics of past and present populations to predict the character of future populations. The future may be only ten weeks away. For example, you may want to forecast the response of all consumers of a certain type to a given offer. The definition of past, present and future populations stays the same – except for time. But as time passes, the world changes. Competitors may launch spoiling campaigns if they have noticed the test. They may launch new products. The government may raise or lower taxes. In the more distant future, the composition of the population changes. So never forget that testing is a predictive activity. The longer term the test, the more careful you need to be about interpreting its results, as many other things could have changed while you were running the test.

> **Warning!**
> Predictions based on test results are **conditional** predictions, i.e. they are conditional on other factors remaining equal. Economists use the term **ceteris paribus** (Latin for 'other things being equal') for this – and they do so frequently, to remind themselves how changeable and unpredictable the world is!

The 'ceteris paribus' problem applies particularly to media advertising in direct marketing. There may be big variations in the level of attention achieved by your advertisement or insert and in the effectiveness of the circulation you attain. The day of the week might be an important factor, and seasonal variations may exist. The exact way in which some of the newer media work is not yet fully understood, so we need to be careful about how we measure their results.

> **Action**
> Do everything possible to ensure the same treatment of test and rollout. Otherwise, external factors may cause variations in results that are very large compared with any 'inherent' difference caused by differences in the pack.

Lists and databases change composition constantly, if for no other reason than that people move house – about 8–12% a year, depending on the state of the housing market. Also, some types of people (e.g. the young, students) move more often than others. In business markets, people move between jobs and companies. If a list or database owner has very good tracking of members of the list or database, and if you can assume that the fact of moving makes no difference to the behaviour of the movers, you might be happy with using a list, a database or a particular selection because a single test result showed that it was better than another. But this may be unwise, particularly if, when the list was tested, another list produced nearly as good a response rate. There is a strong argument for retesting at least annually.

If you are using your own database as the basis for most or all of your activity, testing will normally be carried out on different selections within your database. You should have good measures of the quality of your database, so some of the uncertainties mentioned above will not apply. However, if it is some time since you last contacted many of the customers on your database, you will face the same uncertainties.

Narrowing down what is to be tested

You can't test every option but you can use research and judgement to narrow down the range of options to be tested. Your judgement should be based on your experience of what has worked with which types of customer and product. If details of your past campaign results are computerized or available in an accessible form, you should be able to analyze them and narrow down possibilities early on in the development of your customer management strategy or your campaign. If you're new to direct marketing, choose an agency with lots of experience in your market sector and take their advice.

> **Action**
>
> If your product or concept is completely new, don't expect the test to give you all the answers. Use market research before testing the campaign. It will reduce the risk of testing a flawed concept. Qualitative research among those expected to be the main users of your product or concept is very valuable.

Sampling and inference

Testing is used to generalize from past and present to the future, and from part of your target market to your whole target market.

Sampling and inference

> This process of generalization is called **'statistical inference'**. The term **'inference'** is used for good reason – you can never 'prove' that a future response rate will be x%, you can only infer it. In other words, you can only say that it is **likely** to happen, not that it is **certain**. Test results are **probabilistic**. The smaller the sample you're testing, the less certain you can be that your inference is correct.

Even if you could analyze your entire target market, forecasting its response rate would still be an inference because other things might have changed. But if your target market is composed of thousands of customers or more, analyzing your whole target market is likely to be expensive and time consuming, so you need to test on samples.

▶ Confidence intervals

As tests are probabilistic, you need a separate estimate of the likelihood that your test prediction will be fulfilled. Here, we use the idea of the **'confidence interval'**. For example, suppose your campaign produced a 5% response rate for a particular pack sent to a sample of your customers. You can't be sure that this will be the exact response if you repeat the campaign for your whole market. But you might be able to say that there is a 95% chance that the response rate for the pack would be between 4% and 6% when sent to the whole population. Put another way, there is a 5% chance that response will be outside the 4–6% band.

Use of this kind of language raises problems. Many marketers' knowledge of statistics is confined to the simple analysis and presentation of tables. In testing, slightly more advanced statistical concepts are used. The problem is that although statistics has a strong foundation in common sense, as soon as you use technical statistical terms, your colleagues' eyes may glaze over. They ask for the table or the graph.

> **Action**
> It is **your** job to make statistics intelligible to management – and of course the job of this book to help.

The language of statistics is drawn from sampling theory. This deals with how to choose samples from populations and then to predict the characteristics of the population from the characteristics of the sample.

> Suppose a retail store wants to test the take-up of a unit-linked investment product by its 1.5 million storecard holders. The product has been designed by analyzing competitive offerings and identifying which have been most successful and what extra features could be built in. So the detailed specifications of the product are not being tested, but the way in which it is presented to the target market is. Three ways of presenting it are designed, and a test is set up to discover:

20 / Testing in direct and interactive marketing

1 whether the product would succeed if marketed to the entire card-holder base;
2 if not, whether there are groups within the customer base to whom the product could be marketed cost effectively;
3 which version of the offer draws the greatest response (or 'pulls the best').

Let's focus on Objective 1. If 20 different samples of 1000 are drawn from the population truly randomly (so that everyone has an equal chance of being included), they should have more or less the same characteristics, but they will not be identical. This is because even if each sample is chosen truly randomly, it cannot be guaranteed that each sample will have exactly the same composition. This also applies to their likelihood of responding to the promotion. So, when tested, these 20 samples might give these response rates (rounded to the nearest 0.1%):

- 6 samples gave 2.0%;
- 5 samples gave 1.9%;
- 5 samples gave 2.1%;
- 2 samples gave 1.8%;
- 2 samples gave 2.2%.

These are depicted in Fig. 20.1. Suppose then that a prediction had to be made as to what the result would be if the offer were made to the whole target market. The simple response is to say 2%. But there is obviously a good chance that it might not be 2%. After all, in 70% (i.e. 14) of the samples, the response was not 2%, but greater or less. Perhaps it would be better to say that there is an 80% chance of the response rate falling between 1.9% and 2.1%. This would be a fairer summary of the situation. Could we say that there is a 100% chance (certainty) that the result will be between 1.8% and 2.2%? Unfortunately, the answer is no. The 21st sample (which was not drawn) might have produced a very low or a very high response rate, destroying the neat generalization.

This raises another point. When the expected response rate is as low as 2%, it would be quite easy to draw a sample that contained very few or even no responders. With a sample size of 1000, this means missing out only 10 or 20 people. So the smaller the expected proportion, the larger the sample needs to be to ensure that it is representative. If a response rate of 50% were expected, it would be hard to draw a sample with no respondents or even one with a proportion as low as 25%.

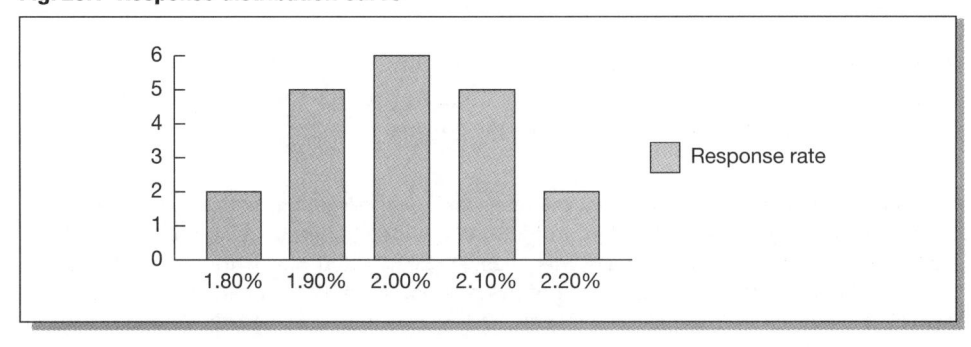

Fig. 20.1 Response distribution curve

Sampling and inference

Obviously, the more samples that are drawn, the more accurate your prediction. But more samples cost more money, which statistics can save. Statistical theory can show what the range of likely outcomes in the total population might be, based on one sample. The larger the sample, of course, the more accurate the prediction. But the prediction should always be a range, with a probability attached to it, as above. As the example also showed, the broader the range, the greater the probability. The range used in a prediction is called a **confidence interval**, since it indicates the range that the predictor is confident about. The probability that the response lies within the range is called the **confidence level**. The four key statistical measures are closely related, namely:

- expected response;
- size of sample;
- significance level (the probability that the estimated range of responses is accurate);
- confidence interval (the upper and lower limits of the estimate for a given significance level).

> Suppose a market research agency is planning a campaign to launch a new market report. It expects the response rate to be 4%. If it wants to be 95% sure that the result, if applied to the whole target market, will fall within the confidence interval of between 3% and 5%, the sample size needs to be much larger than if it wants to be only 90% sure that the result falls within the band 2%–6%. What sample size is chosen depends upon the costs and benefits of the campaign. For example, if breakeven is 1.5%, the company may be happier with the second set of criteria and so be happier with a smaller test cell. **Note that the size of the total population, perhaps surprisingly, does not enter into the calculation.**

The confidence interval can also be expressed as the **error level** you are prepared to tolerate. In the above example, the company might be able to afford an error rate of 2.5%, the difference between the expected response rate (4%) and the breakeven response rate (1.5%).

The formula for determining the size of a test sample is:

$$\frac{C^2 \times R\,(100 - R)}{E^2}$$

where

E = the percentage error from the response rate that you are prepared to tolerate

R = expected response rate

C = constant determined by the required significance level.

Most direct marketers work to a level of 95%. The constant comes from a **distribution table** (see below), which shows the likelihood of outcomes. For example, for 95% confidence, it would be 1.96. The constant is higher for higher significance levels.

The same formula is used to find the effect of changes in the tolerable error rate when you change the size of the test sample.

Distributions

Distributions are a vital asset to statisticians. They are used to generate tables, which allow them to look up what one of the above statistical measures is, given the other three. As four-dimensional tables are quite complicated, they are simplified by using grouped sample sizes (e.g. 500–999) and by using two or three levels of significance (e.g. 95%, 97.5% and 99%). These tables can be bought separately and are also included in statistics textbooks. They are based on the known properties of the distribution of random events. The most common distribution curve used for this is the **normal distribution**.

> **Action**
>
> Always aim for as accurate a prediction as you can afford. Too low a rollout response may mean financial losses. But too high a response may mean that your fulfilment house runs out of stock – not good for your customer service image. However, provided that once the rollout campaign is launched, close track is kept of responses to see whether they are exceeding the prediction, and provided that new stocks can be obtained quickly, you may just want to predict what your lowest response rate is likely to be.

In the retail example above, 90% of the samples produced a response of 1.9% or above. In the market research example, if breakeven was 3%, the company might want to be 99% sure that the campaign would exceed this level. This is called a 'one-tail' test because it concentrates on one tail of the distribution curve, i.e. the proportion of the distribution to the right of 3%.

Testing differences

In direct marketing, you often need to use several samples, perhaps to test different creative expressions, different offers and different selections. Each sample is called a **'test cell'**. You often need to test whether the response in one cell differs significantly from that in another. For example, two samples might have response rates of 1.2% and 1.8%, with 95% confidence intervals of 0.9% to 1.5% and 1.5% to 2.1%. You might want to know whether it is likely that these samples came from the same population. In this case, specific statistical tests are available for the difference between two sampling proportions.

Sampling methods

All statistical inference relies on **truly random** samples (the distribution curves are based on this assumption). Samples that are biased in any way give a poor basis for prediction. In the interests of economy and speed, compromises are sometimes made, but these can be risky. In theory, the only way to produce a truly random sample is to number all the population and pick the sample using a random number table. This is feasible with small samples or where the list or database is computerized. Most computers have random sampling routines.

The most familiar method used is the **one in n** sample. This means picking every nth (e.g. fourth or fifth) name. However, if the names are in any order (e.g. alphabetical) and the length of the list is not known accurately, this approach can omit names from the end of the list if the sample size is given and the proportion to be sampled is over-estimated. For example, this could lead to the omission of many people with overseas names (beginning with letters X to Z!). If male and female names alternate, choosing an even number will lead to a horrendous gender bias.

> **Quota sampling** is a cost-cutting technique. Here, sampling takes place (usually on a haphazard basis) until the quota is reached. A good example of this would be stuffing a leaflet in the first 500 packs sent out, or handing out 500 leaflets to shoppers in a town centre. In theory, quota samples are not truly representative because they are not randomly drawn.
>
> **Stratified sampling** is used where prior information about the population allows it to be stratified. Random samples are then chosen within these stratified groups. This makes sure important groups are represented in the sample. Strictly speaking, generalizing from these samples should be based upon information about the distribution of the stratifying characteristics in the overall population.

Test matrices

To test which factor is producing the response, you must try to hold as many factors equal as possible between test cells. For example, if there are two test cells, each with different offers and different list selection criteria, it will not be possible to say whether any difference in response rate is due to the offer or the selection. If the response rate is the same, it will still be impossible to say whether the result was achieved by the offer or by the targeting, or by some combination of the two. So if two offers and two target markets need to be tested, each pack should be offered to each target market, as in this diagram:

	List M	List N
Offer P	Test cell A	Test cell B
Offer Q	Test cell C	Test cell D

A more economic solution might seem to be this:

	List M	List N
Offer P	Test cell A	Test cell B
Offer Q	Test cell C	No test cell

This assumes that the result of Offer Q on List N can be inferred by the difference between the two offers on List M. This may not be correct, as Offer Q may work relatively better on List N than on List M. When the test is carried out, it might yield these response rates:

	List M	List N
Offer P	2.2%	2.5%
Offer Q	2.8%	2.9%

These should be subjected to two statistical tests:

- Are any of these rates significantly different from zero, given sample size?
- Are the rates significantly different from each other?

> The term 'significantly different' means that the results cannot be explained by random sampling errors and that it is unlikely that the two cells' response rates are the same, i.e. it is likely that the difference was caused by your actions (targeting, offer, etc.).

Split runs and other ways of varying sample treatment

'Split run' is a term used to describe sampling when different inserts are used for a given published medium. With modern inserting machinery, you can alternate packs to achieve a one in n effect for the whole circulation of a paper. The old way of doing it was to physically split the run and insert one pack in one run and a second pack in another run. The same is possible with telemarketing scripts or call guides. In interactive technology, the costs of producing variants, e.g. of text messages, web offers, is relatively low. Indeed, testing may involve the whole customer base because the cost of message delivery is so low. However, note that the more different offers you make, the more difficult it can be to interpret the results.

The control group

In many tests, one cell is designated as a control group, to which you do not promote or for which you do not change your customer management strategy. For example, an airline club card marketing department might send to members of a control group only normal club mailings (whether postal or e-mail) and no special offers. This would allow identification of the overall effect of mailings on flight volumes. Or a credit card company might try a variant on its standard membership solicitation mailing. The control cell would be the standard mailing. In other cases, the control cell may be chosen as the one believed to be the best option. In this case, tabular presentation may be of differences relative to the control cell. To ensure that the control cell produces high levels of statistical validity, a larger sample may be allocated to it.

▶ Response rates vs sales rates

Most of this chapter is phrased in terms of response rates, which measure success in terms of the proportion of customers making a first response. This is a good (but not the only) measure of the success of the initial communication. However, in the end, you are interested in sales. **Every test that can be performed with response rates can also be performed with sales rates**. But the contact strategy that leads to sales may require higher and higher levels of human intervention as the sale nears its completion. This applies particularly to complex industrial products. For example, the sales performance of a lead-generating campaign may be higher in one market segment than another. This might be because the sales force specializing in the first segment was better trained or more highly motivated. This would be visible in the better sales closing ratio (ratio of sales to leads). But would this higher closing ratio necessarily be attributable entirely to better selling, or could the offer design have appealed more to that segment, for example? On this information, there is no way of knowing.

▶ Testing complex contact strategies

The simplest form of testing – of response rates to a mailing or to an outbound telephone call – has been carried out for decades, almost ever since mail order was invented. More complex testing, of multi-stage contact strategies involving older and new media, or complex combinations of newer media, is a newer activity. It has become more common as direct marketing has become involved in achieving a wider range of tasks and working with a greater variety of marketing media (web, mobile telephony) and channels (e.g. retail, sales force). You need to check that tests involving new media ascertain that the messages were actually delivered and responses handled. Tests involving other channels usually take a long time to set up. This is because you need to:

- brief and motivate sales staff;
- distribute materials to a large number of sales points;
- set up systems and procedures for distributing leads to a large number of offices.

Some of these tests could more accurately be described as pilots. Because the costs involved in using different contact strategies vary, simple comparisons of sales rates are not usually appropriate.

> Suppose a company in the business-to-business market wants to compare these three contact strategies:
> 1 direct mail followed by a personal sales visit only to customers stating a definite desire to order;
> 2 telemarketing followed by a sales visit only to those indicating a definite desire to order;
> 3 cold sales force calling.
> (Note the simplifying assumption that there is no drop-out from those customers asking for or agreeing to a sales visit in strategies 1 and 2.)

20 / Testing in direct and interactive marketing

> **eg**
>
> The overall cost per initial contact will rise from the first to the third. But the effectiveness of initial contact will also rise. This would be measured by the chance of moving to the next stage of the sale. Therefore the revenue per initial contact will be much higher. So the only comparison that makes sense must be based on profit (revenue from the sale less the total cost of the contact strategy). Statistical tests can still be applied to such figures, although many of the assumptions underlying these tests may not be valid. It might be better just to use management judgement. Suppose the figures for the three strategies were:
>
> | | 1 | 2 | 3 |
> |---|---|---|---|
> | Number of contacts | 1500 | 400 | 100 |
> | Sales rate (%) | 2 | 5 | 10 |
> | Number of sales | 30 | 20 | 10 |
> | Revenue per sale (£) | 500 | 750 | 1200 |
> | Total revenue (£) | 15 000 | 15 000 | 12 000 |
> | Cost per initial contact (£) | 1 | 5 | 60 |
> | Total initial contact cost (£) | 1500 | 2000 | 6000 |
> | Cost per follow-up contact (£) | 60 | 60 | 0 |
> | Cost of follow-up contact (£) | 1800 | 1200 | 0 |
> | Total contact cost | 3300 | 3200 | 6000 |
> | Total contribution (£) | 11 700 | 11 800 | 6000 |
>
> This shows that strategies 1 and 2 are clearly the most cost effective, with little difference between them. The test shows that a direct sales call by itself is ineffective. However, if the objective were to cover the market thoroughly (perhaps to fend off competitive attack), the direct sales call might be used for companies that are known not to be responsive to direct mail or telemarketing approaches. Their characteristics could be discovered by analyzing the results of the tests of strategies 1 and 2.

> **Action**
>
> Even in a direct mail test, the same approach should also be used. This is because in many direct mail tests, the customer is not paying a fixed sum. So use profit as your preferred measure of success.

One list may draw a much better response than another in terms of numbers of respondents, but a much lower revenue per respondent. This is only for the first sale. If the mailing is being used to recruit new customers, the estimated lifetime value of customers should be used to assess which list is the best.

> **eg**
>
> A book club company selling non-fiction 'household' books (do it yourself, beauty, health, etc.) is investigating the market for romantic fiction. It has just received a research report showing that about 20% of its customers also read romantic fiction. This figure would yield a reasonable business return, but not enough to justify investment in new titles. To make it worthwhile entering this market, it needs to recruit many more new customers. It is considering which lists to rent for this purpose. A demographic analysis of readers of romantic fiction (from the research) suggested that the prime readership group for the product would be women in their late teens to mid 40s. The company decides to trial three lists that list brokers have recommended as containing a high proportion of mail-responsive women in this group. In the test, an identical pack is sent to 10 000 members of each list. The test gives the following results:

	List 1	List 2	List 3
Number mailed	10 000	10 000	10 000
Response rate (%)	3.0	2.0	3.9
Number of respondents	300	200	310
Average value of first order (£)	7.5	12.9	6.9
Total value of first orders (£)	22	2580	2139
Cost per pack, including postage (£)	0.3	0.3	0.3
Total cost of mailing	3000	3000	3000
Loss against first response (£)	750	420	861

On response rate, List 3 looks best, but not on revenue, where List 2 pulls best. However, all hangs on second and later orders, where the situation might be reversed. Also, management might want to use the lower band of the confidence interval rather than the test response rate, to identify the risk.

Advanced statistics

In some companies which have used direct marketing for some time, more advanced methods of interpreting test and campaign results are used, particularly for segmenting within databases and lists, to find out which members are most likely to respond or to buy, or how much they are likely to spend. There are many methods for doing this. One of the most common is regression analysis. It aims to predict outcomes, e.g. the likelihood of someone responding/spending, by deriving an equation. In the above example, the equation to predict the amount likely to be spent by someone on List 1 might be:

Spend = 0.2 (a constant) + 0.3 × (a measure of age) + 0.2 × (number of children) + 0.5 × (number of years of education after 16)

This equation could be used to select from the list next time so as to achieve a higher response rate. Of course, real regression equations are more complex and you need to pay careful attention to the significance of each coefficient (the numbers in front of each variable) and the overall success of the equation in explaining the variation in spend levels (technically known as the R-squared).

More complex methods, broadly grouped under the term '**data mining**', can be used to find out which kinds of customers have responded well or badly to a test. This technique can be used without any hypothesis other than the most general question, 'Which types of customer responded well?' So long as the data about the customers is on the database being analyzed, it can be used to identify whether different behaviour has taken place. '**Cluster analysis**' is similar in its use – it looks for groups of customers who are similar, e.g. in terms of their response or purchasing pattern.

Using gains charts

Before you get really sophisticated, one of the best analysis techniques in direct and interactive marketing is the gains chart. This simply shows how any attribute, e.g. a response, a customer value, is distributed in a sample or a customer base, using a particular variable to classify the analysis. For example, you might want to understand how customers with different income levels responded to a particular offer. So you might classify customers by 'quartiles' (i.e. one quarter of the group) or 'deciles' (i.e. one tenth of the group), both in terms of their income (i.e. the top 25% or 10% by income, the next 25% or 10% by income) and in terms of their response rate to a test or a campaign (i.e. the most responsive group to the least responsive group).

Here is what a gains chart looks like for a test.

Income group (quartile 1 highest)	Number in sample	Average sales rate	Average net value per sale	Total value	Cost per contact	Total contact cost	Profit
Quartile 1	10 000	2%	90	18 000	3	30 000	−12 000
Quartile 2	10 000	6%	70	42 000	3	30 000	12 000
Quartile 3	10 000	7%	30	21 000	3	30 000	−9 000
Quartile 4	10 000	5%	10	5 000	3	30 000	−25 000

This shows that the only income group we should roll out the action to is the 2nd quartile. Normally, we would then redraw the chart showing the most responsive or profitable segment first, and so on. Of course, in practice we might decide not to use income quartiles but some other grouping (e.g. not of same size), and income is only one variable we might choose. In its most advanced form, we might do cluster analysis to identify the responsiveness of different segments to our offers, and then run the test by segment.

▶ Using statistics

Interpretation of tests is not easy. If you are not a statistician, you might interpret test results incorrectly. So if you suspect you don't understand what's going on, refer to a good statistics textbook for this purpose, or even better, to a statistician who understands business – if you can find one!

▶ Summary

Direct marketing's key characteristic is measurability. With some media, such as direct mail, you can measure the response to your campaigns very accurately. However, you often need to predict response, to improve your planning and reduce risk. This chapter has reviewed briefly some of the techniques you can use. These techniques derive from statistical probability theory and the properties of the normal distribution. When we have a test result for a sample market, we can estimate with specified degrees of confidence the likely range of response rate outcomes when the same campaign is run for the whole market. This is because we know whether our test result was significant. We have also examined test designs, including the design of test matrices. We have noted that more advanced statistical techniques, such as regression analysis, are available for predicting responses and analyzing how they differ by market segment, using a range of explanatory variables. Good testing, properly interpreted, is the foundation of financial success in direct marketing, the subject of our next chapter.

21 profitable, cost-effective direct marketing

Planned and actual results

General budgeting

Campaign budgeting

Monitoring and control

Supplier quality as shown by control statistics

Learning from final results

Summary

The only justification for direct marketing is results. For a profit-motivated organization, the result should be immediate profit or events which lead to profit (e.g. good sales leads, recruitment of customers who are or will become profitable). For a non-profit organization, the results should be cost-effective contacts, and for many charities, the expected contribution. In general the focus is on return on investment – the difference between customer value and marketing costs. Of course, you may want to combine these with other objectives (customer care, quality, attitude change). But the prime justification is normally monetary.

Planned and actual results

We show direct marketing financial figures in many ways, for example:

1 a budget showing the expected results of a single campaign or of particular treatments within a campaign;
2 a performance statement showing what happened with a campaign;
3 an analysis of the value of customers recruited by a particular campaign, compared with the revenue or profit they are expected to yield;
4 a comparison of the effectiveness of different media;
5 a database evaluation, showing the value of your customer base, often analyzed by value and loyalty (as shown in Fig. 21.1);
6 an overall direct marketing budget, showing the expenditure required for direct marketing and the overall results likely;
7 an overall direct marketing performance report, showing expenditure on direct marketing and the overall results, perhaps compared with the effectiveness of other marketing communications approaches (whether used in, with or in competition with direct and interactive media).

Short-term justification and campaign evaluation is usually by methods 1 and 2. You may split this into **front-end response** (how many responded with an order) and **back-end performance** (how many actually bought, net of returns and bad debt). This is often called conversion (to sales). For longer-term evaluation, back-end performance may include methods 3, 4 and 5. You can easily raise front-end performance by not selecting for creditworthiness or by giving a valuable premium for response. But back-end performance could be very weak, creating big losses. Longer-term evaluation of a single campaign is usually by method 3. Periodical evaluation of the effect of several campaigns, different media or the entire contribution of direct marketing to your success is usually via methods 4 to 7. Method 7 is used for the longest-term evaluation.

Fig. 21.1 Example of customer base value

		Loyals	Balanced	Switchers	Total
High usage	Number	120k	300k	350k	770k
	LTV	£90m	£90m	£70m	£250m
Medium usage	Number	200k	250k	120k	570k
	LTV	£60m	£50m	£12m	£122m
Low usage	Number	300k	220k	120k	640k
	LTV	£30m	£11m	£6m	£47m
Total	Number	620k	770k	590k	1980k
	LTV	£180m	£151m	£88m	£419m

Note: In this example, the focus is on the different lifetime values of loyal customers, switchers and an intermediate group who occasionally switch, the 'balanced' customers. They are split between different value categories. Whatever dimension you segment by on the horizontal axis, it always makes sense to try to identify the characteristics of different value users.

▶ General budgeting

The contribution of direct marketing to your marketing budget might not be identified separately, particularly if many campaigns use several media. However, direct marketing activities may still need budgets as part of the normal budgeting cycle. Budgeting usually follows a sequence like this:

1. Budgets prepared as part of corporate plan.
2. Implementation of plans and control of expenditure according to budgets.
3. Performance measured and evaluated against budgets.
4. Variances between planned and actual expenditure and revenue statistics identified.
5. Corrective actions taken.
6. Feedback to next period's planning process.

You may have budget hierarchies. Your marketing budget may be part of your overall corporate budget, while there may be a separate direct marketing section in your marketing budget. Campaign budgets will be part of the marketing and/or direct marketing budget.

▶ Realistic budgeting

Budgets are used to:

- communicate;
- motivate;

- allocate resources and accountabilities;
- control and co-ordinate activities;
- report results;
- provide feedback on performance.

You can make sure your budgeting process works:

1. Different budget holders must co-operate and communicate with each other.
2. The objectives which are set for individuals via the budget must be consistent with your company's overall objectives and with the individual's job goals.
3. The feedback developed by the budgetary process must be constructive (i.e. indicate where and how improvement is required), not just punitive.
4. Targets set by the budget must be feasible and mutually consistent.
5. The budget process must be designed to be usable in practice, i.e. not over-complex, and be a normal part of the working process of each department. For example, it must be used to provide internal control as well as to report the performance of the department 'upwards'. It must be used to provide 'what-if' and other planning analyses.
6. Reports and statements of performance must be produced in time for them to be acted upon, and not too late.
7. The process must be accurate, so that people are confident in it.
8. The information must be of the right level of detail to be useful (i.e. more general the higher up the organization, more detailed the lower down). To save time and create focus, a common technique used is exception reporting. This singles out variances from budgets of more than a specified amount for management attention.
9. The budgetary process must be able to cope with new types of activity (e.g. with different timescales, resources, new media).

Campaign budgeting

A budget is a structured plan for the financial aspects of a campaign. It does not summarize other aspects of a campaign. These are covered by the brief and subsequent marketing documentation. The budget should be structured, meaning that it follows a standard format. This ensures that budgeting is done properly, that the figures can be interpreted correctly, and that comparisons with other campaigns can be carried out easily. It also makes it much easier to compare the budget with results.

The elements likely to be included in a direct marketing budget include:

Media

- Press/journal space
- TV time
- Radio time

Agency

- Design
- Copy
- Artwork
- Filming/recording (for TV/radio)
- Consultancy/management

Mail production and despatch

- Initial envelope
- Return envelope
- Brochure/leaflet letter
- Sample
- Lasering (set-up and production)
- Handling and despatch
- Postage
- Premiums
- Customer service correspondence

Telemarketing

- Script design and testing
- Set-up
- Agency costs (if calling subcontracted)
- Direct and indirect calling cost (if in-house)
- Telecoms costs
- Customer service calls

New media costs

- Internet site set-up costs
- Internet content refreshment costs
- E-mail marketing/campaign costs
- Processing costs (manual or automated) to fulfil an Internet application/request
- SMS campaign and processing costs

Fulfilment

- Opening mail
- Order sorting

- Inbound call handling
- Outbound calls (for coupon check)
- Data capture
- Credit check
- Labelling
- Picking, packing and despatch
- Return postage

Product

- Fixed costs
- Per unit costs
- Returns refurbishing costs
- Inventory holding costs (storage, deterioration, etc.)
- Premiums

Internal communications

- Sales staff briefing
- Office staff briefing

Payments and money handling

- Bank charges
- Bad debt (cheques bouncing, invoices not met, etc.)
- Delayed payments
- Collection costs
- Interest charges
- Credit card commission
- Cheque handling costs
- Instalment billing

Overheads

- Rent and uniform business charge
- Staff
- Facilities
- Heat, light, etc.

Sales

- Initial sales
- Impact of offers/promotions
- Returns/uncompleted sales
- Re-order patterns

Financial calculations

- Historical and projected response rate
- Conversion rate (response:fulfilment ratio)
- Average order value
- Proportion acceptance
- Returns/cancellations ratio
- Proportion of returns refurbishable
- Bad debt ratio
- Method of payment analysis

▶ Tests and rollouts

You should have separate budgets for tests and rollouts. Test budgets often show a loss because the fixed costs of the campaign may not be depreciated over a large enough volume. The loss incurred by testing is called the cost of testing. If it is high, you need to re-assess the benefits of testing. For example, if you ran a similar campaign in the same target market and got a response rate that would take the planned campaign well above breakeven, you might decide to run the full campaign without a test. Or you might decide to minimize risks by going for a larger test which, if the response rate was high enough, would cover costs. This shows that when it comes to testing, judgement still has an important role to play.

With some media, particularly some new media, it is possible to test in real time or near-real time. When using DRTV selling, products can be introduced or deleted according to whether they sell enough to make the required profit. This can be measured straight away in terms of phone calls received and number of sales taken. Home shopping channels use this measure to determine the most profitable and strong offers, which in the longer run define their core business, e.g. cosmetics, jewellery, exercise and fitness equipment.

Web-site traffic and click-throughs can be measured from every angle to track the number of hits, the areas of the site visited, and any actions taken. Any change in patterns indicates the effect of web advertising (banner ads and so on), or above-the-line advertising (the URL featured on press ads, outdoor posters, on the radio, etc.). It can also be designed to propose offers to customers according to the response of previous customers or according to the needs of the particular customers using the site. This intelligence and flexibility allows marketing via the Internet to be much more cost effective. However, in the same way as more classic marketing channels, the anticipated conversion to sale is still key to determining the budget. The Internet doesn't differ at all, in that the marketing costs and any offers must be driven from knowing the likely response rate and conversion to sale, likely customer value and their churn rate.

▶ Standard formats

Standard budgeting formats can be used where campaigns have common or repeated elements. The main types of direct marketing campaign have enough repeated elements for standard formats to be used. Frequent users of direct marketing are likely to have standard formats for the following types of campaign:

- a single-offer mail-order campaign;
- a catalogue;
- a mail campaign to generate leads for the sales force or dealers;
- an outbound telemarketing campaign to sell products directly;
- an outbound telemarketing campaign to generate leads;
- a media campaign to sell products;
- a media campaign to distribute catalogues;
- a media campaign to generate leads;
- an e-mail marketing campaign to sell direct or generate footfall to your Internet site;
- an e-mail viral campaign to create brand noise, publicity and awareness;
- an SMS campaign to warm up the target audience and prompt call to action.

▶ Spreadsheets

Computer spreadsheets are ideal for budgeting. Irrelevant sections can be deleted, so you need only one format for all kinds of campaigns. Rows can be deleted or inserted as necessary. Also, where many entries are constant, you can prepare a standard version with these entries held constant, e.g. postage rates on acknowledgement letters, cost per call, assumed response rates. The same model can be used for showing both planned results and actual results, once the campaign is completed.

▶ Planned vs actual results

In a budget, response and conversion rates would normally be based on historical test data. If a campaign involves media advertising, budgeted and out-turn figures might differ as it is not always possible to know what the costs will be for media advertising beforehand. For example, a media buying agency is normally instructed to buy a certain number of TVRs (television ratings) rather than to spend a certain budget.

▶ Simple budgets

Many direct marketing campaigns don't require complex budgets. Suppose you are selling a book at £12, including post and packing. The cost of the book to you is £5.50. The cost of sending the book to the customer is 50p, leaving a gross margin per book of £6. The overheads carried by the promotion will be 10% of revenue, or £1.20 per book. To meet profit targets, you need a profit margin of 15%, or £1.80. This leaves £3 per book to cover mailing costs. The cost of each mailing will be 25p. To meet profit targets, one in 12 mailings (£3 divided by 25p) must yield a sale, or 8.3%. Suppose the highest response rate on any of your previous similar campaigns was 5%. This mailing looks unviable. So you might consider:

- raising the price;
- offering two books;
- using the list of customers who actually bought in this campaign as a list for future campaigns, yielding higher response rates, thereby justifying the mailing on the basis of lifetime value;
- improving the mailing piece to attract a higher response. This would increase the cost per mailing;
- refining targeting, to get a higher response rate.

▶ Monitoring and control

Measurement **during** campaigns helps you check your strategy is working. Measurement **after** a campaign tells you what worked and what did not. In setting up your campaign, make sure the right information is reported at the right time to the right people (i.e. those who are in a position to do something about it). This means:

- deciding what performance indicators are required. They must, of course, be measurable as well as useful;
- making sure these indicators are actually measured. Ideally, they should not require special measuring techniques but be picked up as a normal part of the campaign;
- making sure that results are communicated to the right people;
- ensuring that the actions indicated by these results are taken.

▶ Control information

The control information you need during a campaign includes:

- where your first communication is direct, the number of customers actually selected by the selection criteria (or the number of valid names on a list);
- availability of stocks of initial mailing material, checking that numbers match selection/list numbers;
- volumes actually despatched and timings of despatch;
- where your first communication is through broadcast or published media (including the Internet), that the advertisement/insert was according to schedule, and that the right number of people actually received it;

- numbers responding to your first communication, and categories of response;
- availability of response packs;
- response pack mailings – timing and volumes (applying to every subsequent action step);
- results of response pack mailings (category and timing), e.g. sales.

Flow rates of outbound and inbound communication are very important. They are the key to checking inventory of mailing material. Inbound rates are also critical in forecasting the final result, but obviously can be understood ony if it is known when the relevant outbound step took place.

▶ Information sources for budgeting

The above information comes from many sources. Where it comes from suppliers (e.g. media buying, mailing, response handling), your contract with them should specify provision of high-quality, up-to-date statistics, as should the brief for each campaign. Many companies new to high-volume direct marketing have significant problems in this area. These can be avoided by attention to detail at an earlier stage. If you don't get these statistics from suppliers, you won't know the exact status of your campaign at a particular time.

> **In the real world**
>
> Most of the problems here are caused by clients failing to specify their requirements of suppliers in enough detail. Make sure you brief each supplier on:
> - the data required;
> - the frequency of reporting;
> - procedures for signalling problems.

▶ Contingencies

Contingency plans are required for all sorts of situation, for example, when:

- responses are too low or high;
- problems emerge with stocks of mailing or fulfilment material;
- media schedules are altered for reasons beyond your control.

> **Fast-track**
>
> If response is too high, your fulfilment pack stocks may run out. Can you order extra stocks quickly (make sure you establish this in initial negotiations with your suppliers)? Can a later wave of outbound communication be deferred? Before taking a snap decision, however, the reason for the high volume needs to be established. Was the outbound mailing larger than expected? Was there a special reason why more people than usual might have seen the press advertisement? Has there been a high volume of responses from 'friends and family' as well as from the target respondents?
>
> If your response is too low, check the achieved media schedule, your selection criteria or the list you used. Perhaps there were delays in the outbound communication. Were all the components of the pack included? Did the right response packs go to the right respondents?

Supplier quality as shown by control statistics

The statistics you receive are the key to ensuring quality. If you have used the right selection criteria, chosen the right lists or media, designed your offer and creative well, and so on, your control statistics tell you how well you have briefed your suppliers and how well they have observed the brief. Analyzing control statistics over several campaigns will tell you whether there is a fundamental problem in a particular area. For example, does a particular mailing house always mail out late, or does a fulfilment house always notify stock figures too late? Has your campaign manager's absence on business or holiday caused problems in the management of a campaign, suggesting that a sharing arrangement with colleagues would help?

> **In the real world**
>
> The problem with learning after the event is that by the time results are in, your next campaign may have started. Control statistics are forgotten. So keep them as a permanent record of your campaign's progress. For example, the rate at which responses arrive (**the response curve** – see Figs 21.2 and 21.3) for a particular type of product, target market and medium may help in interpreting early results next time a similar campaign is run.

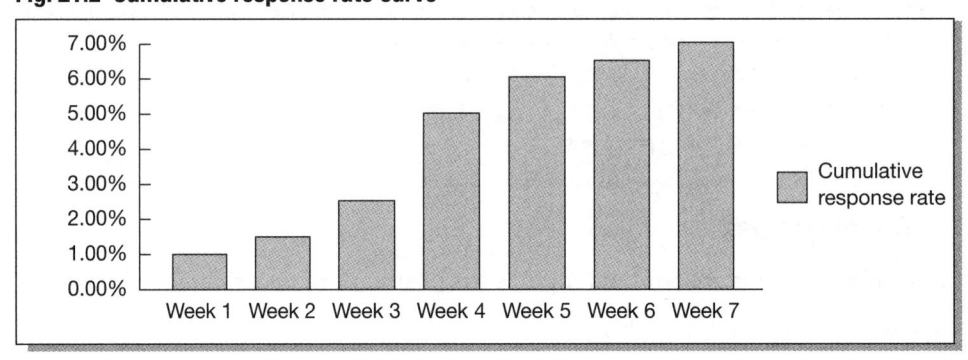

Fig. 21.2 Cumulative response rate curve

Week	Cumulative response rate
Week 1	1.00%
Week 2	1.50%
Week 3	2.50%
Week 4	5.00%
Week 5	6.00%
Week 6	6.50%
Week 7	7.00%

This curve shows how the response rate rises over time, gradually reaching its final level. Such a pattern is normally the result of responses coming in as per Fig. 21.3.

Learning from final results

Monitoring and control during a campaign are closely related to final evaluation, except that:

- during a campaign basic flows and stocks (responses in and packs out) are evaluated;
- after a campaign, rates and ratios (e.g. profit per contact) are usually evaluated.

Fig. 21.3 The classic reverse-J curve of responses

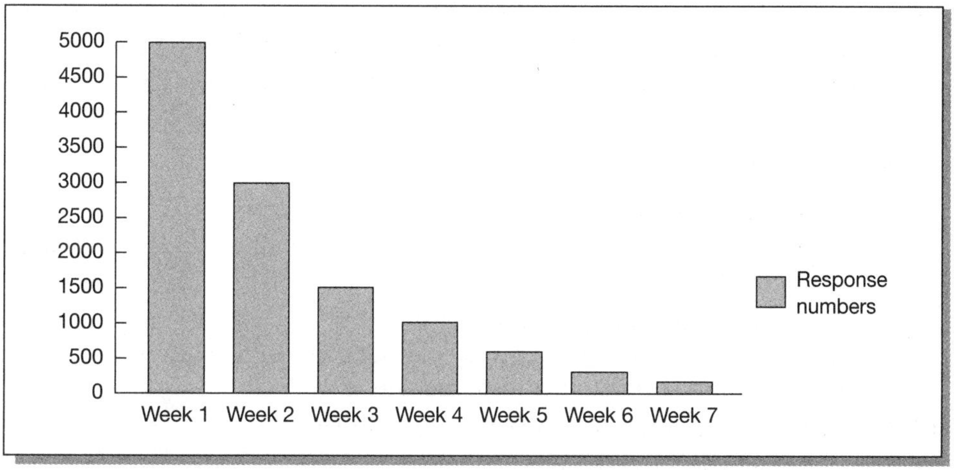
5000
4500
4000
3500
3000
2500
2000
1500
1000
500
0
Week 1
Week 2
Week 3
Week 4
Week 5
Week 6
Week 7
Response numbers

There are many ways you can measure your campaign's effectiveness. Some are non-monetary (e.g. response rates). Some are cost ratios (e.g. cost per response, relative media cost productivities). In the end, the most important results are customer satisfaction and brand support and how these are translated into financial measures, such as revenue and profit.

Intermediate criteria can be used to judge effectiveness. These are based on the **chain of productivity**, the ratios which determine the relationship between input and output. A simple example of such a chain is:

Profit = Unit profit × Number of units sold

Number of units sold = Sales per response × Number of responses

Number of responses = Responses per customer reached × Number of customers reached

Using intermediate measures, you could evaluate your campaign by, for example:

- how many customers it reaches;
- how many responses it generates (of each type);
- number of bookings made;
- extra profit from the campaign;
- how much it increases customer lifetime value.

'Cost productivity' statistics are used to judge the effectiveness of different inputs. They include:

- cost per 1000 mailed or per phone call;
- cost per decision-maker contact;
- cost per lead achieved;
- cost per response;
- cost per conversion;
- cost per sale.

You should compare these for different media. You should also analyze the cost of different elements of the sales process (outbound contact, enquiry handling and fulfilment, concluding sale). These should be set against revenue and margins achieved (including any sales of products which were not the subject of the promotion).

▶ Simple ratios

The most common ratios used here are:

CPM = Cost per thousand – the cost of making a thousand contacts, e.g. mailing a thousand letters.

OPM = Orders per thousand – the number of orders received per thousand contacts. Dividing this by 10 gives % order rate. In a single-step contact strategy, this is equal to the response rate.

CPO = Cost per order – the cost of achieving an order.

The relationship between these is:

$$CPO = \frac{CPM}{OPM}$$

That is, cost per order is equal to the cost of contact divided by the orders per contact. But such ratios don't tell you your return on promotional investment (ROP), which is the ratio or the difference between contribution achieved (back-end revenue less all direct costs including promotional costs) and up-front media or mailing/list costs. The latter is the key measure because it is what you risk before you sell the first item.

The use of the Internet and interactive TV can reduce the cost of initial contact to very low figures. However, the processing of online orders can be costly, especially if manual processing is required. This is often the case, as entirely automated processes are rare. Depending on the product or service, the processing costs and subsequent contacts required can be as high or even higher than with other media. On the other hand, if you are marketing entirely via the Internet (e.g. low-cost airlines, book and CD retailers, and some insurance companies and banks), contact costs are virtually zero. Here, the real costs are those involved in getting users to start and then continue using your web site, and also (in some cases) higher costs of handling returns or claims because you are less likely to be able to be selective about your customers.

▶ Allowable cost per order

Even indicators with such distinguished mail-order pedigrees as 'allowable cost per order' should be used in evaluating only if you are sure that the situations being compared are really comparable. For example, 'allowable cost per order' helps in markets where all campaigns must follow a particular format because extensive testing and years of experience have shown that no other format works. There are many such situations in mail order. All such calculations start with the assumption of a predetermined selling price, but price is determined, via the strength of demand, by your volume and profit targets.

> The steps in using these ratios are:
> 1 estimate your allowable CPO;
> 2 estimate your media CPM;
> 3 divide your CPM by your CPO to give your required OPM;
> 4 divide OPM by 10 to give orders per hundred, i.e. your required response rate.
>
> If you are using direct mail costing £500 per thousand to sell training manuals at, say, £50 and you can afford to spend £10 to acquire each order, you need an OPM of £500/£10 = 50 and a response rate of 50/10 = 5%.

▶ Quality statistics

These include database quality statistics (e.g. gone-aways) and measures of the quality of the response-handling process (e.g. average elapsed time before fulfilment pack sent out).

▶ Setting targets

As you use direct marketing more and more, you get a better idea about what is achievable. Examples include:

- the kinds of response rates that can be achieved in different markets for different types of offer and product;
- the cost levels that can be achieved for particular kinds of pack;
- allowable cost per order;
- conversion rates achievable on leads from particular kinds of campaign;
- rate of growth of active customers (those having bought in a specified recent period) as a proportion of total customers on the database.

You can turn these figures into targets. Although your final campaign result is the most important figure, these other figures provide a check on the quality of different parts of campaign design. You can use these figures as benchmarks to appraise management performance. Examples of the use of such benchmarks include:

- response rates being used as a check on targeting;
- pack cost figures being used as a check on design and print buying;
- conversion rates being used as a check on sales force or telemarketing skills;
- proportion of customers who are active being used as a check on quality of campaign planning.

> **Fast-track**
> Never take such benchmarks in isolation. The classic example is low conversion rates because of high volume but poor quality leads. High pack costs can bring high response rates. High response rates may be due to over-restrictive targeting and small campaigns, leading to high fixed costs being spread over low sales levels.

For these reasons, the prime evaluation is whether the campaign achieves your business objectives, for example:

- to bring in an agreed profit;
- to contact a given number of neglected customers and motivate them to re-contact you;
- to get a given number of users of a competitive product to try your product.

▶ Building your database value

Long-term performance across several or indeed all campaigns should also be evaluated. This evaluation helps answer questions such as:

- Should you recruit a particular customer type?
- How much should you pay to recruit new customers?
- Should a particular medium be used?
- How much credit should be extended?
- How frequently should campaigns be run?
- Is it worth reactivating lapsed customers?
- Which customers are profitable now, and how profitable are they?

Much statistical experience is built into such models. The more experience you have with your database, the more easily you can develop such a model. Spreadsheets are often the best way of representing the model.

▶ Valuing customers

Customers are expensive to acquire and not easy to keep. If you neglect acquisition and retention of customers, you will incur high marketing costs relative to any competitors that take more trouble. Your marketing information system must therefore give an accurate and up-to-date picture of acquisition and retention. The relevant management report is the **customer inventory**. This shows customer gains and losses, classified in various ways (e.g. by type of customer, type of product typically bought).

If acquiring customers is expensive, why do it? Over the period of a customer's relationship with you, the customer may buy many times, across all your product range, which is why we use lifetime or future value estimates. To estimate the future value of a group of customers, you need data on:

- all your marketing contacts with the customer;
- the responses and revenues that result from these contacts;
- the costs associated with each action and response;
- change in status of customers, e.g. between being a customer and not being one, or from being an intense to an infrequent user.

▶ Frequency and recency

The value of your customer base depends on how actively they buy.

In the real world

Suppose all the customers on your database have bought large amounts of a wide range of products at good prices from you. However, if it is a long time since most of them bought (i.e. if recency is poor), the value of your database is questionable. You should hesitate to value the database at all until customers' propensity to buy is tested by a new campaign. The same concerns apply to frequency, amount and category. Don't generalize from behaviour over the last few years if your customers are buying less often and smaller amounts from you each year.

▶ Getting the concept of lifetime or future value accepted

The concept of customer lifetime or future value is well established in companies whose customers are all identifiable and with whom a succession of financial transactions are carried out. These include mail-order and financial services companies. They routinely compare lifetime values of customers recruited from different media or lists and by different offers. Lifetime value is for them a key criterion in choice of list and medium. They also use statistical segmentation procedures to find what differentiates customers with different lifetime values. The variables that account for the difference are then used as criteria for targeting customers within lists or for searching for new lists.

A financial services company might discover that customers with a high lifetime value are married couples with three or more children, living in a particular housing type, with husband and wife both with professional jobs and holding certain store cards (as revealed by a questionnaire). Although this segment might not be large, its high value might warrant specific targeting, e.g. through advertisements in store card magazines, use of store mailing lists, and use of media with higher than average proportions of such customers among their readers.

However, for many companies, lifetime value is a new concept, or one that is poorly understood. In some companies, the pressure to sell 'new business' militates against using the concept. This can distort relationships with customers, and even alienate customers with high lifetime values, as they may be neglected relative to their business potential. This problem can be resolved, although it may take time.

Fast-track

To get the concept of lifetime value accepted:

◆ First make sure that lifetime value statistics are available, at least on a sample, estimated basis.

◆ Carry out tests to show the benefits of the concept, taking care to follow through and measure results.

◆ Demonstrate the financial and customer-satisfaction benefits of the approach, being particularly careful to identify the cut-off points under different strategies.

◆ Propose specific changes to policy in areas where using the concept is likely to pay off best.

Summary

This chapter has shown that the financial aspects of direct marketing are in principle simple. The key point to remember is that your aim is to find out what works, in every element of your campaign, and for whom, in the short and long term. However, this is just the start. You must budget for your campaign to work – using the well-tried direct marketing formulae described in this chapter – and provide contingencies for if it doesn't. However, never forget that your budgets are based on assumptions, and don't be surprised if your campaign doesn't go quite to plan or bring in the exact results you expected. The problem may be in your assumptions, not the market.

22 integrated communication

What is 'integrated communication'?

Media integration

The meaning of integration

Strengths and weaknesses of different media

How integration is achieved

The concepts of integration

Summary

What is 'integrated communication'?

> **Integrated communication** is simply the joint deployment of all marketing communications media in a consistent way. Your aim is to make each medium reinforce the others and avoid confusing customers. Productivity and quality are the outcome of integrated communication.

If you are launching a new product, you may want to create national awareness for it and then find customers. Television and web advertising followed by direct mail and e-mail may be the best way. In consumer markets, the combination of television, mail, retail display and telephone can be particularly powerful. In industrial markets, exhibitions and seminars combined with mail and telephone can have similar power. But for them to exercise this power, they must be planned and executed together. Because they are traditionally planned separately, special attention must be given to project-managing them together.

In the real world
As much direct marketing methodology derives from direct mail practice, the integration of telemarketing, the web, mobile marketing and e-mail is often weak. So ensure that the telemarketing side of your campaigns is properly planned, briefed and managed. This includes working with colleagues across the company to ensure you are all working together.

Integrated marketing communication merges the traditional concepts of different marketing disciplines. The **key thought** and **proposition** of your advertising campaign must be clear, consistent and *must* transfer to your mail piece, your telemarketing script and your web site for all aspects to work well together and for the right 'take-out' (what customers will say about their contact with you) and consumer action (what customers do) to be achieved. The direct marketing concept of 'managed dialogue', in which contacts with your customers occur in a structured way, must be applied to media advertising, which becomes the dialogue's 'front end' – the incentive to your customer to start the dialogue.

Fast-track
As the dialogue with your customers continues, direct mail and telephone must be integrated with other actions, such as the sales call, your Internet site and e-mail marketing campaigns. But be careful to maintain the brand values you have so carefully and expensively established. This means adopting clear rules on copy and presentation in every medium.

Media integration

One of the key aims of your post-campaign analysis is to find out how different media work together best for your products in your target markets. There are few general rules on media integration – what works for you may not work for another company. What works in one target market may not work in another. Much depends upon your customers' media habits, defined largely by their lifestyles. Clearly the aim of your marketing communications is for your advertisements to be seen by as many desired prospective customers possible, and as frequently as possible, to provoke a reaction – a response and sale.

These are the main considerations that determine your marketing communications mix:

- The target customers' media habits – when and what they watch on television, choice of newspaper and magazines, what radio station they listen to, when and why, whether they attend or are exposed to exhibitions and seminars information, and so on.
- How target customers respond to different media. Are they familiar with and users of new media? Do they enjoy responding to e-mails? Or are they more traditional and conservative, perhaps responding well to personal contact by phone or mail? Do they like a lot of information before they decide to buy your product or are their decisions impulse decisions?

The quality of integration of direct with other marketing media has improved due to:

- the diffusion of knowledge about direct marketing techniques into the wider marketing community;
- the transfer of practical direct marketing techniques to other media, for example, the use in leaflet production of print technologies pioneered in direct marketing;
- the use of database marketing to provide the data needed for integrated marketing communications. This is because data is held on customers' responses to all media and can be analyzed not only in classic direct marketing ways (e.g. by type of response) but also using media-based approaches (e.g. by TV area);
- high costs in broadcast and published media, which force advertisers to examine ways of sharing tasks once undertaken by media advertising;
- improved ability to handle multiple-step contact strategies, involving a mix of media, due not only to better understanding of the roles played by different media but also to increasing computerization of the process;
- focus on accountability for marketing expenditure, producing a strong desire to find the most cost-effective media combination.

The meaning of integration

Even the best integrated campaign must ensure the following:

- Your overall campaign must be as effective as possible, i.e. achieve results in terms of its objectives – awareness, trial, purchase, etc. – and as efficient as possible, i.e. achieve results economically.

- Your mandatories must be achieved, e.g. company or product branding must be fully supported and enhanced, so that as few customers as possible are alienated and the foundation for future campaigns is laid and/or strengthened.

However, integration is not just a matter of having integrating campaigns. You might use each medium separately and still be considered good at integration. For example, a continuous programme of television and radio advertising might be used to maintain brand presence, with individual campaigns carried out entirely by direct mail, e-mail or text messaging.

Strengths and weaknesses of different media

A properly integrated marketing communications campaign uses the different media according to their strengths and weaknesses. The suitability of a particular medium for a campaign depends on the nature of the campaign, i.e. objectives, products, offer, target market and so on.

To develop a good multi-media campaign you need to know:

- which media are acceptable and credible to different types of customer;
- which media are right for different kinds of message;
- which media are best for the different tasks involved in moving your customer towards the sale;
- which media are the most cost effective;
- which media have the right volume capabilities (taking into account any time constraints).

Media choice depends on the nature (objectives, target market, desired response) of your campaign, but each medium has general strengths and weaknesses.

▶ Direct mail

Direct mail, like the telephone and other forms of directly addressable media, has all the advantages of personalization. Customers tend to pay more attention to communications that are addressed specifically to them. However, name and address are not the only ways of personalizing. Any reference to facts and ideas that apply to individual customers or small groups of customers increases the 'fit' between communication and customer. Finding generalized but strong benefits that apply to large parts of the market is more difficult than finding benefits that apply to small groups. This is because the needs of customers in well-defined market segments can usually be defined very tightly. The most perfect example of this is when the segmentation is purely by benefit.

> **Fast-track**
> Once the envelope is opened, direct mail has an additional advantage – its power. This is because your reader usually gives it their full attention, if only for a short time. This is an advantage it shares with the telephone. It makes direct mail a good carrier of strong, repeated propositions.

Direct mail can contain a lot of information, far more than an advertisement in broadcast or published media, and far more than in a telephone call. This makes it ideal for the stage of a sales cycle when your customer is already interested and is preparing to make a choice about what to do. Also, if it is important for your customer to qualify themselves as a candidate for your product or service, they may need a lot of information to do this. This information may be best delivered by direct mail.

> **In the real world**
>
> Despite worries about 'junk mail', most direct mail is generally appreciated and respected as a source of information. It is mail that is mistargeted, with offers that are inappropriate for the target market, or that is not properly addressed or personalized that sullies the reputation of direct mail. Properly targeted mail is powerful mail.

The variety of print and design formats possible in a direct mail pack means that direct mail is good at carrying over other media's themes. You can reproduce ideas from your television or press advertising in the copy and illustrations. However, worries about your motives can cause customers to mistrust direct mail. So the tone of your mailing must be carefully judged and consistent with your overall contact strategy tone, to overcome possible mistrust.

A disadvantage of direct mail is reliance on list quality, whether the list is external or drawn from your own database. In an integrated campaign, nothing is as divisive as a high level of complaints from customers that they are receiving two or more copies of a mailing, or receiving mailings intended for other people. Somehow, this is different from customers watching a television advertisement that was not intended for them. The inevitable rivalries between advertising and direct marketing agencies, often played out in front of your senior management, are exacerbated in these circumstances. However, the higher quality your database and the more you update it through frequent promotions and data audits, the less frequently you'll encounter such problems.

> **In the real world**
>
> A disadvantage of direct mail, shared with all published and broadcast media but not with media involving face-to-face or voice-to-voice contact, is its inability to answer the questions of individual customers. This can be partly compensated for by explicit anticipation of their questions in the copy. The lack of limit to the length of copy in a letter allows you to do this.

Direct mail works best in an integrated campaign as a confirmer of branding (through its tone and perhaps through carrying themes over from other media), through delivery of the volume of information needed to move customers through to the next stage in the sales cycle or qualify themselves.

▶ Inserts and tip-ons

Inserts are loose flyers that are inserted (as their name suggests) into newspapers, magazines and other publications. Since inserts normally have several pages and offer good selling space, they are more expensive than off-the-page advertising in the same titles. Due to their size and targetable nature, they also have some of direct mail's advantages. Although not personalizable, they can carry the volumes of information and provide some of the variety of format. They cannot reach individuals as with direct mail, but careful selection of media (and of editions within media) can improve your targeting. With the latest inserting machinery, you can test different versions of an insert within the same publication, while using the same insert in different publications allows quick testing of media. You can also buy inserts regionally at shorter notice than off-the-page advertisements.

Despite their higher unit costs, inserts usually produce several times greater responses than page advertising. This is not just because they stand out more but also because the response device is usually more substantial. Page advertising allows a coupon, with at most a section similar to a small order form. An insert can contain a complete order form. But inserts usually produce lower response rates than direct mail. They may fall out of the enclosing medium or be thrown away immediately. However, with lower costs than direct mail, they play an important role. They often work in conjunction with direct mail campaigns as a trawl for new customers.

Most of these points apply to tip-ons – small cards or mini-brochures that are attached with glue to the page. Typically, they need to be smaller, but have the additional advantage of working together with the page advertising, though care should be taken to minimize print and production costs to manage the end cost per response since marketing costs will be double the usual, with the page advert plus the tip-on.

▶ Page advertising

Many of the advantages and disadvantages of page advertising are implicit in the above. Cheaper than inserts or direct mail, page advertising is excellent for raising awareness or triggering a first response based on limited information. It is a powerful deliverer of branding, although combining delivery of branding with response generation can be difficult. This is because it is hard to produce copy designed to generate a response (focusing the customer on the coupon or the freephone number) which also develops or reinforce branding.

Where prospects already have much of the information they need, page advertising may be the best way for you to reach new customers in a broadly defined market. Technical magazines are a good example of this, e.g. computer magazines, usually dominated by page after page of software and hardware listings.

Fast-track
If you acquire customers through page advertising, find ways to reinforce your relationship with them by direct mail and telephone. This may be done by capturing the name and address and e-mail address and contacting them later. You can also prompt call to actions by e-mail or SMS by requesting this in your advert. Many companies have used this successfully. Some have launched mini communities using this combination of page and SMS.

While direct mail depends on list quality, page advertising depends upon accuracy of circulation figures (achieved as opposed to target) and the position of advertising in the publication and on the page. But low-cost advertising (in poor page and publication positions) can work wonders, particularly if readers are likely to look for the advertisement (e.g. in a special advertising section which self-qualified readers tend to look at). For example, readers about to make a holiday decision tend to examine pages of holiday advertisements.

> **In the real world**
>
> In buying page advertising, you may need to negotiate with a publisher's sales offices. So your advertising effectiveness depends on the quality of your media buying. This in turn depends on good briefing of your media buyers.

▶ Catalogues

If you are selling a wide range of products to customers who are likely to want more than one item, a catalogue may be right for you. However, high catalogue production costs mean you need to qualify customers before giving them the catalogue. Sometimes you will need to distribute the catalogue as the first contact, as part of a test. Of course, for catalogue retailers, wide distribution of the catalogue is the prime mode of generating traffic.

Catalogues can contain vast amounts of information, about your company, your products and the uses to which they can be put. Readers usually view this information as highly credible. The style of a catalogue – repeated statements of product specifications and prices – creates this credibility. But it also creates a weakness – inability to focus on specific products or types of customer, given the volume of information. So catalogues are often the basis for subsequent mail and telemarketing campaigns. These stimulate customers to consult their catalogues. Catalogue price promotions are powerful, as they are based on reductions from a published former price. To verify this, your customer has only to consult your catalogue.

> **In the real world**
>
> Properly targeted customers keep their catalogues and therefore its cost can be depreciated over many contacts. However, this brings the accompanying risk of dating – hence the need for merchandising to be carefully controlled in line with catalogue publishing cycles.

▶ The telephone

The telephone is one of the most flexible media. It can be used either as the core medium or as support to almost any other medium, whether in its inbound form, for customers seeking to progress the sale or have queries resolved, or in its outbound form, to identify and qualify customers and to take orders.

The telephone is a powerful medium. It demands attention (once the connection is made), but intrusiveness can destroy the call. The very power of the telephone means that you can use it to get a high level of commitment from your customers. For new customers, whose relationship with your company has just started, commitment may need to be backed up quickly by written confirmation. Absence of visual contact and immediate written confirmation can weaken commitment, so follow-up must be delivered by other media, such as direct mail or a sales force call. Slow follow-up reduces commitment.

> **In the real world**
>
> The telephone is most acceptable as a marketing medium when used within an existing relationship. Here, quality of commitment is less suspect. If you are using SMS, opt-in is essential as this is a very intrusive and personal media and abuses are likely to be punished by consumers.

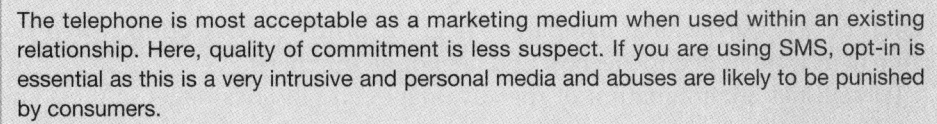

If the first connection is not with the right person, the telephone allows you to find the right person quickly, while a letter may just be returned with no further information. So for customers who have high sales potential but who are hard to track down, the telephone is a good medium. This **interactivity** means that the telephone is excellent for answering questions, handling objections and resolving queries. So it works well as a follow-up to direct mail, which may have delivered the information the customer needs to stimulate the questions.

With modern systems and approaches (e.g. computerized scripting and operator training), telephone is as measurable and testable as mail. It has the added advantage that testing can be carried out in small volumes, limited only by the statistical validity of the sample size. For example, set-up costs for a variation in script are usually less than for a mail pack. Telemarketing is also flexible, so if your customer does not want the product or service promoted by the campaign, an immediate needs analysis allows your contact centre agent to up-sell or cross-sell.

> **In the real world**
>
> High cost per contact is offset by depth and effectiveness of telephone contact. Also, as the telephone is often an excellent substitute for a field sales call costing ten times as much, high cost is usually not a barrier to its use.

▶ Public relations (PR)

Spending on PR has increased dramatically over the past few years, with some companies relying heavily on the medium for their above-the-line exposure. It works well when integrated with direct marketing as it can be linked in with a mail or insert campaign to targeted customers. As a medium on its own it is less effective as it can really only be used to raise the profile of a brand and the company has limited control over the final coverage it gets or the timing of that coverage. If, however, the company uses inserts and a mailed campaign to support any PR coverage it gets, the overall effect can be very powerful as the halo effect of awareness and ability to purchase will increase sales.

▶ Television and radio

These are the least targetable media, but the most powerful at developing branding and generating awareness. They are therefore typically used at the initial stages of an integrated campaign, to be followed up by telephone or mail and thereafter to keep your brand image strong, reinforcing your customers' propensity to respond. The value of television as a response generator has been proved through off-peak, low-cost and long-response advertisements, and with occasional peak-time national campaigns (e.g. for utility privatization, when the campaigns were linked to Freepost and freephone numbers).

Teletext has a combination of the advantages and disadvantages of press and television. Its restricted coverage means that it is most often used as a supplement to other media, for covering known Teletext users. It can give excellent results combined with inbound telemarketing, as the telephone number can be advertised prominently and the consumer can hold the page while writing it down. Because in the UK this segment is up-market, the additional coverage is worth considering.

Interactive television (iTV) is TV enhanced with additional information and functionality for more involvement. Albeit widely available to digital satellite and cable TV viewers, experience with it is still in its early stages. It is not yet as effective as some of the more traditional direct marketing media in prompting sales, though it is a strong reinforcer of brand values and allows far more interaction. As a sales channel iTV is better suited to impulse purchases and trial FMCG purchases, where discounts can be offered to motivate a person to try a new product, or to high-value purchases, where more information and involvement is required before the customer buys, such as with new cars. Again creative and marketing integration is key to ensure the maintenance of brand identity and a smooth sales and fulfilment experience.

> **In the real world**
>
> The disadvantages of Teletext – cost per contact, limited audience and creative limitation – should of course be taken into account, but because the medium is so highly testable, these can be overcome.

▶ The Internet

The Internet is a valuable channel for marketers, both as a platform through which to reinforce their company's presence and optimize existing marketing activity and increasingly as a sales channel. Marketing campaigns are often supported by using a call to action to customers to visit a company's web site, where they can get more information or buy products. Tesco.com is a good example of a functional online ordering site for home shopping and delivery. Habitat.co.uk is an example of a site where goods are displayed for purchase in-store, the beauty being that the stock can be easily updated. Sky.com is an example of a web site that offers a wide range of information as well as the option to purchase Sky TV online. In all cases the corporate identity is clearly defined and communicated as it appears in the high street or on other marketing communications.

Web sites themselves are marketed too. Using banner advertising on other relevant sites and ISP home pages can further boost footfall or hits to the site. Other resulting actions such as downloading images, games, applying online, requesting more information and so on can be measured, allowing you to understand what actions are taking place and to assess exactly what prompts someone to spend time on your site, and ultimately to buy from you.

Information via the Internet can be accessed and requested on demand. This has changed the way we do business, and there is little or no need for face-to-face contact in many business areas (of course not all). However, just as a shop would be branded with the corporate identity, web sites also require integrated design and brand values to optimize marketing spend and make it work harder. As well as web site integration, e-mail marketing should follow suit.

▶ E-mail marketing

Though e-mail is a recent development it is becoming more widely used as a tool to reach individuals in a similar way that direct mail might. Names are collated by viral or other e-mail marketing campaigns, very often by asking people to take part in competitions or to give information on web sites. This information is used to target people with products that fit with their profile. Most of the principles of direct mail apply. E-mail marketing needs to be relevant, pertinent, the offer attractive, and the e-mail timely. It should be personalized where possible, the data correctly spelt and used. E-mailing should also be an extension of your other marketing communications, therefore the tone of voice, branding, font and so on should mimic your brand and corporate identity.

▶ SMS text messaging

SMS is being used increasingly to reinforce the messages of an above-the-line advertising campaign and is also being used on its own where communities of consumers already exist. Policing the use of SMS as a marketing tool is voluntary at the moment, but it is accepted practice that consumers should opt in before they are included in a campaign. Some of the most successful campaigns in recent years have been conducted using text-and-win competitions and information prompt services. For example, *Top of the Pops* sends messages to its opted-in community with news about who will be appearing on the day of the show.

▶ The sales force

The sales force is usually used for in-depth diagnostic work, query resolution and closing the sale, particularly for complex products (e.g. financial services, technical products and services). But sales staff are expensive, so it is important that every customer they visit is a good quality prospect. Your sales force must structure visits to customers as effectively as possible. Visits should take place only when face-to-face presence is needed to initiate contact or move your customer through the sales cycle.

> **In the real world**
>
> You can deploy your sales force in tight combination with other direct marketing approaches. Direct marketing approaches can help sales staff to call on more prospects who really do want to place large orders and fewer prospects who are just 'testing the water'. Time spent looking for new business or servicing marginal accounts can be saved. Information on existing accounts and on new customers can be provided from your customer database. Telemarketers can work closely with field sales staff to deliver more business.

Your customer database can be used to support sales force management, by:

- providing key sales productivity ratios, such as sales per call and calls per day, and data on productivity of individual sales staff;
- aiding sales call and journey planning;
- monitoring customer behaviour, such as buying cycles and order values, so sales staff can establish when customers are ready to buy, how often, and what sort of purchase levels they may reach.

Your database marketing system can achieve the above by:

- gathering and processing leads, whether from the web, via direct mail, trade or national press advertising, telephone marketing, TV and radio, inserted or delivered leaflet, catalogues or exhibitions. These leads are delivered, prioritized, to sales staff, with the assurance that the customer was targeted as a good prospect, has responded to a campaign and has already received information on the product or service;
- rationalizing prospecting, enabling your sales staff to spend more time converting prospects and developing more business with existing customers. The database marketing approach makes it easier for you to identify and reach opportunity markets and segments, ensuring that your sales staff are used for the task for which they are most needed – making the most profitable sales;
- gathering prospect data, enabling your sales staff to plan their own sales efforts and prepare more thoroughly for their approach to the customer. The breadth and depth of customer information gives sales staff a deeper understanding of the customer and their needs, enabling them to tailor their proposals more effectively and to determine sales strategy more precisely, from which customer staff will be called on to what needs to be discussed when they are seen;
- getting information to your customers, helping them to move faster towards purchase, ensuring that sales staff are not just information providers;
- identifying which prospects are 'hottest' and when they are likely to buy. This helps you schedule visits. It also means that customers who want to buy will be dealt with quickly. Your system should ensure that sales staff know when the customer receives the information, preventing waste of time before the call;
- enabling further communications or actions to be triggered automatically (e.g. follow-up sales or service activities) as part of the contact strategy;

- sustaining customer loyalty, reducing the required frequency of 'maintenance' visits, and allowing sales staff to concentrate on moving forward sales cycles or resolving serious problems. Provided the communication is relevant and not for its own sake, many customers prefer maintenance activity to be by mail or telephone. Campaign co-ordination ensures that your customers receive a structured, non-overlapping flow of communication about products and services which meet their needs.

In many campaigns, sales staff are the last link in the chain, the final element of the contact strategy that delivers the business. This does not mean that they have to follow up every lead that arrives. Some leads will be low priority. Others may arrive at a difficult time, when existing customers are crying out for attention. So you should devise a scoring system for prioritizing leads, e.g. according to likely size of order, whether other suppliers have been asked to tender, urgency of requirement. When a high-priority lead arrives, it means that a customer has expressed a need and is expecting to hear from the salesperson.

In the real world

No salesperson should be a market researcher, but the system should provide a streamlined framework to encourage sales staff to help maintain database quality by maintaining data on customer profiles and needs. However, if this is a problem area for you, experience shows that outbound telemarketing is more effective than field sales when it comes to gathering customer data during the sales process.

Many sales forces are supported by a sales office, which may also act as a telesales centre and perhaps take on service functions as well. Staff are normally carrying out one or two basic direct marketing tasks, such as response handling – dealing with inbound enquiries or fulfilment – and ensuring your customers get what they want (e.g. a product brochure, confirmation of order entry, delivery or installation). Many such staff feel their work is cut out just dealing with the existing volume of enquiries coming in. But a customer database can help them by:

- providing improved marketing databases for identifying the best prospects for particular services and products. This means that the leads coming to your offices will be higher quality and that better prospects will be identified for telemarketing campaigns;
- getting leads to your offices quickly, ensuring that they are fresh. This means that the customer is more likely to commit to the next stage of the sales cycle and less likely to have pursued enquiries with competitive suppliers;
- prioritizing leads. This ensures that sales staff know which leads to give attention to first;
- making sure, through careful targeting of campaigns and copy design, that leads are high quality;
- providing a mechanism for following up leads derived from telemarketing campaigns more quickly and effectively;

- in some cases, automatically sending customers the information they need. This enables your sales office staff to concentrate on scheduling sales appointments with the right customers and closing orders. It also enables your telemarketing staff to concentrate on moving the customer to the next stage in the sales cycle rather than providing information;
- ensuring that the leads received contain more relevant information than before, giving staff a flying start in moving to the next stage in the sales cycle;
- improving the basis for monitoring the sales cycle by providing better reports on open orders, etc.;
- facilitating co-ordination of local sales office efforts with those of your other marketing functions – sales staff, other channels, telemarketing, etc., as part of a coherent contact strategy.

In a business where coverage of many small to medium-size customers (business or consumer) is important, where potential sales do not justify a calling sales force but do justify a more proactive marketing stance than setting up a retail outlet and relying on customers to call, using direct marketing enables the sales office to serve as a remote account management office, deploying a combination of mail and telephone. The most important asset which enables this approach to be taken is information on the database which indicates customer potential in terms of what, how much, how frequently and when they buy, and details of how to contact them.

▶ Other media

You can use many other media in an integrated campaign, e.g. to generate leads and reinforce your branding. A steady background of relevant and favourable media comment, generated by a good PR campaign, should be used as cost-effective support to a multi-media campaign. If your industry is one in which exhibitions are used, some visits to exhibitions will be towards the end of the contact strategy, to be followed by a sales force close on the stand or shortly after, while others will be at the very beginning, when the customer is in the search phase of the buying cycle. Poster campaigns, particularly in well-targeted sites, have frequently been used to reinforce multiple-media campaigns. Cross-tracks campaigns aimed at commuters at railway stations are frequently used to reinforce business-to-business campaigns. Sales promotions are often used to add value to the use of other media (particularly print media) and to add strength to the customer's motivation to move to the next stage in the sale.

▶ How integration is achieved

Here's what you need to do to make integration work.

▶ Time

Make enough time to develop your campaign. You will need more documentation for an integrated campaign. Your brief must contain everything that agencies responsible for advertising, direct marketing, sales promotion, exhibitions and sales force motivation need. Your campaign must march according to the communications discipline with the longest lead time. In some cases this may be the exhibition discipline, in other cases direct marketing. If you want to test a new television advertising approach, this discipline may have the longest lead time, particularly if longer-term factors such as wear-out need to be tested.

Integrated campaigns usually require long overall campaign times. For example, the brand awareness component may need to be strongly established before your customer receives a direct communication. So the overall time from campaign conception to completion may be much longer.

▶ Communication and involvement

You will need to involve more agencies and more of your own staff than in a normal single-medium campaign. So make sure that communication between them is high quality. All parties should be involved in the development of the campaign right from the beginning. This helps you avoid ideas that work well in one medium but cause immense problems in another.

▶ Variety of results

Integrated campaigns yield a variety of results and should be designed to do so. Awareness, positiveness of attitude, customer satisfaction with treatment by the company, agreement to a sales visit, receipt of information, agreement to visit an exhibition and, of course, a purchase are all results which might come out of a campaign. These results must be measured – in your sales results and through research.

> **In the real world**
> This variety of results must be planned for and the value of each result understood.

▶ Careful budgeting

Your integrated campaigns should cost less for a given task because each medium is used for the purpose most suited to it. You won't be using direct mail to raise awareness, nor television to generate response. But using several media together tends to increase the minimum effective size of an integrated campaign. Also, some media have a minimum effective volume of usage.

> **In the real world**
> Integrated campaigns tend to be larger and therefore require more careful budgeting.

▶ Planning and control

As your campaign progresses, you need tight planning and control. You need to co-ordinate the timing of different media and control media buying and mailing times tightly. Tight budget control is also essential. You can easily lose financial control in the plethora of activities of a major multiple media campaign. You may find gaps at the last minute (e.g. a piece of print missing) and be tempted to throw money at the problem rather than try to solve it cost effectively.

▶ The integrating manager

You need integrating managers for integrated campaigns – managers who understand the essentials of all marketing communication, not necessarily all the details. But they must have a clear idea of what each medium can do and how it needs to be managed to deliver what it promises. They also need to be effective communicators as they have to work with a variety of people and budget holders across the organization.

▶ Results evaluation

You need to analyze the results of all the media you used in a campaign to see how well they worked in combination. Too much evaluation is 'stand-alone', using different methods for each medium.

> *Fast-track*
> You must develop a common language for measuring and assessing different kinds of performance.

Performance measures that apply to every medium are:

- what customers each medium reached;
- what immediate effect each medium had;
- whether the customer responded, and how;
- what the final outcome was, in terms of sales (or other fundamental objective).

▶ The concept of integration

▶ Branding

> You go to a party and see a sexy guy across the room. You approach him and say, 'Hi, do you want to dance?' That's direct marketing.

> You go to a party and see a sexy guy across the room. You give a friend some money. He approaches the other guy and says, 'Hi, my friend over there wants to dance with you.' That's advertising.
>
> You go to a party and see a sexy guy across the room. You recognize him, walk up to him, refresh his memory and get him to laugh and then ask, 'Do you want to dance?' That's customer relationship management.
>
> You go to a party and see a sexy guy across the room. You stand in an attractive pose, get the guys round you laughing with a few stories, smile at the other good-looking men in the room, and then move up to the sexy guy and ask, 'Do you want to dance?' That's hard selling.
>
> You go to a party, you see a sexy guy across the room. *He comes over* and says, 'Hi, I hear you're a great dancer, how about it?' Now *that* is the power of branding.

The concept that unites all marketing communications and makes your relationship with customers more coherent is **branding**.

> Your **brand** is the complete set of values that your customers derive from your company's offering. These values are created by your marketing mix (of which communication is one part).

It is not just your **current** marketing mix that matters. Customers have memories. Successful deployment of the marketing mix over a period of years leads to strong and positive branding. Your brand remains valuable even after your investment in creating it is reduced. A strong brand can survive weak marketing for a period. However, like any asset, your brand can depreciate, particularly if it is poorly maintained. Investing in a brand usually requires maintaining the value added by the product range and continually reinforcing it with positive messages through promotion and/or customer service. However, the more focused your marketing, the easier and cheaper it is to develop branding. In very large markets, finding the branding which stands out and making it stick in customers' minds is an expensive business. This is because it is expensive to create a product or service that appeals strongly to a large number of people and then to promote it extensively.

In the real world

Creating a brand is considered one of the best and most long-term routes to survival and growth. But creating a brand is not easy. It takes years of hard work. Once established, however, your brand is one of the best barriers to entry by competitors. It is a psychological barrier in your customers' minds that makes them less willing to try other experiences. It also makes them more willing to pay higher prices.

Successful branding also depends on your taking some hard decisions. Perhaps the most important is what kind of brand you want to create, for example:

- classic stand-alone, e.g. Persil, Coca Cola;
- international, e.g. IBM, Kodak, Vodafone, Orange, Sony, Disney, Levi;

- corporate, e.g. Heinz, Volkswagen, BMW, BA, BT;
- corporate range, e.g. Heinz Weightwatchers;
- regional, e.g. English Tourist Board, *Manchester Evening News*;
- youth, e.g. Nike, Playstation, Red Bull;
- children, e.g. Barbie, Thunderbirds;
- classic range, e.g. Clarks Shoes, Covent Garden Soups;
- manufacturer, e.g. Cadbury, Viyella;
- retail, e.g. B&Q, Marks and Spencer, Mothercare, Tesco, Sainsbury;
- sub-brands, e.g. Persil Washing-up Liquid, BA Executive Club, Volkswagen Golf;
- wholesale, e.g. Costco, Makro;
- online service brand, e.g. Lastminute.com, Egg.com and Yahoo, Yell;
- online Internet service provider (ISP) brands, e.g. AOL;
- environmental/social brands, e.g. Prêt à Manger, Ecover, Greenpeace.

You need to distinguish between **company brands** and **product brands**. Company branding is for an entire company, while product branding is for an individual product. Company branding is important where your customers make separate decisions on which supplier to buy from and which product to buy. For example, a package tour operator might want to create a branding associated with high quality of all of its packages and separate branding for its tours to particular areas or at different times of the year.

The key here is to be realistic about what you can achieve with your branding, and in particular whether you want to combine any of the above. Financial services companies tend to combine several of the above in their product brands, often falling between (at least) two stools by combining the (often long) company name with a product description and a hint at the target market.

▶ Brand values

Branding your product is not just a question of a particular set of product features. Nor is it created by a single communication campaign. It is something that exists in customers' minds. The aim of branding is to get **brand values** associated with your **brand name**. This means that whenever the consumer sees your brand name, your brand values are recalled. When your brand name is well established, you can get your promotional messages over much more easily because when customers hear or see your brand name, recognize it and (ideally) recall its values, they are more receptive to further messages. Direct marketing thrives in a strongly branded environment. Your customers are more willing to listen to your telephone message, to open your envelope and to accept a visit from your salesperson.

▶ Brand proposition

You use customer benefits and brand values in the form of your brand's proposition.

> **Brand propositions** are the **words** that express the values and benefits of your brands most succinctly, as the idea that you want to occur in people's minds when they see, hear of or buy your brands.

In an integrated campaign, you must present this proposition across the different media if each medium is to reinforce the others. How you do this depends on how your **creative execution** of the proposition differs across different media.

> **Creative execution** refers simply to the graphical and verbal ideas used to express your proposition, i.e. what your customer sees in your communication. Put more simply, these are the 'words and pictures'.

At one extreme, your creative execution can be fully integrated. You use the same pictures and words in different media. The TV sound track may be modified for use on the radio. The words from the sound track may be incorporated in the mailing copy. The images from the TV advertisement may appear in the brochure or as a backdrop to the exhibition stand. At the other extreme, the brand proposition may be the same but the creative execution very different. Irrespective of the degree of creative integration, your proposition should always be the same in every medium within a campaign.

▶ Tone of voice

Marketing communication speaks to customers, whether through the voice, copy or pictures. The tone of that speech is critical. **Tone of voice** must be consistent with your branding. Cheap and cheerful brands can be communicated in light-hearted tones. Serious brands need to be communicated in serious tones. The tone must be consistent with the **brand personality**.

> **Brand personality** refers to the embodiment of your brand's values in personal attributes, e.g. serious, expert, cheerful, professional, helpful, trustworthy. It gives agencies a lot of help in determining how the product is to be presented.

▶ Brand support

This refers to how your brand is supported by:

- the features of your product or service;
- how it is promoted.

As we emphasized above, both must support your brand.

Summary

This chapter may seem a little theoretical in its concepts. But even a cursory examination of the most successful multiple-media campaign will reveal the importance of sticking to the above principles. Conversely, campaigns that fail in this respect often do so because of failure to observe these rules.

In this chapter, we have stressed that managing multiple-media integrated campaigns depends critically on good management of every element of the campaign. This begs the question of who is going to do the managing – the subject of our next and final chapter.

23 people in direct marketing

Who works in direct marketing?

Direct marketing users in the marketing organization

Who's responsible for the workload?

Staff capabilities

Recruiting direct marketing staff

After the investment?

Supplier management

Should you contract out?

Supplier selection

Agency structure

Rules of good supplier management

Controlling supplier costs

Managing the strategic relationship with supplier

Finalizing contracts

Summary

Despite direct marketing's reliance on technique and technology, especially since the arrival of advanced database and customer contact systems and new electronic media, most direct marketing is still planned and implemented by people. Even when the customer interacts with web sites, e-mail management systems or interactive TV, people are involved in planning and managing the interaction and of course in handling cases that cannot be dealt with automatically. So in this chapter we examine the jobs direct marketers do and how they are best organized.

▶ Who works in direct marketing?

There is of course no ideal direct marketing organization. But certain jobs occur in most direct marketing organizations, although companies take different views on how much expertise they should have and how much their agencies should supply, so some jobs are done either by clients or agencies. The main jobs are as follows.

▶ The direct marketing manager

This is the leader of the direct marketing organization, usually reporting either to a more senior marketing manager (e.g. head of marketing communications or marketing services, marketing director or marketing and sales director) or rarely (usually in smaller companies) to a non-marketing person. In some companies, particularly smaller ones, there is no direct marketing manager, and direct marketing specialists are more junior, reporting in to marketing management (or indeed the only marketing manager). In the smallest companies, there is unlikely to be a direct marketing specialist, and one person will encompass many of the roles described in this chapter. Some large companies believe that direct marketing is so well integrated into their marketing that there is no need for separate senior responsibility and that direct marketing skills are essential for all marketers. So instead of having specialists, they train all marketers in direct marketing and senior marketers are expected to be able to manage direct marketing along with their other responsibilities.

The greatest seniority of specialist direct marketers is in the largest companies and/or those with the most commitment to direct marketing – many more companies are now committed users of direct marketing. The lowest level is achieved in smaller companies and/or those with least commitment.

▶ CRM manager/director

The development of customer relationship management approaches has led to many companies renaming some senior marketing roles and some more junior roles. For example, a senior direct marketer may now be called 'CRM director'. This is not simply a renaming, it usually reflects a broadening of focus away from campaigning to achieve sales volume objectives to focusing on recruitment, retention and development of customers, although the focus on sales volumes and revenues is usually still strong.

▶ The direct marketing specialist

This is the most common direct marketing type. Often recruited from an agency or another user company, the specialist usually carries the burden of developing campaigns and making them work. Many companies put graduate trainees into a junior version of this role, growing them into the specialism through experience and training.

▶ The systems specialist

In smaller companies, much of the systems work is contracted to external suppliers, so they are unlikely to have systems specialists dedicated to direct marketing. In larger companies which have their own customer database, there may be many in-house systems specialists involved in direct marketing. They are usually assigned to support marketing systems by the IT manager. Some will be only temporarily involved, but in large companies a permanent team is needed to support marketing systems and develop them further.

Systems specialists often help integrate direct marketers' work with mainstream marketing, perhaps by drawing customer data from general marketing and sales and administrative systems and feeding back data gathered from direct marketing campaigns into marketing systems. Or they develop decision-support systems which can be used in all marketing contexts (e.g. management reporting systems). IT specialists also play an essential role in liaising with external suppliers such as computer bureaux and data suppliers.

Direct marketers must learn to communicate effectively with their IT department to ensure their requirements are understood. IT departments can easily misinterpret requirements or hold up campaigns, and this can cause serious problems. So it is up to the direct marketing manager to ensure that everyone understands what their roles are in a campaign. Good project management also helps.

New media are very IT intensive and the IT team do essential work in ensuring that, for example, contact centre systems and the web are properly connected with other marketing work.

▶ The media specialist

With an increasing variety of media available, companies that become big users of a particular medium may need to employ specialists in developing and using that medium. This applies particularly to new media. However, other companies take the view that this expertise is best supplied by agencies.

▶ Customer data/customer insight management

As companies have increased the size and complexity of their customer databases, they now need managers who specialize in developing and maintaining customer data and deriving knowledge from it, whether for campaign selections or for developing new customer management strategies. In some companies, customer information from all sources (not just marketing data but also, for example, market research and customer service) is brought together under a new type of manager, who is expected to be familiar with how all these sources should be managed and combined to create customer insight.

▶ The statistician

If you are in the early stages of using direct marketing, your statistical expertise is likely to be supplied as part of a package deal with your direct marketing agency, which carries out (or uses specialist suppliers to carry out) any statistical analyses needed. These analyses are likely to be quite simple, e.g. comparing results of different tests, different selections within a campaign, and so on. As you get more sophisticated in your use of data – particularly if you develop your own database – you may need to use advanced statistical techniques such as data mining to analyze customers and group them into categories likely to be more responsive to different offers. At this stage, the strategic advantage gained from using these techniques may make policy in this area a highly sensitive competitive issue. You may be worried about using external suppliers. Also, the depth of the analysis required means there are real gains in having internal experts. They know your company, your customers, your strategies and your data.

> **In the real world**
>
> Good business statisticians are rare birds. They don't require great skills in statistical manipulation – that is the job of sophisticated computer packages, which even tell them what is worth analyzing. Good direct marketing statisticians must have insight and creativity. They are not statistical purists. They must be prepared to live by the central rule of direct marketing – what works, works. Most direct marketing statistics are 'dirty statistics', which don't observe nice theoretical pure statistical rules, designed to provide scientific degrees of certainty in making predictions rather than find patterns which can be shown to continue (or not!) by testing.

▶ Direct marketing users in the marketing organization

The wider team involved in direct marketing may also include the following.

▶ Users

Users are responsible for putting together campaigns. They may be specialists (direct marketers) or generalists (marketers with other accountabilities but who do some direct marketing themselves, e.g. product managers, sector/segment managers).

▶ Internal customers

Internal customers ask/brief specialists to produce campaigns to meet their needs, e.g. brand managers. This category tends to overlap with users – the difference is that users tend to be more involved in the direct marketing process.

▶ Market research

Market researchers may use data generated by or recruited for direct marketing to reach research conclusions for use in the wider marketing organization. They are also providers of data for customer insight, particularly qualitative research designed to probe more deeply the characteristics of segments identified on the customer database. Some market research teams have been merged with customer database teams and renamed 'customer insight' departments. This is a reflection of an integrated approach to customer information.

▶ Support

These provide various support functions needed by your users and internal customers. They include specialists in print, data analysis systems support (who help marketing staff operate database and campaign management systems) and database management (who ensure that your customer database is the quality and size required to meet your needs).

▶ Senior marketing management

These secure funding, create direction and manage resources.

▶ Who's responsible for the workload?

You can allocate workload between specialists and users in many ways. At one extreme, users may do most of the work and specialists may provide infrastructure (e.g. the customer database, the agency roster, campaign scheduling approaches). In this case, users become 'doers'. At the other extreme, users may brief specialists, who act on their behalf with all suppliers. In this case, they are 'internal customers'. In a large organization, there are also 'influencers' of direct marketing, who can make things easy or hard for direct marketers and users. Senior marketing management usually control the financial resources which allow direct marketers to recruit staff, invest in systems and pay agencies.

▶ Staff capabilities

Although direct marketing management skills requirements are common across most industries, different types or sizes of companies need different capabilities. The major differences are likely to be as follows.

▶ Smaller companies

If your company is small, you probably won't be able to afford many or even any dedicated direct marketing staff. You may even have no marketing staff at all. So your manager responsible for direct marketing will usually be co-ordinating external suppliers (often small themselves) to achieve effective low-cost campaigns. For this, you'll need a hard-working marketing all-rounder who is good at liaising with a wide range of people.

▶ Larger companies

If your company is large, you probably can afford specialists – and you'll need them. Their tasks are likely to be precisely allocated as part of an overall plan. As specialists they will be 'pitting their wits' against their opposite numbers in competitive companies, to gain an advantage over them. They will probably be working as members of a large in-house team which works as much by consensus as by instruction. The team needs to be communicated with, listened to and influenced rather than told what to do.

▶ Consumer marketers

If you are marketing mainly to consumers, you may be an intense user of 'mass-market' media – mail, inbound telemarketing, published and broadcast media, the web. You may also be using consumer data from third parties and need to be familiar with the kinds of analysis carried out on such data to segment the market. Because you are likely to have big contact centres, you will need to ensure that your work is closely integrated with the work of contact centre management.

▶ Business-to-business companies

If you are selling to businesses, you'll still need experience in mass marketing if these businesses are small (whether as final or trade customers). But if your market is mainly larger organizations, your staff will need strengths in telemarketing (especially telephone account management) and using direct marketing in support of sales staff or large agents. In the latter case, your staff need to be strong in communicating, influencing, negotiation and functioning as part of a team. Sales forces are rightfully suspicious of new approaches to marketing which involve addressing people they see as 'their' customers. A simple way of keeping the sales force informed is to add them to the database so they get a copy of all the campaigns which are sent out to customers and prospects.

▶ Long-term relationship marketers

If you aim to develop long-term customer relationships (or have potential for so doing), e.g. if your customers buy often or if you have other products and services to sell after the 'main sale', you'll need database marketing expertise as you'll probably find an in-house customer database cost effective. However, you may still use external help for cleaning and maintaining your data. If your company is constantly developing new businesses, you may find it easier to outsource data management for new businesses, bringing that management in-house as each business matures.

▶ Operations-intense companies

> **Warning!**
> Companies with 'real' operations facilities (whether service delivered through branches or 'hard' product, e.g. manufacturing, transport, product retailing, banking) have more constraints on their flexibility to customer needs (e.g. inventory, capacity, staff training) than companies without such facilities (e.g. direct financial services, mail order).

If you have 'real' operations, you should aim to plan further ahead and remain closely in touch with the inventory or capacity situation and with your people. If you don't have such operations, you may even be able to create products specifically for direct marketing campaigns.

▶ The effect of your company's heritage

This is best demonstrated by example. If you have a strong engineering heritage, your direct marketers need to work closely with engineering management. They need to show them how to market benefits rather than sell features and to design products to fit markets rather than find markets for pre-designed products. A sales force-driven company needs to think of direct marketing as more than just a lead-generating device, but rather as a way of managing markets.

> **Warning!**
> You may find it hard to get sales staff to accept the idea of working to direct marketing disciplines, such as:
> - total accountability for the cost effectiveness of each call;
> - high visibility of this accountability;
> - measurement of effectiveness versus other media for managing customers;
> - structured calling programmes following clear contact strategies, often in combination with other media.
>
> So you may need to develop a long, slow campaign to educate and motivate sales management.

▶ Recruiting direct marketing staff

Too much direct marketing recruitment focuses only on technical direct marketing skills, to the exclusion of management skills and personality requirements. So many direct marketers become real experts at targeting, media selection and judging creative, but are hopeless at managing a complex network of relationships or project-managing a large campaign. Your recruitment should include all marketers.

It is easier to make a good direct marketer out of a good marketer or manager than the other way round. Training in direct marketing is easier to achieve than creating the right personality. Experience can usually be created quickly by a period of secondment to the agency or by taking a junior role on a number of campaigns.

> In a multinational computer company, a programme of telemarketing of a computer supplies catalogue was being extended from the UK to the rest of Europe. The best implementation was in Germany, where the manager was an engineer by training. After he was given proper direct marketing training, his thoroughness ensured that the catalogue was properly produced, suppliers were briefed well and systems worked.

After the investment?

If you've spent good money on recruitment and training, work hard to keep your staff:

- Reward them for achievement. Build evaluation of their campaigns into their appraisal and reward success by increased remuneration and promotion.
- Allow them to work steadily towards success, by giving staff small campaigns to work on initially, then build them to being able to handle large campaigns.
- Manage their workload. Direct marketing succeeds through management of detail. Do not expect staff to succeed with massive workload fluctuations. Give good notice of campaigns.
- Let them contribute expertise to strategy development. Accept and develop their ideas. Give credit for them.
- Let them express how they feel about how they're managed and what they're learning, in work and training.

Supplier management

You're likely to use many direct marketing suppliers, such as:

- direct marketing agencies;
- list suppliers and brokers;
- media buyers;
- computer bureaux;
- letter shops/mailing houses;
- fulfilment houses;
- print creative providers;
- paper and envelope providers;
- premium providers;

- data providers;
- telemarketing agencies;
- print production.

If you have integrated campaigns, the wider circle of suppliers may also include:

- advertising and PR agencies;
- market research agencies.

This wide selection of suppliers means you can achieve excellent direct marketing without a single in-house specialist. You can contract everything out, from customer management strategy through to campaign strategy and implementation to data management. To control this network of suppliers, you may even get most of them to contract with you via your direct marketing agency. At the other extreme, you might handle as much as possible in-house, including traditional agency functions such as copywriting and lay-out design, as many mail-order companies do. The general rule is that the greater the strategic importance of direct marketing to you and the greater the integration required between direct marketing and the rest of the marketing mix, the more is carried out in-house.

Should you contract out?

Advantages

- Lower overheads – your suppliers are hired on a job basis. For best results, a strategic agreement may be required, with longer-term fee commitments. This is likely for conventional agency functions (see below) and database management functions, which both require longer-term relationships. Telemarketing agencies and fulfilment houses also benefit from stable relationships, so consider longer-term contracts here too.
- Lower prices – suppliers constantly compete for work. But costs of competition may lead to higher fees (hidden pitching costs) and constant evaluation of pitches and quotes is time-consuming for you too.
- Variety – new experience is constantly fed into your company, supplementing your own.
- Customer-orientation – in-house staff tend to be less customer-oriented than (some!) agencies which know that if their performance falters, they may lose the contract.

Disadvantages

- Management control and communication problems – suppliers take time to learn to work with you and each other. Frequent changing of suppliers can cause communications problems and loss of job control.

- Strategic control – if your database is kept outside, there may be security risks. If too much policy is generated outside, key skills may not be available in future. Agencies may learn from you, not vice versa.

▶ The key need – close co-operation and strategic understanding

Many models of client-supplier relationship work – there is no ideal. The issue is not how much you contract out but how you handle contracting. Try to remain flexible about this issue and decide on the basis of strategic need and costs. Always aim to manage the relationship professionally, over the long term.

> **Warning!**
> Hiring and firing suppliers from campaign to campaign certainly never works.

Because suppliers need to work with each other over many campaigns, you need teamwork between suppliers themselves and between the suppliers and the various internal departments involved. On each campaign, the team should be brought together at as early a stage as possible, in order to agree the work programme and sort out any potential problems. Many inter-supplier problems are caused by centralization of communication. In practice, it is best if suppliers work closely with each other according to a tight brief from the client (see Chapter 5). This is much better than their having to rely on the client being at the centre of a network of communication.

▶ Supplier selection

Selection of suppliers is an important first step. Consider the following criteria:

- Creativity – do they provide that extra spark but one which is consistent with the brief? For agencies, this may depend on the quality of the creative brief as well as on the quality of creative staff.
- Quality – is their work of a consistently high standard and is this high standard a result of good management rather than chance?
- Reliability – can they be relied upon to perform well every time?
- Ability to observe deadlines – do they meet all their deadlines? If there are problems, do they inform the client quickly enough or try to hide the problems?
- Ability to understand client needs.
- Openness – are they honest with clients?
- Ability to take criticism and bounce back with better solutions.
- Price – do they give good value for money? This does not mean being cheap. Can they account properly for the money that clients pay them?

- Ability to work with others (the client and other suppliers) – do they enter into the team spirit and not try to look good at others' expense? Do they accept problems as team problems?
- Ability to add value – do they execute the brief blindly or do they help achieve more by identifying weaknesses in the brief and remedying them?

Don't hesitate to emphasize **management quality** rather than creativity. Direct marketing relies greatly for its effectiveness on 'managerial' factors. It is good management that translated the strategy of the campaign – targeting, timing, offer, creative and media – into action. In selecting a supplier, it is worth paying close attention to managerial factors such as:

- their management processes;
- the management experience of staff;
- budgetary and costing processes;
- their clients' experiences (e.g. do they deliver on time, of the right quality, within budget?).

▶ Is one-stop shopping an advantage?

Some agencies will offer you a full range of services. The main advantage of this is that inter-supplier communication and control problems are minimized (if **their** internal communications are good!). This can reduce the time to produce campaigns and improve quality, as long as the agency's internal procedures are quality-oriented.

> **Warning!**
> One-stop shopping can be just a ploy to make it easier for the agency to sell. So if you are considering using a one-stop agency, ask for evidence of the agency's internal campaign management procedures, in particular those concerning briefing, campaign project management and financial control. Such an agency should also be asked for reference clients, who can testify that one-stop means more than one juicy contract for the agency. Some agencies offer online tracking for their clients. This means the client can look on the agency's Extranet to see how their work is progressing. This is useful if your company has its own activities to complete, as you will know when to carry out these activities.

▶ Agency structure

The main roles in agencies are as follows.

▶ Account handler/manager/executive

This person is responsible for handling day-to-day liaison with you and ensuring that work is moving through the agency and subcontracted suppliers at the right pace. The account handler is likely to handle more than just your business, unless you provide the agency with enough business to keep an account handler busy. Otherwise, a question for you is whether the handler (and other staff) spend enough time on your account. Account handlers must understand in detail how each department of their agency works. This knowledge is essential to ensuring that work is progressing through the agency. Handlers must also understand your needs and interpret them to the rest of the agency. Handlers therefore spend much of their time in meetings with you and with agency staff, and writing reports, briefs and correspondence.

▶ Planning

This function is responsible for research and bringing together data to support campaign planning. Planners are usually responsible for ensuring that all involved in your campaign understand your market and needs. This understanding is a key part of the brief for the creative team. Planning may also be involved in determining a long-term strategy for you. Planning will usually be closely involved in targeting, media and list decisions and for analyzing response statistics to determine which approach works best. Many planners will have a good grasp of the principles of research. They are useful to bounce ideas against before talking to the creatives.

▶ Creative

'Creatives' are responsible for developing the proposition in response to your brief and the creative execution of that proposition in copy, graphics, scripts, web-site design, etc. In direct mail, this will include the complete pack design, together with incentives. Key members of the creative team are the copywriter(s) and the art director.

▶ Research and information

Most agencies have a research department, which handles desk research and small-scale field work required to check other research or to research campaigns. This department may also subcontract major research (e.g. to measure non-response elements of a campaign).

▶ Studio

The studio produces the artwork, based on the creative execution, for printers to work with.

▶ Media

If you do not use an independent media agency, the agency media team is responsible for cost-effective buying of the right media for your campaign. This requires knowledge of all media, their coverage and effectiveness.

Financial controller

Once, agencies could afford to be slack about budgeting. Now, clients expect value for money. So expect all your money to be closely accounted for. Your agency should have strong financial control, to control their costs and make the most of your money.

Rules of good supplier management

Once your supplier is on board and working with you on campaigns, apply these 'good management' rules:

- Always brief suppliers clearly at the beginning of each campaign and communicate with them thoroughly during development and implementation. Give clear instructions and cover what is to be achieved, by when, by whom and at what cost. As far as possible, suppliers should put response to instructions in writing, e.g. through contact reports, which should summarize their understanding of your instructions. Without these reports, it can be difficult to establish who said what or agreed to do what.
- Develop and explain the criteria by which you'll be judging the supplier's performance.
- Give clear feedback on performance, based on the agreed criteria. Set and stick to high standards.
- Recognize good performance, by stability of future contract and public recognition.
- Punish bad performance, by querying or refusing invoices or negotiating down fees. Eventually, a re-pitch should be asked for. Working closely with suppliers during a campaign should not prevent you being tough if things go wrong. This is the essence of any commercial relationship. Management by fear is not the right approach. Give early warning of potential problems so the supplier has time to correct them. Both you and suppliers benefit from this. However, poor performance which is the result of an agreed experiment should **never** be punished. This is a good way to destroy all creativity.

Controlling supplier costs

It should not be too difficult for you to control supplier costs. For each activity, obtain a proper quote from each supplier. For a competitive tender, compare quotes and select the best value for money, not the cheapest. Take quality into account. If you use a small number of agencies, perhaps on a retainer basis, retain the right to examine their cost structures and compare them with other agencies. For work agencies buy in, set clear cost targets. In all circumstances, use professional negotiating skills – for new contracts, retainer fees and problem resolution.

▶ Cost overruns

There are several reasons for cost overruns, often occurring simultaneously. They are listed below, along with possible solutions.

- ◆ Last-minute copy changes and missed approval deadlines – these changes may be caused by changes in your requirements or be stimulated by inspection of final copy. To avoid this, always take copy seriously well before the final version. Where 'final copy stimulated' revisions are a severe problem, they can be removed by using desktop publishing techniques as an intermediate production stage. Producing something looking very like the final copy helps focus attention. If you detect slackness in this area, it may be because your staff are not budget-accountable. If they are not, make them so. Otherwise, occasionally exercise the ultimate sanction of withdrawing a promotion if the costs overrun too much. If your staff are budget-accountable, they may just be unaware of the costs of late changes. So make them aware early enough for them to avoid them.
- ◆ Lack of criteria for judging supplier costs – in media buying and TV advertising production there are established benchmarks for costs. Such benchmarks are less well established for direct marketing. But when you've run several campaigns, you will have enough data on media, print and telemarketing costs to establish your own benchmarks. If you're new to direct marketing, ask agencies for client references and benchmark quotes against what other clients pay.
- ◆ Lack of negotiation with suppliers – remember you're a negotiator, not just a budget estimator and user. Never make an estimate on the basis of a single quote, although you may do this under time pressure. Train all your buyers in negotiation. Develop a negotiating strategy with each supplier. This includes situations of cost overrun, where additional billing should never be accepted without query and negotiation. Finally, prepare briefs as early as possible to give yourself time to negotiate.
- ◆ Lack of feeling of cost accountability – none of the above will work unless your staff feel cost-accountable. Take leadership on this. Devise a system for cost reporting to indicate where or with whom problems lie. Success must be rewarded in appraisal, visibility and promotion. Ability to manage costs should be seen as an entry-gate to more senior management positions and a natural development of professionalism.
- ◆ Lack of supplier cost-control – many suppliers lack cost-control systems which account properly for your money. If their systems don't do this, ask them to install a system or risk deletion from your list of approved suppliers.
- ◆ Your lack of cost-control system – if you have no proper cost-control system, you will find it hard to control supplier costs.

In a cost-control system you need:

- ◆ proper procedures for recording costs against cost centres;
- ◆ reporting procedures, including simple reports on performance relative to budget and benchmark, and reports on who is over- and under-running on budgets, with exception reports for severe cases;

- budgetary rules, for example, no work without job number and budget cleared, no agreement without negotiation and reference to benchmarks, no change to specifications without cost implications being negotiated and agreed;
- benchmark processes, for example, a database of costs, time-estimates and resulting charges from different suppliers for different kinds of task;
- management processes, for example, clear and fast processes for determining and modifying budgets, so that suppliers are not encouraged to work ahead of budget because budget agreement is not finalized;
- management review. Budgetary performance should become an important item in your management meetings and in your suppliers' review. Issues to be reviewed in this way include whether suppliers, in response to your brief, offer alternatives with significantly different costs and benefits; whether suppliers stick to budgets; whether proper communications budgeting is practised; and whether staff have the right resources and skills.

Managing the strategic relationship with suppliers

You might consider an arrangement with your suppliers in which they receive an annually negotiated fee for their consultancy, account management, planning and creative work. Charge all other items at cost, with no mark-up and only when agreed. In this situation, achieving cost effectiveness depends heavily on fee/mark-up negotiations and on close vetting of the **content** of work, as you are not using competitive tendering. If you use this approach, include in your contracts the installation by suppliers of quality and cost-control procedures (including progress reporting). Publish the estimated and final costs of every campaign as part of the cost-control process, using standard formats (as used in the request for tender). Develop target cost levels from these, and base budget setting on analysis of these costs.

Finalizing contracts

The aim of the contract is to:

- ensure detailed specification of the supplier's deliverable;
- embody it in a form which is an agreed management and legal basis for monitoring delivery, paying and resolving problems.

Your contract with your supplier should flow naturally out of the summarized conclusion to the negotiation. However, the problem with many negotiations is that, accidentally or deliberately, they fail to cover every aspect of the subsequent relationship. You may discover this when the formal contract is being drawn up, and you may need to return to negotiation. There is only one way to avoid this: a persistent, almost dogmatic attention to detail, an insistence that the agreement be fully documented and that it be used as the basis for a contract.

A good contract must be:

- based on a clear understanding by both sides of the requirements of the situation, the resources required to deal with it, the resources actually available, likely problems, and so on;
- clearly committed to by both sides;
- properly documented, with deliverables, timing and resources clearly specified, in a form accessible to and agreed by both sides;
- followed through professionally, so whenever there is a risk of outcomes not meeting requirements, early warning signs stimulate corrective action;
- reviewed afterwards, with any learning points identified and used to improve the relationship;
- correctly positioned in relationship to other agreements (concurrent, past or future).

Obviously, the level of detail agreed and contracted to varies with the type of project and the closeness of the relationship. A close working relationship does mean that you can assume certain things. There may also be a framework agreement against which individual agreements are made.

A good contract specifies:

- what is delivered – at the level of detail needed to ensure that it can be managed and quality-controlled on both sides, including progress checks. This should cover commitments of both sides, not just the supplier's;
- who delivers it (individuals and teams, including contact names and when and how to access them);
- by when – overall and for particular stages;
- at what cost – overall and for individual elements of work (again, the level of detail depending on the type of work and the relationship);
- how you measure delivery, including types of review, milestones etc.;
- whether you pay by inputs (time/resources) or outputs (results);
- prices (of delivered units), fees (where an overall package has been agreed) or rates (where you are paying for resources on a unit basis);
- terms of payment (invoicing, payment period, late payment, interest charges);
- problem handling (what to do if something goes wrong);
- how you want to incorporate learning into the management of the relationship;
- escape clauses – how contract terms might be changed and why.

Summary

In this chapter we have explored some of the main issues involved in managing the direct marketing organization – your own and suppliers'. Direct marketing is

23 / People in direct marketing

more likely to deliver results when a longer-term approach is used, in developing your own direct marketing organization and in managing relationships with suppliers.

Indeed, this applies to most of what we have covered in this book, whether it be in the use of media, in establishing a database or in planning and implementing campaigns.

We hope this book gives you the feeling that direct and interactive marketing is a professional discipline, which can be learned. It is not a witch's cookbook but a series of simple – though not short – recipes. Like all recipes, the more you use it, the better you will get and the more the result will suit your tastes (objectives); used once in a while, as a tactical fill-in, your chances of success are not so high. We hope we have encouraged you to take the route to becoming a cordon bleu direct marketer.

glossary of terms

Call to Action (CTA) The mechanic through which the customer will respond: call now on 0800 321 123, pop into your local retailer, visit Sky.com to book on line today etc.

Above the Line (ATL) Brand advertising. Historically on an invoice the brand advertising was found first. Below the line on the same sheet were any direct marketing jobs. ATL is normally described as media, which is consumed by the masses. It includes TV advertising, off-the-page press advertising, outdoor posters, radio, ambient (pub beer mats, back of toilet doors etc). It also covers sports ground advertising and sponsorships and much more.

DRTV Also known as direct-response TV. This is the use of an advert with a strong call to action, to prompt a response (usually call now and book, pop into your local retailer to buy this now), which is normally time boxed. Used heavily by charities and loan, mortgage companies.

Time boxing This is the act of closing an offer at a certain time to prompt response quickly. This is often used in direct marketing to bring forward the purchase decision to now rather than later which helps meet sales targets. Examples include 'open an account before 31/10/03 and get a free travel alarm clock' and 'buy 2 products and get a third free, offer ends 25/09/03' and 'get 50% off a new kitchen this bank holiday weekend only'.

Cromalin The 4 colour proof generated from the printer, which is an exact copy of what artwork will be printed on your paper. It's important you check for spots and smudges, check the clarity of any pictures used, the edges of letters and images are clear and sharp (fit), and that if using a 4 colour process, they are lined up over each other to avoid a halo of a colour appearing over the word.

Wet proof This is similar to the above but printed on the same stock of paper you are to be using. This provides a real example to check what the quality and colour will be on the final printed result. This is useful if changing your paper stock, or if you want to check the reproduction of an image, such as when using pictures on a press (newspaper) advert.

USP Unique selling point. This is the unique way in which you have an advantage over another, and therefore something which you can market to your advantage. It might be your 24 hour customer service (Barclaycard), personal recommendations of holiday destinations (Trailfinders) or that for transaction you make on your NSPCC credit card, a percentage goes to charity. Whatever it is, use it.

Presstream This is used for posting newspapers, magazines and periodicals. There are specific requirements from the Royal Mail that differ from Mailsort. Presstream must have a title, and date, month or season on the publication. The piece must carry one sixth editorial not related to selling etc. (i.e. It is not really for direct mail purposes)

glossary of terms

Prospect Someone or something which you wish to market your product to. If you have some information about the prospect that makes them more likely to respond, they may be described as a warm or hot prospect (according to how likely you think they are). Typically someone who has made contact with a company previously for information, or has purchased something from a company may be considered a warm prospect. This is due to the relationship or experience, albeit sometimes a small one, which you have established already, and which you can flex again.

URL Uniform Resource Locator. Or web address to traffic people to your web site.

ROI Return on investment. This is the recovery of the initial marketing and overhead costs after a period of time. It can be brought forward by increasing the value of the customer by cross-selling them more products, increasing their transactions with you and limiting the initial investment costs.

LTV This is the lifetime value. This is the total value of the customer for the length of their relationship with you. The longer the customer stays with you, the more they spend and their behaviour whilst they're with you will impact their lifetime value.

Churn Also known as attrition. This is the loss of customers. Retention is the act of retaining these customers, either proactively to give them reasons to stay loyal, or reactively to get them back once they have decided to leave.

RR% Response rate. This is the percentage response from a campaign. This may be measured by the number of calls received from the telephone number advertised, the number of hits to a web site, or numbers of coupons received back. There may also be a number of ways to respond so it's important to measure the total response.

$$RR\% = \frac{\text{number of responses} \times 100}{\text{volume of mktg campaign}}$$

CPR Cost per response. This is the cost of each response. All campaign costs should be included to give an accurate CPR. Normally overheads (cost of call centre staff etc.) is not included as they are picked up by the call centre budget.

$$CPR = \frac{\text{total cost of campaign}}{\text{number of responses}}$$

Where an offer is used (ie. half price), then the cost of the offer should be added to the CPR.

$$CPR = \frac{\text{total cost of campaign} + \text{offer cost} = \text{total CPR}}{\text{number of responses}}$$

CPS Cost per sale. This is the total cost per sale, not response. Naturally not everyone who calls the call centre will want to buy your goods or open an account. They may just want information. Therefore to measure the cost per sale gives an accurate picture, ignoring the drop off from call to sale.

$$CPR = \frac{\text{total cost of campaign} = \text{total CPS}}{\text{number of sales/new accounts}}$$

Again if there was an offer used, then this should be factored into the final CPS again as above.

Conversion rate This is the difference in numbers of responses to the number of sales. Conversion rates typically vary between 20–50% of responses to sales depending on the industry and product. The more complicated the buying process and the product proposition, maybe also the price, all impact the conversion rate.

$$\text{Conversion rate} = \frac{\text{total number of sales} \times 100}{\text{number of responses}}$$

FMCG Fast moving consumer goods. Such as toiletries, grocery items and other supermarket products.

SMS Short Message Service, sent to mobiles.

Marcomms This is short for marketing communications. This is a general term to describe the variety of elements used to market through. They include direct mail packs, press adverts, door drops, inserts, customer letter and so on.

index

ABC classification 140
account executives 380–1
accountability 109, 130–1, 228, 230–1
acquisition programmes 23, 44–9
action plans 69
advertising
  design of display adverts 247–8
  media 33–7
  messages 4–6, 268
  online advertising 222–3, 358–9
  telephone numbers 207–8, 249
aesthetic value 165
agencies 31, 193, 380–2
allowable costs per order 344–5
artwork 273–4
attrition rates 44, 64
automatic call distributors (ACD) 197–8

banner advertising 222, 359
barcodes 278
barriers to market entry 40, 112
benefits 179, 180–1, 267
brainstorming 263
brand marketing 21–2, 115, 157–8, 165, 223, 264, 364–8
break-even volumes 64
briefing templates 69–74
brochures 171
budgeting 334–40, 341, 363
business-to-business marketing 8–11, 21, 250–1, 375
Butlins 226, 227
buying decision 3–9, 10

call guides 205–7
campaigns 23, 59–76, 124, 129–30, 134–6, 291–313
  budgeting 334–40
  cross-campaign planning 309
  development 292, 296–9, 308
  direct mail 176–7, 182–8
  effectiveness ratios 343
  evaluation 292, 333
  implementation 292
  monitoring and control 340–1
  offer strategy 157–63, 298–9
  planning 291–2, 293–5, 306, 309, 364, 381
  quality management 305–8
  resource management 312–13
  roles 311–12
  statuses 310–11
  timing 280, 297–8, 309
campaign managers 75
catalogues 21, 171, 242, 250–3, 356
chain of productivity 343
charities 30, 100, 238
cinema advertising 35
cluster analysis 329
codes of practice 174
cold calling 195
colours 274
communications
  hierarchy of effects models 262
  integrated communication 351–68
  technology 196–201
competitors 39, 65, 266
computer bureaux 31
confidence intervals 321–3
contact centres 196
contact strategies 53–4, 118, 327–9
contingency plans 341
contracting out 234–5, 378–9
contracts with suppliers 384–5
control groups 326

index

control information 340–1, 364
copy length 181–2, 268
core proposition 158
costs 46, 47, 63–4, 67, 109–10, 114–20, 301
  controlling supplier costs 382–4
  of e-mail marketing 232
  productivity ratios 343–4
coupons 244, 246–7
creativity 48, 261–70, 299–300, 381
  briefing template 72–3
credit cards 99, 146
cross-campaign planning 309
cross-selling 50
customers
  ABC classification 140
  acquisition 23, 44–9, 51–2
  dialogue 125
  insight managers 372–3
  internal customers 373
  inventories 346
  lifetime value 24, 45, 64, 346–7
  needs 4, 5, 215–16
  neglected 110–11
  profiles 46, 62–3, 128
  purchasing behaviour 3–9, 144–6
  relationship management 193, 211–18, 371, 375–6
  retention 24, 44, 49–54, 215
  see also databases

data mining 329
data processing 277–8
Data Protection Act 175
data reduction 127
databases 16, 23–5, 43, 79–93, 97–105, 302
  applications 123–5, 129–34
  contact data 88
  and cost savings 114–20
  customer data 79–80, 85–7
  data design 83–4
  data sources 84–5, 127–8
  decision support systems 131
  deduplication of data 89, 91
  integrated system 133–4

merge and purge software 91–2
outsourcing 92
product data 88
quality and maintenance 89–92, 128–9
strategic/tactical use 109–13, 126–7
transaction data 87–8
decision maker contacts (DMCs) 201–2
decision support systems 131
depth interviews 150
deregulation 37–8
dialogue 125, 203–4, 269
direct mail 36, 169–88, 353–4
  artwork 273–4
  campaign management 176–7, 182–8
  data processing 277–8
  effective mailings 177–82
  fulfilment 280–6
  and legislation 173–6
  mailing components 170–2
  mailing houses 18, 31, 102–3, 276–7, 281–6
  mailing lists 10, 32, 91, 302–4, 320
  Mailsort 174, 184, 188, 279
  quality standards 173–6
  response handling 282–3
  stock/pack management 184–6
  targeting 169
  timing 280
  users of 172–3
  volume of mail 183–4, 280
  see also printing
Direct Mail Services Standards Board (DMSSB) 174
direct response television 30, 37, 224–8, 249–50, 358
directors 371
display adverts 247–8
distribution channels 163–5
distribution curves 322, 324
domestic appliance manufacturers 100–1
door drops 36

e-mail marketing 231–7, 257, 359
economic influences 38–9

391

enclosures 172
enquiry management 212
envelopes 171–2, 177, 187–8
executive summaries 60–1
exhibitions 254

FAB analysis 267
fast moving consumer goods 101
faxes 37
field sales forces 21, 109–10, 114, 116, 255, 359–62
financial services companies 30, 98–9
flexography 276
flyers 36
fonts 274–5
formal proposition 159
fragmentation of markets 103
free newspapers 36, 246
free samples 256
free-standing inserts 244
frequent flyer programmes 17
future value of customers 24, 45, 64, 346–7

gains charts 329–30
geo-demographic segmentation 140–1
government marketing 100
group behaviour 7
group discussions 147, 150

hierarchy of effects models 262
high-involvement products 3–4
hypothesis testing 318

inactive customers 50
incremental revenue 117
inferences 320–1
inserts 35, 36, 243–5, 355
integrated communication 351–68
integrating managers 364
interactive television 30, 37, 224–8, 358
intermediaries 19–21
internal customers 373
Internet 19
    e-mail marketing 231–7, 257, 359
    web sites 222–3, 338, 358–9

interviews 150
inventories 115–16, 117

lapsed customers 50
lateral thinking 263
leaflet distribution 35, 246
legislation 173–6
leisure services sector 99
letterpress 276
letters 170, 179, 185
    copy length 181–2, 268
    magic words 180
    paper quality 183
    writing style 182
    see also envelopes; printing
lifestyle questionnaires 141–2
lifetime value 24, 45, 64, 346–7
lists *see* mailing lists
lithography 276
low-involvement products 3–4
loyalty 16–18, 44, 51–2, 111
    retention strategies 24, 44, 49–54, 215

magazines 34, 242, 243, 247–8, 355–6
magic words 180
mail questionnaires 150–1
mailing houses 18, 31, 102–3, 276–7, 281–6
mailing lists 10, 32, 91, 302–4, 320
Mailing Preference Service (MPS) 176
Mailsort 174, 184, 188, 279
management summaries 60–1
managers 364, 371
market entry barriers 40, 112
market research 54, 115, 116, 147–52, 374
market segmentation 139–44, 147, 296–7
market share 66–7
media 33–7, 241
    briefing template 69–71
    broadcast media 30, 34–5, 37, 221, 358
    evaluation and selection 46–7
    integrated communication 351–68
    interactive media 221–8

media specialists 372
messages 4–6, 268
mobile technology marketing 228–31, 258
mobile telephone industry 30
modelling 146
monitoring campaigns 340–1
motor industry 100
multi-media messaging (MMS) 258

needs of customers 4, 5, 215–16
neighbourhood classification data 141
new products 111, 112–13, 161
newspapers 33–4, 243, 355–6
   advertising design 247–8
   free newspapers 36, 246
normal distribution 324

objectives 65–7, 293–5
   of testing 318–19
offer strategy 157–63, 298–9
one-piece mailers 172
online advertising 222–3
order forms 171, 186–7
outsourcing 378–9
   e-mail marketing 234–5

Panadol ActiFast 225, 226
paper suppliers 32
payment modes 146
performance management 63–4, 75
   effectiveness ratios 200–4, 343–4
   interactive television 228
   SMS marketing 230–1
   telemarketing 200–5
   see also costs
personalization 11, 15, 143, 179–80, 236, 268
photographs 253
planning campaigns 291–2, 293–5, 306, 309, 364, 381
political parties 37–8, 100
positioning 266
post-testing 152
postcodes 140
posters 256

power companies 97–8
premium rate telephone numbers 208
press advertising 33–4, 243, 355–6
pricing 161, 165, 253
printing 32
   artwork 273–4
   colours 274
   plate making 275
   processes 276
   typesetting 274–5
prize draws 163
production process 273
productivity *see* performance management
products 3–4, 62
   aesthetic value 165
   benefits 179, 180–1, 267
   choice of right product 160
   concept testing 148
   modifications 160–1
   new product 111, 112–13, 161
   positioning 266
   proposition 157–63, 217, 366–7
   small-value goods 238
   strengths and weaknesses 266
profiling 46, 62–3, 128
profits 67
project files 306
promotions 161–2, 255–6, 300–1
proposition 157–63, 217, 366–7
psychographic analysis 141
public relations 256–7, 357
purchasing behaviour
   businesses 10
   consumers 3–9, 144–6

QCi model 216–18
quality management 173–6, 305–8, 342, 345
questionnaires 141–2, 150–2
quota sampling 325

radio 35, 221, 358
ratio analysis 200–4, 343–4
   see also performance management
recruitment 376–7

regression analysis 329
relationship management (CRM) 193, 211–18, 371, 375–6
renewal cycle 50
resource management 64–5, 312–13
response rates 15–16, 149, 327–9
response-based segmentation 142–3
retailers 18, 102, 115, 116
retention strategies 24, 44, 49–54, 215
 see also loyalty
returned orders 202
revenue strategies 116–17
Rimmel 227–8
rollout budgets 338

sales forces 21, 109–10, 114, 116, 255, 359–62
sales offices 114–15, 116
sales promotions 161–2, 255–6, 300–1
sales rates 327–9
sales seminars 254–5
sampling 320–6
segmentation 139–44, 147, 296–7
seminars 254–5
service delivery systems 165
shopping channels 250
situation analysis 61
size of test samples 323
small-value goods 238
SMS marketing 19, 228–31, 257, 359
social grade definitions 140
social influences 7, 39
specialists 372
split runs 326
spreadsheets 339
staff capabilities 374–6
statistical analysis 146, 147, 318–30, 342, 373
strategy 67–9, 109–13, 126–7
 creative strategies 265–9
 offer strategy 157–63
 testing 132
stratified sampling 325
suppliers 29, 31–3
 contracts 384–5
 cost control 382–4

management 377–8, 382, 384
 selection 379–80
support functions 374
symbolic proposition 157, 159
systems specialists 372

targeting 4, 16, 20, 46, 169, 212, 241–2, 296, 301–4, 306
targets 204–5, 345–6
telemarketing 191–208, 356–7
 call guides 205–7
 call management 200
 communications technology 196–201
 contact centres 196
 dialogue 193–4
 objectives 195
 productivity ratios 200–4
 strengths and weaknesses 192
 targets 204–5
Telephone Preference Service (TPS) 195, 208
telephone selling 19, 37, 191
telephones
 advertising telephone numbers 207–8, 249
 automatic call distributors (ACD) 197–8
 premium rate numbers 208
 questionnaires 152
 toll-free calling 193, 198
Teletext services 221
television 30, 34, 37, 221, 248–50, 358
 interactive 30, 37, 224–8, 358
 shopping channels 250
test budgets 338
test cells 324
test matrices 325–6
testing 132, 148, 152, 184, 317–30
 objectives of 318–19
 size of test samples 323
text messaging 19, 228–31, 257, 359
through-the-line advertising 243
timing 280, 297–8, 309
tip-ons 245, 355
toll-free calling 193, 198

trade marketing 20
training 308
travel industry 30, 99
typesetting 274–5

up-selling 50
utility companies 97–8

volumes 66–7

water companies 97–8
web sites 222–3, 338, 358–9
welcome cycle 49, 212
wireless marketing 237
writing style 182

THE DEFINITIVE BUSINESS PLAN 2e

Richard Stutely

ISBN 0 273 65921 9

A good business plan is the difference between success and not even getting the chance to try.

This international bestseller is the ultimate guide to business planning.

Whether the goal is raising start-up or development finance for a new business, requesting venture funding from a corporate parent or directing operational management, *The Definitive Business Plan* will help you deliver the information that the decision-makers are really looking for.

Visit our website at
www.business-minds.com

MARKETING AND COMMUNICATIONS

Books to make you better at getting your messages across...

Read This
Robert Gentle
0273 656503

Information overload. Everyone has too much to read. So, what's going to make people read what you write? Simple, clear, commanding writing – that's what. Here's how.

Viral Marketing
Russell Goldsmith
0273 659057

Viral marketing is hot. This is the first practical, informal, informative, easy-read guide to explain what it is, how to do it and how to measure success.

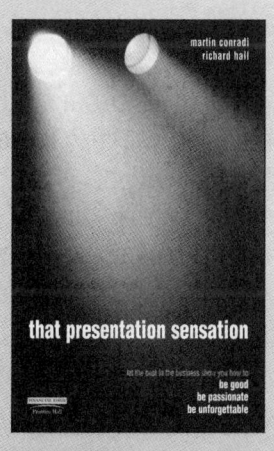

That Presentation Sensation
Martin Conradi
0273 654748

For the presenter, a presentation can be a make or break, career-turning experience.
This inspirational book shows you how to be unforgettable – packed with advice and ideas from leading business people who already are.

Available at all good bookshops and online at
www.business-minds.com

The Definitive Guide to Managing the Numbers

The executive's fast-track to mastering spreadsheets, budgets, forecasts, investment metrics...

Richard Stutely

ISBN 0 273 66103 5

They made you a manager because you're good at what you do. What you do isn't numbers. Until now. From now on, the numbers matter – they're what you'll be judged by. Understand the numbers and you'll become a better manager.

Internationally best-selling author Richard Stutely takes you step-by-step through the areas where numbers and managers meet. He reveals all the shortcuts and tricks and shows you how to use Excel to simplify the process and crosscheck your results.

When you put down the book, you will not only be able to produce an outstanding set of financials, you will also have a much clearer understanding of what they mean and how to use them to be a more effective manager. You won't fear the financials ever again. Moreover, you won't fear dealing with people who make numbers their business. Learn to talk their language; win the arguments; never be intimidated by another finance meeting. Get ready to beat the beanies at their own game.

Available at all good bookshops and online at
www.business-minds.com